MORE, Charles

Britain in the
twentieth century

D0541093

BRITAIN IN THE TWENTIETH CENTURY

CHARLES MORE

PEARSON
Longman

Harlow, England • London • New York • Boston • San Francisco • Toronto
Sydney • Tokyo • Singapore • Hong Kong • Seoul • Taipei • New Delhi
Cape Town • Madrid • Mexico City • Amsterdam • Munich • Paris • Milan

PEARSON EDUCATION LIMITED

Edinburgh Gate
Harlow CM20 2JE
United Kingdom
Tel: +44 (0)1279 623623
Fax: +44 (0)1279 431059
Website: www.pearsoned.co.uk

First published in Great Britain in 2007

© Pearson Education Limited 2007

The right of Charles More to be identified as author of this work has been asserted by him in accordance with the Copyright, Designs and Patents Act 1988.

ISBN-13: 978-0-582-78483-3
ISBN-10: 0-582-78483-2

British Library Cataloguing in Publication Data
A CIP catalogue record for this book can be obtained from the British Library

Library of Congress Cataloging in Publication Data
A CIP catalog record for this book can be obtained from the Library of Congress

10 9 8 7 6 5 4 3 2 1
10 09 08 07

Set by 35 in 10.5/12.5pt Ehrhardt MT
Printed and bound in Malaysia

The Publisher's policy is to use paper manufactured from sustainable forests.

CONTENTS

List of boxes   vi

Timeline   viii

General elections 1900–1997   xii

Preface   xvi

Chapter 1   Britain in 1900   1

Chapter 2   Liberal high tide: Politics 1900–1914   13

Chapter 3   The First World War   29

Chapter 4   Changing tides: Politics between the wars   49

Chapter 5   The search for peace: Britain and the world 1918–1939   73

Chapter 6   Society 1900–1939   89

Chapter 7   The Second World War: Battles and strategy   117

Chapter 8   The Second World War: Politics and society   137

Chapter 9   The years of consensus? Politics 1945–1974   151

Chapter 10   Thatcherism and after: Politics 1974–2000   177

Chapter 11   Britain and overseas 1945–2000   200

Chapter 12   Society 1945–2000   222

Afterword   252

Appendix   UK population and earnings   264

Index   266

LIST OF BOXES

Politics and government

Liberal welfare reforms	18
Suffragists and suffragettes	23
The abdication of Edward VIII	67
Houses and plans	154
Northern Ireland	179
Local government in the twentieth century	189
The Civil Service in the twentieth century	192
The Liberal Party 1945–2000	195

Society and economy

War, women's work and women's status	46
Economic depression	60
Religion in Britain 1900–1945	91
Living with unemployment	100
Health and health care	105
Rationing and consumption	144
The economy 1951–1973	160
Rural Britain 1945–2000	226
Religion in Britain 1945–2000	233
The media	244
Crime in twentieth century Britain	249

People and politics

H. H. Asquith	31
David Lloyd George	41
Ramsay MacDonald and British socialism	55
Stanley Baldwin	58
George V	63
Neville Chamberlain	82
Winston Churchill	126
Clement Attlee	157

Harold Macmillan   165
Harold Wilson   169
Margaret Thatcher   183
Ernest Bevin   202
Anthony Eden and Suez   206
Queen Elizabeth II   247

Military affairs

Douglas Haig   35
The Royal Navy, the RAF and rearmament   86
The Battle of Britain   118
The Battle of the Atlantic   120
Strategic bombing   122
Alan Brooke and the Mediterranean Strategy   131
The Blitz   143
The nuclear option   213

TIMELINE

1900	General election; Conservative government; Lord Salisbury Prime Minister (PM)
1901	Queen Victoria dies; Edward VII becomes King
1902	Balfour PM
1904	*Entente Cordiale* with France
1905	Balfour resigns; Liberal government; Campbell-Bannerman PM
1906	General election; Liberal government; Campbell-Bannerman PM
1908	Asquith PM
1910 (Feb)	General election; Liberal government; Asquith PM
1910	Edward VIII dies; George V becomes King
1910 (Dec)	General election; Liberal government; Asquith PM
1911	Parliament Act strips Lords of its blocking powers
1914 (Aug)	Germany invades Belgium; fails to respond to British ultimatum; Britain and Germany at war
1915	Coalition government; Asquith PM
1916 (July)	Battle of the Somme begins
1916	Second Coalition government; Lloyd George PM
1917	USA declares war on Germany
1918	Representation of the People Act
1918 (Aug)	Battle of Amiens; start of the 'Hundred Days'
1918 (Nov)	Armistice ends fighting
1918	General election; Coalition government; Lloyd George PM
1919	Treaty of Versailles
1920	Partition of Ireland
1922	Southern Ireland (Eire) gains independence
1922	General election; Conservative government; Bonar Law PM
1923	Baldwin PM
1923 (Dec)	General election
1924 (Jan)	Labour government; MacDonald PM
1924 (Oct)	General election; Conservative government; Baldwin PM
1925	Locarno Treaty
1926	General Strike
1929	General election; Labour government; MacDonald PM
1931	National government; MacDonald PM

1931	Britain leaves Gold Standard
1931	General election; National government; MacDonald PM
1933	Hitler becomes German Chancellor
1935	Peace Ballot
1935	Baldwin PM
1935	General election; National government; Baldwin PM
1936 (Jan)	George V dies; Edward VIII becomes King
1936	Remilitarisation of Rhineland
1936 (Dec)	Abdication of Edward VIII; George VI becomes King
1937	Chamberlain PM
1938	Munich Agreement
1939 (March)	Germany invades Czechoslovakia
1939 (Sept)	Germany invades Poland; fails to respond to British ultimatum; Britain and Germany at war
1940 (May)	Coalition government; Churchill PM
1940 (May/June)	Dunkirk evacuation
1940 (June)	Italy declares war
1941 (June)	Germany invades Russia
1941 (Dec)	Japan declares war on Britain and USA; Germany declares war on USA
1942 (Jan)	Fall of Singapore
1942 (Oct)	Battle of El Alamein
1943 (May)	German and Italian surrender in North Africa
1943 (July)	Invasion of Sicily
1943 (Sept)	Italy surrenders
1944 (June)	D-Day – invasion of Normandy
1945 (May)	Germany surrenders
1945 (May)	Conservative government; Churchill PM
1945 (July)	General election; Labour government; Attlee PM
1945 (Aug)	Japan surrenders
1946	Nationalisation of coal mining
1947	India and Pakistan gain independence
1948	Inception of National Health Service
1948–1949	Berlin Airlift
1949	North Atlantic Treaty
1949	Devaluation of sterling
1950	Outbreak of Korean war
1950	General election; Labour government; Attlee PM
1951	Festival of Britain
1951	General election; Conservative government; Churchill PM
1952	George VI dies; Elizabeth II becomes Queen
1953	Korean war ends
1954	Rationing ends
1955	Eden PM

1955	General election; Conservative government; Eden PM
1956	Suez crisis
1957	Macmillan PM
1958	Formation of European Economic Community (EEC)
1959	Formation of European Free Trade Association (EFTA)
1959	General election; Conservative government; Macmillan PM
1963	De Gaulle blocks British entry to EEC
1963	Douglas-Home PM
1964	General election; Labour government; Wilson PM
1966	General election; Labour government; Wilson PM
1967	De Gaulle again blocks British entry to EEC
1967	Devaluation of sterling
1967	Britain ends 'East of Suez' defence commitment
1969	Voting age lowered to 18
1970	General election; Conservative government; Heath PM
1971	Decimalisation of currency (formerly £1 = 20 shillings; 1 shilling 12 pence)
1972	Sterling floats
1973	Britain joins European Community
1973	Oil price rise
1974	Miners' strike
1974 (Feb)	General election; Labour government; Wilson PM
1974 (Nov)	General election; Labour government; Wilson PM
1975	Referendum on EC membership; affirmative vote
1976	Callaghan PM
1976	IMF loan to Britain
1978–1979	'Winter of discontent'
1979	Scottish and Welsh referenda on devolution fail to approve it
1979	General election; Conservative government; Thatcher PM
1981	Foundation of Social Democratic Party (SDP)
1982	Falklands war
1983	General election; Conservative government; Thatcher PM
1984–1985	Miners' strike
1987	Single European Market established
1987	General election; Conservative government; Thatcher PM
1989	Berlin Wall opened by East Germany
1990	Britain joins Exchange Rate Mechanism (ERM)
1990	Major PM
1991	Break-up of Soviet Union
1991	Gulf war
1991	Maastricht Treaty
1992	General election; Conservative government; Major PM
1992	Sterling leaves ERM – 'Black Wednesday'
1994	IRA ceasefire

1994	Privatisation of coal mines
1995	Labour revises Clause IV of its constitution
1997	General election; Labour government; Blair PM
1997	Devolution for Scotland and Wales agreed in referenda
1998	'Good Friday' agreement over devolved Northern Ireland assembly
1999	Reduction in numbers of hereditary peers voting in House of Lords

GENERAL ELECTIONS 1900–1997

Cons = Conservative; Lab = Labour; Lib = Liberal; IN = Irish Nationalist; SNP = Scottish National Party; PC = Plaid Cymru.

Percentages of vote rounded so may not sum to 100.

Date	Party	MPs	% of vote
1900 (Oct)	Cons	402	51
	Lab	2	2
	Lib	184	45
	IN*	82	2
	* most Irish Nationalist MPs were unopposed 1900–1910		
1906 (Feb)	Cons	157	44
	Lab	30	6
	Lib	400	49
	IN	83	1
1910 (Feb)	Cons	273	47
	Lab	40	8
	Lib	275	43
	IN	82	2
1910 (Dec)	Cons	272	46
	Lab	42	7
	Lib	272	44
	IN	84	3
1918 (Dec)	Coalition Cons	335	33
	Coalition Lab	10	2
	Coalition Lib	133	14
	Other Cons	23	3
	Labour	63	22
	Lib	28	12
	Irish Unionist	25	3
	IN	7	2
	Sinn Fein	73	5
	Others	10	5

Date	Party	MPs	% of vote
1922 (Nov)	Cons*	345	38
	Lab	142	30
	National Lib	62	12
	(i.e. ex-Coalition Lib)		
	Lib	54	18
	Others	12	3
	* includes Northern Irish Unionists 1922–1970		
1923 (Dec)	Cons	258	38
	Lab	191	31
	Lib	159	30
	Others	7	2
1924 (Oct)	Cons	419	48
	Lab	151	33
	Lib	40	18
	Others	5	1
1929 (May)	Cons	260	38
	Lab	288	37
	Lib	59	23
	Others	8	1
1931 (Oct)	Cons	473	55
	National Lab	13	2
	Lib	68	10
	(all above in National government)		
	Lab	52	31
	Independent Lib	4	1
	Others	5	2
1935 (Nov)	Cons*	432	54
	Lab	154	38
	Lib	20	6
	Others	9	2
	* includes Liberal Nationals 1935–1966		
1945 (July)	Cons	213	40
	Lab	393	48
	Lib	12	9
	Others	22	3
1950 (Feb)	Cons	298	44
	Lab	315	46
	Lib	9	9
	Others	3	1
1951 (Oct)	Cons	321	48
	Lab	295	49
	Lib	6	3
	Others	3	1

Date	Party	MPs	% of vote
1955 (May)	Cons	344	50
	Lab	277	46
	Lib	6	3
	Others	3	1
1959 (Oct)	Cons	365	49
	Lab	258	44
	Lib	6	6
	Others	1	1
1964 (Oct)	Cons	304	43
	Lab	317	44
	Lib	9	11
	Others	–	1
1966 (March)	Cons	253	42
	Lab	363	48
	Lib	12	9
	Others	2	1
1970 (June)	Cons	330	46
	Lab	287	43
	Lib	6	8
	SNP/PC	1	2
	Others	6	1
1974 (Feb)	Cons	297	38
	Lab	301	37
	Lib	14	19
	SNP/PC	9	3
	Others*	14	3
	* includes Northern Irish Unionists 1974–1997		
1974 (Oct)	Cons	277	36
	Lab	319	39
	Lib	13	18
	SNP/PC	14	4
	Others	12	3
1979 (May)	Cons	339	44
	Lab	269	37
	Lib	11	14
	SNP/PC	4	2
	Others	12	3
1983 (June)	Cons	397	42
	Lab	209	28
	Alliance (Lib/SDP)	23	25
	SNP/PC	4	2
	Others	17	4

Date	Party	MPs	% of vote
1987 (June)	Cons	376	42
	Lab	229	31
	Alliance	22	23
	SNP/PC	6	2
	Others	17	3
1992 (Apr)	Cons	336	42
	Lab	271	34
	Lib Democrat	20	18
	SNP/PC	7	2
	Others	17	3
1997 (May)	Cons	165	31
	Lab	419	43
	Lib Democrat	46	17
	SNP/PC	10	3
	Others	19	7

Source: D. Butler, 'Electors and Elected' in Halsey and Webb, (eds) *Social Trends* (see Chapter 1)

PREFACE

This is a book about the public life of the British people. It is about which political parties they choose to govern them and about the decisions the governments they elected have taken. It is about Britain's relations with the outside world. It is about major decisions that people have taken for themselves but which have affected the nation's collective life – such as the number of children in a family, or how individuals spend their money. And it is about the things that have impinged on people's lives but have been partly beyond the control of either individuals or governments – war and economic shocks, for example. It examines the ideas people have had about certain things that have affected public life, such as class and national identity, but it is not primarily about people's private lives and thoughts. So it is a political, social and economic, but not a cultural, history.

The use of some terms may be unfamiliar to non-British readers. 'The 1900s' means the period 1900–1909 (or, loosely, 1900 to the First World War). 'Interwar' means the period between the two world wars, and 'post-war', after the Second World War. 'Liberal' and 'Conservative' with initial capitals mean the political parties of those names. The views they have been associated with are discussed in the relevant chapters. Uncapitalised, 'conservative' can mean politically right of centre (the location of the centre, of course, changing over the century – and broadly moving to the left until the 1980s), or simply reluctant to change, and the context should make clear which. As the Liberal Party faded, 'liberal' came to mean mildly left of centre; for the last 50 years or so it has been particularly associated with liberal social attitudes. Neither word, in Britain, denotes an extreme position and hence one can have, for instance, liberal Conservatism without that being a contradiction. Finally, 'America' and 'the USA', and between 1922 and 1991 'Russia' and 'the Soviet Union', have been used interchangeably.

A book like this is dependent on the work of many other historians. There is a list of useful books covering the whole period at the end of Chapter 1. At the end of other chapters 'Further reading' indicates the most important sources. In the case of books of essays by different writers, I have listed individual essays where they are a particularly important source, and otherwise I have listed the book.

I owe a debt of thanks to two anonymous referees for their valuable comments, and to my wife, Hilary, for her support.

Chapter 1

BRITAIN IN 1900

Monarch and Empire

On 22 January 1901 Queen Victoria died at the age of 81, having reigned for over 63 years. The personification of the nineteenth century lived until the beginning of the twentieth. Although her name is immortalised in the adjective Victorian, her importance to Britain lay not in the real power she wielded, which was limited, but in her position as a focus of loyalty and as a constitutional monarch.

Britain has good claims to be the first real constitutional monarchy. In its modern form, this means that the monarch is ultimately subordinate to an elected body, the House of Commons. This subordination had been more or less accepted by the time Victoria came to the throne, and over the next 60 years much of the monarch's remaining real authority was eroded. The government was established by its ability to command a majority in the House of Commons. The Crown retained some real power in its ability to ask one party leader or another to attempt to form a government, but the occasions for using this power were infrequent, because party discipline was tight. So it was usually obvious which party would command a Commons majority and which party leader would become Prime Minister. Once in office, the Crown by convention accepted its government's policies, even if the monarch did not like them. The Crown retained the right to 'be consulted . . . to encourage . . . [and] to warn', in Walter Bagehot's phrase.[1] Bagehot was a journalist, but his dictum came to be seen as official doctrine.

The monarch's elevation above politics had important consequences. Politics had become increasingly polarised between the two major parties, the Liberals and the Conservatives. By remaining aloof from all this, the monarch avoided criticism from either side and was increasingly seen as a benevolent mother (or when Victoria was succeeded by her son Edward VII, father) of the nation. Victoria herself in later years had increasingly favoured the Conservatives, but Gladstone, the Liberal leader, had loyally kept silent and the monarchy was perceived as officially neutral. Positive feelings about the monarchy were buttressed by the spread of popular newspapers and magazines which carried, mainly respectful, news of the royal family. Always a focus of loyalty to many, by 1900 the monarchy probably commanded more widespread support than at any time since the late sixteenth century.

To many Britons in 1900, sentimental loyalty to the monarch was strengthened by her position as ruler of the British Empire. In 1900 the Empire was at war. Small-scale wars, mainly punitive expeditions against unsubdued native peoples in Africa or the Indian frontier, were not unusual. The Boer war, which had broken out in South Africa in 1899, was a much bigger affair. It was an attempt to subdue the independent Boer republics of inland South Africa, and the Boers, farmers of Dutch origin, had initially scored considerable successes. It was to take three years to finish Boer resistance, although by 1900 Britain had gained the upper hand.

In spite of the Boer war, the British Empire in 1900 was at or near its peak. It covered one-fifth of the habitable land surface of the globe. Like the Crown, it was a focus of loyalty for many Britons. Its protection provided one of the rationales for the British navy, by far the largest in the world. It provided jobs for the sons of middle-class professionals, although as it was staffed remarkably economically the jobs were not that numerous. And it had a considerable economic significance for Britain. However, its vast size and spread can lead to an overestimation of its importance. It had many limits.

The Empire was extremely diverse. Most important, in terms of their impact on popular consciousness and on Britain's own economy, were two very different entities. One was India. Victoria had been declared Empress of India by Benjamin Disraeli, the Conservative Prime Minister, in 1877 and the title seemed to add an additional lustre to Britain's possession of this part of the Empire. Hugely populous – it had almost 300 million inhabitants in 1900 – large parts of it were ruled by a small number of British administrators assisted by Indian clerks and police. Other parts were quasi-autonomous states under their historic ruling families. British rule was backed up by two armies, an Indian army – with British officers – and elements of the British army. All this was paid for by India. Apart from largely paying for herself, India was import-ant to Britain economically. It is often assumed that the importance of India, and other parts of the Empire, was in the supply of raw materials to Britain, but this was not the case. Britain bought raw materials from all over the world and enjoyed no special advan-tages in buying them from the Empire. India did, however, act as a huge market for British manufactures. These were paid for partly by India's exports to other parts of the world. Thus India helped to buttress Britain's position as the world's second largest manufacturing nation.

The second great segment of the Empire comprised the 'White Dominions', a term becoming popular for Australia, New Zealand, Canada and tiny Newfoundland, then independent of Canada. From the 1840s onwards, these had been granted effective self-government, and therefore they were not 'ruled' by Britain in any real sense. While they were important markets for British goods, their main economic significance to Britain was as destinations for emigrants. Between 1900 and 1914 net British and Irish emigra-tion to these countries totalled almost 1.4 million, and they overtook the USA as the prime destination for such emigration. (Net emigration is after counting those who returned in the period.) While there were people in these countries – Irish emigrants in Australia, the long-established French settlers in Canada – who remained ambival-ent about their membership of the British Empire, most of the inhabitants were enthu-siastic. Britain herself, as the 'mother country', was also a focus of their loyalty, hardly surprising as a large proportion of their population had actually been born there.

The Empire also comprised a mass of miscellaneous smaller colonies, the term usually given to the non-Indian territories which were directly ruled by Britain. (Confusingly, the White Dominions were also often called colonies.) Some of these, such as Nigeria, had only just been welded together as one entity and were governed to a considerable extent by their traditional rulers. Others, such as Ceylon, contained a large British commercial presence in the form of plantation owners or managers – in Ceylon's case the crop was tea. South Africa itself was more complex in that the Boer farmers had different aspirations to later British settlers, the most influential of whom had substantial mining interests.

While the Empire was a focus of loyalty within Britain, it did not command such widespread support as did the Crown. A substantial portion of the Liberal Party had been publicly opposed to the Boer war. The Conservatives, already in power, had called an election in 1900 and had won a smashing victory, suggesting that voters who favoured the Empire exceeded in numbers those who were lukewarm or against it. But the fact remains that, although there was much patriotic support for the Empire, enthusiasm for it was not universal.

Late nineteenth century imperialism affected Britain's relations with other countries. British foreign policy at this time is sometimes described as one of 'splendid isolation', but the phrase is misleading. Foreign policy was essentially pragmatic. As the world's largest trading nation it was not in Britain's interests to be on bad terms with anyone in the long run. However, events sometimes got in the way, and one of these was the rapid expansion of the Empire in the late nineteenth century, which antagonised other nations. In the short term the most important of these were France and Russia, also imperial powers. France and Britain collided in Africa, while Russia's expansion southwards into Central Asia came up against Britain's attempts to safeguard India's north-west frontier. The resulting quarrels led to a period of foreign policy isolation for Britain at the end of the century. The way out of this had major long-term consequences.

Some imperialists had believed that, by constructing a world-wide Empire, Britain could be rendered invulnerable. By 1900 it was apparent that this dream would never become a reality. Strong though the Royal Navy was, as other nations industrialised and built up their own navies it became increasingly unable to police the entire world. Britain had already effectively ceded control of the seas around the Americas to the USA. In the East, Britain saw advantages in friendship with Japan, whose economy and navy were both expanding rapidly. The Japanese alliance of 1902 was the result. It was defensive, with each nation pledging to help the other if it was at war with more than one other nation. If Japan went to war with Russia, which it did two years later, Britain would not get dragged in.

More important was Britain's changing attitude towards Europe. As late as 1901 Lord Lansdowne, the Foreign Secretary, had proposed an alliance with Germany against Russia. But Germany was a problem. Its foreign and imperial ambitions had become increasingly grandiose under the reckless and unstable Wilhelm II. Its ambition to develop a large navy, although still unfulfilled, was also a threat. In the circumstances, most British politicians accepted that easing imperial tensions was the safest course of action, and the *Entente Cordiale* of 1904 with France was the result. It was strongly supported by the cosmopolitan Edward VII, but he was not the prime mover. The *entente* was in no sense a military alliance, being designed essentially to settle imperial rivalries in Africa. Nor was it intended as a threat to Germany. As before, Britain's interests lay in world peace, not war.

Prosperity, poverty and the role of the state

Britain's interests lay in peace because of her supremacy in trade, even though the USA had dethroned Britain as the largest industrial nation. This supremacy was in part because of Britain's abolition of tariffs on most imports in the mid-nineteenth century, which had encouraged world-wide tariff reductions and a trade boom. Free trade became a cornerstone of Britain's self-image. It meant cheap imported food, albeit at the expense of British agriculture. In turn, Britain was the world's largest exporter of manufactured goods, while British citizens had built up large holdings of shares and bonds in foreign railways, mines and other assets. Britain's biggest export products were the goods on which she had built her own industrial revolution: textiles, heavy engineering products such as locomotives, ships and coal. In addition, she was the world's greatest provider of the services necessary for trade: shipping, insurance and banking. This pattern was replicated in Britain's economic geography. The wealthiest areas were those where trade or heavy industry was dominant.

Wealthiest of all was London. It was a centre of trade, of much manufacturing (although not heavy industry) and of financial services such as banking and insurance. It was also the place where many of the wealthy chose to live. Outside London, wages were highest in the industrial areas: Lancashire produced coal, machinery and, most of all, cotton textiles; Yorkshire, coal, machinery and wool textiles; South Wales, predominantly coal; the Midlands engaged in engineering, a vast range of other manufacturing activities and coal mining; the North-East, in shipbuilding, engineering and coal mining; and the Scottish Lowlands, in all these activities. The production, use and export of coal was the common denominator (Figs 1.1 and 1.2). The wage levels of the men, and in textiles some women, in these areas made the British working class the best paid in Europe. There was a paradox, however. Working-class health in these areas was poor: no better, and often worse, than in other areas where wages were lower. The best overall measure of this is height, since adult height is a reflection of childhood and adolescent living conditions – that is, a combination of housing conditions, the prevalence of disease, other environmental factors such as air quality and the nutritional value of food intake. While figures for the past are not precise, the average height of working–class men was probably 4 to 5 inches less than the 5 feet 10 inch average of men today. The relatively high wages of many workers were counteracted by overcrowded housing, a poor urban environment and the paucity of medical services for many people.

Of course, as Britain was a relatively advanced society, hospital and medical provision was widespread, although very basic for the really poor since they had to rely on the Poor Law, originally set up as a safety net for the destitute. This function still existed, although it was unpopular since it often meant confinement in workhouses,

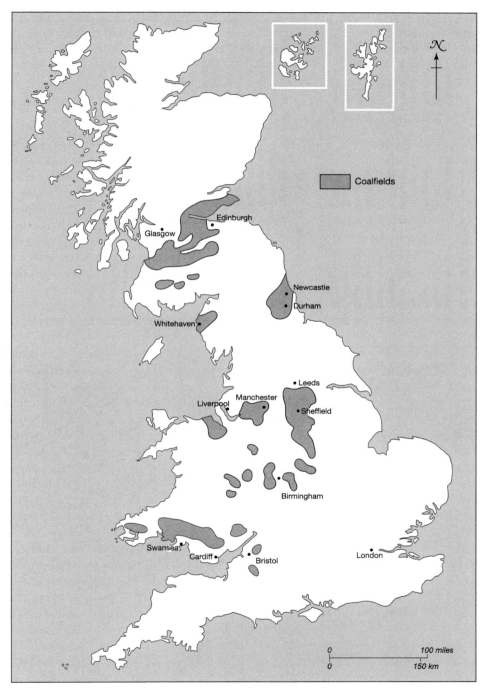

Figure 1.1   Coalfields in Britain
Source: More, G., *Industrial Age*, Longman (1989 and 1997)

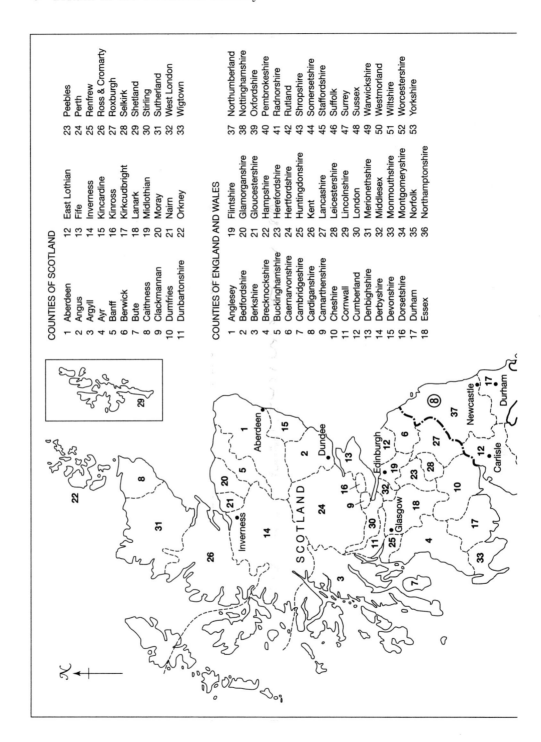

COUNTIES OF SCOTLAND

1	Aberdeen	12	East Lothian
2	Angus	13	Fife
3	Argyll	14	Inverness
4	Ayr	15	Kincardine
5	Banff	16	Kinross
6	Berwick	17	Kirkcudbright
7	Bute	18	Lanark
8	Caithness	19	Midlothian
9	Clackmannan	20	Moray
10	Dumfries	21	Nairn
11	Dunbartonshire	22	Orkney

23	Peebles		
24	Perth		
25	Renfrew		
26	Ross & Cromarty		
27	Roxburgh		
28	Selkirk		
29	Shetland		
30	Stirling		
31	Sutherland		
32	West London		
33	Wigtown		

COUNTIES OF ENGLAND AND WALES

1	Anglesey	19	Flintshire
2	Bedfordshire	20	Glamorganshire
3	Berkshire	21	Gloucestershire
4	Brecknockshire	22	Hampshire
5	Buckinghamshire	23	Herefordshire
6	Caernarvonshire	24	Hertfordshire
7	Cambridgeshire	25	Huntingdonshire
8	Cardiganshire	26	Kent
9	Carmarthenshire	27	Lancashire
10	Cheshire	28	Leicestershire
11	Cornwall	29	Lincolnshire
12	Cumberland	30	London
13	Denbighshire	31	Merionethshire
14	Derbyshire	32	Middlesex
15	Devonshire	33	Monmouthshire
16	Dorsetshire	34	Montgomeryshire
17	Durham	35	Norfolk
18	Essex	36	Northamptonshire

37	Northumberland
38	Nottinghamshire
39	Oxfordshire
40	Pembrokeshire
41	Radnorshire
42	Rutland
43	Shropshire
44	Somersetshire
45	Staffordshire
46	Suffolk
47	Surrey
48	Sussex
49	Warwickshire
50	Westmorland
51	Wiltshire
52	Worcestershire
53	Yorkshire

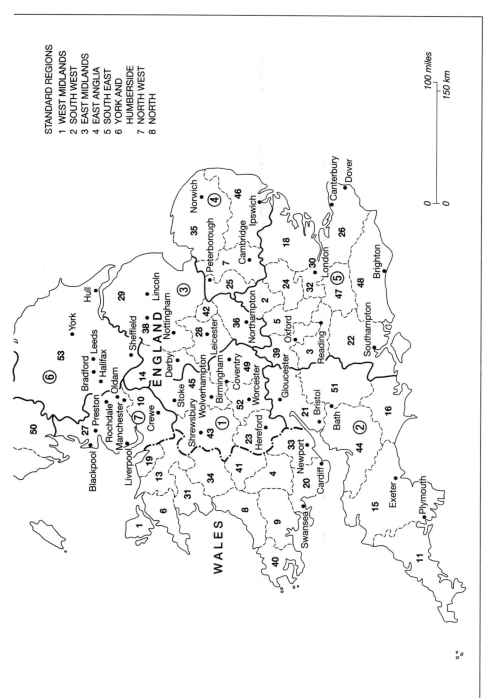

STANDARD REGIONS
1 WEST MIDLANDS
2 SOUTH WEST
3 EAST MIDLANDS
4 EAST ANGLIA
5 SOUTH EAST
6 YORK AND
   HUMBERSIDE
7 NORTH WEST
8 NORTH

100 miles
150 km

Figure 1.2   Great Britain: counties and major towns
Source: More, C., *Industrial Age*, Longman (1989 and 1997)

usually grim mid-Victorian buildings. But there was no welfare state as we know it today. There was no form of state social insurance for unemployment; no additional benefits for families with young children; no old-age pensions. Such insurance as did exist was provided through individual subscriptions to friendly societies, insurance companies and trade unions. The middle classes and better-off manual workers could afford such subscriptions, but a large proportion of the population only paid them at a minimal level, if at all.

The absence of state social welfare did not mean a complete absence of state intervention. Intervention of various kinds had developed since the mid-nineteenth century, often in response to obvious problems or glaring abuses rather than as a result of major ideological shifts. For many years there had been legal limits on working hours for some groups of workers, many of whom were children. By 1900 the state also provided substantial resources for lower-level, then called elementary, education. It was thought appropriate to intervene on behalf of children, partly because they were not able to help themselves, but also because it was accepted that it was financially difficult for parents to provide them with an adequate education. Similarly, Poor Law medical services had developed, not just for the destitute but for a wider population, because of a similar pragmatic acceptance of their inability to provide for themselves. Both the Poor Law and education were provided through locally based authorities (the churches also provided education), although central government provided much of the money for education. It was generally agreed that such local provision was the correct approach. Local government in larger towns had also become increasingly concerned with the provision of services such as water, gas and electric tramways which had proliferated in the 1890s, as well as the control of building standards and street widths, and the provision of cleansing and sewerage services. Larger towns had their own councils; county councils, covering small towns and rural areas, had only been set up in 1888 and were usually less active.

Municipal action of this kind had developed for two reasons. In the case of gasworks and tramways, because town councils thought they could make money out of them. In the case of building regulations, water and sewerage, because the appalling conditions of mid-Victorian cities had led to a widespread realisation that some collective control over environmental conditions was needed. In modern terms, there was a 'market failure' caused by the fact that misuse of the environment did not contain financial penalties; either collective provision was needed or, at the very least, control over private provision. Like the protection of the weak and vulnerable, remedying market failure was seen by most as a limited but necessary exercise. It did not impinge on the duty of the able-bodied population – that is, most people – to look after themselves for most of their needs.

However, there was a growing number of those who believed the state should have a wider role. The Boer war had resulted in a sudden need for more recruits than usual for Britain's small army. One consequence was a large number of rejections of such recruits for medical reasons. A side effect of the war, therefore, was a heightened debate about 'national efficiency'. Concern about the subject was not new, as from the 1880s there had been worries about 'urban deterioration'. The poor physical condition of many town-dwellers had led to a whole quasi-scientific theory: urban children grew up with poor physique which they transmitted to their children in a vicious cycle of decline. The theory was based on a faulty conception of genetics, as acquired characteristics cannot be inherited. However, the poor physique of many of the urban working classes was a reality. Concerns over urban deterioration coalesced with other fears and aspirations to lead some thinkers to much more expansive ideas. Some of these ideas played upon notions of the 'race' and its possible deterioration, from poor living conditions or other causes. A discourse of race – that is, a set of beliefs and debates about its importance – was well entrenched in 1900. This incorporated the notion that the British race, or more generally the Anglo-Saxon race, was superior to others – but its superiority might be under threat. (Other countries had similar discourses about themselves.)

Politics and parties

Social welfare was seen as a means of rebuilding superiority by improving working-class conditions, and elements of both political parties were attracted by these ideas. On the Conservative side these included some of the Liberal Unionists. This was a group of mainly right-wing Liberals who had broken away in 1886 and allied them-selves with the Conservatives; it included a socially progressive wing under Joseph Chamberlain, known as Radical Joe. The Liberals too had a socially progressive wing. Known as the New Liberals, some were influenced by ideas of national efficiency while others simply extended the traditional Liberal sympathy with the underdog. What united them was a belief that 'liberty' was not just political and religious, but was social and economic too; and if people lacked the means to acquire even the basics of adequate housing and medical care, they did not have social and economic liberty.

The conception of national efficiency tied in to the ideas of some contemporary philo-sophers about the nature of the state. They saw it as an organic community to which the citizen owed duties. This idea was very different to most British thinking about the state, which derived from the great seventeenth and early eighteenth thinker John Locke. Locke saw the state as a body which existed to guarantee the peace and liberty of the people. It was their servant, not their master: an abstract entity which owed them rights. Most people in 1900 had probably never heard of Locke but held ideas about the undesirability of too much government interference which had been indirectly influenced by him or his followers.

At the same time, the notion of Britons as free and autonomous citizens was tem-pered by patriotism, encapsulated by the reverence attached to the Crown. Patriotism embodied a different, and older, brand of communitarian thinking. In this the British people, while free citizens, were also part of an 'imagined community' (a term coined by Benedict Anderson) – that is, the British nation.

The two major political parties can in part be categorised by the degree of their support for each of these contrasting – although not necessarily competing – ideas. The Liberals were more strongly attached to the Lockean tradition, the Conservatives to the communitarian. But there were many overlaps, while some in both parties were attracted, and others repelled, by the newer ideas of an organic community. The beliefs of traditional Liberals, often called Gladstonian Liberals after the great Liberal leader who had died in 1898, were underpinned by the Lockean conception that every able-bodied adult male in Britain had the right to be independent (Locke paid less attention to women). To be independent was to be free to vote and to worship as one wished. It was assumed that such people would support themselves and their family, so state aid was not only unnecessary but actually pernicious. To be able to support oneself, the cost of living needed to be as low as possible; therefore, taxation should be low, which was an argument for a minimal state. This conception had become so pervasive in the 1860s and 1870s that it had been accepted by many Conservatives, although their stress on freedom was less marked. So new ideas about state intervention confronted older but still strongly entrenched ideas about the sharp limits which should be placed upon it.

There were, of course, other reasons for the distinctions between parties. One was the Conservative stress, implied by their name, on the necessary slowness of change. Constitutionally, Conservatism stood for the status quo. So they opposed Home Rule for Ireland, meaning Irish autonomy in their domestic affairs. Ireland was then an integral part of the United Kingdom, but many Irish disliked this arrangement. Liberal support for Home Rule had been instrumental in causing the Liberal Unionist breakaway which had led to Home Rule's defeat in 1886. (Subsequently, for many years, Conservatives often referred to themselves as Unionists, and for a period the word was incorporated into the party's official name, the Liberal Unionists fading away as a separate entity.) The Conservatives also supported the existing powers of the House of Lords, then consisting almost entirely of hereditary peers, which included the power to defeat all government legislation except, by long-established custom, legislation involving government revenue (money bills). A later Home Rule bill during the Liberal government of 1892–1895 had passed the Commons but had been defeated in the Lords. In spite of their support for the anti-democratic powers of the Lords, Conservatives broadly accepted the idea of a wide franchise. The extension of the franchise which had taken place in the nineteenth century had seemed to bring as much electoral advantage to them as it had to the Liberals. But in spite of this extension, in 1900 over one-third of adult males could not vote in parliamentary elections, and neither could women.

There were two other dividing lines between the parties. The Conservatives had become increasingly associated with the Empire, particularly after the alliance with Chamberlain, who combined his social progressivism with imperialism. While some Liberals were almost as enthusiastic about the Empire as the Conservatives, many others, following Gladstone, saw an expansionist imperialism as both expensive and potentially denying to others the liberty they so strongly supported for themselves. It was these Liberals who had opposed the Boer war. The other dividing line was religion. Formally, the Church of England was the Established Church; that is, the Church whose rights were enshrined in law, whose senior bishops sat in the House of Lords and of which the monarch was the head. (In Scotland, the same was true of the Presbyterian Church, which had a different form of government, with no bishops; so the monarch belonged to different churches in the two countries.) But England and Wales had also become, with the Glorious Revolution of 1688–1689, a religiously tolerant state, to be followed later by Scotland. Toleration was gradually extended and made more effective while the Church of England's privileges were restricted. Nevertheless, the Liberals were still perceived as the party which fought for the rights of nonconformity; that is, the numerous Protestant churches – Methodists, Baptists and others – which were independent of the Church of England. Since many Liberals were Church of England, the Conservative Party was not associated with the Church so strongly as Liberalism was with nonconformity, but the Conservatives still presented themselves as the 'Church' party.

To most MPs, party activists and voters, the ruling issues in 1900 were the constitution, the issue embodied in the debates over Irish Home Rule and the powers of the Lords; religion; and the Empire, the issue which was most prominent in the 1900 election itself. Welfare was not at this time a major concern, even though the Boer war was to push it up the agenda by exacerbating concern over urban deterioration. In 1900, however, one other event foreshadowed the importance of social welfare to the twentieth century British state, even though at the time its significance seemed little more than the biblical cloud which was no bigger than a man's hand. This was the foundation of the Labour Party, known initially as the Labour Representation Committee (LRC).

In contemporary language, 'labour' meant organised associations of working men and also encompassed the wider issues of manual workers' relationship with society. As Britain industrialised and as more urban workers got the vote, labour had risen up the political agenda. By 1900 its significance was further heightened because British trade unions were among the largest and most powerful in the world. That did not actually make them very large and powerful, but even so a significant proportion of key groups such as engineering and cotton workers, and miners, were unionised. Unions of skilled, or well-paid, workers such as these were not in themselves particularly in favour of social welfare measures. Their members tended to agree with the ruling consensus that it was the duty of adults to provide for themselves – which they did in part by belonging to a union. Nevertheless, unions of unskilled workers did attach more importance to such issues and, for reasons of solidarity, skilled unions tended to go along with them. More important for most unions was their legal position. They were concerned that their ability to carry out strike action and make it effective could come under attack. These fears were exacerbated in the 1890s by unfavourable legal judgments and by employer attempts to reduce union influence.

Although the Conservatives had in recent years trodden carefully with the unions, and there were union members who were Conservative, the Liberals had historically been closer to them. In part, this was because Gladstone had successfully presented himself as the representative of the independent-minded common man. However, although there were a few working-class Liberal MPs and other Liberals who were sympathetic to 'labour', many Liberals were far more concerned with their traditional causes. Uncertainty as to how far either of the two main parties would support the unions, therefore, promoted the idea of an independent body to represent labour interests, namely the LRC. Among the founding bodies, apart from various trade unions, were two socialist parties, the Social Democratic Federation (SDF) and the Independent Labour Party

(ILP). The SDF, a Marxist body, soon left; the ILP remained. But socialism in Britain was still a tiny movement, exemplified by the fact that, in spite of the alliance of two socialist parties and the unions, the LRC got just two MPs elected in 1900.

Britain at the beginning of the twentieth century was a country of contrasts. It had a long-standing tradition of constitutional government, but many men, and all women, still lacked the right to vote in parliamentary elections. For most of the time the monarch was removed from politics, but another unelected institution, the House of Lords, still had considerable power. Britain ruled the largest Empire in the world but was fearful of international isolation. Its economy was the world's second largest, its working men among the best paid and its trade unions the strongest, but state social welfare was rudimentary, the physique of the working classes poor and trade unionists constantly concerned about their status.

Note

1. Bagehot, W., *The English Constitution* (London: Kegan Paul, 2nd ed., 1873), p. 75.

Further reading

Books used for the whole period are listed below. Brown, J. and Louis, W. (eds), *The Oxford History of the British Empire: The Twentieth Century* (Oxford: Oxford University Press, 1999) is invaluable for its subject. Floud, R. and Johnson, P. (eds), *The Cambridge Economic History of Modern Britain* (Cambridge: Cambridge University Press, Vols 2 and 3, 2004) is authoritative, although some chapters are quite technical. Halsey, A. and Webb, J. (eds), *Twentieth Century British Social Trends* (Basingstoke: Macmillan, 2000) contains huge amounts of data; an earlier edition, Halsey, A. (ed.), *Trends in British Society since 1900* (London: Macmillan, 1972) has also been used. Johnson, P. (ed.), *Twentieth Century Britain: Economic, Social and Cultural Change* (Harlow: Longman, 1994) has many useful essays. McKibbin, R., *Classes and Cultures: England 1918–1951* (Oxford: Oxford University Press, 1998) is a book of enormous interest; its importance is such that it should be mentioned here although it does not cover the whole period. Matthew, H. and Harrison, B., *Oxford Dictionary of National Biography* (Oxford: Oxford University Press, 2004) is a priceless source. More, C., *The Industrial Age: Economy and Society in Britain 1750–1995* (Harlow: Longman, 2nd ed., 1997) covers a wide range of topics. Ramsden, J., *The Age of Balfour and Baldwin 1902–1940* (London: Longman, 1978), Ramsden, J., *The Age of Churchill and Eden 1940–1957* (Harlow: Longman, 1995) and Ramsden, J., *Winds of Change: Macmillan to Heath 1957–1975* (Harlow: Longman, 1996) are not only comprehensive histories of the Conservative Party but illuminate British politics for the period. Reynolds, D., *Britannia Overruled: British Policy and World Power in the 20th Century* (Harlow: Longman, 2nd ed., 2000) is a thought-provoking survey. Zweiniger-Bargielowska, I. (ed.), *Women in Twentieth-Century Britain* (Harlow: Longman, 2001) contains many valuable essays.

Other sources for this chapter are as for Chapter 2.

LIBERAL HIGH TIDE: POLITICS 1900–1914

The political process

Britain's major political parties, and the policies they have adopted when in government, have always been subject to a variety of influences. Smaller parties have found it hard to prosper under the 'first past the post' electoral system, so the large parties have accommodated many shades of opinion among their MPs and activists. The views of business and other pressure groups have been recognised as legitimate influences on policy. Britain's strongly entrenched Civil Service has meant that the views of senior civil servants have been a significant factor. The press has also been important. In the 1900s, local papers were far more concerned with politics than most are now: the Conservatives had been increasing their influence in the national and local press, but many newspapers still followed a Liberal tradition. Politicians used the press to 'place' stories in order to gauge public opinion or to bring an issue into the open. Relationships between politicians and the newspapers which supported them were probably closer, and less critical, than today. Lloyd George, for instance, had links with several, such as the high-minded *Manchester Guardian* (the ancestor of today's *Guardian*) and the less high-minded *News of the World*.

Ultimately, however, in the 1900s, as today, politicians depended on the support of voters. But while voters had the ultimate sanction, the traffic in influence was not one-way, since voters were influenced by what politicians said. This was especially the case as, to a greater extent than today, self-image was formed in part by allegiance to a political party. So politicians and voters were engaged in an endless dance, in which the movements of each reacted on the other; but it was a dance with no set rules, so that the movements continuously, if often slowly, changed. Sometimes they changed suddenly, because of one other factor which was always latent in politics: an external shock. Such shocks might be economic, or they might be generated by foreign affairs, or they might be domestic shocks such as the periodic upheavals over Ireland.

Conservative woes

The Conservatives' great electoral victory of 1900 was won in the wake of apparent victory in the Boer war. The war, however, dragged on for two more years, one of an increasing number of problems which eroded the party's popularity.

Of course the Conservatives, with their allies the Liberal Unionists, did not depend for their electoral victory simply on a wave of popular patriotism, or what was called at the time jingoism. The traditional basis of Conservative support was agriculture and the 'rural interest', encompassing landowners, farmers and the tradesmen and professional classes of villages and small country towns. Their tendency to vote Conservative was solidified by the strength of the Church of England in most rural areas. There was not, in fact, much else besides sentiment and custom to make agriculturalists vote Conservative. The party had long since dropped its support for agricultural protection – that is, tariffs on imported foodstuffs. Subsequently, Britain had become the greatest free-trade nation in the world, helping to give its working classes cheap food and thus a relatively high standard of living. Resurrecting protection would be a bold move.

Agriculture was rapidly declining in importance and no political party could exist simply on the support of the rural interest. The real strength of the Conservatives, after the redistribution of constituencies in 1885 had created something close to the modern pattern of single member seats, had lain in the expanding suburbs of large towns and in the South of England generally. Conservative supporters in these areas included many clerks, shopkeepers, members of the professional classes and businessmen and was summed up in the phrase 'villa Toryism'. Religion was a less important factor here than an active imperial appeal, and a passive conservative one. The active appeal came at a time when both the sentimental and practical attractions of Empire were at their height. The Empire promised jobs, and many of the professional classes had a relative in imperial service, or in the army or navy. To those in lower social groupings, the Empire held out possibilities of emigration. In addition, imperial glorification had grown steadily. It ranged from Victoria's promotion as Empress of India, to the widespread imperial coverage of popular newspapers, to the boys' books of G. A. Henty which often had an imperial theme. The passive appeal played on fear of change. The Liberals were represented as the 'dangerous' party: the party which had attacked property by instituting graduated death duties in 1894 (duties which, in fact, left the vast majority of estates untouched); the party which was intent on overturning established constitutional arrangements by giving Home Rule to Ireland; the party which wanted to allow special privileges to nonconformists. In addition, and an argument that played well with many working men, the strong temperance lobby within Liberalism was represented as a threat to that innocent British pleasure, the pub.

However, working men supported the Conservatives for reasons other than the freedom to drink. Religion was a factor. The working classes went to church less than the middle classes, but even so there was a strong popular conception of Protestantism as an integral part of Britishness. In Liverpool, where Irish immigration had been extensive throughout the nineteenth century, the result was a city divided by Protestant/Catholic sectarianism. Local Conservatives capitalised on this and in 1900, of Liverpool's nine parliamentary seats, eight were Conservative. This association with rabid anti-Catholicism was rare, but the rest of Lancashire, where the Church of England was stronger among the working class than in most industrialised areas, had a strong Conservative presence. Here, however, workers' religious allegiances may have been less important than those of employers. Many workmen, both in Lancashire and elsewhere, had identified themselves closely with their employers in the nineteenth century. This identification was diminishing, but it was still strong and it helps to account for working-class Conservatism. Although many employers were nonconformist and Liberal, many were Church of England and Conservative and their workers often voted the same way.

The two years taken to wind up the Boer war chipped away at the Conservatives' self-promoted reputation for running the Empire competently, but it was other issues which were to lead to the party's worst defeat since the modern Conservative Party came into being in the nineteenth century. The 1902 Education Act was intended to bring order to the administrative mess of English and Welsh education, and thus help to promote 'national efficiency'. The separate providers of elementary education, the churches and the 'School Boards' set up in 1870, were put together with the hitherto independent grammar schools under the control of local councils. The scheme was logical but infuriated nonconformists because Church of England and Catholic schools would now receive large sums from the rates yet be free to appoint their own teachers and give denominational religious education. (Scottish education was not denominationally split and did not receive the same treatment.) The Conservatives' attempts in 1904 to reduce the number of pubs by compensating publicans who surrendered the licences needed to sell alcohol was a slap in the face for temperance enthusiasts, also often nonconformist, who saw it as rewarding evildoers.

These Conservative measures tended to solidify opposition from people who were naturally inclined to vote Liberal anyway. Far more important was the Conservatives' debate over protection, initiated by Joseph Chamberlain. The messy winding up of the Boer war had not reduced Chamberlain's keenness for imperialism. In 1903 he launched his policy of 'Tariff Reform', a title chosen to distance it from old-fashioned protection. Tariffs would be put on foreign foodstuffs and manufactures, but not on those from the Empire. So the 'White Dominions' would be welded together in a racially homogeneous bloc, while tariffs would also raise money which could be used for social reform.

The desire for social reform was strengthened by the debate over national efficiency which the Boer war had stimulated. The improvement in living conditions for the working classes would ensure a healthy race which would keep the Empire strong. Conservatives also saw social reform as essential to ameliorate labour, and this aspect of the policy became increasingly significant. However, as the party which claimed to defend property, they did not want to do this by raising ordinary taxation. Tariffs neatly filled the fiscal gap.

It seemed brilliant, but it helped to smash the Conservatives' electoral hopes for the next decade. The White Dominions were not actually keen on full-blooded imperial preference, as the policy came to be called. And, in Britain, belief in free trade was to many Liberals an ideological commitment, not just an argument for cheap food. It went along with a belief in international harmony, opposition to aggressive imperialism and support for a peaceful foreign policy. For many other people, including some Conservative MPs and many working-class voters, free trade was primarily a policy which ensured cheap food – but it was still very important. Some 80 per cent of Britain's wheat was imported, as was much meat; over 50 per cent of the average working-class budget, it was estimated, was spent on food. The equation between cheap imported food and real income levels was an easy one to make.

Tariffs had a real appeal to many Conservatives, as well as to the agricultural interest, and the appeal to imperial loyalties is obvious. But more people were lukewarm or actively hostile. Moreover, in 1903 social welfare still had a relatively small place on most voters' agenda, so this aspect of tariff reform was not a trump card for Chamberlain. The Conservatives split, although not on the scale of the Liberals in 1886, and 17 Conservative and Unionist MPs defected to the Liberals, including, most famously, Winston Churchill. The Conservative position was not helped by their leader, Arthur Balfour, who had replaced his uncle, the rocklike Lord Salisbury, in 1902. Balfour hedged his bets in the controversy over tariffs and satisfied no one. However, Ewen Green has pointed out that the Conservative Party did not settle the tariff issue even after Balfour resigned as leader in 1911. Nor was Chamberlain solely to blame for the 1906 electoral débâcle, since tariffs had wide support in the party. Rather, its continued electoral failure owed itself to the scale of the problems which confronted it in adapting to new electoral demands.

Liberal triumphs

Balfour resigned as Prime Minister late in 1905. The election in early 1906 produced a huge victory for the Liberals and a correspondingly dire defeat for the Conservatives and Liberal Unionists. The Liberals had triumphed more through Conservative unpopularity than because of their positive appeal. Liberal MPs were in some ways even more divided than the Conservatives. Some kept to Gladstonian ideals of the minimalist state, although an increasing proportion were sympathetic to New Liberal ideas of social reform. Some were strongly anti-imperialist – they had been nicknamed pro-Boers during the Boer war – while others were imperialist. Furthermore, these divisions cut across each other so there were a number of groupings. Many Liberals were in the middle, accepting moderate state intervention but hostile to this involving excessive expenditure.

Liberal voting support came from all classes, but there were predictable strengths and weaknesses. Support was strong among nonconformists, of course, but the party's real strength by 1900 came from the working class, and this support was solidified by working-class hostility to tariff reform. Nevertheless, most Liberal MPs were middle class, and many were Anglican, so it would be wrong to see Liberalism as exclusive. It would also be wrong to see voting for either party as overwhelmingly dictated by class position or by religion. Many people voted for what they believed were certain fundamental characteristics of each party: for instance, that the Conservatives were the party of patriotism, or Liberals the party of peace. The fact that much voting was dictated by class or religion, however, did have an impact on the Liberals' geographical support. It was strongest in Wales, which was predominantly nonconformist and, in its mining areas, working class; and in the working-class areas of the other industrial regions.

The Labour Representation Committee (LRC), renamed in 1906 the Labour Party, was still only a minor political factor in the election, winning 29 seats. Even this small number would have been less had there not been a non-competition agreement with the Liberals. The fact of such an agreement emphasises that, in spite of the involvement of socialist parties in the formation of the LRC, the early Labour Party was very moderate. Many of its MPs were the type of working men who could still be found elsewhere as active Liberals – nonconformist, sober, skilled workers. At this stage many Liberals saw Labour as essentially a junior wing of the Liberal Party, both working towards the same 'progressive' causes. This was the so-called Progressive Alliance.

Once in power, the problem which the Liberals did not have to worry about was imperialism. This seems paradoxical, given that their own deep divisions over imperialism at the time of the Boer war had contributed to their defeat in 1900. However, by 1906 aggressive imperialism had shot its bolt. It had shot it partly because there was hardly anywhere else left in the world to bring into the Empire. But it had also shot it because of its failure to achieve rapid success in the Boer war. With expansion of the Empire off the agenda, Liberals could concentrate on running it efficiently and with some regard for the views of the native population – although in South Africa that excluded blacks. The Morley–Minto reforms in India, named after John Morley, the Secretary of State for India, and Lord Minto, the Viceroy (India's ruler, appointed by the government), were one result. In 1909 the India Councils Act, as the reforms were formally called, increased the power of legislative councils and their Indian representatives. It was not conceived of as a step towards independence, but it showed that there were limits to the influence wielded by the rhetoric of Anglo-Saxon racial superiority.

Finding a path through the jungle of imperialism turned out to be surprisingly easy, and it kept Liberals of all shades of opinion happy. It was more difficult to do this in domestic policy. The new Liberal government had two main approaches. On the one hand were bills to remedy what were seen as the wrongs of the Conservative legislation on education and licensing. These were rejected by the House of Lords. The attempts were a necessary sop to the nonconformists, and the rejections became elevated by the Liberals into a policy in their own right. The Lords had already shown themselves, over Home Rule and other issues, as irredeemably Conservative. By provoking them into rejecting more Liberal legislation, it was hoped that there would be unstoppable public support for reform of their right to reject bills from the Commons.

The Liberal government's other route to fulfilling its supporters' aspirations was welfare reform. Not only was this desired by the New Liberals, but it would also steal the clothes of the Chamberlainites. It was, however, going to cost money – important when the Liberals had criticised the Conservatives for profligacy and tax-raising during the Boer war. The early reforms (see box, 'Liberal welfare reforms'), therefore, were either cheap, like school meals and medical inspections, or in the case of old-age pensions the intention was to pay for them with money saved on defence. However, the savings were not as great as anticipated and a trade depression cut revenue in 1908–1909, so higher taxes were needed. The combination of this fact with the Lords' opposition to other Liberal reforms provided the ingredients for a powerful political cocktail.

Politics and government: Liberal welfare reforms

Although it is convenient to group the Liberal welfare reforms together, different ones were motivated by different factors. One important theme of the early reforms was the welfare of children. This was in line with the attention paid by reformers on both sides of the political spectrum to 'national efficiency'. Local authorities were given permission to provide free school meals to needy schoolchildren by an Act of 1906, although they did not have to. This apparently small measure was significant because it was a step in distancing state welfare from the Poor Law, which was perceived as stigmatising those who made use of it. In 1914 a new Act compelled local authorities to provide such meals. In 1907 they were required to provide medical inspection for schoolchildren, continuing a trend begun in 1893 when education for blind and deaf children had to be provided. Energetic local authorities started to provide school clinics on a large scale. Finally, in 1908, the Children Act embodied a raft of reforms. In this case the impetus was not only national efficiency but also simple humanitarian feeling. The Act established separate juvenile courts and remand homes for children under 16. It also policed the everyday behaviour of children more rigorously by, for example, making the sale of tobacco to children an offence. At this stage no one saw any link between smoking and specific diseases, although it was regarded as an activity that was acceptable for adults but not for children.

School meals and medical inspections were meritorious social welfare measures. They were also cunning political moves, because they addressed national efficiency concerns but, as they were largely paid for by local authorities, cost the national Exchequer very little. Those Liberals who opposed too much state interference and spending had their fears partially assuaged because under the first Act local authorities had to agree to provide school meals, giving a further line of defence against excessive spending. The other early Liberal reform, old-age pensions, was of course more expensive. One solution would have been pensions paid for by contributions, but this was either a long-term measure or would still mean expensive state financing for an interim period while the contributions built up. Non-contributory pensions at a low level were the solution. Since the pensions were so low, these would still provide an incentive for most people, except the very poor, to save through friendly societies or trade unions. The pensions were restricted in other ways. The age limit was 70, not an age to which many working people lived; and above a certain income level the pensions tapered off. In spite of the restrictions, around 500,000 people received the pensions in 1909 when they became payable.

The next stage of reform was, in part, an attempt to grapple with the inadequacies of labour markets. Here Churchill, at the Board of Trade, worked with civil servants who were themselves keen to push changes. Contemporary diagnosis pointed to an unskilled residuum of workers who were often underemployed – a typical national efficiency concern. As a response, in 1909 labour exchanges were introduced to spread information about job vacancies. However, poverty surveys had shown that many workers were poor simply because of low wages and so trade boards, which fixed minimum wages in 'sweated' industries such as clothing, were set up. The final element in these reforms was unemployment insurance, covering workers in the cyclical trades of shipbuilding, engineering and building. Employers and workers paid contributions whilst the state administered the scheme through labour exchanges. Introduced in 1912, this scheme, like the others, was relatively modest both in its scope and its expense.

In contrast, health insurance was a large-scale measure. Both this and unemployment insurance were influenced by other such schemes in Germany, Australia and elsewhere, and it is important to realise that Britain was neither unique, nor even first, in establishing such schemes. The same concerns which lay behind them in this country were at work elsewhere. In the health scheme the state added a contribution to that paid by employers and workers, and in theory all those earning under £160 a year – practically all manual workers and some others – were included, a total of 15 million people. In practice, some small employers probably evaded payment. The scheme provided access to treatment by a doctor, although hospital treatment, with the important exception of tuberculosis, was not covered, nor was the wage earner's family. Most importantly, the scheme provided sickness benefit for six months. In this indirect way wives and children did benefit.

The first Prime Minister of the new government was Henry Campbell-Bannerman. He proved a clever politician, but by 1908 he was seriously ill and his place was taken by the Chancellor of the Exchequer, H. H. Asquith, who was widely recognised as the leading parliamentary figure of the day (Fig. 2.1). It fell to Asquith and his successor as Chancellor, David Lloyd George, to devise a method of breaking through the opposition of the Lords to Liberal legislation.

The Lords' long-established custom of not interfering with money bills seemed to provide one solution. Asquith and Lloyd George's plan was to make the 1909 Budget itself a centrepiece of reform, by making a virtue of the need to increase taxation. If the Lords confronted the government, it would have a strong case for reforming them. If not, desirable social reforms could be financed. The Budget put forward increases in taxation on unearned incomes, a measure calculated to appeal to long-standing radical prejudices against those who did not need to work for their living; a 'supertax' on incomes over £5000; increased death duties; and taxes on increments in land value. There were other measures but these were the main ones which aroused Conservative hostility. From the Liberal point of view, the Budget's political cleverness lay precisely in its 'class' nature, which the Conservatives attacked. It solidified Labour's support for the government, while presenting the Liberals as a party that transcended class because wealthy Liberals were willing to shoulder an extra burden of taxation. Finally, the new principle of differential taxation on incomes would allow the Liberals to introduce new social welfare measures without increasing general taxation levels. Thus the whole argument for tariff reform would be undercut.

The Conservative argument, of course, was the mirror image of this. To them the Budget showed clearly that future welfare measures, in the absence of tariff reform, would depend on attacks on capital – in other words, in the heightened language adopted, would be 'socialistic'. The Conservatives therefore gave their support to overturning the convention by which the Lords did not interfere with money bills and, in November 1909, the Lords threw out the budget.

A series of complex political shifts were seen in 1910, which for the Liberals had one aim in mind – the ending of the Lords' veto. The Liberals called an election in January over the rejection of the Budget. They lost a large number of seats and ended up level pegging with the Conservatives and Liberal Unionists combined, but the Liberals had Labour as allies, now 40 strong, and the Irish Nationalists, with over 80 seats. To the latter, removal of the Lords' veto was essential to gain Home Rule. So the Liberals were still able to form a government. Asquith then brought forward a Parliament bill, which excluded the Lords entirely from financial questions and gave them the ability to reject other legislation twice but no more. As a quid pro quo, the maximum parliamentary term was to be reduced from seven to five years. (This provision was suspended during the two world wars.) If the Lords rejected this and the Liberals and their allies

Figure 2.1   Asquith as elder statesman: a post-war portrait as the 1st Earl of Oxford and Asquith. Private collection/The Bridgeman Art Library

won another election, Edward VII agreed to create sufficient Liberal peers to outvote the Conservatives in the Lords. Then he died. The new King, George V, tried to find a way out through party cooperation, but it was not forthcoming. He therefore repeated his father's undertaking and a second election was held in December 1910, with virtually identical results. The new Liberal government was armed with the King's guarantees, and enough Conservative Lords caved in to ensure the bill's success in 1911.

With the Lords issue settled, the government could now embark on more ambitious welfare measures (see earlier box, 'Liberal welfare reforms'). Like the earlier ones, these were prompted by the increasing influence of New Liberalism within the Liberal Party, as well as being part of the continued effort to outflank reforming Conservatives. The Labour Party also had to be taken into account. Many of its MPs were still broadly sympathetic to the Liberals and were willing to support a Liberal government – as long as it showed that it kept the interests of working people in mind. So social reform became something of a necessity for Liberals, to prove their pro-labour credentials and head off challenges from the left, as well as from the right. Finally, the reforms that were undertaken owed a considerable amount to the combination of genuine reforming zeal and lust for power shown by Lloyd George and Winston Churchill – the latter of whom had emerged, after leaving the Conservatives, as a left-leaning Liberal (Fig. 2.2).

Figure 2.2   Lloyd George in his prime, and a youngish Churchill: 1910. © Hulton-Deutsch Collection/CORBIS

Welfare reforms continued to be politically controversial, as the vast numbers of upper- and middle-class employers of domestic servants were faced with the expense of buying stamps, the method of registering contributions for health insurance. Nevertheless, with the Lords no longer an obstacle, the scheme passed, together with unemployment insurance, in 1911, coming into effect in 1913.

In spite of the prominence historians give to the welfare reforms, to many Liberals the old nonconformist concerns were still vitally important. One such concern was the disestablishment of the Welsh Anglican Church. Three-quarters of Welsh Protestants were nonconformist, and the establishment of the Anglican Church was an obvious anomaly. The bill was passed in 1914 and, suspended due to the war, brought into effect in 1920. The monarch was now head of an episcopal church in England, a presbyterian church in Scotland, and had no such position in Wales and Ireland.

The 'strange death of Liberal England'?

The title of this section is also the title of an influential book by George Dangerfield, published in 1935. Dangerfield's book was written in the context of the troubled years of the 1930s, in which many people saw the years before 1914 as a lost period of peace, prosperity and liberal values. Dangerfield instead portrayed it as a period of tension and difficulty in which these values came under attack. He had three main themes: strikes, suffragettes and Ulster.

In 1900 unions encompassed around 15 per cent of the male workforce, and by 1914 this figure had risen to about 30 per cent, with around 8 per cent of women workers unionised by that date. Much of this growth came towards the end of the period and was accompanied by a wave of strikes. In 1911 unskilled and semi-skilled workers such as dockers and carters joined in short strikes, and there was a brief national railway strike. Then in 1912 there was a five-week national miners' strike – miners previously had often gone on strike but only on a local basis. A continued high level of strikes was seen in 1913 and 1914. At times, particularly during the railway and coal strikes, there was considerable government concern. In the same period an odd political-industrial movement called syndicalism gained some influence, particularly in the large and powerful engineers' union, the Amalgamated Society of Engineers, and among the South Wales miners. Syndicalism was an offshoot of anarchism, calling like the latter for the collective ownership of property and the withering away of central government. But syndicalism saw the future organisation of society as lying firmly in the hands of producers, organised in trade unions. Strikes would be the weapon to bring this about. However, syndicalism's direct involvement in the strike wave was very limited and it had no appeal to most trade union leaders.

Most historians agree that the main motives for the strikes were economic. The period from 1900 to 1910 had seen a stagnation or only a very slow rise in real wages. (The old belief that there was actually a fall has been shown by Charles Feinstein to be incorrect.) On the other hand, demand for British industrial products and coal was growing rapidly and, by 1911, unemployment was quite low. Many working people saw prices rising but no increase in their own prosperity. Discontent built up and, since low unemployment meant that strikes were likely to have a greater impact, they did indeed occur. Such conditions also encouraged increases in union membership as unions provided the organisation to make strikes effective. In addition, the Liberals themselves promoted unions.

In 1906 the government had passed the Trades Disputes Act, which removed the penalties imposed on strike action by earlier legal judgments. Passing this was a sop to the Labour Party, but it had a wider significance. The government signalled that there was no political animus against the working classes. They were free to use their industrial muscle without legal penalty. Later, the government intervened directly to help settle the rail dispute, and as a result the railway companies, hitherto firmly anti-union, now had to accept their influence. The government also intervened to facilitate a national minimum wage in coal mining, encouraging the growth of union membership in the poorer coalfields which stood to gain most from such an agreement.

Suffragettes are discussed in the accompanying box, 'Suffragists and suffragettes'. The most intractable and threatening of the government's problems was Ireland, and in particular Ulster. Irish Home Rule was a policy the Liberals had inherited from Gladstone. In 1886 the Liberals had split over it and in 1893 the Lords had scuppered it. But the 1910 elections had left the Irish Nationalists holding the balance of power in Parliament. With the Lords' veto now emasculated, the government had no excuse not to pursue Home Rule to completion. As its name implies the policy fell short of independence. The Westminster Parliament would retain control of defence and foreign affairs; in return for domestic hegemony the Irish would have a reduced representation, of 42 seats, in Westminster.

Politics and government: Suffragists and suffragettes

Demands for female suffrage went back well into the nineteenth century. Old-fashioned constitutional theory held that the exclusion of some adults, women or men, was acceptable because those who had the vote represented the views of those who were excluded, through poverty, frequent changes of address which prevented registration, or because of their sex. Even after the electorate had been substantially expanded in 1884, only about 60 per cent of men had the vote. Increasingly, however, this older view was challenged and the call for the inclusion of all men often included within it the call for female suffrage. The oddness of excluding women was pointed up by the fact that they could vote in school and Poor Law board elections if they were rate payers.

The old-established National Union of Women's Suffrage Societies (NUWSS) under Millicent Fawcett was joined in 1903 by the Women's Social and Political Union (WSPU), organised by Emmeline Pankhurst and her daughter Christabel. The WSPU took a more militant approach, starting with the persistent heckling of anti-women's suffrage politicians. Its followers were nicknamed 'suffragettes' to distinguish them from the suffragists of the NUWSS. Both groups were mainly middle class, but increasingly

▶

working-class women became involved, particularly in Lancashire where they formed their own organisation.

In early histories of the subject, the patient work of the NUWSS was overshadowed by the glamour of the WSPU and its leaders. The Pankhursts combined charisma with a tactical shrewdness exemplified by their ability to capitalise on local initiatives. Militancy developed after the 1906 election into demonstrations and stone throwing. After one arrested suffragette in 1909 went on hunger strike, the WSPU took up this tactic. It confronted the government with a dilemma – unwilling to risk

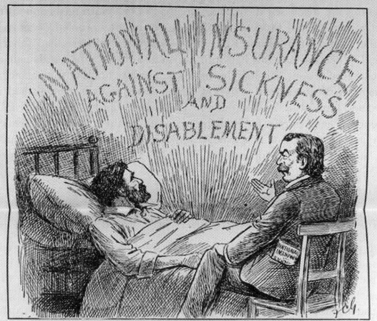

THE DAWN OF HOPE.

Mr. LLOYD GEORGE'S National Health Insurance Bill provides for the insurance of the Worker in case of Sickness.

Support the Liberal Government
in their policy of
SOCIAL REFORM.

Published by the LIBERAL PUBLICATION DEPARTMENT (in connection with the National Liberal Federation and the Liberal Central Association), 42, Parliament Street, Westminster, S.W., and Printed by the National Press Agency Limited, Whitefriars House, London, E.C.
LEAFLET No. 2382.]   28/6/11.   [Price 5s. per 1000.

Figure 2.3   Liberal progressivism: 'Doctor' Lloyd George administers Health Insurance

a suffragette dying, they resorted to forcible feeding which also aroused controversy. It was actions such as these which George Dangerfield seized on, his book elevating the significance of the WSPU as a threat both to the government and to Liberal principles in general (Figs 2.3 and 2.4).

The reality was more complex as historians over the last 30 years have shown. The WSPU never had as many members as the suffragist organisations, and by 1914 its effectiveness was declining. However, many women did not see themselves as exclusively 'suffragette' or 'suffragist', and moved between organisations. In that sense there was more support for militancy than it might seem from membership figures, but

Figure 2.4   Liberal reaction: the 'Cat and Mouse Act', as it was nicknamed, of 1913 provided for imprisoned suffragettes on hunger strike to be released and then rearrested. Image courtesy of The Advertising Archives

few women would actively participate in it. Traditional historiography also suggested that women's contribution during the war was critical to changing politicians' minds. But this, too, is something of a myth. A fair number of politicians had always been pro-suffrage and, before the war, support was growing in the Labour Party and among many Liberals. The resistance of the pre-war Liberal governments was stiffened by Asquith's hostility to votes for women, a reflection of his social conservatism and his pessimism about the intellectual ability of most people besides himself. Asquith's influence was broken by the war. Given the existing support for suffragism, adding women voters to the proposed extension of the male franchise in 1918 ceased to be a significant issue. Masculine prejudices were assuaged by confining women's right to vote to those over 30 (the male age remained at the traditional 21). This ensured a male–female majority in the electorate of 60:40. But the exclusion was so illogical that voting ages were equalised in 1928 – a process helped by the fact that the Conservative majority in Parliament were by now satisfied that women were just as, or more, likely to vote Conservative as were men.

In the nineteenth century there was a shared interest between the British and Irish landed classes, because the defence of the latter's land seemed inseparable from the defence of British landowners' interests. But the Conservatives' own policy from 1886 had eroded this link to insignificance. They had accepted that Irish tenant farmers would never be reconciled to landowners, and therefore subsidised the buying out of tenancies. As a result, the basis of opposition to Irish Home Rule completely changed.

Opposition was now centred in Ulster, the historic name for the north-eastern counties of Ireland in which about half the population were Presbyterian. Their origins went back to Scottish settlement in the sixteenth and seventeenth centuries. In the nineteenth century Ulster had been the only part of Ireland to industrialise on a large scale. It was therefore religiously, and to some extent economically, distinct. Ulster Presbyterians, led by Edward Carson, were adamantly opposed to Home Rule. They were militantly anti-Catholic and saw any quasi-independent Irish state as potentially embodying the influence of Catholicism. Their opposition was not, however, just religious. It drew on a history of mutual hostility which went back to the time of the original settlement.

In 1912 Ulster Protestants pledged in a covenant not to accept Home Rule. Their opposition was supported by the Conservatives. The Conservatives had a number of fairly flimsy constitutional arguments to back them up; the strongest was that radical new arrangements should not be imposed on a large minority such as the Ulstermen. Andrew Bonar Law, a Glasgow iron merchant, had taken over from Balfour as Conservative leader in 1911. Law was a low-key personality but an effective speaker. He fuelled the flames by declaring in 1912 that he 'could imagine no length of resistance to which Ulster can go in which I should not be prepared to support them'.[1] Nevertheless, the Home Rule bill, having been ritually rejected twice by the Lords, was ready to go before the Commons for a third decisive time in 1914. A possible compromise solution lay in partition, with Ulster excluded from Home Rule. But more extreme Irish nationalist opinion – which the moderate nationalist leaders could not ignore – rejected such a solution. A pro-Home Rule paramilitary body, the Irish Volunteers, grew rapidly to rival Carson's Ulster Volunteers.

The situation in the summer of 1914 was undoubtedly difficult, with drilling and surreptitious arming by both groups of volunteers and indications that the army was not completely loyal. Various compromises, such as temporary exclusion for Ulster, having failed, the government had to push ahead with the whole bill. And then the First World War broke out. Asquith suspended Home Rule for the duration of the war. The Nationalists had no option but to go along with this, since bringing down the government would do them no good, but it strengthened the hand of the extremists.

Was there a 'strange death' of Liberal England in the years 1910–1914? No historians now agree with all of Dangerfield's original argument. The 'problem' of the suffragettes would have been solved at some stage by giving women the vote. The strike wave marked a significant step in the evolution of trade unionism but was not a challenge to the government. The real challenge was Ulster. But the Conservatives had their own divisions over it, and because of this it is likely that a compromise would eventually have been fixed up between the British political parties.

However, the 'strange death' can be given another meaning. The Liberal Party was undoubtedly severely wounded by the 1920s and almost moribund by the 1930s. Since the 1960s there has been much debate about this decline: was it an inevitable result of the rise of the Labour Party, and therefore latent before 1914 but not manifest then, or was it due to external contingencies, notably the First World War? To many historians in the 1950s and 1960s it seemed inevitable that the Labour Party, which at least in theory embodied the aspirations of working people, would have taken over from the Liberals whether or not there had been a war. A necessary part of this argument is the belief that, as politics became more polarised along class lines, the Liberals, who attempted to straddle the class and ideological divides, would have lost support to the Conservatives on the right as well as Labour on the left.

Certainly the Conservatives increasingly attempted to define themselves as 'anti-socialist' and thus became attractive to many middle-class Liberals who were concerned, for instance, about higher rates arising from greater local government responsibilities. In some areas before the war there was Liberal–Conservative cooperation against Labour on local councils. However, this went against the grain of national politics. Here, as we have seen, the Liberals increasingly pushed a social reform agenda. In 1971 Peter Clarke changed the terms of the historiographical debate by arguing that this New Liberalism meant that the Liberal Party potentially had a vibrant future, since it was attending to the social welfare demands of the wider labour constituency. The analysis of by-elections in the immediate pre-war period certainly suggests that the Labour Party was not making much electoral progress, and if it wanted a future this would have to be in conjunction with the Liberals.

More recently, Ewen Green and others have argued that the whole period from 1900 to 1914 saw a crisis of Conservatism as much as of Liberalism. Imperialism had been the great Conservative rallying cry of the late nineteenth century. But with the arrival of Labour as a political force, and the perceived need to articulate a social reform agenda, imperialism was not enough. Tariffs seemed to provide a way out, as they strengthened the Empire but also raised money for social reform. Many electors, however, did not like tariffs, while the Liberals could raise as much money and annoy fewer people by selective tax increases aimed mainly at the wealthy. But in the end all these arguments about the political prospects of parties in the years before 1914 are hypothetical. World war broke out and domestic politics were disrupted.

What is true about the period from 1900 to 1914 is that the terms of political debate had changed. The central issues of mid- and late nineteenth century politics – the constitution, religion, the Empire, foreign policy – remained important. But social reform, as one way of coping with the aspirations of working people, was now firmly on the political agenda, and with it went an inevitable increase in the role of the state. To that extent one kind of liberal England, the liberalism of Gladstone which had seen the minimal state as the best way of enhancing the opportunities of the individual, had died.

Note

1. Quoted in Koss, S., *Asquith* (London: Allen Lane, 1976), p. 135.

Further reading

Clarke, P., *Lancashire and the New Liberalism* (Cambridge: Cambridge University Press, 1971) and McKibbin, R., *The Evolution of the Labour Party 1910–1924* (Oxford: Oxford University Press, 1974) are still classics; the latter can be supplemented by Tanner, D., *Political Change and the Labour Party 1900–1918* (Cambridge: Cambridge University Press, 1990). Green, E., *The Crisis of Conservatism: the Politics, Economics and Ideology of the Conservative Party 1880–1914* (London: Routledge, 1995) contains a thorough exposition of the argument summarised in the chapter. Harris, B., *The Origins of the British Welfare State* (London: Palgrave Macmillan, 2004) is a good recent guide. Packer, I., *Lloyd George* (Basingstoke: Macmillan, 1998) is a succinct and thoughtful recent biography. Pugh, M., *The Making of Modern British Politics 1867–1945* (Oxford: Blackwell, 3rd ed., 2002) is extremely useful for this and later periods.

Other sources: Brown and Louis, *British Empire* (see Chapter 1); Dangerfield, G., *The Strange Death of Liberal England* (London: MacGibbon and Kee, 2nd ed., 1966); Dutton, D., *A History of the Liberal Party in the Twentieth Century* (Basingstoke: Palgrave Macmillan, 2004); Feinstein, C., 'What Really Happened to Real Wages? Trends in Wages, Prices and Productivity in the United Kingdom, 1880–1913', *Economic History Review*, Vol. XLIII, pp. 329–355 (1990); Holton, S., 'The Women's Movement, Politics and Citizenship from the late 19th century until about 1918' in Zweiniger-Bargielowska, *Women* (see Chapter 1); Hunt, E., *British Labour History 1815–1914* (London: Weidenfeld and Nicolson, 1981); Joyce, P., *Work, Society and Politics* (Brighton: Harvester, 1981); Liddington, J. and Norris, J., *One Hand Tied Behind Us: the Rise of the Women's Suffrage Movement* (London: Virago, 1978); McKibbin, R., Matthew, C. and Kay, J., 'The Franchise Factor in the Rise of the Labour Party' in McKibbin, R., *The Ideologies of Class* (Oxford: Oxford University Press, 1991); More, *Industrial Age* (see Chapter 1); Pugh, M., *The March of the Women: A Revisionist Analysis of the Campaign for Women's Suffrage, 1866–1914* (Oxford: Oxford University Press, 2000); Ramsden, J., *Balfour and Baldwin* (see Chapter 1); Shannon, R., *The Crisis of Imperialism 1865–1915* (London: Hart-Davis, MacGibbon, 1974); Thane, P., *Foundations of the Welfare State* (London: Longman, 2nd ed., 1996).

Chapter 3

THE FIRST WORLD WAR

Britain and Europe 1904–1914

In the early 1900s Britain's diplomatic position seemed favourable. As shown in Chapter 1, the *Entente Cordiale* of 1904 with France had been designed to ease international tension. Yet within ten years Britain was at war with Germany. What went wrong?

In part, Germany did. In the early 1900s Germany was viewed as too unstable to be a partner for Britain but was not seen as an enemy. Quite soon this changed. Germany's naval build-up was already a challenge, since Britain believed that it was essential that her fleet should be superior, both to protect trade and to defend herself against invasion. The German fleet was militarily pointless but, once the build-up had started, it attracted powerful support within Germany and became difficult to stop. The fleet was not the only problem, however; it was seen by the British Foreign Office as just one symptom of a German desire for European domination. The Foreign Office's conclusions were influential and reflect the impact of permanent civil servants on policy.

Nevertheless, when the Liberals came to power British foreign policy could have gone down the classic Gladstonian path of peace and an avoidance of foreign entanglements (not that Gladstone had always been successful in this). This path was favoured by many Liberals such as Campbell-Bannerman, the Prime Minister. But Campbell-Bannerman had to accommodate the Liberal Imperialists, of whom the brilliant Edward Grey was a leading light. On the formation of the Liberal government in 1906 Grey became Foreign Secretary and took the alternative path, that preferred by the senior civil servants at the Foreign Office. This set less store on morality and more on defending what were seen as Britain's essential interests. More and more, it appeared that these were to ward off the danger of Germany becoming dominant in Europe. It was a reversion to the classic British policy of maintaining a 'balance of power'.

One of Grey's first actions was to approve 'military conversations' with France. The French had become increasingly concerned about German ambitions, and it suited them to make the *entente* into something more solid. They found the British willing, because of their own fears. The conversations gradually hardened into a plan for Britain to send a 150,000-man army to France if the German threat seemed serious enough. It was not, any more than the *entente*, a treaty obligation, but naturally the French saw it as implying a strong level of British support. Then, in 1907, Grey engineered an *entente* with Russia. Described as a 'convention', it aimed to reduce friction along India's northern frontier. Since Russia was France's ally, and that alliance was viewed by Germany as its biggest threat, this exacerbated Germany's fears.

As Germany continued to build up her navy, the Liberals faced strident demands for more battleships. Even the anti-war radicals supported the navy and, though the Liberals disliked the spending implications, Lloyd George, the leading radical, joined Asquith and Grey in accepting the need to build more ships. The crisis was temporary, but the German refusal to back down added to British distrust. More important was the new focus of European rivalry, the Balkans. The disintegration of the Ottoman Empire, which had once controlled the Balkans, presented European countries with threats and opportunities. The ramshackle Austro-Hungarian Empire saw it as an opportunity to assert itself by annexing Bosnia-Herzegovina. This stoked the resentment of Serbia, the strongest of the new Balkan states, and her supporter Russia. Germany supported Austria, her oldest ally.

By 1914, although the Austro-Serb rivalry simmered, Anglo-German relations had improved. In practice, whatever the Germans did with their navy the British were confident that they could build more battleships. The Germans, too, were now less concerned about naval rivalry; but they were still desperately worried about encirclement by Russia and France, both of which were enlarging their armies. When the Austrian heir, Archduke Franz Ferdinand, was assassinated in Sarajevo on 28 June by a young Bosnian Serb, the Austrians and Germans acted. Supported by the Germans, the Austrians presented the Serbs with an ultimatum in late July. Either the Serbs would bow to the ultimatum and therefore tacitly accept Austrian supremacy, or war would ensue. If the latter, the Serbs on their own would be crushed; if Russia intervened to support Serbia, Germany would fight her and France before they built up their armies. Serbia refused to knuckle under and Russia mobilised her forces. Germany declared war on Russia and, in line with previous plans, on France.

Britain joined reluctantly. Grey had tried to mediate in late July and the Cabinet was divided. The French had put moral pressure on Britain, and the Foreign Office convinced Grey that Britain should support France, but this might not have been enough for other Liberals if German military strategy had not tipped the balance. Given a war on two fronts, Germany's aim was to knock out one enemy as soon as possible. The target was France, the method an overwhelming attack on France's north-west frontier, through Belgium and Luxembourg. Belgian neutrality had been guaranteed by Britain and other powers in 1839. It was a technicality, but an important one, and enough to convince most of the Cabinet to support war. Britain's ultimatum to Germany expired at 11.00 pm on 4 August.

Britain's involvement in the First World War was severely condemned by a small minority during the war, and by a larger number of people after it. Critics saw the war itself, and Britain's involvement, as a consequence of the naval arms race, or of the 'secret diplomacy' behind treaties and inter-state agreements.

Most historians, including most German historians, now accept that Germany's pre-war behaviour was the main impetus behind war. Under Wilhelm II's erratic direction, German foreign policy constantly aimed to score points off others. German fears of Russia and France had some basis in reality, but there is no evidence that they would have attacked without provocation. The naval arms race was not a direct cause of war; rather it illustrated Germany's aggression, as did the nation's strategic plan. Faced with

People and politics: H. H. Asquith

Henry Asquith is an enigma. He presided over a reforming government but was himself socially conservative and pessimistic about his countrymen and women. Before the war he opposed women's suffrage. In 1918 he said, 'The number of people who really think in any age or country is very limited.'[1] Yet most people considered him the only possible leader of the Liberals in the pre-war years.

Asquith's strength lay partly in his mastery of Parliament, but most of all in his ability to remain calm in crises. He preferred to wait until the moment was ripe before putting forward a solution. He believed that delay would soothe dissent, but to delay so consistently showed very strong nerves. It was a formidable achievement to navigate through the crises of the 1909 Budget, Lords reform and Ulster.

During the war, Asquith's dislike of overhasty action led to criticisms of his slowness to change. But he also resisted drastic change because he was unwilling to compromise Liberal principles too much and, in fairness, only very few people foresaw the size and scale of the war effort which would eventually be required. In 1915 he agreed a coalition with the Conservatives, thus avoiding the danger that the Liberals would bear the whole responsibility for the war, which seemed to be increasingly stalemated. But he insisted on retaining the voluntary principle for recruitment – a bedrock of Liberalism, since conscription was seen as smacking of continental authoritarianism. However, the insatiable demands of the Western front for troops led to conscription for single men being introduced in January 1916, with general conscription being introduced in May of that year. This and continued Irish problems eroded support for Asquith, and in December 1916 he was ousted by Lloyd George (see box, 'David Lloyd George').

He retained the support of many Liberals and, at the end of the war, resisted Lloyd George's invitation to join the Coalition. As a result, the Liberal Party split and Asquith lost his seat in the 1918 election. In spite of this, his prestige was such that he led the weakened non-Coalition Liberals again when re-elected in 1920, and continued until 1926 after Lloyd George and his followers had returned to the fold. Asquith provided little real leadership, however. The complex reasons for Liberal decline are discussed in Chapter 4, but Asquith in his later years did not help.

His epigrams will endure. He immortalised the 1918 election as the 'Coupon Election' (see Chapter 4). And when Bonar Law was buried in Westminster Abbey near the tomb of the Unknown Soldier, Asquith cruelly nicknamed him the Unknown Prime Minister.

the possibility – not the actuality – of attack from one country (Russia), Germany invaded another (France) by way of two neutrals (Belgium and Luxembourg). The belief that Germany was an aggressive nation which needed containment had a strong basis, and British policy towards Germany had aimed at containment through firmness, not war. However, the policy had a corollary. If Britain was to maintain credibility in the future, it had to deliver on the expectations it had aroused.

A 'Gladstonian' foreign policy would have avoided this pitfall. But such a policy might have made Germany even more overconfident and aggressive; it would certainly not have guaranteed European peace. Furthermore, Germany's violation of Belgian neutrality was enough in itself to persuade many Gladstonians of the rightness of war.

The course of the war

By the Royal Prerogative the government could, and did, declare war on behalf of the Empire, as well as the United Kingdom. There was overwhelming support in the White Dominions and little opposition elsewhere. Dominion troops were eventually to provide around 20 per cent of the total British and Empire forces, and Indian troops – used extensively on the Western front in 1915, and then mainly in Mesopotamia – another 20 per cent. So the Empire was a major part of the war effort, although for convenience 'British' will usually be used to refer to both British and Empire troops.

The British army had been reformed by Richard Haldane, the Liberal Secretary for War, into a well-trained but small force. At the outbreak of war the British Expeditionary Force (BEF) crossed the Channel and, in accordance with the earlier staff talks with France, was positioned on the left wing of the French armies. There was little understanding of the German intentions, based on the famous Schlieffen Plan of a few years earlier, which were to advance in strength through Belgium and northern France – that is, on the Allies' left. So the British, themselves advancing into Belgium, stumbled upon a vastly superior German force, against which they fought defensive battles at Mons and Le Cateau. With the French they were forced back, regrouping on the River Marne near Paris. The Germans were by now exhausted, since the Schlieffen Plan, however elegant conceptually, imposed huge strains on the troops as they marched long distances. At the Marne they halted and then retreated. During the autumn, both sides moved crabwise towards the Channel in an attempt to outflank one another. After a bitter defensive battle around Ypres in Belgium, the British remained in this area for the rest of the war, although they gradually extended their sector of the front southwards. In late 1914 and into 1915 the trenches, which defined the front until 1918, took shape as both sides sought protection from the combined killing machine of rifle, machine-gun and artillery fire. All armies had already suffered appalling casualties, although British casualties were fewer as the army was smaller. Even so, by the end of November 1914 there were 90,000 British killed and wounded.

French and German initiatives dominated in 1915, since the British army, although rapidly growing, was still too small to make a major impact. The Germans soon went on to the defensive on the Western front (Fig. 3.1), as the line of trenches from the coast to the Vosges came to be called (it was actually only western from the point of view of Germany), and instead attacked Russia and Serbia. The French engaged in costly and ineffective attacks on the Western front. Late in 1915 the Battle of Loos, the first major British offensive against German troops, was planned as part of a wider Anglo-French attack. It, too, was a costly failure. The main British initiative in 1915 was directed against the Ottoman Empire (whose core was to become modern-day Turkey), which

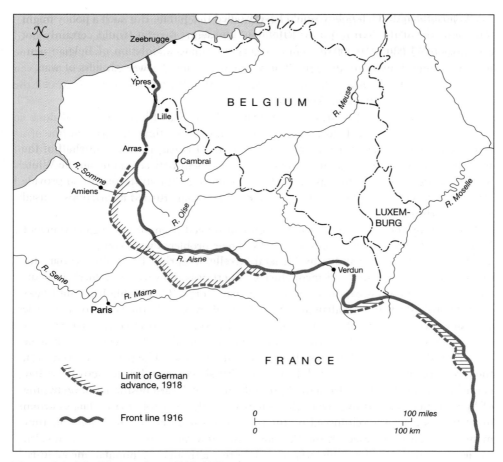

Figure 3.1 The Western front 1916–1918
Source: Adapted from Jamieson, A., *Europe in Conflict*, Hutchinson (1967), p. 141

had joined the war on the side of the Central Powers, as Germany and Austro-Hungary were known. This was the Gallipoli campaign, an attempt to gain access to Constantinople, the capital. It was partly born in the fertile brain of Churchill, then First Lord of the Admiralty. This campaign also failed and Gallipoli was evacuated in January 1916. The war with the Ottoman Empire sputtered on until 1918. It involved romantic escapades by T. E. Lawrence and his Arab irregulars in the Hejaz in modern-day Saudi Arabia; a hopelessly ill-judged expedition into Mesopotomia (modern Iraq) which ended in disaster; and finally a successful offensive in Palestine by General Allenby. But it was essentially a sideshow.

In 1916 the German High Command switched its attention to the Western front again, and in an attempt to bleed France to death launched a huge offensive at Verdun. Partly to take the pressure off Verdun the British army, by now over 1 million strong, was induced to take the larger part in a joint Anglo–French offensive on the River Somme. The first day of the battle, 1 July 1916, was disastrous for the British, who suffered casualties of 57,000 – 19,000 of whom were killed. Subsequently, however, the Somme became a long drawn-out struggle. The Germans suffered fewer casualties, but even to them it was the *Blutbad* – bloodbath. Along with a Russian offensive, it forced the winding up of their attack on Verdun.

Through the years of bloodshed, Germany's High Seas Fleet, which had done so much to poison relations before the war, spent most of its time in port. On one of its rare excursions, however, it was intercepted by the British, resulting in the Battle of Jutland on 31 May 1916; the first, and only, engagement between large fleets of dreadnought battleships. Jutland was tactically inconclusive, but strategically it confirmed British control of the surface of the seas. Instead Germany turned its attentions to submarine warfare.

On land, by the end of 1916 the French had indeed been almost bled dry, both by Verdun and by their own ill-judged attacks. Their problems were compounded by yet another offensive, commanded by General Nivelle, in spring 1917. The British share of this, Arras, was costly and inconclusive. There was, however, one local success at Vimy Ridge which was captured by the Canadian Corps. This highlighted the increasing role of Australian, Canadian and New Zealand troops. By the last two years of the war they provided a significant proportion of the Allies' most effective infantry.

The French part of the Nivelle offensive was another disaster. Exhausted and demoralised, many French troops effectively went on strike. The perceived need to take the pressure off the French led Haig, the British commander, to activate a long-cherished plan to break out from the Ypres salient, an awkward position around the town of Ypres which was left over from the defensive battles of 1914–1915. Haig's commitment to this plan was reinforced by the serious threat posed by German submarines, many of which were based on the Belgian coast a few miles from Ypres. The resulting battle was, to the military historians, 3rd Ypres, although in popular memory it is Passchendaele. Fought in the summer and autumn of 1917, it had a similar minimal result in terms of ground gained and heavy cost in lives lost, as did the Somme.

Meanwhile, at sea, Germany now pursued unrestricted submarine warfare, meaning the sinking of merchantmen irrespective of nationality. For this and other reasons, America came into the war on the side of the Allies. From the military point of view, the results were slow to materialise as the Americans took time to assemble and train an army. The immediate effect of Germany's initiative was very serious as merchantmen sinkings dramatically increased. Still hugely dependent on imports, Britain's situation temporarily looked grim, but the institution of convoys cut losses and the submarine threat receded.

Throughout 1917 Russia's military value had been declining. The Czar had been deposed in March, then the Bolshevik Revolution effectively ended Russian resistance. Germany could pull back troops from the East and at last take the offensive again on the Western front. The threat of American reinforcements added to German urgency. A series of offensives began with the *Kaiserschlacht* – the Kaiser's Battle – on 21 March 1918. The British had extended their line further to relieve the French, and the

Military affairs: Douglas Haig

Douglas Haig, commander of all the British armies on the Western front from December 1915, has been both praised and damned by historians. A. J. P. Taylor represents the largely critical views of the 1960s. John Terraine was a strong supporter. One recent historiographical trend has been to draw attention to the successes of the 'Hundred Days', leading to a more favourable assessment of Haig's overall command (Fig. 3.2).

The evidence against Haig is formidable, however. Although he could write well, he was famously inarticulate in conversation, and thus found it difficult to explain himself to politicians in Britain. In late 1917 Lloyd George virtually gave up trying to communicate with Haig, and instead kept him short of troops to discourage offensives – unfortunate timing in view of the German plans to attack. Haig's choice of staff at his headquarters was spectacularly bad; his intelligence chief General Charteris fed Haig

Figure 3.2   Douglas Haig, looking military. © Hulton-Deutsch Collection/CORBIS

▶

ridiculously overoptimistic assessments of the decline of German morale, which Haig never seems to have seen through. Haig has been praised for encouraging all-out attack in the summer of 1918, when the German army finally gave way. But he had been attacking for two years, for the most part fruitlessly: if you always gamble on red, it will sometimes come up. Finally, Haig persisted in believing that the army could fight and win breakthrough battles. Subordinates such as Henry Rawlinson and Herbert Plumer disagreed, but the difficulty of communicating with Haig meant that differences were not resolved. Almost certainly Haig was wrong. Until 1918 the Germans had such defensive strength that breakthroughs were highly unlikely. Therefore, Haig's post-war justification for his strategy – that it wore the Germans out – was disingenuous, since it was not the rationale he put forward at the time.

Haig had merits. His focus on the Western front, however mistaken his tactics, was probably correct. The war was not going to be won in Italy or further east. He never panicked. And – not often mentioned – the British army's logistics, as they would now be called, were efficient. Troops were fed and supplied effectively and medical services were much better than those of the French.

Haig had powerful political backing within the Conservative Party and his replacement was never really an option. If it had been, a better choice might have been Plumer, of Second Army. Plumer was in appearance a caricature – plump, red-faced and white-moustachioed – but he was efficient and understood the problems of fighting on the Western front. Plumer, and Rawlinson of Fourth Army, were much more realistic than Haig in assessing what could be achieved by attacks on the German army of 1916 and 1917.

German attack mainly fell on the weak British Fifth Army. The Germans advanced 40 miles before the attack petered out. In April they attacked in the north and regained all the ground they had lost at 3rd Ypres, and more; Haig issued his famous 'backs to the wall' order urging no further retreat, but it was exhaustion rather than Haig's order that halted the Germans. Finally, in May, a third German offensive again hit weakened French and British units and once more German troops reached the Marne.

The offensives had been far more successful than any others on the Western front since 1914, but they had taken a heavy toll on the German army. Germany's domestic economy had also been seriously weakened by the British naval blockade and so, in spite of their military failures, by 1918 the Allies had material superiority. American troops added to the pressure on Germany as a series of Allied attacks forced the Germans back. But it was British and Empire troops which played the single biggest role on the Allied side, winning a series of victories from August onwards known collectively as the 'Hundred Days'. From the late summer, domestic discontent in Germany increased and the High Command lost hope. Germany sued for an armistice, which started at 11.00 am on 11 November. By a strange irony, British troops had just reached Mons where, for Britain, the fighting had begun over four years earlier.

Dilemmas of the Western front

It was not inevitable that the Western front should have dominated the land-based activities of Britain and France to the extent that it did. Early in the war, the so-called Easterners pushed for an attack on Turkey, which resulted in the Gallipoli campaign. In late 1915 a Franco-British expedition was sent to Salonika in Greece to relieve Serbia. It got nowhere, being held up by determined resistance from the Bulgarians who had entered the war on the side of the Central Powers. Finally, there was the possibility of reinforcing the Italian campaign against Austro-Hungary. Italy had entered the war on the Allied side in 1915, embarking on three years of attritional warfare as bloody as anything on the Western front.

The problem with both Gallipoli and Salonika, even if they had succeeded, was that they led nowhere. Turkey was essentially peripheral, although it tied up a large number of British troops. Therefore, a more vigorous drive to oust the Turks from Palestine and Mesopotamia might have been justified, as it would have freed these troops for the Western front. The elimination of Bulgaria would still have left the Allies hundreds of mountainous miles from the heartland of Austro-Hungary, let alone Germany. Reinforcement of Italy would have inevitably led to the German reinforcement of Austro-Hungary and the likely continuation of stalemate on the Italian front. The lure of by-passing the bloodbath of the Western front tempted politicians, but was resisted by generals who believed that the war could only be won on the Western front. But the result of their efforts, for three and a half years, was stalemate there too.

By the 1930s the view was becoming established that the pounding on the Western front had entailed pointless slaughter and that this was partly due to the inefficiency of the higher commanders. *Journey's End*, the 1929 play by R. C. Sherriff, himself a junior officer in the war, vividly represents this in microcosm. In it, two officers are killed as a result of an ill-judged trench raid. By the 1960s such views had become pervasive and were encapsulated in A. J. P. Taylor's works. In these, the Western front battles between 1915 and 1917 were represented as much the same – that is, one hopeless Allied offensive after another. The main reason for this was the stupidity and rigidity of the commanding generals. There were counter-arguments, notably in the books of John Terraine, while subsequent academic debate had become more nuanced. Some historians, such as John Bourne and Gary Sheffield, have viewed the British war effort quite favourably, although others remain more critical. But the popular view is still one of heroic but largely pointless sacrifice.

The problem for the attacker on the Western front has often been represented as the virtual impossibility of crossing the fire-swept ground of no man's land to the enemy's trenches. And indeed, this was the main reason why the first day of the Somme was the bloodiest day in the history of the British army. The Germans were well dug in and, although the British artillery bombardment had been long drawn out, it was not intensive enough to smash up the German dugouts. When it ended, the Germans emerged to man the firing line. Many British units never reached the enemy trenches or else suffered such heavy losses that they were helpless when they got there (Fig. 3.3).

Figure 3.3 Prelude to slaughter: the 16th Middlesex Battalion assembling before the Somme attack; they would suffer 522 casualties.

In most battles, however, troops did successfully cross no man's land and survived in considerable numbers. As time went by, tactics evolved to facilitate this. Artillery bombardments became shorter and more intensive, temporarily numbing the enemy. Troops lay out in no man's land during the bombardment so the distance to the enemy's line was minimised. Light machine guns, which could be pushed up in the attack to provide covering fire, proliferated. The biggest problems usually came when the attackers had reached, and taken, the enemy's first-line trench.

Behind the first-line trench lay support positions, and in them waited troops ready to counter-attack. Counter-attack was an integral part of German tactical doctrine, and it meant that one wave of attackers was not enough. More troops had to be ready to move up in support: they would pass through the first wave, take on the counter-attack forces, and penetrate the trench lines further back. If they did not, the first wave was stranded in the old German front line, defending it from the wrong side against determined counter-attacks. But to deploy large numbers of support troops strained transport and logistics. If the attack was launched from a salient, as at 3rd Ypres, space for support troops to form up was limited. German tactics also evolved. Since crowded front-line trenches were vulnerable to artillery fire, their defensive systems came to consist of mutually supporting strong points, often extending miles back, with an even greater emphasis on counter-attack. Attacks on such systems had to be in strength and be well coordinated with both the supporting troops and the artillery. None of this was easy in the broken-up landscape of the battlefield, with little effective communication since battlefield radios were in their infancy.

New technologies made a difference. By 1918 the Allies had established air superiority, which was useful in harassing the retreating enemy during the Hundred Days. But aircraft had little impact on the earlier German advance, suggesting their overall influence was still marginal. Tanks had been deployed in the later stages of the Somme battle but only in small numbers. The first mass tank attack, Cambrai in November 1917, had been a localised success, but German counter-attacks soon gained all the ground back by more conventional means. Another mass tank attack marked the start of the Battle of Amiens on 8 August 1918 – the battle which proved to be the start of the Hundred Days. It was an important Allied victory, which became known as the 'black day of the German army'. But on the second day, two-thirds of the tanks were out of action, mainly through mechanical failure, and they played a diminishing part in later successes. Tanks were still too unreliable to have a major impact on the battlefield.

The Allies also established superiority in an old technology, artillery. This was partly quantitative: by 1918 the Allies had 30 per cent more guns than Germany. British gunners had also established superiority in the techniques which enabled them to locate enemy guns. Quantitative and qualitative superiority in artillery were very important: the German guns could be neutralised by counter-battery fire and the German front line could be pounded too. Even so, defence in depth still presented a formidable obstacle, as at 3rd Ypres, where Britain had artillery superiority but still could not break through.

After the war, Haig referred to the 'wearing-out battle,'[2] which lasted for four years until the Battle of Amiens. A more familiar term for it is the strategy of attrition, the argument behind this being that an army of the size and effectiveness of Germany's could only be beaten by a gradual chipping away. This argument, of course, cut two ways. Allied losses were consistently heavier than German losses, and by early 1918 both British and French forces were seriously denuded. This was the most likely reason for the size and speed of the German breakthroughs in the spring. While the Germans' more sophisticated tactics are often given the credit for their success, tactics were not enough when confronted by strong British defences in the northern sector of the March offensive. The German breakthrough against Fifth Army was achieved against forces which were very thinly spread, so there were virtually no troops available to counter-attack. Similarly, improved British tactics are sometimes said to be the reason for the successes of the Hundred Days. For much of the war, British tactical rigidity, in part imposed because most troops had little previous training, was noted by the Germans who thought the French were more flexible. But their superior tactics achieved little for the French against German defences. British tactics became more flexible but, as with the German breakthrough, it seems unlikely that this was crucial. It was more important that the Germans, like the Allies earlier in the year, were desperately short of men by the summer of 1918. British artillery superiority helped to crack up the German front line, and the Germans now lacked defence in depth and the ability to make effective counter-attacks.

Was this a final vindication of the strategy of attrition? Not really. By the summer of 1918 there was a number of other reasons for Allied success on the battlefield. The Germans had lost heavily in their own offensives; they persisted in keeping large numbers of soldiers in the East because of their expansionist ambitions there; and the Americans were by now pouring in troops who engaged a large slice of the German army. Allied material superiority supplemented these factors. This material superiority owed itself, in part, to the British naval blockade of Germany.

Fleets, blockades and submarines

In spite of the pre-war plans which gave the BEF a small role, practically everyone envisaged that, in a continental war, Britain's main role would be maritime. She would fulfil her traditional function of supporting her continental allies financially, and blockading the enemy to deprive them of food and raw materials. Elements of this conception survived. What was not conceived of, apart from the huge land commitment, was that Britain herself would be blockaded.

Britain's blockade was quite effective because the German High Seas Fleet remained resolutely in harbour. In the end, however, professional pride led the Germans to sortie out in an attempt to ambush a segment of the British fleet that was on patrol. But better British intelligence meant the ambushers were themselves ambushed. Around 6 o'clock on the evening of 31 May 1916 the High Seas Fleet ran straight into Britain's much larger Grand Fleet. The actual battle was something of an anticlimax. The High Seas Fleet soon disengaged itself, having suffered heavy punishment but losing only one major ship. By contrast the British lost three, all lightly armoured battlecruisers. This was the Battle of Jutland. The conventional verdict is that it was a tactical defeat for the British but a strategic victory. Even this seems pessimistic. The British lost more ships and more men, but several German ships had to spend months under repair. So it was probably a tactical draw. It was undoubtedly a strategic victory for Britain. The High Seas Fleet made a few more excursions but it was clearly unable to alleviate the British blockade by destroying British sea power.

Far more threatening to Britain than the High Seas Fleet was the German war on commerce. Surface raiders had been a nuisance in the early months of the war but had gradually been eliminated. Submarines (in German, *unterseebooten* – U-boats) were a different matter. Originally they were expected to act as surface raiders, stopping a merchant ship, ensuring the safety of crew and passengers and only then sinking the vessel. Neutral ships were theoretically safe. The Germans chafed at the restrictions this imposed and in 1915 began sinking vessels without warning. But neutral, particularly American, public opinion was too much for them and this first campaign was ended. By early 1917, however, with the land war on the Western front at an apparent *impasse*, Germany decided on unrestricted submarine warfare even if it brought America into the war. The campaign began on 1 February 1917. On 6 April of that year the United States declared war, in large part because of the German action. But also in April, allied merchant shipping losses rose to 880,000 tons. It was the highest monthly total of either of the world wars, and was practically a year's worth of British construction in wartime conditions. Clearly it could not go on.

The answer was convoy. The story, promulgated by Lord Beaverbrook, that Lloyd George imposed it single handedly on the Admiralty, is a legend, like many stories about

Lloyd George. But the Admiralty was reluctant to institute it, pessimistically seeing all sorts of problems, and Lloyd George provided his usual galvanising impetus to its rapid adoption. Convoy worked because it emptied the oceans. Previously, U-boats would wait and a vessel was likely to come along. Now vessels were concentrated in a few square miles. They were far harder to find and, furthermore, there were escort vessels to protect them, although detection of submarines underwater was difficult due to limited technology.

People and politics: David Lloyd George

David Lloyd George was a self-made man, setting up a successful solicitor's practice in North Wales after a modest lower middle-class upbringing. He was elected for the constituency of Caernarvon Boroughs in 1890, only stepping down in 1945. He was a superb speaker with an enormous capacity for work. What his other positive attributes were is still a matter for debate.

Lloyd George started on the radical wing of the Liberal Party. He opposed the Boer war and supported classic nonconformist issues such as Welsh disestablishment. In 1906 he became President of the Board of Trade and then Chancellor of the Exchequer, replacing Asquith, in 1908. As Chancellor he drove forward welfare reform and the attack on the House of Lords. In 1914 Germany's violation of Belgian neutrality persuaded him to support war.

When the first Coalition was formed under Asquith, Lloyd George pressed to become Minister of Munitions (Fig. 3.4). The Ministry was itself set up partly at his instigation, in order to take control of munitions production from the War Office, which he thought to be inefficient. In August 1914 Asquith had appointed Lord Kitchener as Secretary of State for War. It was a typically clever Asquithian political move, since it gave the government an important non-party figure, England's leading general, in this position. Kitchener realised the need for a large land army and took steps to bring this about, and he had actually secured a major increase in munitions production. But in the long term far more would be needed and the War Office's reliance on existing contractors meant that this would be difficult to achieve. Lloyd George deserves credit both for seeing the need and for his willingness to take responsibility. Himself a chaotic administrator, he drafted in large numbers of businessmen to organise output.

Lloyd George's accession to the prime ministership in December 1916 again owed itself in part to his genuine belief that Asquith was not providing dynamic enough leadership. Lloyd George did not want Asquith to go, but he did want him to cede control of the war effort. Lloyd George resigned – he was by then Secretary of State for War, Kitchener having been drowned while on a mission to Russia – and persuaded Bonar Law to resign as well. Asquith also resigned, probably anticipating that he would still be the only option as Prime Minister. But Lloyd George had the support of the Conservatives and enough Liberals, and it was therefore he who formed the new Coalition. Whereas Asquith's Coalition had been dominated by Liberals, now it was Conservatives who held the major offices.

▶

PUNCH, OR THE LONDON CHARIVARI.—April 21, 1915.

DELIVERING THE GOODS.

Figure 3.4 Lloyd George harnesses labour and capital to deliver munitions: a Punch cartoon of 1915. *Punch* library

In spite of all the criticisms of Asquith, not much actually changed. This was partly because Britain's war effort was already near its peak, helped by Lloyd George's own efforts as Minister of Munitions. It was also because the government, like the French and the Germans, was a prisoner of the Western front. Although Lloyd George formed a small War Cabinet there was no change of strategy. The failure of Gallipoli meant that military action on other fronts had little political backing. But even more important, the realities of war meant that the Western front had to be the centre of attention.

After the Coalition's post-war election victory (see Chapter 4), Lloyd George and the Conservatives were locked in an uneasy alliance, each dependent upon but not fully trusting the other. Lloyd George deserves credit for his energetic efforts to ameliorate the harshest French demands at Versailles, and for subsequent attempts – albeit unsuccessful – to build European understanding. In other ways, though, the Coalition's hand-to-mouth policy bears the stamp of expediency.

He inherited the leadership of the – now much diminished – Liberals after Asquith retired in 1926, and again deserves credit for his attempt to steer them towards a more positive economic policy in the late 1920s. But they could not achieve an electoral break-through and he left the leadership in 1931.

Why did Lloyd George, with his many gifts and his enormous personal charm, inspire such distrust among many politicians? He was a strange mixture. He retained a traditional Liberal concern for the dispossessed, but he seemed to have less and less concern for the Liberal belief in personal freedom; hence his support for draconian measures during the war and during the post-war Irish struggle for independence. The former were probably justified, the latter not. He was undoubtedly unscrupulous, saying different things to different people. But in fairness his ends – social welfare, winning the war, post-war international settlement – were worthy ones. And his 'sale' of Honours to various unsavoury recipients – using the money for his private political fund – was another black mark, although it was only an exaggerated version of what had always gone on. Ultimately his reputation must depend on his contribution during the war. This was enormous, although most evident in his galvanising efforts in the first two years than during his prime ministership.

The British blockade was far more effective than the German one. There were many leakages via neutral countries, especially Scandinavia and Holland, but in 1915 German imports had almost halved. However, Germany provided more of her own food resources than Britain; and she already either possessed, or had seized in occupied territories, critical raw materials such as coal and iron ore. Nonetheless, the British blockade had a cumulative, if slow, impact. In 1916–1917 Germany faced its 'turnip winter' when food shortages were endemic. And undoubtedly the German army by the end of the war was far less well equipped than the Allied forces, with fewer guns and very few lorries. Lorries were unimportant when the static front lines of 1915–1917 could be directly served by rail, but were potentially of value in the mobile warfare of 1918. Even so, Niall Ferguson has argued strongly that, in spite of problems, the German home front was not the cause of the German collapse.

Many historians see Allied military victory, achieved on the battlefield, as an ultimate explanation of the German surrender – for the Armistice was effectively a surrender. Like many debates in history, this one has tended to become polarised: in this case between those who support this line of argument – although they usually disagree as to the actual mechanism of military victory – and those who hold that the problems of the German home front, caused in part by the British blockade, were decisive. Multicausal explanations lack conceptual elegance but may, in this case, be the best available. By the late summer of 1918 Germany was facing discontent at home, had a relatively less well-equipped army and fewer men. In addition, Austro-Hungary was on her last legs, again partly as a result of the blockade. Improved British fighting skills helped in achieving military success, but it is difficult to separate them out as a factor from material superiority and the increasing American contribution. All of these together contributed to the crisis of confidence in the German High Command, which took the initiative in demanding peace.

Britain at war

To succeeding generations, one of the central facts about the First World War was the carnage on the battlefields. Over 700,000 Britons died; another 1.7 million were wounded. Most of the casualties were soldiers, although 15,000 merchant seamen were among the dead. Death was distributed across the classes. Casualty rates among junior officers, mainly middle and upper class, were double those in the ranks.

The fighting man's experience was not all of death and wounds. Units rotated in and out of the front line, and many parts of the front were relatively inactive for much of the time. Many men spent the war as 'lines of communication' troops concerned with supply. Nevertheless, the strain of Western front fighting when a big battle was in progress was intense. Lengthy artillery bombardments had to be endured; the infantry might have long periods of continuous action as they attacked, regrouped to face counter-attacks and so on. What motivated men to go on?

Not all did. By the later stages of the war, there is testimony to a proportion of men lying low during attacks when they thought they could get away with it. And there were accepted limits to the sacrifices expected in defence. Around 20,000 British soldiers became prisoners on the first day of Germany's March 1918 offensive, many in isolated strongpoints which were surrounded in the German advance. To continue to resist in those circumstances would have meant certain death. But the British army never experienced large-scale collapse, as sections of the French army did in 1917.

Pride in the local regiment is sometimes given as an explanation for cohesion in the British army, but it is not a very good one. Initially volunteers often joined local regiments but later men were drafted into whatever unit needed them, irrespective of where they came from. There were probably a number of reasons for the tenacity of British soldiers. Officers led from the front, as their casualty rate attested. This was accepted practice in the pre-war army, and once practices are accepted peer-group pressure tends to keep them going. Grievances about food or medical attention never became extreme because of the army's efficient logistics. And, for most soldiers, there was some sense, however obscure, that the war was worth fighting.

Measuring the strength of such ideas is impossible but some inferences can be made. Two and a half million men volunteered before the introduction of conscription, an indication of patriotic feeling. Local pride was part of that patriotism, and here the ability of many volunteers to join local battalions (sub-units of regiments) was important. These were the so-called Pals battalions. But there was also a sense among many that German aggression, particularly the attack on Belgium, was unfair, and among some that liberal values were under threat. As the war went on, the strength of these initial feelings and motives diminished. They were replaced, however, by the impact of the press and film. A glance at contemporary newspapers shows that the mess of the battlefield, and the casualties, were not played down; but they were rendered in a heroic and self-sacrificing light. Similarly, the widely seen documentary *The Battle of the Somme* was realistic in its depiction of battlefield conditions, although omitting the horrific casualties of the first day. But what comes over most strongly to the audience is the comradeship between ordinary soldiers, their decency towards prisoners and the immense power of British artillery. The strength of patriotism reflects the strength of belief in the 'imagined community' of Britain (see Chapter 1).

Effective self-censorship by the media gave the conscripts of the second half of the war a motive to fight. It also helped to maintain civilian morale. But, just as the army had also to be reasonably well fed and supplied, so did civilians. Britain started with advantages. Much munitions and army clothing production could be met from the country's existing large engineering and textile industry resources, at the expense of exports rather than of civilian consumption. High demand for labour also kept up working-class wages. The losers included war widows, doubly so because the recompense for their loss was a miserable pension. The middle classes had mixed fortunes. Those who owned businesses could benefit from rising prices, and later in the war accusations of profiteering were rife. But those with salaries, such as clerks and schoolteachers, often did badly: most were not trade union members and did not receive regular increases. Even worse off were those on fixed incomes such as private pensions.

Behind the human face of war lay economic facts, and there were two major problems. Food imports were one, as merchant ship sinkings began to increase. The problem was tacked with Lloyd George's usual vigour. Apart from convoy and food rationing, there was a big increase in arable acreage in 1917 and 1918. But food and other imports were only possible if Britain could pay for them, and the problems of doing so consti-tuted the other economic crisis. The need for dollars had risen massively as exports fell and imports from America rose. Britain also acted as a banker for her allies, whose financial position was even weaker. By early 1917 there was a real possibility of Britain's credit in America running out, thus severely jeopardising the war effort. Germany's declaration of unrestricted submarine warfare, by helping to push America into the war, averted this crisis. As with the Schlieffen Plan, Germany took a huge gamble. Once again it lost.

The growing influence of Lloyd George can be seen as a replacement of freedom by organisation, a dichotomy identified by A. J. P. Taylor as running through the British attitude towards the war. This parallels the dichotomy between those who believed in an organic state and those who did not (see Chapter 1), but it is not quite the same. Organisation could be seen as necessary to win the war and therefore to preserve liberty, rather than as implying that the state was necessarily superior to the individual. Thus, while Conservatives tended to favour organisation and Liberals freedom, plenty in both parties, like Lloyd George himself, straddled the divide. In practice, no one had conceived of such a war and no one had a blueprint for running it, so government controls were usually responses to particular problems rather than an organised limita-tion of freedom. Even the theoretically draconian powers of the Defence of the Realm Act (DORA), passed at the beginning of the war, did not stifle press debate, the expres-sion of anti-war views and significant numbers of strikes. More specific measures included rent control, which was instituted in December 1915 as a response to spiralling rents in large industrial and shipbuilding towns and consequent civilian discontent. The Munitions of War Acts of 1915 and 1916 enforced dilution – the release of skilled engin-eering workers from repetition work so they could concentrate on skilled tasks, with unskilled men and women taking over their old work.

Society and economy: War, women's work and women's status

It is often said that the First World War permanently changed the nature of female employment in Britain. In fact, change was temporary. After the war the old patterns were reinstated. There were adjustments – more women did secretarial work, for instance – but the war did no more than accelerate existing trends.

By far the largest single change for women was the growth in the numbers working in existing engineering firms or in new plants making shells, fuses and so on. Women and unskilled men often took on parts of the jobs that skilled men – that is, those who had served an apprenticeship – had been doing. The latter's rights to reclaim their work after the war were the subject of specific agreements. The process was known as dilution. It did little to foster women's skills, because the work they did was usually just one part of the normal work of a skilled man. And it did not open up long-term opportunities, because the wartime agreements were honoured after the war. The mainly young and unmarried women who had worked in war industries went back to their traditional jobs, or got married and left paid work, as they would have done before the war.

There were more permanent changes in women's legal position. Voting rights for women over 30 were conferred in 1918 (see Chapter 2). Under the Sex Discrimination Act of 1918 women could become jurors, magistrates and lawyers, while the extension of national insurance after the war included women wage earners. But, on the other hand, reforms to make divorce easier, and equally available to women as to men, were prepared before the war and delayed until 1923 because of it.

While lip service was paid by men to women's war work, basic attitudes towards women's roles did not change much. The proliferation after the war of 'marriage bars' – preventing the employment of married women – in certain occupations, notably teaching, illustrates this. They were supported by male trade unionists. More positive changes for women were primarily the result of the gradual liberalisation of society and the law. The war may have sometimes accelerated them, but it was not their main cause.

The continued strength of belief in freedom limited government powers in other ways. Rationing was not instituted until it was urgently needed at the end of 1917. Taxation rose, but not nearly as high as in the Second World War. As a result, almost 90 per cent of the cost of the war had to be met by borrowing, much of it from the banks. Borrowing in this way did not reduce consumer demand, and the almost unlimited demand from both government and private spending led to rapid price rises. A Ministry of Reconstruction was set up in 1917, and a series of reports on post-war policies, which endorsed more state intervention, were published. But the limited time for discussion meant that pre-war assumptions still remained deeply rooted. The need for reconstruction did not become internalised in people's minds as it did in the Second World War.

While most people accepted the encroachment of government into everyday life during wartime, a residue of political opposition to the war and to coercive government legislation remained. At its core were the true believers in a Gladstonian foreign policy, most Liberal and a few Labour, united in the Union of Democratic Control (UDC). The UDC was never influential, however. Lloyd George, by far the most prominent member of the radical Liberal left, had become the apostle of organisation. In the Labour Party, too, most MPs supported the war.

Labour's support was important because dissent among workers was potentially the most dangerous threat after the Germans. The pre-war years had been marked by labour militancy. Patriotism mitigated this, with strike-prone groups such as miners among the most eager to join up. But the wartime combination of rising prices and heavy demands for labour inevitably led to forcefully expressed demands for wage increases. Workers were conciliated in various ways. Rent control was one. Dilution, which undercut trade union agreements over the tasks which skilled workers usually undertook, was softened by an agreement to end it after the war. The first Coalition brought the Labour Party into government for the first time, and the Lloyd George Coalition increased the number of Labour ministers. Nevertheless, 1917 saw a series of large-scale strikes led by local shop stewards, discontent being focused around traditional skilled workers' concerns such as wage differentials with the less skilled. With official Labour and trade union leaders on its side, the government could buy off the strikers but imprison some of the leaders under the DORA. What was most remarkable was not the strikes, but the willingness of most working people to continue to support the war.

Notes

1. Quoted in Terraine, J. (ed.), *General Jack's Diary 1914–1918* (London: Cassell, 2000) p. 298.
2. Quoted in Koss, *Asquith* (see Chapter 2), p. 102.

Further reading

Bidford, S. and Graham, D., *Firepower: British Army Weapons and Theories of War 1904–1945* (London: George Allen and Unwin, 1982) is an outstanding analysis of army doctrine and tactics in both world wars. Bourne, J., *Britain and the Great War 1914–1918* (London: Edward Arnold, 1989) is an excellent short survey. De Groot, G., *Blighty: British Society in the Era of the Great War* (London: Longman, 1996) covers the home front. Prior, R. and Wilson, T., *Command on the Western Front: the Military Career of Sir Henry Rawlinson 1914–1918* (Oxford: Blackwell, 1992) helps to understand the slow evolution of the higher command's thinking. Strachan, H., *The First World War* (Oxford: Oxford University Press, Vol. 1, 2001) will be irreplaceable when all volumes are published and has been used here especially for the causes of the war.

Other sources: Dunn, J. C., *The War the Infantry Knew* (London: Abacus, 1994; 1st ed., 1938); Dutton, *Liberal Party* (see Chapter 2); Evans, R. and Pogge von Strandmann, H. (eds), *The Coming of the First World War* (Oxford: Clarendon Press, 1990); Ferguson, N., *The Pity of War* (London: Allen Lane, 1998); Middlebrook, M., *The Kaiser's Battle* (London: Allen Lane, 1978); More, C., *Skill and the English Working Class 1870–1914* (London: Croom Helm, 1980); Otte, T., '"Almost a Law of Nature"? Sir Edward Grey, the Foreign Office and the Balance of Power in Europe 1905–1912' in Goldstein, E. and McKercher, B. (eds), *Power and Stability: British Foreign Policy 1865–1965* (London: Frank Cass, 2003); Packer, *Lloyd George* (see Chapter 2); Prior, R. and Wilson, T., *Passchendaele: The Untold Story* (London: Yale University Press, 1996); Pugh, *Making* (see Chapter 2); Reynolds, *Britannia* (see Chapter 1); Sheffield, G., *Forgotten Victory: The First World War: Myths and Realities* (London: Headline, 2001); Taylor, A. J. P., *The First World War* (London: Hamish Hamilton, 1963); Terraine, J., *Business in Great Waters: the U-Boat Wars, 1916–1945* (London: Leo Cooper, 1989); Terraine, J., *Douglas Haig: The Educated Soldier* (London: Hutchinson, 1963).

Chapter 4

CHANGING TIDES: POLITICS BETWEEN THE WARS

Introduction

The beckoning world of post-war politics held many possibilities. The war had produced an unstoppable impetus towards universal male suffrage. The Representation of the People Act 1918, often known as the Fourth Reform Act, enfranchised the many men who had not had the vote, for instance because they were not householders in their own right, and women over 30 (see Chapter 2 box, 'Suffragists and suffragettes'). With no opinion polls, who this vast new electorate would favour was unknown. Trade union membership had grown rapidly during the war and the Labour Party had been in office as part of the wartime Coalition. Would it now continue on this constitutional path, or follow the pre-war syndicalist line of direct industrial action, or be influenced by Russia's Bolsheviks, and how many of the new electorate would follow it?

In practice, the surge of post-victory patriotism benefited the Conservatives most of all in the election which followed the war, and thus the war seemed to free them from the box which some historians think constrained their pre-1914 electoral chances. But their electoral success was in conjunction with Lloyd George, proclaimed as the 'man who won the war', as Prime Minister. Could they maintain their popularity without him? The continuing split between Lloyd George and Asquith resulted in a group of 'Asquithian' Liberal MPs and a group of Coalition Liberals. Would the Liberal Party surmount this split? Asquith nicknamed the endorsement given the Coalition Liberals 'the coupon', in a disparaging reference to ration coupons, and the election of December 1918 became the 'Coupon Election'.

The Coalition

The renewed Coalition won a smashing victory, although on a low turnout. It was dominated numerically by Conservative MPs, but with a substantial Coalition Liberal minority. The Asquithian Liberals were decimated, and Labour with 59 seats became the effective opposition. It was a government of glittering talents. Apart from Lloyd George, it contained Churchill, the brilliant lawyer Lord Birkenhead, the Conservative Party leader Bonar Law and Austen Chamberlain, Joe's eldest son. Yet in spite of its talents, the four years of the Coalition had no obvious theme. Part of the reason for this was the need to cope with an endless series of problems.

Huge wars cause huge financial and economic disruption, with lasting effects. The Coalition's first instinct was to continue the wartime policy of spending and borrowing. Large armed forces were kept up to maintain Britain's foreign policy commitments, while optimistic plans for reconstruction were on the drawing board. There was a particular focus on housing. Lloyd George's slogan 'Homes Fit for Heroes' epitomises its importance, which stemmed in part from ideas that had germinated before the war. Existing small-scale 'garden cities' and 'garden suburbs' provided more space, fresher air and larger gardens than most housing. To reformers, such benefits should be available to all but, at inflated post-war prices, subsidies would be needed. Other reconstruction plans, such as those for education, were also potentially costly. The apparatus of government had itself become more expensive as the state's responsibilities increased: the number of civil servants doubled, from 58,000 to 116,000, between 1914 and 1923.

Government spending contributed to the continuation of rapid wartime inflation in 1919 and 1920. Prices were also driven up by a world-wide boom, as consumers and firms unleashed their pent-up spending power. By late 1920 prices were around two and a half times those of 1914. The boom contained a large speculative element and reversed itself rapidly in late 1920. Throughout 1921 prices fell, wages were forced down and unemployment rose.

In 1920 unemployment benefit had been expanded to cover most manual workers. The expansion took place at a time of full employment when its potential cost seemed limited. As unemployment rose the scheme fell into deficit, which had to be met by the government, while many unemployed quickly exceeded their benefit entitlement. The benefit period was extended, although even so many people had to be relieved by the Poor Law. Unemployment, and the consequent dependence of many on one or another form of benefit or relief, was to become a permanent interwar phenomenon.

With unemployment relief pushing up government spending, press and political pressure for economy became intense, led by the *Daily Mail* and supported by many Conservative MPs. The press played on middle-class dislike of taxation, which had real causes. For many of the middle classes, a combination of inflation and higher taxation had drastically cut their accustomed standard of living. The government responded with a committee, headed by Sir Eric Geddes, a businessman turned government minister. The drastic economies recommended by the committee in 1922, nicknamed the 'Geddes axe', were politically difficult to resist. 'Reconstruction', already moribund, was now buried.

The hopes of reconstruction had extended to industrial relations: wartime conciliation had put labour in an apparently strong position; progressives in all parties believed there should be more opportunities for employer-worker discussions; anti-union employers and the political right were on the defensive. However, some of organised labour's demands were fantastic in the economic circumstances of the time. The government combined some goodwill towards labour with a desire to defuse the more extreme demands by temporising. Committees, commissions (a grander name for the same thing) and conferences were a means of doing this.

The miners' claim for a six-hour shift, when eight hours had been the norm, was one fantastic demand. It was coupled with a demand for nationalisation, now on the political agenda as the Labour Party supported it. In 1919 a Coal Industry Commission, with representatives nominated by the different interest groups, predictably produced split reports on the various claims. A seven-hour shift was awarded, while nationalisation was rejected. Early in 1921 the government announced that it would end its wartime control of the mines in March. With coal prices rapidly falling, the employers posted big wage reductions. At that point the miners tried to activate the 'Triple Alliance' of themselves, railwaymen and other transport workers, first mooted before the war. But the miners' refusal to compromise on certain issues led the others to back out. This was 'Black Friday', seen by the left as a defeat for the working classes. In reality, strikers would have confronted a government which was determined and well pre-pared, in support of the miners who, for many years before 1921, were among the best paid manual workers. The reluctance of others to support them was not surprising.

The National Industrial Conference, also of 1919, was more harmonious. Its proposals for a maximum working week, excluding overtime, of 48 hours – a big reduction on the 56 which had been common before 1914 – was immediately accepted. But pro-posals for state intervention to reduce unemployment ran into the sand, and the trade union representatives to the conference eventually resigned.

Apart from its domestic problems, the Coalition had simultaneously to deal with difficult foreign policy issues, discussed in Chapter 5. An issue which was neither strictly domestic nor foreign was the status of Ireland.

At the outbreak of war, the activation of Home Rule in Ireland was delayed, in part because of the threats of resistance from Ulster. Early in 1916 armed rebellion broke out in Dublin – the Easter Rising. The British decision to execute 14 of the leaders sparked off widespread discontent and a wholesale shift of electoral support to Sinn Fein, which stood for complete independence. Outside Ulster, Sinn Fein dominated the Coupon Election in Ireland. Their MPs refused to take their seats at Westminster, constituting themselves as an Irish parliament, the Dail, which in 1919 ratified the Irish Republic declared in 1916. A tragic, confused and bloody three years ensued.

The early stages consisted of psychological as much as actual warfare, aimed at break-ing the morale of the Royal Irish Constabulary (RIC). Many policemen resigned. Then resistance was stepped up using familiar techniques evolved over centuries of Irish anti-landlord campaigns – the revolver attack on individuals, the ambush on isolated roads. The Irish Republican Army, which became the military wing of Sinn Fein, carried these out. To restore order the British recruited ex-soldiers and officers, mainly from England. These were the 'Black and Tans', so-called because they wore khaki uniforms with the RIC's black belts, and the Auxiliaries or Auxis. Both used disreputable and often violent methods, the Auxis particularly so.

The Coalition pressed ahead with a new Home Rule bill, and in 1920 Ireland was formally partitioned: the six counties of the north-east, part of historic Ulster, became Northern Ireland (Fig. 4.1). Its Protestant-dominated parliament had complete con-trol over its domestic affairs, and it also sent some MPs to Westminster. The Dail, how-ever, rejected Home Rule and virtually ran Southern Ireland as British administration broke down. Amidst increasing violence, there was widespread British condemnation of the Black and Tans and the Auxis. With George V also exerting a moderating influence, the Coalition's hard line softened. In July 1921 a truce was arranged, and in December 1921 a treaty was signed. The Coalition preserved a figleaf of British sovereignty by refusing to recognise the Republic and insisting on Ireland becoming a Dominion. The

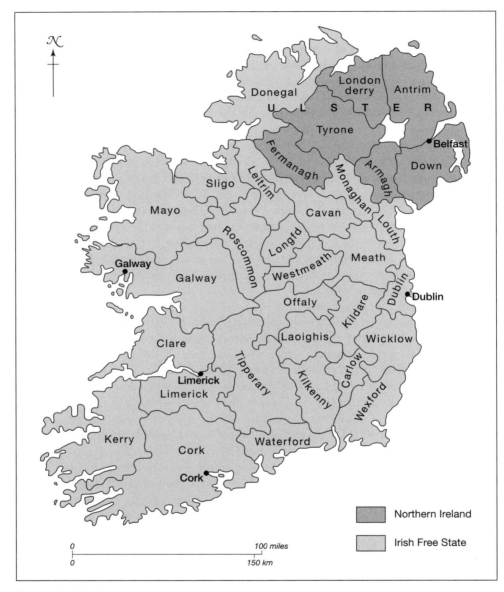

Figure 4.1 Irish partition
Source: Cootes, R. J., *Britain since 1700*, 2nd ed., Longman (1982), p. 226

British handed over the government in January 1922, but from the summer another bitter year of fighting followed in the new Irish Free State as hardliners opposed the terms of the treaty. For Britain, however, the Irish problem was solved. A blind eye was turned to Protestant domination in Northern Ireland, which condemned Catholics there to second-class status for 50 years.

Bonar Law had resigned from the Coalition in 1921 because of ill health. By 1922, with an election not far away, discontent among Conservatives was increasing. There was Lloyd George's reputation for underhand dealing. But more important was the fear that, if the Coalition won another election, the Conservative Party would be lost in an amorphous fusion with the Coalition Liberals. Law recovered and, now out of the government, had a free hand. He was reluctant to ditch Lloyd George, his old wartime comrade, as personally they were on good terms, but he eventually backed the rebels at a meeting of Conservative MPs in October. (The meeting originated the name, still in use today, of the 1922 Committee of Conservative backbenchers.) Lacking Conservative support, Lloyd George resigned. At the subsequent election, the still divided Liberals, and Labour, split the anti-Conservative vote and Law became Prime Minister.

To Charles Loch Mowat, whose *Britain between the Wars* was the first modern history of the period, the end of the Coalition marked the end of the 'reign of the great ones, the giants of the Edwardian era and of the war'.[1] It is an optimistic verdict. The Coalition made some egregious mistakes, particularly in their handling of Ireland, and in failing to control the post-war boom until it was too late. But they had a difficult hand to play. Ireland was never going to be easy. In the post-war world some policies had to be undertaken for which there was a high financial price. And some sections of labour, in a strong position at the end of the war, persisted in making demands which combined impracticability with selfishness.

Labour in power

The fall of the Coalition and the success of the Conservatives at the election did not immediately usher in a period of political stability. In late 1923 another election saw the Conservatives lose their majority in Parliament. Their defeat paved the way for Labour to form a government. It only lasted until late 1924 but was of huge symbolic importance. Labour's brief first period in office raises two questions, one important but the other fundamental.

The important question is why the Conservatives threw away their hold on office. The ostensible reason was to allow an election over tariffs which, in the context of continuing unemployment, were potentially more attractive to the electorate than before the war. However, Stanley Baldwin, who had become Conservative leader when Law's illness reached its final stages, was probably more subtle than to have just one motive. By putting tariffs on the agenda again, he showed that the Conservatives cared about unemployment and had a remedy for it. In addition, he isolated Lloyd George from the Conservative ex-Coalitionists who were holding aloof from government. The context here was Baldwin's fear of Lloyd George as a charismatic figure who, while semi-detached from the Liberals, could always spring a dangerous surprise. Now Lloyd George was forced to return to his Liberal roots and defend free trade. What Baldwin miscalculated was free trade's continuing appeal and, as a result, the Conservatives were defeated.

The fundamental question is why it was Labour and not the Liberals who were the chief beneficiaries of the Conservative misjudgement. The Liberals, reunited after the Asquith–Lloyd George split, gained seats but remained smaller than Labour. As suggested in Chapter 2, some historians have seen Liberal decline as proceeding inexorably from the rise of class feeling. But others believe that, up until the war, the Liberals had been successfully turning themselves into a party which could appeal to a working-class interest in social reform. Certainly the Liberals' pre-war electoral performance remained reasonably robust. Such historians see the Liberals' subsequent fall as due to the demoralising effects of war on a party many of whose activists believed strongly in peace, together with the corrosive effects of the split.

Another line of approach achieved some prominence in the 1970s and 1980s, mainly as a reaction against class-based explanations of change. This approach, associated with Maurice Cowling, sees 'high politics', the interaction within a small group of politicians, as crucial to political outcomes. In this account of change, Conservatives and Labour took a decision to destroy the Liberals. They could do this by refusing to ally themselves with the weakened party, instead exposing it as a powerless centre party which there was no point in supporting. There is plenty of evidence that some politicians had this outcome explicitly in mind. In late 1923 Austen Chamberlain, formerly a Conservative supporter of fusion with the Liberals, wrote 'our business now is to smash the Liberal party';[2] Labour's Ramsay MacDonald had very similar sentiments, and Baldwin's actions after the 1923 election helped. He did not resign but returned to face the Commons, at which point the Liberals supported Labour. Therefore, Labour came into office as a minority government, incapable as Baldwin saw it of doing much harm. But by putting Labour in, the Liberals alienated middle-of-the-road electors.

No one could deny that politicians behaved in the way they did and thus helped to ease Labour's path to office, but this does not explain how Labour gained 191 MPs in the first place. Here class is a partial although not a complete explanation. After the war, mining constituencies swung behind Labour. While this trend was developing before the war and can partly be attributed to the growth of class feeling and the slow decline of nonconformity, the extent to which 'class feeling' meant growing solidarity between the working class as a whole is questionable. Before the war, industrial relations in some mining areas such as Durham had been good, fortified by high wages and employer paternalism. The economic turmoil of the war and its aftermath sent coal prices soaring and then, from 1921, into an almost permanent slump. The owners, with their profit margins slashed, now took a much harder economic line. The miners' reacted similarly, at first with huge wage claims, and then with fierce opposition to wage reductions. Their interest, quite understandably, was to extract the maximum amount of money from whoever ran the mines and hence their support for nationalisation: it would replace private owners with the state, which had deeper pockets.

So, in the prosperous pre-war days, the coal owners had normally met wage claims, industrial peace usually reigned, 'class' was not an issue and miners mainly voted Liberal. After the war it became impossible to reconcile the different economic interests. The divergences became cloaked in the language of class, but the real issue was the miners' pay packets.

Labour took over other Liberal strongholds, notably inner-city constituencies. Here many poorer voters were enfranchised for the first time in 1918. Although pre-war Liberal social reform had been in their interests, the mixed messages coming from the split Liberal Party of 1918–1923 may have helped Labour, which also stressed social reform, to capture these votes and constituencies. In such constituencies, class was an explanation for change, but elsewhere there were other factors behind Labour support. Much of the Gladstonian element of the Liberal Party, who put international peace at the centre of their beliefs, went over to Labour. All the chief Liberal leaders had supported the war, so MacDonald's opposition to it was now a real attraction to internationalists.

In 1918 Labour had appeared to make itself into a socialist party when as part of its constitution it had adopted the famous Clause IV, the promise to 'secure for the producers by hand and by brain the full fruits of their industry, and the most equitable distribution thereof that may be possible, upon the basis of the common ownership of the means of production and the best obtainable system of popular administration and control of each industry and service'. Clause IV was adopted as a rallying cry for socialists in the party, and appealed to trade unions such as the miners who had nationalisation as an aim. However, it was vague and had no time scale, so in practice committed the party to little. Most Labour leaders and supporters, were not extreme, and the interest of trade unions in nationalisation was essentially because they saw it as the best way of protecting their members' interests rather than as a step towards a socialist millennium (see box, 'Ramsay MacDonald and British socialism').

People and politics: Ramsay MacDonald and British socialism

Can there be a sadder story in modern British politics than the career of Ramsay MacDonald?

He was born illegitimately in 1866 in Lossiemouth, Scotland. He became a pupil teacher and then a journalist, which led him into early Labour politics. His apparently contradictory characteristics made him a formidable political force: he could woo audiences with compelling oratory, yet was an efficient organiser and a shrewd and sometimes ruthless political operator (Fig. 4.2).

MacDonald was unusual among British politicians in that he had a developed philosophy. He was also unusual in that his ideas were almost the exact opposite to the way most supporters of the Labour Party usually behaved. MacDonald believed that the state was an organic unity, and therefore that individuals were less than the state (see Chapter 1). This led him to a gradualist philosophy – as organic bodies evolve, so would states – and therefore the transition from capitalism to socialism would be slow. His ideas are often seen as woolly, but one idea was clearheaded – he downplayed class, seeing that workers had different interests, for instance as consumers, not just a class interest.

Most supporters of the Labour Party were happy to subscribe to MacDonald's idea of gradual change. Many of them were not even socialist, or not what is usually meant by socialist, and few of those who were wanted to see the rapid overthrow of existing society. But, in contrast to him, many supporters of the party, especially those who were also trade unionists, held the classic liberal view that individuals and their interests were superior to the state. As Robert Currie has brilliantly demonstrated, this led to the primacy that British trade unions have placed on putting their members' perceived interests ahead of everything else.

In spite of this fundamental difference, MacDonald's oratory had immense appeal to many ordinary people. Perhaps one reason for this was that his benevolent ▶

Figure 4.2   Ramsay MacDonald with Philip Snowden, Labour's 'iron chancellor', in 1929. MacDonald once described Snowden as resembling a 'being of a thousand years looking very young for his age'. © Hulton-Deutsch Collection/CORBIS

progressivism was attractive to many ex-Liberals, especially nonconformists. This appeal was accentuated by MacDonald's internationalism and love of peace. After the euphoria of victory and the immediate desire for revenge on Germany, a reaction against the blood toll of the war quickly set in. During the war MacDonald had joined the UDC, and had been vilified at the time. But unlike the Liberals, among whom the Lloyd George–Asquith split had caused bitter divisions, Labour remained united as a party even though most of the leadership disagreed with MacDonald and supported the war. He remained party treasurer and, in 1922, was elected party leader by the other Labour MPs.

As the main text shows, MacDonald was one of the chief actors in the replacement of the Liberals by Labour. His triumph should have come in the second Labour government of 1929–1931, but economic depression turned it to ashes. MacDonald himself might have considered a more flexible economic policy, but he came up against the free-trade, balanced-budget inflexibility of Philip Snowden, and did not have the energy or expertise to argue against him. In his last few years as National Prime Minister, MacDonald continued to influence foreign policy, but otherwise he was little more than a figurehead, while his speeches became notoriously vague. Increasingly isolated, vilified by the Labour Party and never having really got over the death of his wife Margaret in 1911, he stepped down from the prime ministership in 1935.

Domestically the first Labour government did little except for a Housing Act, usually known by the name of the Minister of Health John Wheatley, which gave more generous support to municipal housing and had a considerable impact. In foreign policy it did more, for instance by working for disarmament. Foreign affairs were important because Labour claimed the old Liberal mantle of the party of peace. Labour's inaction was partly enforced. They were in office with the support of the Liberals, whose patience could not be tried too much. But it was also deliberate. It was in its interests to present itself as a 'safe' party, because long-term electoral success depended on it capturing moderate voters from the Liberals. What better way to appear safe than by doing very little?

Labour was forced out over a technical issue relating to its handling of a court case involving a Communist journalist, J. R. Campbell. It would in any case have gone quite soon, because the Liberals were preparing to vote against treaties the government had concluded with the USSR. The 'red scare' stoked up by these issues was further fuelled by the Zinoviev letter, a document apparently showing Russian plans for stirring up class war in Britain. It was probably a forgery, although Zinoviev was quite capable of writing such a letter. It was undoubtedly used unscrupulously by the right-wing press, although most historians think its effect on the election was limited. The Campbell case and the Russian treaties gave enough ammunition anyway for an anti-socialist campaign. The Conservatives, having again dropped protection, had fulfilled their strategic plan and were the safety-first option, with voters switching to them from the Liberals in large numbers. The Labour vote actually increased, although they lost seats. It was the Liberals who collapsed, to just 42 MPs.

Calm and storm: 1924–1929 and the General Strike

During the turmoil of the interwar years, 1924–1929 saw a brief period of calm, punctuated in 1926 by the General Strike. Stanley Baldwin, now Prime Minister after the Conservative election victory of 1924, was one reason for this calm (see box, 'Stanley Baldwin'). For the trade unions the strike was cathartic, and after it they moved decisively away from any attempt to challenge the government.

The strike arose directly out of the problems of the coal industry. It became a general strike, however, because the Trades Union Congress (TUC) had committed itself to supporting disputes in which large numbers of workers were involved. For most union leaders, this commitment to sympathetic strikes was not an attempt to politicise industrial relations. It was simply seen as a logical extension of unions' industrial powers. In practice, it was a blank cheque to the miners.

Coal miners had secured an improvement in wages in 1924 on the back of a temporary upsurge in coal exports. In 1925, with exports again in decline, the owners attempted to end the agreement. The government offered a subsidy for nine months while an enquiry was held into the industry. While this was partly a response to pressure by the TUC which threatened to block the movement of coal, it gave Baldwin the moral high ground in any future confrontation. The enquiry, headed by Sir Herbert

People and politics: Stanley Baldwin

Stanley Baldwin came from a wealthy iron-making family. The family firm's paternalistic attitude towards its workers strengthened Baldwin's own tolerant views and put him firmly on the left of the Conservative Party. He combined this orientation with a belief in the virtues of British constitutionalism and a romantic love of the English countryside. Taken together, his views enabled him to deploy a formidable rhetoric in pursuit of his ends (see Chapter 6, 'Identities: local and national').

Right-wing Conservatives disliked Baldwin's moderation and his reaching out to labour, but to many in the party these were made acceptable by his simultaneous appeal to older values. He skilfully used the name of Disraeli, the great nineteenth century Conservative leader, to help legitimate his inclusive social policies.

Baldwin was more than just a wielder of effective rhetoric. Both contemporaries and historians agree that he was a man of genuine goodness. In 1925 he courageously headed off strong Conservative efforts to pass anti-union laws, famously ending his speech, 'Give peace in our time, O Lord.'[4] After the General Strike he had to make some concessions to the right, but these were limited. Between 1930 and 1934 there was much party and newspaper opposition to Baldwin's moderate India policy (see Chapter 5), which he faced down.

Yet Baldwin was also extremely shrewd and in many ways very modern. Although temperamentally very different, he bears some striking similarities to another successful interwar politician, Franklin D. Roosevelt. Both mastered the new medium of radio and used it to project themselves as speaking individually to millions in their living rooms. Both delegated detail and relied on personal contact and skilful speech-making to wield influence. Both could be devious but had as one of their basic motivations a strong Christian faith. And both aimed to stabilise situations which they saw as deeply threatening to western civilisation: Roosevelt, the Depression; Baldwin, the threat of extremism to constitutional government.

By 1940 Baldwin was vilified, unfairly, as one of those most responsible for Britain's unpreparedness for war. He then suffered from historians' disenchantment with the whole interwar period as one of drift. More recently, historians such as John Ramsden and Philip Williamson have restored Baldwin's reputation. He is seen as immensely important in the transformation of the Conservatives into a party which successfully occupied the middle ground of British politics, keeping their own core vote but also taking votes from the Liberals. Undoubtedly his rehabilitation is justified. But Baldwin's reputation lies as much in his contribution to Britain's social and political cohesion as in his contribution to one party (see conclusion of this chapter).

Samuel, produced little on which the miners and owners could agree. This was unfortunate as its plans for reconstruction of the industry were a possible basis for agreement between the government and the TUC. The owners, however, wanted sharp wage cuts while the miners were unwilling to accept any reductions, which the government also saw as necessary. Both sides were obstinate. In 1924–1925 the miners had reasonable wages by the standards of most workers and could have made concessions, but the owners made the pill excessively bitter by proposing a return to an eight-hour day.

With deadlock between the two sides, the coal owners issued wage reduction notices and the TUC's General Council prepared to support the miners. After confused negotiations with the government broke down, the strike, which included transport workers, printers and workers in electricity, gas and heavy industry, began on 4 May 1926. With mild weather it caused no major problems. There was little violence, partly owing to the generally conciliatory stance by the police and most local union officials. Emergency plans had been prepared by the Coalition back in 1920, and with the government moving food successfully, helped by middle-class volunteers driving lorries and unloading ships, the strikers were on a hiding to nothing. The General Council had put itself in the position of defending a state of affairs – miners' existing pay levels coupled with their refusal to negotiate realistically – which most trade union leaders privately thought indefensible. The strike was called off on 12 May, although fears about employer retaliation kept many men out for a few more days. In spite of this lingering resistance, many employers, such as those on the railways, used the unions' defeat to reduce staffing levels. The coal owners hardened their position still further, and the miners drifted back to work from the summer, most quickly in the Midlands where a breakaway moderate union, the Miners Industrial Union (often called the Spencer Union after its founder), started up.

Right-wing Conservatives wanted a counter-attack on the unions, but Baldwin held the line against stringent anti-union laws. A 1927 Act effectively outlawed sympathetic strikes and made it necessary to opt in to the political levy which unions paid to the Labour Party, rather than opting out as before. This cut Labour's income, but the unions had escaped lightly. With legal curbs remaining weak, trade unionism outside the coal industry remained quite buoyant. Unlike coal owners, many employers saw benefits in standardised wage levels. These avoided time-wasting individual bargaining with workers and minimised competition from rogue employers who wanted to cut wages. The TUC's response to the strike was to build on the often positive relations with employers and to try to develop a wider common ground. The Mond–Turner talks of 1928, named after an industrialist and the TUC chairman, were one such initiative. They did not lead to much but were symbolic of a new mood of cooperation.

The General Strike and its aftermath overshadow the fact that this was a mildly reforming government, not a reactionary one. Baldwin set the tone but the details were left to a very different character, Neville Chamberlain (see Chapter 5). His speciality was reform of administrative structures, deeply boring to most historians and history students but often necessary. With it went an interest in social amelioration. In 1925 he introduced contributory pensions at 65, on the same principle as pre-war health insurance; these bridged the years of old age until the original Lloyd George scheme cut in, at 70. Then, in 1929, he reformed local government. Counties and county boroughs (the then arrangement gave larger towns, as county boroughs, and cities similar powers to county councils) took over the Poor Law, managing its Poor Relief functions through Public Assistance Committees. Local authorities could also take over and develop Poor Law infirmaries, a rudimentary public hospital system, although outside London they were slow to do so. In addition, Chamberlain initiated the formula method of making central government grants to local government, a method which, by taking account of factors such as unemployment and the local value of property, allocated more money to poorer areas. So, while the government had no more success than Labour in dealing with structural unemployment (see box, 'Economic depression', below), it tried to do something about its social consequences.

1929–1931: depression and crisis

With unemployment remaining stubbornly high, a swing against the Conservatives was likely in the election due in 1929. The Liberals, now led by Lloyd George, campaigned on a Keynesian-type platform of public works (see box, 'Economic depression'), but having lost so many core constituencies to Labour they could not gain many seats. Labour emerged as the largest single party, but still without an overall majority. Once again, rather than attempt a Conservative–Liberal alliance, Baldwin chose to allow Labour to take office.

Society and economy: Economic depression

The interwar years saw severe and lasting unemployment, beginning when the boom ended in 1920 and, in some areas, lasting all the way through to 1939.

The main reasons for this were well known at the time, but it was not so obvious how to deal with them. After the war cotton textiles, historically around a quarter of British exports, suffered increasing competition from the cheap labour producers, Japan and India; at the same time, higher tariffs in European countries disrupted exports there. Coal exports also came under increasing pressure from cheap producers such as Poland, while coal-fired ships slowly gave way to oil-firing and diesels. Jack Dowie has also pointed to the impact of the cut in working hours from 56 to 48 instituted in the post-war euphoria of 1919, which raised labour costs. One other major possible reason was the decision to return sterling to the Gold Standard, which had been abandoned in 1919 after the post-war inflation. This meant a return to the old pre-war parity of $4.86 to the pound, which was achieved in 1925. The argument for this was that stability would help to restore confidence to the world financial system, in which Britain had been the most important participant. Historians have mixed views over the direct effect of this. It pushed up the price of British exports, having a particular impact on coal, demand for which was sensitive to small price differentials. On the other hand, it reduced the price of imports and thus benefited consumers in Britain. The problem lay partly in the indirect effect of the policy: to support sterling, interest rates were raised and kept high, therefore depressing demand.

The impact of all these things – because no single one was paramount – had a devastating effect on what had once been areas of working-class prosperity such as South Wales, the North-East and the West of Scotland. They now became semi-permanently depressed, with high levels of unemployment, and many younger workers migrated elsewhere. Lancashire suffered too, but less so as its economy was more diversified.

To this structural unemployment, as economists call it, was added the effect of the world depression which began in 1929 and reached its peak in the winter of 1932–1933. The causes of this are debated even now, but most historians accept that they lay outside Britain. Whatever the reasons, Britain suffered as export markets declined still further, exacerbating the problems of the depressed areas. The registered unemployment level, which is the one usually quoted, reached 22 per cent of the workforce in 1932. Underlying unemployment was less, about 16 per cent, since workers who did not pay unemployment insurance, such as domestic servants, and who therefore did not appear on the register, were less likely to be unemployed.

The depression remains one of those facts of British history, like the two world wars, about which most people are aware. However, it is important to realise that Britain did not suffer as badly as many other countries. America and Germany among industrialised nations, and food producers such as Australia and Canada, all experienced far worse, the last two because of the catastrophic fall in the price of wheat. These price falls benefited British consumers. Another factor which mitigated the worst of the depression was the large size and financial strength of British banks: unlike America and Germany, Britain suffered no banking crisis. Finally, when Britain was forced off the Gold Standard in 1931, the need for high interest rates was removed. They subsequently fell sharply, stimulating borrowing for mortgages and, therefore, house building. This and relatively high consumer incomes contributed to rapid economic improvement from 1933. But since export demand was still low, the depressed areas remained depressed. It was in the South and the Midlands, and more patchily elsewhere, that industries such as vehicles, light electrical assembly and clothing boomed.

The depression has often been blamed on the strength of financial interests in Britain who believed that financial stability, narrowly conceived of as meaning a balanced budget and adherence to the Gold Standard, was essential. This is a generalised version of the old Labour argument that the 1931 crisis was a 'bankers' ramp' (see main text). This diagnosis implies that there would have been two possible remedies. One was to run an inflationary monetary regime, a remedy which had been killed off during the Coalition and buried by the return to gold. The other was the more sophisticated, and arguably non-inflationary, remedy of John Maynard Keynes. This called for the alleviation of depression by government spending financed by borrowing, rather than taxation. It was only published as a formal economic theory in 1935, although Keynes had been advocating it for a number of years.

Financial interests, namely bankers and the set of institutions collectively known as the City of London (geographically, they were mainly located there), did advocate financial stability. But it is important to realise that their views commanded widespread support, among both economists and the general public. Furthermore, the ideas were not always as stupid as has been suggested since. In the 1920s governments believed that the main road to economic recovery was to restore world trade in general, and reduce European tariff barriers in particular. Even in the 1930s, although the task was now much more difficult, that remained an aspiration. If successful, these ideas would

▶

have benefited everyone and not just bankers. However hopeless they may seem in retrospect, it was very human to think that the pre-1914 economic system, which had seemed to work so well, would do so again if restored. In the meantime, after 1931, the government accepted the desirability of sterling devaluation and low interest rates (see main text) and was not, therefore, completely wedded to economic orthodoxy.

In contrast, government spending on a huge and politically impossible scale would have been required for Keynes's remedies to have had a real impact. The most efficient form of government spending to reduce unemployment in the depressed areas was rearmament, which in the later 1930s started to have an effect. In the early 1930s, however, it was disarmament which held centre stage. From an economic point of view this was unfortunate: building a couple of battleships would have done far more for unemployment in Clydeside and Tyneside than any amount of spending on roads, the usual remedy advocated by Keynesians.

Labour's minority status made little difference, because their policies offered no shelter against the economic blizzard which was about to start. The world depression pushed unemployment ever upwards, but the Labour Chancellor, Philip Snowden, believed in strict economic orthodoxy, meaning a balanced budget. As unemployment benefit payments rose, this was impossible to achieve without drastic tax increases, unacceptable to the Liberals and Snowden himself. By 1931 there was a budget deficit which brought Labour up against another fundamental constraint: international bankers.

In the eyes of orthodoxy, a budget deficit meant the danger of inflation; and inflation threatened the value of sterling. To see inflationary dangers in the situation of 1931, when world-wide commodity prices were plummeting and millions were out of work, nowadays seems a fantastic misconception. But it is important to realise that, although it was bankers who dictated terms, this orthodoxy was almost universal at the time. Thus, in 1933, Clement Attlee, the future leader of the Labour Party, criticised the National government for running a budget deficit.

The explosive content of the 1931 crisis was provided by the general economic and financial situation. It was detonated by a committee, headed by the businessman Sir George May, and set up early in 1931 at Liberal instigation to recommend economies in public expenditure. The May Committee reported on 31 July, recommending heavy cuts in spending, including the reduction of unemployment benefit. The committee was undoubtedly excessive in its demands for cuts. However, historians who lambast the 10 per cent cut which was eventually made, neglect the fact that, since the benefit rate had been set, prices had decreased by about 12 per cent. After the report there followed negotiations within the government, with the other party leaders, and between the government and the Bank of England as to what cuts would be acceptable.

With uncertainty exacerbated by the May Report, investors began moving money out of London, thus threatening the international parity of sterling (see box, 'Economic depression'). A big international loan to Britain seemed essential but depended on a certain level of cuts being achieved. The Cabinet split down the middle over what cuts it would accept, and on 23 August the party leaders all saw the King although,

Lloyd George being ill, it was Sir Herbert Samuel who represented the Liberals. George V, with his personal closeness to MacDonald and his consistent belief in the inclusion of all classes, encouraged MacDonald to continue in government even if Labour as a party did not. Samuel supported this and Baldwin fell into line. The new National government, led by MacDonald, comprised a few Labour MPs, most Liberals (but not Lloyd George) and the Conservatives. The rest of the Labour Party went into opposition.

People and politics: George V

Monarchs get short shrift in most textbooks on modern British history. Apparently consigned to the sidelines of the constitution by Bagehot's dictum, quoted in Chapter 1, it is tempting simply to leave them out. But there is a strong case for saying that twentieth century monarchs have been extremely significant and that, of them all, the unassuming and reticent George V was the most important (Fig 4.3).

Figure 4.3   George V, looking like an ordinary middle-class citizen. © Hulton-Deutsch Collection/CORBIS

Edward VII was both too grand and too old to modernise the monarchy. Although George disliked change, and although the flummery of the court did not alter much during his reign, the monarchy modernised in other and important ways.

Crucially, he oiled the adjustment of politics and government to the Labour Party. The acceptance by other political leaders of the inevitability of the first Labour government obviously helped; George was not faced with the dilemma in which the Conservatives had placed him over Lords reform. Nevertheless, his genuinely warm greeting to the first Labour ministers, which set the tone for future relations, was his own doing. It helped to emphasise, to the Labour Party, to the country and to the more reactionary Conservatives, that Labour was now an established part of the political fabric.

George also showed himself surprisingly good at public relations. Not obviously interested in soccer, he regularly attended Cup Finals – then even more than now the highlight of the football year. It was a peacetime complement to the endless reviewing of troops which he undertook during the war. And in 1932 he was persuaded to the radio for the first Christmas address, universally acknowledged to be a great success.

George also had finely tuned antennae for anything which might actively damage the monarchy. He agreed to jettisoning the family's German name in favour of Windsor – an inspired choice – in 1917. It was also his decision not to give asylum to the Russian royal family at the same date. This refusal is sometimes put down to fear of the reaction in Britain, but it may reflect the fact that George was both more liberal and more intelligent that he is often given credit for. His writings show him to be more racially tolerant than most of his generation, while his biographer Kenneth Rose found 'not a trace of . . . anti-semitism',[4] which was then, if usually in a mild form, common in Britain.

While some of George's enormous popularity was inherited from the later years of Victoria and from Edward, much can be attributed to the persona he constructed. This had an impact which overshadows his occasional formal constitutional interventions. Here the most important were his eventual acquiescence in the Liberal plan to create peers in 1911 and his promotion of a National government in 1931. Although he bears some direct responsibility for the latter, and for keeping MacDonald as Prime Minister – and thus splitting the Labour Party – it does not seem to have born him a grudge. On the contrary, the *Daily Herald*, the Labour newspaper, devoted as much space to the royal family as did its Conservative rivals. It was his unifying influence, perceived by Labour and by millions of ordinary people, that was George's great achievement.

Subsequently, Labour constructed two myths about the crisis: that it was a 'bankers' ramp'; and that MacDonald had plotted for some time to form a National government. ('Ramp' is an old-fashioned term meaning an underhand deal.) But, as noted above, it was not just bankers but practically everyone, including many in Labour, who believed in balanced budgets. As for MacDonald, there is no hard evidence that he had any plans beforehand or that he particularly wanted to carry on at the time. While his considerable vanity was touched by the King's appeal, he was also an unhappy man who craved rest. The most likely interpretation is that he responded to an appeal to his duty.

Duty was the watchword in the formation of the National government. The King, most politicians and the large majority of citizens who voted for the government in the subsequent election believed that there was a desperate crisis and that a common spirit of sacrifice could overcome it.

Ironically, financial confidence was not restored and, with no further international loans forthcoming, Britain was forced off the Gold Standard in September 1931. Sterling now 'floated' – that is, its value fluctuated, after an initial fall. While this fall made exports cheaper, there was little immediate benefit to Britain because of the collapse of the world economy. The Conservatives pressed for an election as there were now strong arguments for their favoured tariff policy. Given the breakdown of the world economy, free trade offered little. Instead, British industries could be reconstructed behind the shelter of tariffs. An election would give a mandate for tariffs and entrench the National government's position. It did, the government receiving 14.5 million votes to Labour's 6.6 million. The figures were a measure both of the huge support for the government and of the large bedrock constituency Labour had now gained. Emergency tariffs were brought in after the election, regularised early in 1932, and increased later that year, although remaining low by world standards.

National government 1931–1939

The National government has often had a bad press from historians. In part this has stemmed from criticism of appeasement and the extent of Britain's rearmament. In part it has stemmed from the continued high level of unemployment. And in part it has stemmed from the success with which Labour subsequently depicted the pre-war Conservatives as an uncaring party, a picture which the post-war Conservatives tacitly endorsed by adopting many Labour policies.

Appeasement and rearmament are dealt with in Chapter 5, and the roots of unemployment are explained in the earlier box, 'Economic depression'. In fact, economic recovery was rapid after 1933. This owed little to tariffs and more to the decline in interest rates made possible by floating the pound. The Treasury also became converted to the idea that a modest increase in prices would be beneficial, so long as it did not lead to uncontrolled inflation, as price rises would raise profits and thus encourage investment. Apart from sterling devaluation, one way of raising prices was by encouraging cartelisation and price-fixing agreements in industry. This dovetailed with existing ideas about 'rationalisation' into larger economic units, which encapsulated the belief that competition was frequently wasteful, and also that large corporations could secure economies in operation.

One early result, promoted under the Coalition, was amalgamation in 1923 of the pre-war railway companies into larger groups. Then, in 1926, the Central Electricity Board was created. It did not supply power but controlled its distribution and rapidly constructed the National Grid, a visible example of Conservative enthusiasm for centralisation. In the 1930s this was manifested in the London Passenger Transport Board of 1933. In inception, this was a product of the Labour administration, but the National government carried it through. The buses and tubes were not completely nationalised, as private bondholders remained, but effectively they were publicly controlled. Amazingly to today's eyes, London Transport became regarded as a model for the world. A similar but smaller measure was the creation in 1939 of the British Overseas Airways Corporation from two private companies. Bodies of this type were known as public corporations.

Agriculture saw the development of cooperative marketing schemes, again using a Labour Act of 1931, in some cases under the protection of tariffs or of physical quotas limiting imports. Subsidies were paid to farmers for some products, notably wheat. However, in coal mining the legacies of sectionalism were much stronger. Labour had passed a modest reorganisation bill in 1930 which the National government carried forward, but it had little impact. Attempts to give it teeth were stymied by the coal owners' opposition, but in 1938 the government did nationalise the rights of landowners to the royalties arising from coal mining. Other price-raising initiatives in steel and cotton also involved agreements between producers. Whether such initiatives had much impact on unemployment is debateable, but the ruling ideas of most experts made a Keynesian policy of heavy spending on public works seem impossible.

Even so, the National government's policies represented a change in the mindset of politicians and civil servants, in which the necessity for significant government intervention in the economy was recognised. They also represent an acceptance of the political impossibility of launching a direct attack on workers by encouraging substantial wage cuts. Instead, price increases became a roundabout means of achieving some reduction in real wages, although in practice economic recovery meant profits and wages grew in the 1930s. The government's policies were, therefore, a logical counterpart to Baldwin's consensual approach to organised labour.

Although the Conservatives became saddled with the opprobrium later directed towards the government, it was in theory National throughout. From 1931–1935 the label was fairly genuine. The 'Samuelite' Liberals left the government over the extension of tariffs in late 1932, but a number of Liberal MPs led by Sir John Simon stayed on. (These 'Liberal Nationals' remained as permanent allies of the Conservatives until 1966, after which the last of them officially joined the Conservatives.) The Labour contribution was small but genuine in that MacDonald's internationalism at first remained dominant in foreign policy. But most importantly the Conservative leaders accepted that the government was National not party political. It chimed in with Baldwin's inclusive Conservatism in a way that the post-war Coalition, with its sometimes authoritarian approach and the permanent whiff of scandal attached to Lloyd George, never did. And Neville Chamberlain, Chancellor of the Exchequer from 1931–1937, saw himself as a genuine reformer and not a typical Conservative. After 1935, when Baldwin replaced MacDonald as Prime Minister, and particularly after the election of that year when the numbers and influence of the other two governmental parties dwindled, the government became more obviously Conservative.

The National governments left a legacy of modest social reform. A Labour Housing Act, the Greenwood Act of 1930, which provided a subsidy to local authorities for rehousing families cleared from slum properties was followed up, and around 340,000 subsidised local authority houses were built under its auspices. This was dwarfed,

Politics and government: The abdication of Edward VIII

Edward had become King on George V's death in January 1936. By the autumn it became clear to the Cabinet that Edward was friendly with, and might marry, an American, Mrs Simpson, once divorced and about to be divorced again (she was on 27 October). Protestant morality asserted itself. While Britain's divorce laws had become less stringent after the war, divorce was still rare. The Cabinet believed that marriage by the Head of the Churches of England and Scotland to a divorcee would not be tolerated by the bulk of public opinion. When public opinion finally knew of the matter – not until very late in the crisis – some sympathised with Edward but probably more were against him, while the Dominion governments were strongly opposed. So the Cabinet's judgement was broadly correct.

The constitutional position was that, if Edward insisted on remaining King and marrying Mrs Simpson, he would be rejecting the advice of his government – a major constitutional challenge, giving the monarch's theoretical subservience to Parliament. He gave way on this but held firm on the issue of marriage and the outcome was his abdication on 11 December 1936.

If it is seen as the replacement of one constitutional monarch, with little real power, by another, then the abdication seems of little importance. The potential ramifications of the affair, and the fact that the theoretically almost powerless George V had at times wielded considerable influence, make it more significant. Edward VIII was a weak character, some of whose reported views indicated a lack of judgement. He was, in fact, probably too weak for the vague Nazi sympathies which some have attributed to him to have been activated, even if the suggestions are correct. But his replacement by his younger brother Albert, whose intellectual limitations were offset by his sense of duty and strict constitutional propriety, was an undoubted gain.

As King, Albert became George VI, confusingly as there was another royal brother called George, killed in an aircrash in the Second World War. One of George VI's chief assets was his wife Elizabeth, best known today as Queen Elizabeth the Queen Mother, the name taken during her long widowhood. George VI's obvious desire to do the right thing, and his wife's enormous charm, helped the monarchy to remain a focus of unity throughout the Second World War. They also made a positive impression on American opinion, important before and during the war.

One less positive aspect of the abdication was to reinforce the barriers which kept Churchill out of office. This was entirely self-created. Churchill, active at that point in trying to construct a united political front in Britain against fascist aggression, indulged in one of the spectacular political misjudgements which punctuated his career by associating himself with a group of 'King's friends' and speaking in favour of giving Edward more time to make up his mind. The result was to strengthen the resolve of influential members of the Cabinet to keep Churchill out.

however, by the private housing boom stimulated by low interest rates: over 1.8 million were built between 1931 and 1939. The most striking social reform was the Holidays with Pay Act of 1938. This increased the number of workers entitled to paid holidays – usually of one week – from 3 to 11 million.

To most people, it is what happened in Germany in the 1930s, not what happened in Britain, that seems important. But the absence of political drama in 1930s Britain is also important in its own way. In spite of economic depression, neither fascism nor communism made a significant impact. The British Union of Fascists (BUF) was founded in 1932 by Oswald Mosley, a charismatic political maverick who had broken away from Labour. In 1934 the *Daily Mail* began to support Mosley. However, this was followed by the infamous Olympia rally in June, at which Mosley's stewards beat up hecklers. Violence at political meetings, once accepted in Britain as part of the rough and tumble of democratic politics, had died out after the war and its renewal was seen as unEnglish. Practically every newspaper was quick to condemn the Fascists, and the *Mail* soon fell into line. Mosley had never had much support, but he was now finished as a serious political force. Among mainstream Conservatives, MPs with extreme-right sympathies were conspicuous by their rarity. A maximum of 30 have been identified, and a number of these only had peripheral links; only four expressed support for Fascist methods at Olympia.

Communism in Britain had equally shallow roots. The Communist Party of Great Britain (CP) was founded in 1920 from a union of various small socialist parties. Labour persistently refused the CP the right to affiliate, as well as discouraging individual Communists from joining the Labour Party. Communism enjoyed some intellectual support in the 1930s because of the apparent success of Soviet industrialisation – its huge failures were less well publicised – and, later, because of the growing threat of European fascism. But the popular appeal of the peace movement (see Chapter 5) was far greater. Labour did shift to the left, committing itself to the nationalisation of major industries if it came to office. But this was also an attempt to differentiate itself from what became perceived as the spinelessness of the MacDonald era. Ultimately it was Labour's centre that was strengthened as the left-leaning Independent Labour Party – one of Labour's founding bodies – broke away and then rapidly declined.

The failure of the CP is highlighted by the fate of the National Unemployed Workers Movement (NUWM), led by a Communist, Wal Hannington. This gained considerable support in 1931, with a membership of around 40,000, but the marches it organised against the Means Test (see Chapter 6) in late 1932 attracted just 2000 participants. Disliked though the Means Test was, refusal by the Labour Party and trade unions to cooperate with what they saw, rightly, as a Communist front organisation meant that the NUWM had little real impact.

Another failure was the Liberal Party. At national level, the remaining independent Liberal MPs were reduced to a rump in 1935. In the 1920s the party had already lost its effective independence in municipal politics in many towns, forming alliances with the Conservatives, while Labour was making gains. Although 1931 was a setback for Labour, it soon recovered and by 1934 was winning borough councils throughout the country, not just in its industrial heartlands. The remaining Liberal council seats, however, were rapidly falling, to the benefit of both the other parties. Ramsay MacDonald's dream of smashing the three-party system was effectively fulfilled.

1918–1959: conclusion

The interwar period was one of economic turmoil, a growth in state responsibilities and political transition. Economic turmoil – post-war inflation, followed by structural unemployment and the deep depression of 1929–1933 – needs no further discussion. The role of the state was hugely increased during the war, but much of this was undone again in the years of cutbacks, 1921–1922. In the long term, the effects of the war on the state were more complex.

After it, middle-class taxpayers faced a far higher tax burden. The standard rate of income tax, 5 per cent for most of the 1900s, had risen to 30 per cent after the war. Taxpayers were understandably reluctant to shoulder still more taxation, and so, in order to avoid antagonising them, Conservative and National governments set a limit on significant spending rises. On the other hand, by acclimatising the middle classes to this higher burden, the war removed the constraints on raising money for social reform experienced by pre-war Conservatism. So interwar Conservative governments could proceed with modest social reform on the basis of existing taxation levels. However, government spending was skewed in certain directions, and again the war was partly the cause. Housing became the watchword of post-war reconstruction, for no very good reason because housing in Britain was better than in most continental countries. A new rhetoric was initiated, in which housing became partly the state's responsibility. At the same time, rent control, another wartime expedient, had reduced the incentive for private developers to supply houses. Housing, therefore, became the target of expensive post-war subsidy schemes, which further reduced cash for other purposes. In other potential areas of public intervention, spending was permanently tight. As a last gasp of reconstruction, the school leaving age was raised from 13 to 14 in 1921, but otherwise little was achieved in education between the wars.

Nevertheless, the acceptance of greater government responsibilities in many areas was one hallmark of the interwar years. Almost universal unemployment benefit, pensions at 65, industrial reorganisation, public corporations and the nationalisation of coal royalties joined housing subsidies in extending the role of the state. The war and its aftermath influenced the direction and timing of the first and the last, but they all had diverse intellectual and social roots going back before the war. *Laissez-faire* had already been significantly eroded in the 1900s, for a variety of reasons discussed in Chapters 1 and 2. After the war, a continuing emphasis on size and scale, and a further downgrading of the importance of competition, helps to explain the Conservative and National governments' acceptance of industrial reorganisation and public corporations. Then, from 1931, the Treasury accepted that a level of economic management involving a floating pound and the manipulation of interest rates was desirable.

How far were all the above measures a move towards the 'organic state' dreamed of by some thinkers in the 1900s (see Chapter 1)? To such thinkers, citizens' obligations came before their rights. But in both the rhetoric and the practice of interwar Britain rights continued to be important and obligations were downplayed. The idea of conscription in peacetime, for instance, continued to be anathema and Britain reverted to a volunteer army. New though unemployment benefit was, to the unemployed it quickly became a right. One reason for this continued emphasis on rights was that many of these measures were a response to labour – both to what political parties conceived working people as desiring and to what organised labour demanded. Working people, and organised labour, did not consider that rights entailed corresponding obligations, over and above those traditionally expected of patriotic and law-abiding citizens.

Adjusting to labour had, of course, itself begun before the war, but it became much more urgent after. This adjustment is often represented as an institutionalisation of class conflict. The historian Elie Halevy wrote in 1919, 'We shall see the class struggle, acclimatised on English soil, adapting itself to the traditional party system.'[5] His comment was prescient but puts class in too elevated a position. While class rhetoric was employed by trade union leaders, their real objectives were traditional – the improvement of their own members' living standards. And while the unions helped to finance the Labour Party, as a parliamentary party Labour established its own agenda which was distinct from that of union leaders. This was partly because the roots of many MPs were in radical liberalism, which gave them other concerns besides class, and partly because of MacDonald's influence. But it was also because the Conservative leadership, notably Baldwin, chose not to make class an issue. The Conservatives could have retreated to a right-wing laager, but they did not. Their moderation, of course, suited them politically. The Liberals became marginalised, while the Conservatives did not alienate their own working-class voters.

Moderation was also politically advantageous simply because many voters in Britain, working and middle class, were moderate. This can be inferred from various indicators. The votes of the millions who continued to support the Liberals in the 1920s were in part a vote for moderation. Similarly, in the 1930s, the huge support for the peace movement and the League of Nations (see Chapter 5) suggests that millions of women and men saw virtue in moderation, as does the weakness of the BUF and the Communists. This electoral moderation was mirrored by the great institutions of the country. During the General Strike the churches urged conciliation. Most big employers, outside coal, preferred negotiation with trade unions to confrontation. And the unions themselves, with the exception of the miners, were usually equally pragmatic.

On the face of it, newspapers bucked the trend to moderation. From around 1900 the press had begun to change in character, becoming more commercial, and after the war this process accelerated. Newspapers lost their close links with parties and became more subject to the whims of their owners. The *Daily Mail*, owned by Lord Rothermere, briefly supported Fascism; and both it and the *Daily Express*, owned by Max Beaverbrook, ran other anti-moderate campaigns, for instance attacking Baldwin's leadership of the Conservatives in 1930–1931. Beaverbrook and Rothermere were as much concerned with scoring points off each other as running concerted campaigns, however, so more moderate papers probably had equal influence. *The Times*, whose small circulation was outweighed by the reverence attached to it abroad, usually steered a conciliatory course. The *Daily Herald* had a large circulation and combined support for Labour with extreme patriotism. The *Daily Telegraph*, establishing itself as the newspaper of the prosperous middle classes, was quick to condemn BUF brutality at Olympia. The local press, less political than before the war, was still the main organ of news for many people, who were therefore immune from the hysteria of the *Mail* and the *Express*.

While forces for moderation in British life were strong, they cannot be isolated from the moderation of political leadership. Most historians now see language as a vital influence in its own right, validating some attitudes and putting others off-limits. The language deployed by the three most influential political actors gained added influence from its symbiosis. MacDonald's rhetoric of gradualism made it easier for Baldwin to sell conciliation to the Conservatives. And George V's support for moderation helped both leaders represent themselves to their parties as in the mainstream of constitutional development. By a tacit and partly unconscious alliance, the three together made political extremism seem just that – extreme, disreputable and unBritish.

The argument in this chapter is that, after the post-war period of uncertainty, an essentially moderate Conservatism conciliated working people, abetted at times by an essentially moderate Labour Party which conciliated everyone else. Of course, Conservatism also worked in the perceived interests of its middle-class supporters, by restricting public spending and setting some limits on organised labour's activities. But it made no serious attempt to undermine the labour movement. There are other interpretations of the period. In the classic left-wing narrative, the working-class were fobbed off with unemployment benefit, which damped down social conflict but did nothing positive, while economic policy was dictated by financial institutions (see earlier box, 'Economic depression'). A more sophisticated version of this has been put forward by Ross McKibbin. To him, organised labour was seen by most Conservatives as an enemy. The Conservative Party relied for its mass voting support on the lower middle classes and non-unionised working classes, influenced by the predominantly right-wing press.

Many Conservative supporters no doubt were opposed to trade unions. But the leadership's more moderate course, although underpinned by Baldwin's personal beliefs, was steered in part because it was thought to appeal to voters. And the evidence suggests that it did appeal: that many voters were moderate. This implies that McKibbin may exaggerate the left/right split.

Notes

1. Mowat, C., *Britain Between the Wars 1918–1940* (London: Methuen, 1955), p. 142.
2. Quoted in Ramsden, *Balfour and Baldwin* (see Chapter 1), p. 155.
3. Quoted in Ramsden, *Balfour and Baldwin* (see Chapter 1), p. 277.
4. Rose, K., *King George V* (London: Weidenfeld and Nicolson, 1983), p. 87.
5. Quoted in de Groot, *Blighty* (see Chapter 2), p. 317.

Further reading

Currie, R., *Industrial Politics* (Oxford: Oxford University Press, 1979) contains important insights. McKibbin, R., 'Class and Conventional Wisdom: the Conservative Party and the Public in Inter-War Britain' and 'Why Was There No Marxism in Great Britain?', in McKibbin, *Ideologies* (see Chapter 2) are both thought provoking. Ramsden, *Balfour and Baldwin* is excellent. Pugh, *The Making* (see Chapter 2) and Thorpe, A., *A History of the British Labour Party* (London: Palgrave, 2nd ed., 2001) are valuable surveys. Williamson, P., *Stanley Baldwin: Conservative Leadership and National Values* (Cambridge: Cambridge University Press, 1999) is exceptionally important.

Other sources: Booth, A., 'Britain in the 1930s: a Managed Economy', *Economic History Review*, Vol. XL, pp. 499–522 (1987); Cook, C., *A Short History of the Liberal Party 1900–1992* (London: Macmillan, 4th ed., 1993); Cowling, M., *The Impact of Labour, 1920–1924* (Cambridge: Cambridge University Press, 1971); Dowie, J., '1919–20 Is In Need of Attention', *Economic History Review*, Vol. 28, pp. 42–50 (1975); Dutton, *Liberal Party* (see Chapter 2); Lawrence, J., 'Fascist Violence and the Politics of Public Order in Inter-war Britain: the Olympia Debate Revisited', *Historical Research*, Vol. 76, pp. 238–267 (2003); McKibbin, *Classes* (see Chapter 1); McKibbin, *Labour Party* (see Chapter 2); Marquand, D., *Ramsay MacDonald* (London: Jonathan Cape, 1977); Moore, R., *Pitmen, Preachers and Politics* (Cambridge: Cambridge University Press, 1974); More, *Industrial Age* (see Chapter 1); Packer, *Lloyd George* (see Chapter 2); Peele, G. and Cook, C. (eds), *The Politics of Reappraisal 1918–1939* (London: Macmillan, 1975); Richardson, H. and Aldcroft, D., *Building in the British Economy between the Wars* (London: Allen and Unwin, 1968); Stewart, G., *Burying Caesar: Churchill, Chamberlain and the Battle for the Tory Party* (London: Weidenfeld and Nicolson, 1999); Tanner, D., Thane, P. and Tiratsoo, N. (eds), *Labour's First Century* (Cambridge: Cambridge University Press, 2000).

Chapter 5

THE SEARCH FOR PEACE: BRITAIN AND THE WORLD 1918–1939

The post-war world

A long shadow falls over European history in 1918 – the shadow of Hitler's future rise to power.

It is tempting to regard everything that happened in Europe from the end of the First World War as in some sense connected with the Nazis' victory in 1933 and its sequel. To believe this, however, is almost certainly wrong. Much that happened after the war did bear on Hitler's rise, in particular the failure to achieve lasting political and economic stability in Germany. But how far Germany's travails between 1918 and 1933 directly led to Hitler's coming to power is something which historians still debate. What is indisputable is that much of the energy of British statesmen and diplomats in the same years was directed towards attempts to settle the legacies of the First World War.

In the immediate post-war period, demands for the punishment of Germany had been widely voiced in Britain, not least by Lloyd George himself. By the opening of the Peace Conference at Versailles in January 1919 more moderate counsels tended to prevail, and Lloyd George accepted that an excessively harsh peace would make it difficult to rebuild a stable Germany. The French, however, wished to weaken Germany, and the very different British and French attitudes were to become a persistent theme. Nevertheless, in June 1919 Britain agreed to guarantee the French frontiers against aggression – in effect to offer a military alliance. This depended, however, on a similar Franco-American agreement, which was not ratified since the United States retreated into isolationism. As a consequence, the Franco-British alliance was never concluded. Without this cement, there was constant mistrust throughout the 1920s between the two former allies: France was anxious to keep Germany weak; Britain was anxious to see Germany restored to normality, albeit stripped of her pre-war militarism.

Reparations – that is, the payment by Germany of money or goods as a recompense for war damage – was perhaps the biggest single post-war issue. The huge scale of reparations was bitterly resented by Germany and their practical implementation was destabilising. Britain had originally supported France over reparations, but in 1922 further discussions over an Anglo-French alliance foundered, in part because of disagreements about them. Germany had defaulted almost immediately. France wanted to take a tough line, Britain a conciliatory one. In 1923, after further defaults, the French occupied Germany's biggest coal and steel producing region, the Ruhr. Britain's dislike of this and associated French political interference in Germany eventually persuaded the French to agree to a further reparations settlement, the Dawes Plan, which scaled down Germany's payments. With Germany herself now becoming more conciliatory, the way was open towards what was hoped would be a permanent settlement. This was the Locarno Treaty of 1925, in which Britain, Italy, France, Belgium and Germany guaranteed the mutual frontiers of the three latter powers, and Germany accepted the demilitarisation of the Rhineland. (It was named after the Swiss resort on Lake Maggiore where it was agreed.)

Because Locarno was ultimately a complete failure, it is difficult to conceive today of the importance attached to it at the time. After the European turbulence of the past few years – encompassing not just Anglo–French disagreement and the occupation of the Ruhr, but also German political instability and hyper-inflation – a new era seemed to have dawned. Unfortunately it was a false dawn. Germany's continued payment of reparations, even at a scaled down rate, involved an infusion of American loans to Germany. These dried up in 1928, helping to precipitate a recession in Germany which preceded the world recession of 1929 onwards. Furthermore, Germans, and not just those on the right, continued to feel that Versailles was unfair. On the other hand, Britain's conciliatory line encouraged Germany to continue a covert programme of military research and officer training which laid the groundwork for future rearmament.

Achieving post-war settlement in the Near East, the old term for Turkey east of the Bosphorus, Egypt and the former territories of the Ottoman Empire stretching from the eastern Mediterranean coast to the Gulf, was almost as testing. The Treaty of Sèvres in 1920 was intended to settle the region. (Egypt and the other former territories are dealt with in the next section.) In Turkey, the treaty was to be enforced by Greek military action, but in 1922 the Turks routed the Greeks and the French refused to provide further support for the Allied occupation of Chanak, guarding the Dardanelles. It was concern over the implications of further British resistance to the Turks which sparked off the Conservative backbenchers' overthrow of the Coalition. Ironically, the British held firm at Chanak and settlement was ultimately reached. The new Turkey was subsequently to become the least troublesome of the defeated powers.

Immediately after the war, one of Britain's biggest headaches was not the defeated states but her former ally, Russia. The Russian Revolution had brought to power a government which not only took Russia out of the war, but also preached world revolution. However remote a Bolshevik revolution in Britain seems in hindsight, at the time it excited many people's fears. (Bolshevism was the term then generally used for communism.) And it was partly because of fears of a Bolshevik takeover in Germany that Britain was so concerned about that country's post-war stability. One riposte to Bolshevism was to intervene directly in favour of the 'White' counter-revolutionary forces in Russia. Munitions and a few troops were sent in 1918–1919, with no ultimate effect since the Whites were defeated. Pragmatism prevailed and a trade agreement was concluded with Russia in 1921. The Labour government of 1924 formally recognised the Soviet government, a convenient sop to Labour's left wing. This in turn provided political ammunition for the Conservatives, as did Soviet propaganda in Britain and the Empire. Subsequently, relations with the Soviet Union fluctuated up and down, but by the early 1930s it had become accepted as a fact of life. Stalin's concentration on industrialising Russia made relations easier because there was less Soviet emphasis on international troublemaking.

The Soviet Union was a minor factor in international relations. A major factor was the League of Nations. The League was part of the post-war settlement because it was pushed by the American President, Woodrow Wilson. Ironically, when the USA became isolationist after Versailles, it refused to join the League, thus weakening it at its inception. It is tempting now to see the League as devised in order to bore GCSE students, forced to memorise its petty triumphs and much bigger failures, but throughout the 1920s and into the first half of the 1930s it was taken with the utmost seriousness by diplomats and politicians. In 1926 a Foreign Office memorandum put the League's Covenant first among British commitments. The Covenant bound members to respect each other's independence and territorial integrity; nations resorting to force would face sanctions. Locarno was, in effect, an acceptance by the signatories of existing obligations under the League strengthened by Britain and Italy's military guarantee. (Germany was not at that point a member of the League but became one after Locarno.)

The League was taken seriously in part because there was a genuine revulsion against war by most people, including politicians. Therefore, support for the League went along with support for disarmament, and here there was a political agenda. Arms were expensive. Given Britain's greatly enlarged post-war financial commitments, reducing military spending was politically expedient and supported by practically all political actors save the right wing of the Conservative Party and the military themselves, who had never had much political clout in Britain.

Whatever politicians' personal beliefs, they also took the League seriously because it had enormous public support. The League was not Woodrow Wilson's personal invention; it had already been mooted in Britain during the war, and with the post-war revulsion against the old alliance system the League seemed a far better substitute. Public support for peace seemed vindicated by the Briand–Kellogg Pact of 1928, a pact renouncing war between the signatories (except for self-defence, a rather important reservation) to which Britain subscribed. This was to be reinforced by a world disarmament conference, planned from the late 1920s although not held until 1932. By the early 1930s the League of Nations Union – the cheerleader for the League in Britain – had over 400,000 subscribers. So popular was the League that no party could stand aloof from the Union. Many Conservatives were rather sceptical of the League, but even so senior members of the party held honorary positions in the Union. Before 1914, while few people actually wanted war, only the radical wing of the Liberals, and part of the then-small Labour Party, were positively anti-war. By the end of the 1920s public support for peace, disarmament and the League was overwhelming.

Empire and Commonwealth

Britain's age of imperial expansion was now firmly over. It had been on its last legs since the Boer war, and its aftermath, had dissipated Joe Chamberlain's dream of an African imperial heartland. The First World War, and its aftermath, was the death blow. The Empire actually became larger, as Britain took control of chunks of the former Ottoman Empire (Fig. 5.1); but the control was subject to League of Nations' mandates which called for an advance to independence. This was symptomatic of a trend of thought.

Figure 5.1   The British empire 1919
Source: Adapted from Taylor, A. J. P., *English History 1914–45*, Oxford University Press (1965)

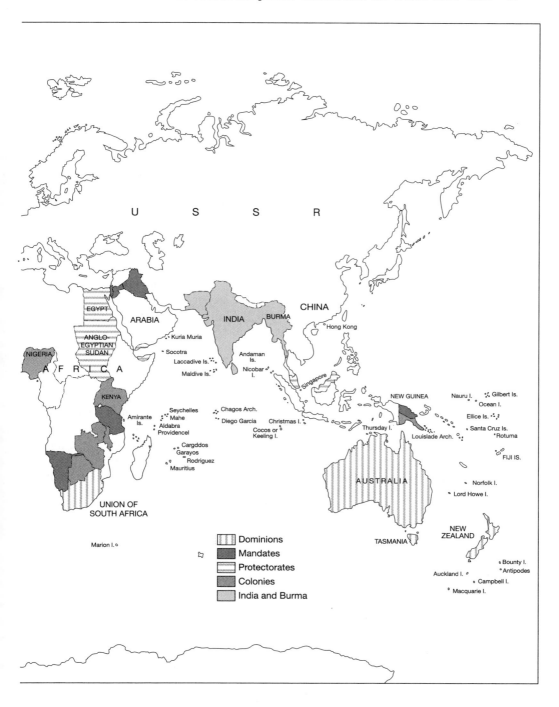

U　S　S　R

EGYPT

ARABIA

INDIA

BURMA

CHINA

Hong Kong

Kuria Muria

ANGLO-
EGYPTIAN
SUDAN

Socotra

Andaman
Is.

NIGERIA

Laccadive Is.

A F R I C A

Maldive Is.

Nicobar
I.

KENYA

Singapore

NEW GUINEA

Nauru I.

Gilbert Is.

Ocean I.

Amirante
Is.

Seychelles
Mahe
Aldabra
Providencel

Chagos Arch.

Diego Garcia

Christmas I.

Cocos or
Keeling I.

Ellice Is.

Thursday I.

Santa Cruz Is.

Rotuma

Louislade Arch.

Cargddos
Garayos
Rodriguez
Mauritius

FIJI IS.

AUSTRALIA

UNION OF
SOUTH AFRICA

Norfolk I.

Lord Howe I.

Marion I.

Dominions

Mandates

Protectorates

Colonies

India and Burma

TASMANIA

NEW
ZEALAND

Bounty I.

Antipodes

Auckland I.

Campbell I.

Macquarie I.

India and the colonies were increasingly seen as a trust under which Britain, albeit slowly, would develop in them the conditions for greater administrative and political participation by non-whites. But there were countervailing influences which restricted progress, particularly in Africa.

The First War had also seemed to prove the cohesion of the wider Empire, including the 'White Dominions', evidenced through their unstinting support for Britain. Defence of the Empire and the sea lanes which bound it together was therefore perceived as being as important as before the war. These two views of Empire – as a trust, albeit with economic advantages for Britain, and as a brotherhood of nations, again with economic advantages – coexisted and were widely supported. The Empire had become more or less depoliticised. One major reason for this was the decision taken by the Conservative leadership to occupy the centre ground of politics. In other circumstances, the Empire might have remained a political battleground. As it was, the major interwar political battle over Empire – the battle over India – was fought within the Conservative Party.

The White Dominions, most importantly Australia, Canada and New Zealand, provided the strongest thread of imperial continuity during the period. South Africa was a Dominion, but the large anti-British element among its white population made its relationship with Britain fragile. Eire – from 1937 the name for the Irish Free State – was so detached that by the late 1930s it was unclear whether it was a member of the Commonwealth or not. Newfoundland could not pay interest on its debt and in 1934 Britain took over its administration; it joined Canada in 1949.

Even with the White Dominions, however, Britain's relationship evolved. The term 'Commonwealth', implying partnership, increasingly replaced Empire, while the word 'White' became less popular as plans for India to become a Dominion developed. In 1926 the Dominions were defined as 'autonomous countries within the British Empire, equal in status', and this was codified in the 1931 Statute of Westminster, in which Dominion parliaments could repeal or amend any Act of the United Kingdom applying to them. So, while the sentimental fabric of Empire remained strong, constitutionally the Dominions were determined to assert their autonomy. This attitude extended to trade. Since the late nineteenth century the Dominions had erected tariff barriers. When Britain finally ditched free trade in 1931, the way seemed open to an Empire united by trade as well as sentiment, a long-held dream of many Conservatives. But the outcome was a mouse, the Ottawa agreements of late 1932. Britain gave concessions to Empire produce; in return the Dominions pushed up their tariffs even further and gave small concessions to Britain. This final insult to free trade was enough to make Philip Snowden and some Liberals, the Samuelites, leave the National government, but it yielded few advantages for Britain. Empire trade increased but did not return to the level of the 1920s.

No one in Britain conceived in the 1920s and 1930s that India would become independent as early as 1947. But the ruling trend of thought, and the pressures of Indian nationalism, led to steady change. The 1909 Act had laid the foundations for Indian participation in government. The 1919 Government of India Act established elected state and national legislative councils, but real power still lay with the state governors and the Viceroy. The limits of the Act made it unpopular with nationalists, who kept up pressure on the government in various ways, such as Gandhi's civil disobedience campaign of 1930–1934. There were a series of reports and conferences, leading to a further Government of India Act in 1935, which provided for much greater autonomy for elected provincial governments (and for the separation of Burma from control by the Indian government). While Gandhi's party, Congress, opposed British initiatives because they did not go far enough, it did participate in the post-1935 Act elections, held in 1937, and gained control of several provinces. And there were substantial elements of educated Indian opinion which supported British plans for India.

Baldwin had consistently supported a progressive policy in India, although much of the early running was made by the Labour government of 1929–1931. The National government took the policy forward. In doing this Baldwin and Sam Hoare, the minister responsible for India, faced persistent opposition within the Conservative Party, orchestrated in part by Churchill – one reason why he played no part in 1930s peacetime governments. Baldwin's insistence on supporting a bipartisan and progressive policy was another facet of his liberal brand of Conservatism.

There was no conception in Britain that her African colonies would progress in the foreseeable future to self-government. In a few cases, colonies were still seen as areas which British companies or settlers might exploit. But there were also important counters to this attitude. In West Africa, the Colonial Office believed in developing peasant agriculture and thus opposed mining companies which made demands on agricultural labour and capitalists such as William Lever who wanted to set up large-scale plantations. The governmental structure in the region mainly worked via existing native rulers. This 'Indirect Rule' was not, however, so much progressive as designed to restrict the influence of the educated and westernised Africans from the coastal cities. By the late 1930s such people, hitherto often pro-British, were beginning to resent their inability to gain political advancement.

Eastern and Central Africa were climatically more favourable for white settlement. But Colonial Office pressure, again, restricted white settler influence in Uganda and Kenya. In Southern and Northern Rhodesia (now Zimbabwe and Zambia) far more land went to whites. Africans might become mineworkers – usually in low-paid jobs due to colour bars – but were more often restricted to marginal agricultural land.

Britain's role in its African colonies, therefore, was a mixture of racism, the enlistment of indigenous power structures, the acceptance of white economic pressure in some cases and the whole tempered by a Colonial Office which had a sense of 'fairness' and was often resistant to white pressure groups. This illustrates the influence civil servants could wield, especially when the policy area was not one about which politicians were likely to feel strongly. India excited, equally, liberals of all parties, who saw it as the touchstone of British willingness to cede democracy to non-whites, and old-fashioned imperialists, who saw it as the cornerstone of British rule. Africa, often the subject of very recent imperialism, did not inflame the British political imagination in the same way.

The former Ottoman territories controlled by Britain were Palestine and Mesopotamia (modern–day Iraq). The latter became nominally independent in 1932, although Britain retained political influence. Britain also exercised a protectorate over Egypt, another nominally independent country. Full Egyptian sovereignty was established in 1936, but Britain retained substantial military forces around the Suez Canal. Two other vital Mediterranean possessions were Malta and Gibraltar, both naval bases. Behind Britain's interest in the region were two common denominators. One was the Empire, for the Suez Canal was the artery for trade to India and the East. The other was oil from Iraq and Persia (the then common name for Iran). Much oil was shipped via the canal, and the oil companies in both countries were partly British controlled. While oil had not replaced coal as the major source of energy, it was vital for the Royal Navy itself, was increasingly used for merchant shipping and was also necessary for petrol and as a chemical feedstock. So the Mediterranean was the first line of defence both for Empire trade and for Britain's oil supplies.

East of the Suez Canal, the Empire and its trade routes were still important, but Britain had to accept compromises in her ability to guard them. Japanese naval power in the Pacific had been accepted since before the war, cemented by a defensive alliance. But the USA distrusted Japan, and Britain considered good relations with America more important than the Japanese alliance. It was dropped in 1921, and Britain accepted the US initiated four-power treaty (the USA, Britain, Japan and France) guaranteeing existing possessions in the Pacific region. Britain also planned to guard its trade routes in the East by building a huge fortified naval base at Singapore, completed in 1938. Singapore seemed strategically vital as it lay between Japan and the Indian Ocean, guarded Malaya and its rubber and was within reasonable distance of Australia.

It was Japan, not Germany, which provided the first major disturbance to dreams of universal peace and world disarmament. In 1931 the Japanese invaded Manchuria. The 'Ten Year Rule' – that British defence budget estimates should be framed on the assumption of no major war within ten years – was suspended in 1932 in response to this. Conscious of her weakness, however, Britain actually did very little in the Far East, even though in 1937 Japan embarked on an attempt to conquer China. Britain's policy towards Japan became one of 'showing a tooth': relying on some increase in the navy, and the completion of the Singapore base, to deter Japanese aggression.

In the 1920s and 1930s, as before the war, there were those who saw a strong Empire as central to Britain's future. They included Max Beaverbrook, the owner of the *Daily Express*, a proponent of free trade within an otherwise tariff protected Empire, and Maurice Hankey, the secretary to both the Cabinet and the Committee of Imperial Defence (CID) from 1919–1938. But such voices were never dominant. Free trade was still the strongest economic ideology until 1931, and after Britain instituted protection the Dominions were too wedded to their own high tariffs to make Empire preference effective. Similarly, the strength of the belief in disarmament, coupled with the perceived need for economy, kept military spending low until the mid-1930s. Pressure to increase it only became overwhelming when Germany became a threat and Europe became centre stage. So the Empire was important; but to most people it was never that important.

Rearmament and appeasement

In 1935 George V encapsulated the views of millions when he said, 'I will not have another war . . . I will go to Trafalgar Square and wave a red flag myself sooner than allow this country to be brought in.'[1] These millions had expressed their own views in one of the most extraordinary canvasses of popular opinion ever carried out, the Peace Ballot of 1934–1935. Organised by the League of Nations Union, almost half a million activists distributed questionnaires and over 11 million adults returned them. They gave overwhelming support to the League of Nations and mutual disarmament. They also voted three to one, with 20 per cent abstaining, for restraint of aggression by force if necessary: so it was not by any means a pacifist ballot. But the continued support for disarmament, two years after Hitler's accession to power, shows how deeply rooted was hatred of war.

Internationally, attempts at world-wide disarmament were predictable failures. The long-planned World Disarmament Conference of 1932–1934 got nowhere, with Germany withdrawing from it, and from the League, in 1933. The combination of the Japanese threat and alarm over Germany's attitude was the signal, at the end of 1933, for serious governmental consideration of rearmament, in spite of the public's attitude. There were no straightforward answers. The threats were still vague – Germany herself was still technically bound by Versailles – and numerous interests and views were involved in deciding on a course of action. The navy, for instance, was particularly concerned about Japan, a threat which, conveniently, suggested a concentration on naval rearmament. The Foreign Office view was most influenced by its senior civil servant, Sir Robert Vansittart. He saw Germany as the biggest threat.

Vansittart's influence helped to make this official government policy, but the ultimate shape of rearmament was influenced as much by Neville Chamberlain, then the Chancellor of the Exchequer (see box, 'Neville Chamberlain'). Chamberlain wanted rearmament to be as economical as possible. He also wanted to assuage the growing public fears about air attack. So in 1934 he put the emphasis on air rearmament.

While Germany was recognised as the major threat, attitudes towards it were strongly influenced by two factors: the deep-rooted view in Britain that Germany was badly treated by Versailles and was entitled to rectification of her grievances; and a misunderstanding by many people of the nature of the Nazi regime. These views were exemplified by *The Times*. In the 1930s *The Times* was effectively a semi-official mouthpiece of the government. Like other serious newspapers, but rather more so in that foreign governments saw *The Times* as having a quasi-official position, it was a conduit by which the government could inform the outside world of its attitudes and views. These views were not always identical – Vansittart, for instance, thought very differently from Chamberlain. So the views of *The Times'* editor, Geoffrey Dawson, and his senior staff became a factor in their own right, strengthening the hand of those within the government in favour of appeasing Germany. In 1932 a leader in *The Times* stated that, 'In this country practically everyone will agree – and the British government agree – that the German claim to equality of status is substantially a good one.'[2] And the next year the chief leader writer, A. L. Kennedy, wrote in his diary, 'A struggle is beginning between

People and politics: Neville Chamberlain

Neville Chamberlain, Joseph's youngest son and the half brother of Austen, was bitterly attacked during and after the war as the architect of appeasement. Subsequently, some historians have come to his defence, but others are still highly critical.

Chamberlain attached great importance to his family's liberal roots, even though Joe had broken away from the main Liberal Party, as a Liberal Unionist, back in 1886. As Minister of Health in the 1924–1929 Conservative government, Chamberlain sponsored important reforms (see Chapter 4) (Fig. 5.2). However, his reputation does not depend on his domestic achievements. As Chancellor of the Exchequer between 1931 and 1937, Chamberlain was faced with the cost of rearmament. He saw it as his duty to influence its direction, thus involving himself in defence and foreign policy. When he became Prime Minister after Baldwin finally retired in 1937, the Foreign Secretary, Anthony Eden, wanted closer links with France. Chamberlain stuck to the policy of avoiding too many foreign entanglements. Eden resigned early in 1938 and Chamberlain became even more dominant in foreign policy. His pursuit of appeasement was only reversed in 1939 (see main text).

The verdict on Chamberlain and appeasement must take into account the fact that the broad lines of his policy had deep roots in interwar British foreign policy, and

Figure 5.2 Neville Chamberlain (right of picture) with Stanley Baldwin (centre) and Jimmy Thomas, a Labour minister who came over to the National Government: 1932. © POPPERFOTO/ Alamy

widespread support. However, Chamberlain deserves much of the severe criticism he has received. His belief, in contradiction to consistent Foreign Office advice, that a lasting settlement could be achieved by a series of concessions was clearly wrong. Having said that, it is less clear that by the late 1930s any move – even a firmer stand at Munich – would have staved off ultimate war. Chamberlain's arrogance also led him to eschew the offer made by Britain's two most prominent trade unionists, Ernest Bevin and Walter Citrine, of union help in speeding up rearmament. Chamberlain's determination to dominate the government led him to anticipate the late twentieth century art of spin, using a press officer to brief against ministerial colleagues whom he considered might pose a threat to his policy.

Any criticism of Chamberlain must not simplistically write him off as a typical right winger. His social concern was genuine. His desperation to avoid war was commendable. But his belief that only he knew the right way to do it was not.

Goering and Goebbels, the extremists, against Hitler, backed by Rosenberg, who are moderates.'[3] There were 'moderates' and 'extremists' in the Nazi regime, but Kennedy exemplifies the persistent tendency in 1930s Britain to place Hitler in the wrong camp. In reality, he was the most extreme of all.

So while there was concern about Germany, and a realisation that it was a potential threat, there was also a strong belief that Hitler, the 'moderate' in the Nazi government, would be satisfied by rectification of the 'injustices' of Versailles. These were the diplomatic foundations of the policy of appeasement, one of the most emotive words in history. Originally, the word simply meant a search for peace. It came to mean achieving this through rectifying Germany's perceived injustices. But originally, since most people in Britain thought rectification correct, this had no negative connotation. As late as 1936 Anthony Eden, later seen as one of appeasement's chief opponents, could use the word positively.

Appeasement had domestic, economic and tactical aspects as well as diplomatic ones, and the relative importance of all these has been the subject of endless debate among historians. Its domestic aspects were tied up in part with the public hostility to war. By slowing down the early stages of rearmament – although, of course, there were other factors – Britain's military strength was weakened, which from 1935 made her nervous of the risk of confrontation with Germany. The economic argument for appeasement instead of all-out rearmament was that, if war did break out, Britain needed to be strong economically in order to supply her allies. This meant keeping up her exports to earn foreign currency, and large-scale rearmament would divert resources from export industries while sucking in imports. An additional argument in the later 1930s was that shortages of skilled workers were becoming evident in key industries such as aircraft building. Finally, by the late 1930s, when Germany had passed from being a potential to being a real and obvious threat, there was a tactical argument for appeasement – that Britain needed time to rearm properly.

The situation was further complicated by Italy. Although Mussolini had been the first Fascist dictator, Italian relations with Germany were poor during Hitler's early days in power. In April 1935 the 'Stresa Front' (Stresa is a resort on Lake Maggiore) united Italy, France and Britain in condemnation of German rearmament. But later in 1935 Mussolini attempted to realise his grandiose imperial ambitions by attacking Abyssinia (modern-day Ethiopia), almost the only African state not already a colony. The League of Nations attempted economic sanctions, but they were ineffectual. However, the Stresa Front had been broken and Mussolini was now more inclined towards Germany. Almost immediately after, the Spanish civil war (1936–1939) began, further polarising European politics as Germany and Italy supported the right-wing General Franco. Italy's steady drift towards Germany made appeasement more attractive because, with Italy in the German camp, the threat now appeared much greater. It also divided and weakened those opposed to appeasing Germany, since some of them, including Vansittart himself, favoured appeasing Italy as a lesser threat which needed to be detached from Germany.

Germany's rearmament, which the Stresa Front had condemned, was formally announced in March 1935, although in practice it was already underway. Then, in March 1936, Hitler remilitarised the Rhineland and withdrew from the Locarno Pact. While the French considered opposing remilitarisation by force, Britain was against this. The demilitarisation of the Rhineland had been, in many British eyes, one of the injustices of Versailles. Hitler's next major challenge was the *Anschluss* – the German occupation of Austria, ostensibly by invitation, in March 1938. Chamberlain, by now Prime Minister, protested against the occupation but conceded that there was little Britain could do. Hitler turned his attention to Czechoslovakia, which was to become the best-known victim of appeasement.

Czechoslovakia had a substantial German minority, the Sudeten Germans, who were a legacy from its status until 1918 as a part of the Austro-Hungarian Empire. The Sudetens, or some of them, had begun a noisy Nazi-sponsored campaign to join Germany. This would weaken Czechoslovakia economically and strip it of its defensible Bohemian borderlands. As Hitler's demands for an urgent resolution of the issue grew, Chamberlain engaged in hectic diplomacy. France had treaty obligations with Czechoslovakia, but it was as eager to avoid war as Britain and therefore supported Chamberlain's mediation. Chamberlain achieved some modification of the German demands at his final meeting with Hitler, at Munich. But in essence Hitler had won hands down. Germany had obtained the Sudetenland lock, stock and barrel.

Chamberlain returned from Munich on 1 October 1938 believing that he had obtained 'peace for our time'; the public and the press for the most part agreed with him and welcomed him. Belief in disarmament was dead, but few wanted war. However, both the government's and the public's opinions quickly changed. Hitler had asserted that the Sudetenland was the last of his territorial demands, but his subsequent aggressive attitude belied this. In February 1939 Britain publicly pledged support for France in case of war. In March Hitler invaded the rump of Czechoslovakia, occupying the Czech lands and leaving only a pro-German Slovak government which was 'protected' by Germany. The British government's reply on 31 March was to guarantee support to Poland, German's likeliest next target, if attacked. This effectively ended 20 years of unwillingness to make any commitments east of the Franco-Belgian/

German frontiers. Appeasement was not dead, however, since Poland's actual frontiers were not guaranteed, thus leaving the possibility of adjustment in Germany's favour. Nonetheless, the guarantee was a distinct hardening of British attitudes. To back this up, the army was to be massively increased in size, and in April conscription for military service was introduced – unprecedented in peacetime Britain.

The guarantee would be even more effective if Russia joined the Franco/British/Polish alliance. It was already linked by treaty with France and an attempt was made by Britain to construct an agreement. Russia, however, assumed that the Polish guarantee ruled itself out as a western partner against Hitler. Furthermore, the Chamberlain government was lukewarm about a Soviet alliance. While part of the reason for this was anti-Communist prejudice, part was the reasonable judgement that Stalin was an unreliable partner and that, after the recent purges of its officer corps, Russia was not likely to be of much use as a military ally. So Russia signed the infamous Nazi-Soviet Pact in August 1939, ensuring – so Stalin hoped – that it would stay out of a European war.

Poland was now presented by Germany with peremptory demands which she was not willing to meet, and incidents were manufactured as a pretext for invasion, which Germany launched on 1 September. It seems likely that Hitler half-expected Britain and France to give way again. Although Chamberlain delayed before declaring war – a delay which drew an angry response from many MPs – he had by now come to realise that Hitler could not be trusted. Britain's ultimatum to Germany, insisting on withdrawal of her troops from Poland, expired at 11.00 am on 3 September. Britain and Germany were at war.

Once war had started, the existing critics of appeasement were joined by many others who suddenly discovered that the policy had been wrong all along. To criticism of appeasement was added criticism of rearmament – that it had been too slow and inadequate. These criticisms were reinforced after the war by Churchill's memoirs, in which he could, given his reputation, rewrite history almost as he liked. Since then, there have been many modifications by historians of this simple story of right (Churchill and a few other anti-appeasers) versus wrong (Baldwin, Chamberlain and other members of the government). Nevertheless, it has enormous staying power in popular representations of history.

Rearmament was relatively slow at first but was substantial in total. Defence expenditure reached its low point in 1932, at £103 million. In 1935, the first year after rearmament became declared policy, it was £137 million and by 1938 had reached almost £400 million. It had risen to 8 per cent of national income from 3 per cent in 1933. In spite of all the criticisms, rearmament policy cycled through a series of expedients to come up with results which could have been much worse. The initial, and crucial, focus on air rather than naval rearmament illustrates this. Chamberlain pressed for it in 1934 as the option which was cheapest and would best satisfy public opinion. Inflated estimates of the strength of the German air force then led to the commitment being reinforced. The air staff wanted more bombers, but Inskip (see box, 'The Royal Navy, the RAF and rearmament') swung the emphasis towards fighters – an indisputably correct decision. Naval rearmament was correspondingly slow, but the navy was far better equipped

Military affairs: The Royal Navy, the RAF and rearmament

After the First World War Britain accepted, in the Washington Naval Treaty of 1922, a major limitation of the Royal Navy. Behind this lay a realistic assessment of Britain's needs in the post-war age. With the German fleet no more and the Soviet Union posing no military threat, the navy did not need to be as large as in its Edwardian prime. It would now be roughly equal to the US navy, although each was larger than any other fleet. And when in 1934 a decision was made as to where to put rearmament priorities, it was the Royal Air Force (RAF) which was favoured (see main text). The navy was by no means neglected, however. Between 1932 and 1938 spending on it increased from £50 million to over £130 million, and by the late 1930s five new battleships and many other vessels were under construction. However, the additional threat from Japan meant that the navy still perceived itself as overstretched. This was one factor behind the naval treaty with Germany in 1935, which limited Germany's surface ships to 35 per cent of British tonnage. The treaty has often been criticised as legitimating Germany's gradual overturning of Versailles, but it appeared to secure a degree of certainty for Britain by limiting the navy's potential commitments.

Recent historiography has portrayed the Royal Navy as realistic in its planning for future possible wars. It underestimated air power but so, too, did most navies. It did, however, possess six aircraft carriers, although several were old and unsatisfactory, and others were being built. It did not underestimate the potential German naval threat, including that from submarines; but it placed too much confidence in its underwater sound detector apparatus, ASDIC, and failed to prepare adequately for the fact that most attacks were launched when submarines were surfaced. What it could not have anticipated, as no one else did, was that after 1940 the substantial French fleet was neutralised and that Germany could base submarines on the French Atlantic coast.

The emphasis put on air rearmament stemmed from the widely held belief in the early 1930s that 'the bomber would always get through'. The belief was correct. What was wrong, however, were the pessimistic assumptions about the moral and material damage caused by bombing, for cities and people proved far more resilient than was thought possible; and the failure to realise that effective defences could wreak heavy punishment on attacking forces. For these misconceptions the leaders of the RAF bear a heavy responsibility. During the First World War British aircraft had been among the pioneers in providing support for ground forces. But the RAF was intent on carving out a role for itself, and strategic bombing, as opposed to tactical support for ground forces, seemed the way to do this. The prime exponent was Hugh 'Boom' Trenchard (so-called because of his loud voice, rather than his love of bombing), head of the RAF until 1929 and subsequently influential behind the scenes. The RAF accepted that the enemy's bombers would get through. Britain's defence would lie in the deterrent value of an even larger bomber force.

The initial stages of rearmament, therefore, saw an emphasis on bombers. However, the rising cost led to a review in 1937, led by Sir Thomas Inskip. His committee understood the potentiality of radar to aid defences against bombing and put a firm priority on building fighters.

The emphasis on air rearmament might have been disastrous. If the RAF had had its way, Britain would have possessed huge numbers of mediocre medium bombers. Fortunately, the swing to fighters took place at just the right time, when modern Spitfires and Hurricanes were coming into production. Inskip has had a bad press as an appeaser and Chamberlain yes-man. In fact, he, his committee and the much-maligned Treasury which instituted the review had performed a major service.

than the other services to start with. And the basic decision to put Germany first, and Japan on the back-burner, was correct in global terms. The mistake here was the belief that Singapore would enable Britain to maintain her position west of Malaysia.

The backdrop to the slowness of rearmament has already been sketched out. Public opinion was overwhelmingly against it in the early 1930s. The threat of air attack, and press agitation led by the *Daily Mail*, led to more public support, particularly for air rearmament, from 1934, but the Peace Ballot shows how strong a hold disarmament still had on the public. The Liberal and Labour parties were also against rearmament; only in 1936 did the latter adopt a less hostile attitude. Finally, there was the belief that Britain needed to maintain her economic strength to play an effective part in a future continental war, although Christopher Price has argued that this was misconceived. One of its products was an attempt to rebuild the international economy by reducing trade restrictions, a policy desired by the USA. To play her part in this, Britain expended much of her gold in 1938–1939 in defending the value of sterling, which was being sold internationally because of the fear of war. Price suggests that Britain should instead have instituted exchange controls in 1938, relying more on her own and the Empire's resources and less on attempting to satisfy America. The argument, which extends back in time to John Charmley's critique of Britain's wartime relations with America (see Chapter 7, 'Friends and allies') is interesting but partial, since even if such actions were feasible they would only have taken effect quite late.

Appeasement must be seen in a whole set of contexts. The British view that Germany had been treated unfairly at Versailles has already been discussed, as has the role of public opinion. An important backdrop was the whole conception of foreign policy, as realised in the 1920s and early 1930s. Britain was unwilling to subscribe to the series of alliances which France constructed with Eastern European states, partly because it did not think Germany such a threat and partly to avoid what were seen as excessive commitments. Once the British mindset was in place – the mindset which relied on the limited commitment of Locarno – it was hard to forget it. From the mid-1930s there was another major factor, the belief that Germany had obtained air superiority. (It is now apparent that, taking the French into account, this was wrong.) Given the fear of air attack, appeasement became in part a policy of buying time for air rearmament to take effect.

In retrospect, the really big misjudgement was over Hitler's intentions. While Vansittart and Churchill were correct in their judgement of the German threat, even they underestimated Hitler, seeing him as simply the latest and most malign expression of Prussian militarism. Although Prussian militarism was a factor, Hitler added a lethal ingredient. Whether his ultimate aims were European or even world hegemony, as some argue, or whether he proceeded more opportunistically is really irrelevant. Given the right circumstances, his ambitions would never be sated.

Misjudging Hitler is hardly a crime, and ultimately that was the chief mistake of the appeasers. In retrospect, the most realistic alternative would have been a far more decisive commitment to France, and its original policy of containing Germany, much earlier on. By the later 1930s France was racked by internal political strife and had become as unwilling as Britain to risk military measures. And ironically, it was France's anti-German policies of the 1920s which, by exacerbating Germany's economic troubles and by stoking up resentment against Versailles, helped to bring Hitler to power.

Notes

1. Quoted in Rose, *George V* (see Chapter 3), p. 387.
2. Quoted in Martel, G. (ed.), *The 'Times' and Appeasement: the Journals of A. L. Kennedy 1932–9* (Cambridge: Cambridge University Press, 2000) p. 55.
3. Quoted in *ibid.*, p. 87.

Further reading

Brown and Louis, *British Empire* (see Chapter 1), for the Empire. Ceadel, M., 'Attitudes to War: Pacifism and Collective Security' in Johnson (ed.), *Twentieth Century Britain* (see Chapter 1) discusses the Peace Ballot. Neilson, K., 'The Defence Requirements Sub-Committee, British Strategic Foreign Policy, Neville Chamberlain and the Path to Appeasement', *English Historical Review*, Vol. CXVIII, pp. 651–683 (2003) contains a good survey of recent historiography. Reynolds, *Britannia Overruled* (see Chapter 1) for a recent overview.

Other sources: Bell, C., *The Royal Navy, Seapower and Strategy between the Wars* (London: Macmillan, 2000); Charmley, J., *Churchill: The End of Glory* (London: Hodder and Stoughton, 1993); Gibbs, N., *Grand Strategy* (London: HMSO, 1976, Vol. 1); Kennedy, P., *The Rise and Fall of British Naval Mastery* (London: Penguin, 1976); Kennedy-Pipe, C., *Russia and the World 1917–1991* (London: Arnold, 1998); Kershaw, I., *Hitler* (London: Allen Lane, Vol. 1, 1998; Vol. 2, 2000); McKercher, B., 'Austen Chamberlain and the Continental Balance of Power: Strategy, Stability and the League of Nations 1924–1929' in Goldstein and McKercher, *Power and Stability* (see Chapter 2); Maido, J., 'The Knockout Blow Against the Import System: Admiralty Expectations of Nazi Germany's Naval Strategy, 1934–39', *Historical Research*, Vol. LXXII, pp. 202–228 (1999); Marquand, D., *Ramsay MacDonald* (London: Jonathan Cape, 1977); Medlicott, W., *British Foreign Policy since Versailles, 1919–63* (London: Methuen, 2nd ed., 1968); Packer, *Lloyd George* (see Chapter 2); Price, C., *Britain, America and Rearmament in the 1930s* (Basingstoke: Palgrave, 2001); Rhodes-James, R., *Anthony Eden* (London: Weidenfeld and Nicolson, 1986); Shay, R., *British Rearmament in the Thirties: Politics and Profit* (Princeton: Princeton University Press, 1977); Stewart, *Burying Caesar* (see Chapter 4); Thompson, N., *The Anti-Appeasers* (Oxford: Oxford University Press, 1971).

Chapter 6

SOCIETY 1900–1939

Identities: local and national

In the 1900s some of the most fundamental characteristics of the British people were remarkably uniform. They spoke the same language, with the notable exception of about half of the Welsh, who spoke their native language, and a few Gaelic speakers in the Highlands and Islands of Scotland. Most were Christian, the great majority being Protestant, and most were white. This relative uniformity in language, confession and ethnicity was a contrast to many European countries. Nevertheless, it concealed varying local, and in some cases religious and ethnic, identities.

Most people, most of the time, had very localised lives. They travelled limited distances, either to work or to play. Commuting any more than a few miles from work was confined to wealthier businessmen. The middle classes might travel long distances to seaside holidays, but only a few of the working class took holidays away from home. Even when they did, they mainly travelled quite short distances – Londoners to Southend or the Kent coast, Lancastrians to Blackpool. Of course this immobility must not be exaggerated. People did travel quite long distances on day trips by cheap excursion trains. More importantly, many people moved in search of better jobs. Migration from country to town, prevalent from before the Industrial Revolution, continued on a large scale as the urban population grew. However, even this tended to be mainly short distances. Many Southern farm labourers ended up in their local town and, if they went further, their journeys were more likely to end in Bristol or London than in Manchester. The same pattern applied in the Midlands and the North. There were some longer-distance migration flows when demand for labour was particularly strong. The booming South Wales coalfield drew migrants from counties such as Devon and Shropshire, for example.

Such flows on a large scale were exceptional, however. Most people, once they were past young adulthood, were more likely to stay in an area than move. Once established, there were powerful forces encouraging identification with a locality. Until the 1920s more people read local newspapers than national, and so for many people, in a pre-radio and television age, 'news' was what was filtered through the local media. Local papers then concerned themselves with the wider world more than most do today, but inevitably they also reflected local issues. Identification with a locality, perhaps just a parish or small town but often also a wider region, was fostered in other ways. One was the regional accent, spoken with greater or lesser emphasis by most people below the level of the upper middle classes. Accent and speech pattern was not just a source of local identity in its own right. In certain areas a strong and self-conscious literary tradition grew up. This was most marked in Wales, where poetry, history and periodicals in Welsh all flourished, and in Scotland to some extent. But there were also regional traditions, primarily of song and popular verse and stories published in cheap editions, particularly in Lancashire, Yorkshire and the North-East.

Another type of localism was fostered through support for sports teams. There had been a massive upsurge in competitive games-playing in Britain in the second half of the nineteenth century. Behind it lay the relatively high working-class standard of living, which allowed enough disposable income – and Saturday afternoons off – to encourage patronage. Other factors were the relatively small distances between big urban centres, which allowed easy team travel by rail (few supporters travelled at that time), and cheap newspapers which carried match reports. Football was the most popular game, with the hierarchy of professional teams not dissimilar to today, although the smaller Lancashire towns were more prominent. Crowds regularly reached 40,000 or more. However, there was also the distinctive Rugby Union tradition of South Wales and a few parts of the West Country, and Rugby League across a swathe of Lancashire and Yorkshire. County cricket attracted far larger crowds than it does today, and local cricket leagues also flourished in the North of England and the Midlands.

Localities in Britain, therefore, had a certain common identity through accent, shared sporting loyalties and a diffuse local loyalty fostered by the local and regional press. To certain well-defined groups, however, their location in Britain was much less important to their sense of identity. Irish migration to Britain had been heavy throughout the nineteenth century and still continued. By 1900 Irish outweighed native English and Scots in the Catholic Church, which itself was one part of a distinct Irish identity. People of Irish origin were mainly to be found in Lowland Scotland, particularly the west, London and Lancashire, particularly Liverpool. They tended to form distinct communities, partly because of earlier, and continuing, discrimination. The latter also led to some occupational specialisation, with Irish predominating in certain jobs, for instance some types of dockwork, in areas of Irish settlement. This Irish and Catholic identity was fostered by the growth of Catholic football teams – Celtic in Glasgow and Hibernian in Edinburgh being the best known – while in Liverpool the Scotland Road parliamentary division regularly returned an Irish Nationalist MP, T. P. O'Connor.

Jewish identity manifested itself in a very different way. Immigration, mainly from Eastern Europe, was substantial in the late nineteenth century and continued into the twentieth. As with the Irish, there were certain well-defined destinations – particularly the East End of London, but also Liverpool, Manchester, Leeds and Glasgow. Unlike the Irish, however, there was an existing Jewish community which was wealthy, activist and Anglicised, and fostered poorer Jews' cultural assimilation through charitable intervention. Of course, Jewish identity survived in other ways, since Orthodox Jews were more resistant to assimilation, whilst even secular Jews tended to be found in specific occupations, such as clothing manufacture, which flourished in inner cities. But Jews' relative cultural assimilation is illustrated by the fact that Jewish political loyalties straddled the Liberal/Conservative divide.

For most people, while local identity was strong, it was subsumed within a wider national identity. That national identity rested on both shared cultural assumptions and practices, and on certain deeper beliefs. Professional sport has already been mentioned as promoting local loyalties. But because support was so widely shared, it was also a common interest for men throughout Britain. Another widely shared leisure interest, extending across the gender divide, was music hall, which became known in the new century as variety and encompassed music, dance and comedy. For adolescents and young men and women, ritual Saturday night parades, leading it was hoped to a regular walking-out partner, were also a standard feature of British towns and cities. However, these were being supplemented, and to some extent replaced, by one new and very important leisure activity, the cinema. Still in its infancy in 1900, by the First World War there were around 3,000. Most were small and programmes were short, but this made them cheap and accessible, and they had a particular appeal to the young. The pub was still central to many men, however, although by the 1920s alcohol consumption had declined. In rural areas, which were partially isolated from many of the influences described above, it remained one of the few foci for social life.

Among the beliefs which were important in establishing a sense of national identity was religion. While Protestantism was the dominant confession, it was divided amongst a number of different denominations, as was shown in Chapter 1. Nevertheless, to many a shared sense of being Protestant was still important, even if this was often conceived of in terms of not being Catholic rather than in any very positive way. That is not to suggest that negative feelings towards Catholicism were usually violent. Except in Northern Ireland and occasionally in Glasgow and Liverpool, the days of anti-Catholic riots were over. While religion was important in many people's lives, however, to many others it was not central as an organised belief system (see box, 'Religion in Britain 1900–1945'). Perhaps more important than Protestantism as an ideological cement, at least for men, was the political system.

Society and economy: Religion in Britain 1900–1945

Although we do not have precise knowledge about late nineteenth century church-going, the best guess is that there was some fall, but that it was very slow. This pattern of very slow decline continued into the twentieth century. Contrary to what many people think, there was no sudden lapse into atheism, nor did the wars have any discernible long-term effect one way or another. About 32 per cent of the population were members of Christian churches in 1900 – that is, had a formal affiliation, as opposed to the much larger number who were baptised; about 24 per cent were members in 1950. Since the population was rising, actual numbers of church members increased slowly until the 1930s. But only Catholicism saw a substantial rise in numbers, by about one-third, reflecting the continuation of Irish migration to Britain.

Geographically, nonconformity was extremely strong in Wales. Other areas of strength included parts of the West Country, Lincolnshire and urban Yorkshire and the North-East. There were occupational and class factors in this pattern. Working-class

▶

areas, especially mining areas, usually tended towards nonconformity. However, the patterns of nonconformist membership from its earliest days had not been determined so much by class as by the failure of the Anglican Church to adjust its parish structure quickly enough to cater for rapid industrialisation and urbanisation after 1750. Once such areas had been lost to Anglicanism they did not return. Outside them, many working-class people were Anglicans. Scotland had an entirely different religious structure, with most people adhering to one form or another of Presbyterianism.

In spite of periodic revivals – for instance, an intense nonconformist one in Wales between 1903 and 1905 – and missions, not many non-worshipping adults became active Christians. Active church membership was usually hereditary. Nevertheless, the churches, and Christianity, still played an important part in people's lives in a number of ways besides worship. For active members all the denominations provided talks and social functions. Since active nonconformists, in particular, were often serious-minded teetotallers, such activities filled the gap in their social lives which the pub, the music hall and the cinema filled for others. In the countryside, the Anglican Church supplemented the pub in providing a meeting place, particularly for women, although the number of extra-church activities depended a great deal on the dedication of individual clergymen and their wives.

Even for those who did not go to church regularly, certain religious ceremonies were important. In 1900, 84 per cent of all marriages in England and Wales were religious. By the 1930s the figure was still above 70 per cent, and in Scotland the proportion was persistently around 10 per cent higher. In England and Wales, about three-quarters of such marriages were Anglican. This indicates that technical adherence to the Church of England was much higher than its share of church membership, which was about 40 per cent, suggests. It also suggests that many people had a core of religious belief. Children often had some experience of Sunday school, since even non-churchgoing families might send their children to these for a few years. Elizabeth Roberts' oral history of Lancashire towns leads her to believe that most people, or at least most women, subscribed to basic tenets of Christian belief, to the belief that sin should be punished but also to its ethical injunction to 'love thy neighbour'.

On the other hand, religion as a vital element in political life made its last major appearance in the 1900s, with the disputes over the 1902 Education Act and Welsh disestablishment (see Chapter 2). In that sense Britain had already become a much more secular society earlier in the century.

This sounds paradoxical since in the 1900s Britain had two dominant, and opposed, political parties. But the Liberals and the Conservatives were not opposed in the same way as some continental political parties, which had fundamentally different views about the constitution or the status of religion within the state. By the twentieth century both British parties had a shared belief in a wide franchise, and both supported the fundamental characteristics of the British Constitution: a constitutional monarchy; parliamentary supremacy; and separation for most purposes between Church and state, whatever the formal status of the Anglican Church and its incursions into education. Some in the Labour Party opposed one other area of agreement between the other two, the private ownership of property. But many other Labour supporters were difficult to distinguish from advanced Liberals, so the party's existence did not significantly change the underlying consensus. The terms of the political debate in Britain therefore acted to reinforce a certain conception of national identity. To actively support either of them was to tacitly subscribe to a view of politics, and life, as give and take, rather than as winner takes all. This dovetailed into a conception of Britishness which overrode ethnicity and religion, to emphasise equality under the law in a free society. As David Feldman has put it, '. . . in political argument the symbolic centre of the nation remained the institutions of the state which guaranteed individual freedoms. The focus of the nation was . . . Parliament, the constitutional monarch and the liberties they ensured.'[1] Thus the 'imagined community' of Britain (see Chapter 1) was not just an abstract British nation but one which, for many, embodied constitutionalism.

This positive conception of a free society overrode, for most of the time, differences between Liberals and Conservatives, nonconformists and Anglicans, and Scots, Welsh and English. It was a positive conception in which the monarch played an important part as one of the guarantors of liberty. As shown in Chapter 1, the monarch also played a rather different role, as a sentimental embodiment of other aspects of British life. The Empire, too, played an ambivalent part in the conception of Britishness, since it tended to embody ideas of racial superiority as well as more egalitarian notions of a brotherhood of (white) Dominions.

One immediate result of the First World War was to enhance popular support for the Empire, as imperial troops came to fight, first at Gallipoli and then in France. In 1916 an 'Empire Day' (24 May) was instituted. And after the war a last surge of emigration took place, particularly to Canada. Then, as markets in Europe stagnated in the 1920s, the Empire's economic attractions were enhanced. But from 1929 economic depression, which was even worse in Canada and Australia than in Britain, cut emigration and limited the Empire as a market for British goods. And politically, by the mid-1930s the interest of British people in overseas was far more likely to be held by events in Europe. So while the war temporarily revived the apparent centrality of the Empire to British identity, this was not to last.

A much more profound effect of 1914–1918 on the national psyche was the revulsion against war, which reached its peak in the early 1930s (see Chapter 5). The more militant side of British patriotism, which had been most evident during the Boer war, was at a discount. The change was most strikingly expressed by George V's declaration in 1935 that, 'I will not have another war.' Instead, a gentler patriotism emerged, a nostalgic identification with a rural England, Scotland or Wales. As a literary genre this was already in being before the war, for example in the 'Highways and Byways' series of travel books and Rudyard Kipling's stories set in Southern England. It burgeoned after 1918. The genre extended from the Batsford series of illustrated books, to the hugely popular later novels of Francis Brett Young, to the newspaper columns and travel books of H. V. Morton. In the 1930s Morton wrote for the *Daily Herald*, the Labour newspaper, suggesting that this ruralism had a cross-class appeal.

Stanley Baldwin was a friend of Brett Young and Kipling's cousin, and often appealed to this rural nostalgia. But Baldwin linked it to a conception of 'national character' which,

Philip Williamson has pointed out, was to him equally or more important. Baldwin associated the British character with individuality, even to the point of stubbornness, tempered by an ability to cooperate engendered by centuries of constitutional government. While Baldwin's conception was tailored to the political views he wished to put across, it was similar to that found among many other interwar authors. This idea of national character was clearly related to the 'imagined community' which emphasised Britain's heritage of constitutional government and individual freedom.

Baldwin was always careful to associate 'national character' with Scotland and Wales as well as England. Nonetheless, interwar Scotland had another potential imagined community in Scottish nationalism. Up to 1914 Scotland had had a strong imperial identification. Numerous Scottish emigrants went to Empire countries, while Scotland provided a relatively large proportion of the army, which policed the Empire. In addition, Scotland was particularly strong in railway engineering, shipping and, perhaps because of Scottish thrift, overseas investment. All of these in one way or another linked Scotland closely to the Empire. And all helped to generate wealth, creating a thriving middle class, which was not attracted to nationalism of anything other than a mild and apolitical nature. After the war, with the drying up of emigration, and with economic depression, this imperial identification began to wane and the Scottish National Party was founded in 1934. But the old ideas died hard and its initial appeal was very limited. Welsh nationalism was even weaker. Pre-1914 Welsh grievances over religion (see Chapter 2) had been subsumed within Wales' strong Liberalism. Between the wars this survived in Welsh speaking areas, while in much of South Wales economic problems, and Labour, came to predominate.

Both nationalism and semi-mystical appeals to a people's rural essence had a potentially darker side: fascism. The British Union of Fascists (BUF) was not particularly ruralist, but there was a ruralist tinge to some components of the British far right. However, its support was limited. Anti-semitism certainly existed and in a mild form was widespread in Britain. It dovetailed with many people's assumption of racial superiority. The 1905 Aliens Act, which restricted the freedom to enter Britain, was largely a response to the immigration of poor Jews from Eastern Europe. The Act offered a right of asylum, but this was withdrawn by a further Act of 1919. Nonetheless, David Feldman suggests that the positive British conception of a free society was an important counter to anti-semitism. The effects of the belief in Anglo–Saxon racial superiority were constrained by the assumption that British citizens, whatever their origin or religion, were free before the law. Therefore, the potentiality for freedom must extend to peoples outside Britain. Thus most opinion in Britain was revolted by the Nazi persecution of Jews. Asylum was reintroduced in 1933, although the cost of funding the 30,000 German Jewish refugees admitted was born by British Jews not the government. In 1938 a more liberal policy was adopted and 25,000 more Jews were admitted before the war.

Political moderation was a final and important factor in interwar national identity. In this, Baldwin played a major part, and his appeal to timeless rural values shows that these could be used to reinforce moderation rather than extremism. And although Labour had replaced the Liberals as the main alternative to the Conservatives, the way in which this had occurred, and the nature of the Labour Party, if anything strengthened moderation (see Chapter 4). It was joined to the established emphasis on constitution-alism and individual freedom. After the General Strike, George V mused that 'not a shot has been fired and no one killed. It shows what a wonderful people we are!'[2] After the militancy of the immediate pre- and post-war periods, he, Baldwin and Ramsay MacDonald had helped in the construction of moderation. As the 1930s wore on, it was to become reinforced as an aspect of British identity, in contrast to the Europe of the dictators.

Work, income and consumption

By 1900 Britain was a predominantly urban country – far more so than anywhere else in the world. Almost 80 per cent of its inhabitants were urban, and this proportion did not subsequently change much. Much of the population was concentrated in six great conurbations – that is, almost continuous urban areas. London with over 6 mil-lion people was the largest. The Lancashire conurbation around Manchester, the West Midlands and the Clydeside conurbation centred on Glasgow housed another 5 mil-lion between them.

The conurbations were marked not just by a concentration of housing, industry and railways – they were also incredibly smoky. In a country fuelled almost entirely by coal, towns of any size had an almost permanently darkened atmosphere, while a constant rain of soot fell on buildings. To outside observers, British towns looked depressingly uniform. The nineteenth century parts were built mainly of brick, which was cheaper than stone and could be shipped in by rail to areas which did not have natural resources of clay. Whether built of brick or stone, the soot meant that they were shades of brown and grey (Fig 6.1).

Most urban dwellers, and 80 per cent of the whole population, were working class. This strictly socio-economic definition is based primarily on occupation: manual, or blue-collar, workers were counted as working class. It does not relate to people's self-image or their views about society. But Britain also had a substantial middle-class popu-lation in relation, for instance, to continental Europe. This arose because Britain almost entirely lacked peasant farmers, usually placed in a separate social category. Most British farmers rented their land from large landlords – the aristocracy and gentry – and employed farm labourers. So in socio-economic terms, most farmers were middle class and farm labourers working class.

Farm labourers in the 1900s were financially almost at the bottom of the heap. Their average wage in the South and Wales (the latter being the only large region in Britain to have significant numbers of peasant farmers) was very low, although much improved on its nadir in the mid-nineteenth century. High urban wage levels throughout the Midlands and North kept up agricultural workers' wages there, although in general urban wages were always higher. London workers had the highest earnings, but London workers paid high rents. Outside London, urban workers in the South earned relatively low wages. In terms of total income and wealth, however, the South, and especially London, came out on top. This was because the wealthy middle class and aristocracy

Figure 6.1   A street in Newcastle: until the 1950s, steam, smoke and soot epitomised urban Britain. © Hulton-Deutsch Collection/CORBIS

tended to concentrate there. Such people often had large holdings of securities, for British citizens owned a considerable proportion of the world's wealth. Not only did they own most of Britain's own capital – the land, the railways, the government's own debt which it had issued over the years and the housing – but they also owned foreign securities. By the eve of the First World War the latter total amounted to around £4,000 million, making Britain the world's largest creditor nation.

Below the upper middle class – wealthy businessmen, better-off professionals and those who had a substantial income from securities – was a large penumbra of other middle-class groups. Shopkeepers, those in lower managerial jobs, schoolteachers and clerks fell into this category. Of course, there were many differences between them: bank clerks, for instance, had relatively well-paid and secure jobs which might lead to promotion, while other clerks might earn no more than manual workers. In most cases, the income earner was male. Young women from the lower ranks of the middle classes, however, worked in teaching, nursing, better-quality shops and, increasingly, clerical work (where they were initially known as 'lady typewriters'). Most of these left work on marriage. A very limited number of upper professional jobs were opening up for women, for instance as doctors.

Skilled workers formed around 30 per cent of the occupied male population in 1911, the date of the last census before the First World War. Miners, who comprised another 9 per cent, would now be classed as semi-skilled, although this was not then a term in common use. Miners in most areas, along with skilled workers, were the highest paid manual workers. There were large numbers of skilled workers in engineering and shipbuilding, two of Britain's great export industries, building, printing and a host of miscellaneous trades. Most skilled workers were classed as such because they had served an apprenticeship, usually of five years, although in some occupations such as steel-smelting skilled men worked their way up via semi-skilled positions. The great bulk of non-apprenticed workers, including most textile and clothing workers and many railwaymen, were semi-skilled, earning an intermediate level of wages. Below them were the 15 per cent of the male workforce who were unskilled – labourers on roads and building sites, porters, van drivers' assistants and so on.

Poorer even than farm labourers were most casual workers. Much dockwork was casual and below that were men who picked up odd jobs washing cabs, grooming horses and in a variety of seasonal occupations. They might have comprised up to 10 per cent of the London workforce but were far less prevalent in most industrial towns.

In most of these occupations, women were non-existent or rare, but they were common in textile factories which provided the best-paid female jobs. Most unmarried working-class women, however, were found in jobs which were exclusively or mainly female – laundresses, dressmakers (both hand and, increasingly, machine workers) and around 2 million domestic servants. Around a third of women did paid work, the proportion being so low because most women left work on marriage. Female participation had fallen in the nineteenth century and was to rise later in the twentieth, so this was a perhaps unique period when the ideal of the married woman in the home was realised.

Women's earnings were usually about two-thirds of male earnings in comparable occupations, although the low-paid nature of most women's work meant that the average of all female wages, relative to male, was lower still. The contemporary rationale for lower female pay was that men needed a wage which enabled them to keep a family but women did not. This was buttressed by arguments that women workers were less productive, for instance because they took more time off. Historians have tended to see the differential as mainly due to prejudice.

It is difficult to discover much about labour mobility but, given the importance of work to most people both economically and in terms of self-esteem, it deserves research. The author's investigation of a sample of 250 unemployed men, mainly manual workers, in York in 1910 suggests a fair degree of stability. Workers had spent, on average, seven-and-a-half years in the last job they held. York was probably fairly typical of industrialised Northern and Midland towns, although employment in Southern England might have been rather less stable.

Most savings were accumulated by the middle classes; only a few organisations provided guaranteed pensions, so saving for old age was seen as essential. And, of course,
the very wealthy had such a large income that all except the most extravagant were
hard put to spend it, and perforce had to save some. Most workers saved relatively
little, although a fair number might accumulate enough to buy a house or small shop
to provide an income in retirement. Even so, owner-occupiership of houses was quite
rare among all classes; on the usual estimate, around 90 per cent of people rented, although
this figure may be exaggerated. As a result, while income inequalities were substantial,
wealth inequalities were even more so. In the 1920s, when inequalities would have diminished somewhat, 10 per cent of the population owned 88 per cent of the wealth.

Workers tended not to save partly because their incomes were too small to make it
seem worthwhile. Many skilled workers, the best equipped to save, had less incentive
as they could rely on unemployment benefit and other financial relief from their
unions. Until the Liberals brought in unemployment insurance in 1912 – and then only
for a few occupations – other workers had to cope with unemployment by pawning
clothes or furniture, borrowing from family or appealing to charity. Only *in extremis*
would families go on the Poor Law, the ultimate safety net. For casual workers and
others with insecure jobs or low earnings, coping like this was a way of life. Poverty was
also a function of family size, and even better-off working-class families with several
young children could be poor. Poverty was also the fate of most working-class widows,
especially if they had young children, and of many of the working-class elderly, even
after old-age pensions.

The sociologist Seebohm Rowntree carried out a famous survey in York in 1899
in which he found that around 15 per cent of the working-class population lived in
poverty, defined as an inability to procure an adequate level of housing and nutrition.
Rowntree's findings were often quoted but his methods were relatively imprecise. A
better survey was done a few years later by A. L. Bowley in a range of towns. He found
poverty levels differed sharply, from 29 per cent in Reading, a typical Southern town,
to 9 per cent in the prosperous shoe manufacturing town of Northampton and just
6 per cent in Stanley, a coal-mining town in Durham.

Bowley's findings point to the fact that many working-class people in the 1900s were
relatively well off, at least by the standards of contemporary continental Europe. Many
in the working classes, as well as in the middle classes, could afford a reasonably com-
fortably furnished house. There would be linoleum and rugs on the floor rather than
bare boards, gas for lighting and cooking and perhaps a piano in the front room. Electricity
was rare outside the homes of the wealthier middle classes, and heating was usually by
coal fires. Housing had improved greatly in average quality in the previous 40 years.
Local authorities had passed by-laws specifying street and pavement width, so modern
houses were less crowded. Most modern houses, too, had their own water supply and
water closets, although in working-class housing outside earth privies were still common. On the other hand, the rapid increase in population meant that relatively few
low-quality houses from an earlier period were demolished. As a result, many people,
not just the poorest, still lived in poor-quality accommodation. Housing standards also
varied regionally, and did not correspond with regional wage levels. The North-East

and parts of the North-West had poor housing, while Lowland Scotland, notably the Glasgow conurbation, was even worse. Poor housing, earth privies, narrow and dirty streets, and smoke all contributed to the environmental degradation which stunted working-class height, as was shown in Chapter 1. On the other hand, the Edwardian period did see increasing attempts by local authorities to deal with these problems.

The immediate impact of the First War on income and employment was positive for many, but its longer-term effects were much less so. Initially the war, and the inflationary period which followed it, led to full employment and buoyant working-class incomes. Wage increases were often flat rate, so that lower paid workers benefited more. With deflation from late 1920, this was partially reversed, but nonetheless the very high skilled/unskilled wage differentials of pre-war were permanently reduced. Many of the middle classes, however, with fixed incomes from pensions, rents or securities, suffered severely from inflation. Income tax, too, had risen substantially and affected the better-off middle classes, although not many below that level. As prices fell in the 1920s the middle classes regained ground. The number of servants – there were still 2.6 million in 1931, men and women, mainly employed by middle-class households – underlines how income inequalities ultimately did not shift very much. A much more fundamental change affected landowners. Their economic position had been weakened since the 1870s by 30 years of agricultural depression, which a small recovery in the 1900s did little to alleviate. Then death duties were sharply increased as a result of tax rises under the Liberals and in the war, while the latter with its horrifying casualty rate for officers meant many wealthier families had to pay them. The final ingredient of change was post-war inflation which temporarily pushed up land values. Many landowners sold up and rural society changed for ever as far more farmers now owned their land. But after the boom, they too suffered as agricultural prices slumped again. Only in the 1930s was limited economic stability restored to agriculture by price support schemes.

The chief impact of depression, though, was on the working classes. The longer-term result of the war was to weaken Britain's staple industries of coal, cotton, heavy engineering and shipbuilding, as export markets crumbled (see Chapter 4). So some of the most prosperous pre-war groups of male workers – Durham and South Wales miners, Clydeside and Tyneside shipbuilders and Lancashire cotton spinners – sank down the earnings league. Apart from the depths of the depression between 1930 and 1933, however, workers in the Midlands and London, with their huge range of industries, many producing for the buoyant home market, were reasonably prosperous. Migration patterns therefore changed, with these areas now becoming magnets for inmigration. Welsh workers travelled to London, although many stopped permanently at Oxford, which had become a car-making town with Morris Motors, or the light industrial town of Slough. Scottish steelworkers migrated to Corby in Northamptonshire, where a big new steelworks was established. Migration was not as great as it might have been, however, due to unemployment benefit and controlled rents for those who stayed in their existing houses.

For those in work, real incomes in the 1920s and 1930s increased as food prices fell. Furthermore, employment became more stable for many, in spite of depression. David

Society and economy: Living with unemployment

How did people cope with the severe and lasting unemployment of the interwar years? And why was there so little violent reaction and organised mass protest?

Because of the fall in primary product prices, real incomes for those in work were buoyant and therefore demand in many sectors – consumer goods and retail, for instance – held up. So there were always new jobs available in these and other sectors, at least outside the most depressed regions, and thus for many people spells of unemployment did not last long. This was particularly the case for adolescents. Their wages were lower, making them more attractive to employers, and they were better able to move. Bob Thorne, from Abercarn in South Wales, worked in a shop there until, in 1930, when he was 16, he moved to another retail job, with Sainsbury's in Oxford. In January 1933 he was made redundant and walked to London. There he teamed up with another youngster from South Wales and they joined the army. Both his movements and the type of work he found were typical of many.

Those who were condemned to long-term unemployment were mainly older men or men with young families in the most depressed coal-mining, shipbuilding and steel-making areas. In 1931 the 'means test' was established by which, after 26 weeks, unemployment benefit was cut if the family already had a certain level of resources. The means test was intrusive and was also resented because of the belief that benefit had been paid for by insurance. But just 20 years before, the even more disliked Poor Law was the only relief available to the unemployed with no other resources.

In spite of benefit, long-term unemployment ground down men in the most depressed areas, although many could find some solace in the associational culture – nonconformism, music and sport – of once prosperous areas such as South Wales and Durham. Families suffered too. Bernard Harris has shown that the nutritional status of all children in such areas – not just those of the long-term unemployed – was poor because low wages and intermittent unemployment affected virtually everyone. Nevertheless, the availability of a basic income drew the teeth of discontent. It was change to the established position which was most controversial. In 1935 the government tried through the new Unemployment Assistance Board to standardise relief for those whose insured benefit had expired. Some lost out, and it was this change which drew most protest and led to an upgrading of the scheme's benefits. The most famous protest, the Jarrow March to London of 1936, epitomised the peaceful nature of most reactions to unemployment. Jarrow was a Tyneside shipbuilding town with appalling unemployment – over 70 per cent in 1935. Far from being a radical protest, the march by some of the town's unemployed was widely supported, including in conservative Surrey which had 'adopted' the town.

Vincent examined the career history of a sample of men, weighted according to geography, social class and occupation, most of whom worked during the interwar period. No less than half had lifetime jobs – that is, they worked for the same employer from young adulthood to retirement or near retirement. Vincent calls these 'Gold Watch' jobs. One reason for this stability was the reluctance of employers to lose experienced workers. Thus during the depression employers put many workers on to short-time working, rather than sacking them. The growing consolidation of British industry into large firms may also have fostered stability. In the interwar years such firms dominated the railway industry, chemical, soap and margarine manufacture, heavy electrical engineering, car-making and banking. Civil Service jobs, increasing in number, were also associated with lifetime employment.

As shown in Chapter 3, many of the changes in women's work during the First War were temporary. So the pattern of female employment in the interwar period was not hugely different to that of 1900. Wage differentials with men had been reduced somewhat, but in 1939 average women's wages were still only 52 per cent of men's. Fewer women were employed in textiles because the industry had declined, while the number of women in secretarial jobs had continued to increase. But, as before, the ideal was of the husband in paid work and the wife looking after the home, although for working-class women that was not always possible.

In spite of depression, most people's living standards improved in the interwar period. But the change was slow and limited, so consumption patterns also changed only slowly. Free trade, allied to the steep fall in the cost of international transport in the late nineteenth century, had already spread middle-class dietary habits down the social scale. White bread and not very interestingly cooked meat were British dietary staples, although meat was too expensive for the poorest to eat it regularly. The most popular diversification was fish and chips, the standard British takeaway up to the 1960s. The drink of choice for everyone, but particularly women, was tea. The majority of men also drank beer, often in large quantities. Although there were many local breweries, the railway network had fostered the rise of national brands such as Bass, the army's favourite beer. Scotsmen supplemented these drinks with whisky, which was also favoured by the upper middle classes throughout Britain.

For many people, particularly the middle classes, better housing was an important item of consumption. The 1930s' housing boom mainly involved the construction of middle-class houses. By the late 1930s it is estimated that around 30 per cent of housing was owner-occupied, and much of the increase from pre-war was in new, middle-class, housing. But, in addition, much local authority construction was of houses in relatively generously laid out estates, and by 1938 some 10 per cent of all houses were local authority owned. They attracted working-class tenants, although high rents meant these were mainly skilled workers, or those in steady jobs, and their families. New houses, however, did not mean a surfeit of household appliances, since only the simplest ones were at all common. Fridges were almost unknown; vacuum cleaners were more common but were probably bought mainly by a middle-class market. Most new houses were electrified, although this was mainly used for lighting.

New housing meant that, for many, leisure increasingly revolved around the home (see next section, 'Women, men and families'). But consumption was an integral part of what was perhaps the prime female leisure pursuit outside the home both before and after the First War: shopping. Of course, for most working-class women shopping was a necessity, although also an opportunity to exchange news and gossip. But for better-off working-class women, comparison shopping for semi-luxuries was a real possibility, and for middle-class women an occupation which became more time con-suming as one moved up the social, and income, scale (Fig. 6.2). Arthur Shadwell, *The Times*' Industrial Correspondent, noted in 1906 'the multiplication of drapers' shops which can be witnessed in every great town . . . they are women's shops and they live on "look and pick" . . .'.[3] The relatively slow change in real incomes meant that shop-ping patterns were likely to have remained similar for most people after the war. Although the distance travelled to the shops, for those living on new estates, must have dictated

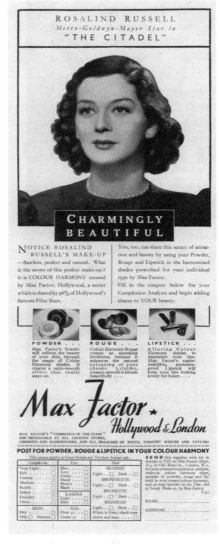

Figure 6.2   Cosmetics represented the prosperous side of the 1930s, as did films, women's magazines (the advert is in *Woman*, June 1938) and multiple retailers such as Boots. Image courtesy of The Advertising Archives

some reduction in the frequency of shopping, this would have been mitigated by cheap bus travel. And for all consumers, except those patronising the cheapest shops or markets, errand boys abounded, delivering goods to the door once the choice had been made.

Much of the interwar increase in consumption, however, went on services rather than goods. From the 1890s the electric tram had reduced the price and increased the convenience of urban transport. Buses supplemented trams from the 1900s, coming into their own after the First War. Buses and coaches meant that inexpensive days out in parks or local beauty spots became easier. They also boosted the growth of large cinemas in town centres or suburban shopping streets. Cheap bus travel also enabled the explosive growth of large dance halls. Locarnos, named after the 1925 treaty (see Chapter 5), and other exotic-sounding *palais* sprang up and public dancing became a major leisure pursuit for the working and lower middle classes, and an important venue for meeting the opposite sex.

The interwar railways also emphasised, even more than before, cheap holiday and excursion travel. For most people, holidays with pay arrived only at the end of the period, in 1938, and this meant that holidays of a week or more, outside Lancashire, remained largely a middle-class prerogative. But excursions to the seaside, to beauty spots or to amusement parks such as Belle Vue in Manchester were another big element in discretionary spending.

For most people, even at the end of the period, mobility did not extend much beyond the bus, tram or train. The exception was the bicycle, which was already popular before the First War and had significantly enhanced job opportunities, particularly for rural workers, by enhancing the radius of travel. It became even more common. The British motorcycle industry became the world leader, but the motorbike's general discomfort and unreliability limited its spread. By the 1930s middle-class consumers were buying cars for leisure, but their use was still limited by cost. Many cars, then as now, were essentially for work – doctors, even before the First War, were among the chief early purchasers. Businessmen and commercial travellers – salesmen – followed them. By 1939 there were around 2 million cars on the road.

Women, men and families

There was much continuity between 1900 and 1939 in the basic structures of married life. The average age of marriage remained virtually static, at around 25 for women and 27 for men. Newly married couples throughout the period from 1900 to 1939 usually set up as a separate household, rather than live with their extended family. Most women, middle or working class, would give up paid work when they married, although there were exceptions, particularly in Lancashire where it was common for young wives to continue working in the cotton industry. And many working-class married women continued to earn small sums of money: they took in lodgers, did homework such as sewing, took in laundry or did basic cleaning (charring) in offices or other people's houses. The need to clean a house and look after children in the days of coal fires and few labour-saving appliances helps to explain why most married women did little or no paid work if they could afford not to. Middle-class married women did have more leisure, of course, but lower down the social scale most would employ no, or only one, servant so still had their own household tasks. Those with higher incomes had more servants – and correspondingly spent more time organising them.

Family limitation first became evident in the 1860s. Then it was mainly a middle-class phenomenon, but it rapidly spread down the social scale. By the 1900s miners and agricultural workers were the only large social groups where it was not widespread. With a general lack of knowledge of artificial contraception, withdrawal or just going without sex must have been the most common methods of limitation. Nevertheless, there were many exceptions among all social classes, so there were still many large families in Edwardian Britain.

The war did not affect the trend towards smaller families, but it did cause irrevocable changes for many individual families. Single-parent families had always been common due to high Victorian mortality, but they were becoming less common as mortality declined. The war temporarily reversed that trend. And the fall in the number of young men meant that the number of lifetime spinsters, already quite high because of the existing sex imbalance, rose even further. This meant fewer children. For those who did marry, the small family had become the norm by the 1930s and there were fears of long-term population decline.

The causes of the decline in family size are amongst the hardest historical phenomena to unravel. The decline in infant mortality was surely a factor (see box, 'Health and health care'), since families could now be much more certain that, with only two or three births, they would not lose their children in infancy. A significant underlying cause must have been a shift to more companionate marriage, since discussion between husband and wife seems almost mandatory if families were to be limited. This helps to explain the slow fall in family size among agricultural labourers and miners, whose cultural isolation may have slowed the development of such marriages. By the inter-war period, even these groups were experiencing decline. Equally important was the framework within which such a discussion went on. Husbands and wives were making a trade-off between the satisfaction of having children and the satisfaction of better housing, more material goods – or better conditions for the children they did have. The last factor was partly imposed upon parents because longer schooling – the school leaving age had gone up to 14 in 1921 – lengthened the period during which children brought no income into the family.

Many working-class mothers had been domestic servants and it is tempting to see this as a mechanism for transmitting to working-class families a middle-class ideal: one or two children, neatly tucked up in their own bed rather than sharing as many children in large and poor families had to do. Finally, by the interwar years, knowledge of artificial means of birth control was spreading. Nevertheless, the evidence is that, for both middle- and working-class families, considerably more than half did not use such methods in the interwar period. Birth limitation was still achieved by traditional methods. There is contradictory evidence about abortion, the birth control method of last resort – and at that time illegal. Elizabeth Roberts and other historians believe that its occurrence was limited.

Society and economy: Health and health care

The twentieth century saw an extraordinary improvement in health, evidenced by dramatic falls in mortality. At the beginning of the century the expected lifespan for a woman at birth was 52, for a man 48. By the end the respective figures were 79 and 74. The rise in life expectancy owed itself in part to the continuation of public health improvements which had started in the later nineteenth century. Sizeable towns had Medical Officers or Health and Sanitary Inspectors. Where these officials were dedicated and properly financed, they had a major impact, because much disease was transmitted via 'nuisances' as they were called at the time – earth privies, drains leaking into wells and a generally dirty urban environment.

Medical intervention, by comparison, was much less important in saving lives than it was to become from the 1940s onwards. Injuries could be treated with some effect in hospitals since the use of antiseptics in the late nineteenth century, but the development of useful drugs was much slower so the dangers of many common diseases remained. Here again, public health helped by more rigorous isolation when there were epidemics. The hospital system itself was of very variable standard in 1900. The coverage of voluntary hospitals, supported by donations, was limited. Otherwise for general hospital care there were only Poor Law hospitals. Some, for instance in London, were good, but most were underfinanced and seen as little more than dumping grounds for poor people who had become helpless in their old age.

There were significant changes over the next 40 years. Voluntary hospitals diversified their funding through employer-administered hospital subscription schemes, which meant that working-class patients no longer had to rely on charity for access. Poor Law hospitals were increasingly taken over by local authorities as a result of the 1929 Local Government Act. Local authorities already provided specialist hospitals such as mental hospitals and tuberculosis sanatoria, and the more active ones improved the general hospitals they came to control. Decent hospital provision remained very patchy, but recently historians such as Steven Cherry have shown that there were progressive parts of the hospital system.

Doctors outside the hospital system, the general practitioners (GPs), were a different matter. At the beginning of the century many working-class people relied on folk remedies, hospital dispensaries or patent medicines which were becoming big business. GPs were given more work by the 1911 Health Insurance Act (see Chapter 2), which paid for wage earners to access their services. Doctors, however, were stuck in a system in which practices were bought and sold. The mechanism for combining practices was not there so doctors tended to soldier on alone. Those who could afford it bought practices in middle-class areas where they mollycoddled and overcharged their patients. Those who could not were often overworked. A. J. Cronin's 1937 novel *The Citadel* paints a devastating if melodramatic picture of the deficiencies of interwar general practice. Probably the most effective areas of primary health care were clinics for children set up by progressive local authorities.

In spite of the weaknesses in health care, mortality rates declined sharply, particularly infant mortality in the 1900s. In England and Wales it was 154 per 1,000 live

▶

births in 1900, falling to 105 in 1910 and 56 in 1940. Falling birth rates were a factor, since this improved maternal health. But this should not be pushed too far, since falling mortality has also been seen as a factor encouraging families to have fewer children. However, it is quite possible that the two processes, once underway, had a positive feedback effect on each other. The cleaning up of towns must have been a factor, but better nutrition from the late nineteenth century, which benefited mothers' health, was also important. There were, however, still big class differentials in health. And industrial areas were less healthy, a problem exacerbated in the interwar period because unemployment meant poorer child nutrition.

Extra-marital sex was almost certainly a minority activity, but probably a growing one. Illegitimacy rates in England and Wales in 1900 were very low – around 4 per cent – although they were over 6 per cent in Scotland, partly because it was more rural and rural illegitimacy rates were higher. These rates remained similar throughout the interwar period, but when in 1938 the relevant statistics were first collected, it was found that about 15 per cent of all children were born less than nine months after marriage. The implication is that pre-marital sex quite often occurred but in many cases was followed by marriage. Survey evidence suggests that about 20 per cent of women growing up in the 1900s and 1910s had pre-marital sex, but that this had rises to a third or more in the interwar years. However, similar evidence suggests that the popular view that, for most women in the period, knowledge of sex was quite limited and sexual relations frequently unsatisfactory is more or less true.

It is difficult to generalise about husband-wife relations. In spite of the adjustment indicated by the growth of family limitation, the Victorian ideal of 'separate spheres' – the man's the public, the wife's the private (that is, the household and family) – still held to a large extent before the First World War. This is related to the 'male breadwinner' model of marriage, although the latter does not necessarily preclude a couple sharing leisure activities and interests. And local cultures, family influence and individual personality meant that there was no universal pattern.

Actively religious families, for instance, had a shared interest and shared activities. In many other families where the husband did not drink, or only drank a small amount, husband and wife might do things together, especially if these were related to child-care. Contemporaries remarked in the Edwardian period on the armies of young parents going for Sunday walks with their families. Such families were probably most prevalent among the lower middle class and the 'respectable' working class. 'Respectability' was well understood but hard to define. It had some relationship with income but was also associated with not drinking much, or any, alcohol. Heavy drinking could, fairly obviously, be a cause of poverty, but highly paid workers in heavy industries such as shipbuilding often drank heavily. A male drinking culture could lead to limited interaction between wife and husband, as well as fostering male violence, one marker of 'roughness' – the opposite to respectability. Many husbands might not drink much, however, but still have a limited relationship with their wives. Then, as now, men and women often had different interests. Ross McKibbin has shown how Edwardian Britain was already a nation of, mainly male, hobbyists. Men might be obsessed with their garden, with handicrafts of some kind, with politics or simply with reading the sports pages. Women would concentrate on household tasks, the children, sewing or reading. Of course there were things inside the house, such as reading aloud or making music, which could be done together. But when gardens were often small or non-existent, houses mainly rented, which militated against DIY improvements, and low incomes prevented many outside activities, the scope for doing many of the things which now bring husbands and wives together was limited.

The continuing interwar shift to a more companionate marriage may be related to the move that many families made in those years to new suburban houses, often in substantial gardens. But far more families, especially working-class families, did not make that move and so the connection can only be partial. Making this move has often been linked to more private lifestyles. Geography certainly had an influence on this trend, in that it was physically more difficult to walk from such houses to local shops and so such trips were less frequent. Thus there seems to have been less sociability between neighbours in new suburbs. On the other hand, such sociability was most evident in stable working-class communities, and many communities had never been stable. The poor London mothers surveyed by Mrs Pember Reeves in 1913 seem to have interacted relatively little with their neighbours. Furthermore, working-class sociability had an obverse, the sometimes unwelcome control of powerful matriarchs over neighbourhood life. So some women may have preferred the greater isolation of a new suburb, although undoubtedly others disliked it.

One antidote to isolation was to join voluntary organisations, and one feature of new suburbs, both middle and working class, was a burgeoning of clubs and societies. Among the most popular were gardening clubs, reflecting the greater opportunities for this in new suburbs. There is plenty of testimony that, in such suburbs, the house and the garden became more central to family life and a shared interest between husband and wife. However, there were many other activities, growing in the Edwardian years and coming to fruition after the First War, in which families or young people could jointly participate. With one and a half million bicycles sold annually by the 1930s, cycling was a widespread pursuit, although cycles were probably still too expensive for poorer families to buy for children. Even more universal were family excursions, by train, bus or for the better-off middle classes by car. These were discussed in the previous section, as were two other widely shared activities – the cinema and dancing. One other, this time within the home, was listening to the radio and gramophone, although women were more frequent radio listeners than men. By 1937 some 80 per cent of households had radios.

The British Broadcasting Company was founded in 1922 and was reformed as a state chartered body, the British Broadcasting Corporation (BBC), in 1927. It was financed by licence fees, then payable for radios, and was headed by the formidable John Reith. Reith wished to educate – but he was forced also to entertain because of competition from continental stations supported by advertising, notably Radio Luxembourg. So the BBC came to mix variety programmes, which drew on the music hall format, light and classical music, and serious talks which were often surprisingly popular. Reith was socially and politically cautious, avoiding controversy with the government by generally agreeing with them. But, in spite of this, the BBC was seen as, and to some extent was, neutral and independent. In spite of his dour reputation, Reith had built an enormously successful institution.

For many working-class families, however, little changed between the wars. They lived in the same type of house, heated water on the kitchen stove for a bath and used outside privies. Household practices were transmitted via older women, usually the daughter's mother, near whom new married couples tried to locate. The centre of male life, for many, continued to be the pub, although in the South, particularly London, working-class women regularly patronised pubs. Alarms over heavy drinking in the First World War led to sharp reductions in Britain's free and easy opening hours – restrictions which only started to be eased again in the 1980s. Partly as a result, drink consumption continued to decline, but for a substantial minority of men heavy drinking on a Saturday night, sometimes followed by violence towards their wives, was still a familiar pattern of behaviour.

Another long-standing activity which went along with the pub was betting on the horses. Since the late nineteenth century cheap newspapers had allowed the intense study of form, and thus betting was a time-consuming hobby but not one which involved much expenditure by most participants, since a fair proportion would come back as winnings. Off-course credit betting was legal but off-course cash betting – and few punters actually went to race meetings – was illegal, in an ineffectual attempt to control working-class gambling. In fact, it just made it more exciting, as a network of 'bookie's runners' collected bets and kept a look-out for police. Just after the Second World War Seebohm Rowntree, still writing sociology books 50 years after his first one, observed street betting from a London police car. As the car came into sight, 'knots of men in street after street broke up and ran, like sparrows scattering at the approach of a cat'.[4] Even with gambling, however, a new, more family oriented variety developed rapidly between the wars. This was the football pools, in which the stake was collected after the results were known, thus technically making them credit operations and therefore legal. Like betting on the horses, the pools involved a satisfactorily time-consuming study of form. They quickly became enormously popular, and 10 million people were enrolled with the pools' operators in the 1930s.

More activities were shared within families, but there were limits to the rise of the companionate marriage even in new suburbs. As late as 1951 a survey in Oxford revealed that working-class women judged husbands' merits primarily by whether they earned a steady wage, were punctual and did not drink too much. This was the case in a long-established inner city area and on a modern suburban estate. This attitude influenced decisions about separation and divorce. The latter, expensive and difficult, was hardly an option at all for the working classes before the First War, and even after the war it was not common for anyone. Significant numbers of working-class married couples were separated, however. But in the Edwardian period at least 50 per cent of these were reunited, usually because the husband's financial situation improved. Both this and the 1951 survey indicate the continuing importance to most people's idea of marriage of the husband as the breadwinner.

Growing up

In the 1900s parental interaction with children was often limited. Aristocratic and upper middle-class children routinely had nannies. In larger working-class families the eldest daughter would be drafted in for much of the care of infants, while in many working-class families the wife's mother was close at hand and, as often today, would more than likely help with children. But in many families, large and small but perhaps more the latter, there is plenty of testimony to fathers as well as mothers engaging actively in family life. Part of this engagement involved the growing emphasis on Christmas as a child-centred festival. A. J. Cronin, the novelist, remarked how Welsh miners in the 1920s made much of Christmas: '. . . the front room in each house [was] locked against the children, festooned with paper streamers, toys hidden in the drawers of the chest . . .'.[5]

The growing ubiquity of toys in the interwar period is another indicator of growing child-centredness. In the early 1900s George Sturt noted that in his Surrey village girls rarely had dolls, but that change was occurring. Between the mid-1920s and the mid-1930s spending on toys rose by about one-third, at a time when prices were falling. Toys were becoming more complex. This was the golden age of Meccano, a constructional toy, and of model trains. In new suburban houses, the size of gardens meant that children's play outside could coexist with gardening. The leisure of inner city children, however, changed less. Cars were still rare enough in poorer areas for the street to continue as the arena of children's pursuits. Girls' traditional street games continued, as did boys' intense participation in street football.

We know too little, though, of the spectrum of children's activities and the influences on them. Between the wars, reading matter diversified through the expansion of comics, the childhood analogue of cheap newspapers. The meaning conveyed to children by the comics' heroes, some of them like Billy Bunter located in a public-school world remote from most of their readers' experience, is impossible to recreate. Perhaps children simply found them funny, which was after all the intention. Surveys suggest that a surprising number of children of all classes also read and enjoyed serious authors such as Dickens, although they may have been influenced in this by what they had to read at school. For older male children and adolescents of all classes, sport provided an endless source of recreation. As with men, this was not so much by playing it as by following it through newspapers. Sport gave unlimited scope for three male obsessions, with statistics, lists and hero-worship. For adolescent girls, the nearest equivalents were popular music, dancing and films. Although all three were decried as fostering American influence, the reality was more complex. Popular music was effectively international. Swing, American in origin, was the dance music of the interwar period, but dance technique was most influenced by Victor Sylvester, who was British. And although American films were more successful, there were important British stars in the 1930s, particularly Gracie Fields and George Formby.

Children in the 1900s mainly left school at 13, an age which had been steadily pushed up since the mid-nineteenth century. Officially, the great majority were by then literate, although most working-class children received no more than this 'elementary' education, as it was called. Grammar schools for older boys, which levied fees, were largely patronised by the less well-off middle classes. They were often small and inefficient. For the upper middle and landed classes there were the misleadingly named 'public' schools – in fact private and also fee-paying. The Conservative reforms of 1902 were meant, in part, to refinance smaller grammar schools to enable them to provide a better education. In 1907, 25 per cent of all grammar school places were made free if a qualifying exam was passed. Even so, only a tiny proportion of working-class children went on to grammar school education. Opportunities for girls beyond the elementary level were particularly limited. There were good quality fee-paying girls' schools for middle-class parents, but equally many old-fashioned ones with a limited curriculum.

The 1902 reforms have been criticised for preventing the development of technical secondary schools, which a few local authorities had set up, but the criticism is misplaced. There were very few such schools and, although the reforms may have temporarily set back some good work in technical education, in general they lifted standards and, in a limited way, promoted social mobility. Much technical education was delivered via evening classes. The number of students in these grew rapidly throughout the 1900s, from 550,000 in 1900 to over 1.4 million in 1910, around 40 per cent of whom were girls. Furthermore, although apprenticeship training varied in value according to the occupation and the firm, in better firms it was genuinely useful and was often combined with technical education.

The standard age for leaving elementary school went up from 13 to 14 in 1921 – the one element of the optimistic ideas for post-war educational reconstruction which survived. Although elementary schools in the interwar years became more child centred – the term 'primary' education came into common use – there was little change in the basic structure of education. The biggest reduction in class sizes had occurred before the war, with pupil–teacher ratios declining from 48 to 37 between 1900 and 1910. They shaded down more gradually to 31 in 1938. The proportion of working- and lower middle-class children going on to grammar or independent school increased, from about 5 per cent of those born before 1910 to about 12 per cent of those born in the 1920s. The latter figure compares with around 50 per cent of children from the professional and managerial classes. But evening classes remained the main route to post-elementary education and the number in those did not change much.

Education has often been seen as reinforcing the class system by impeding social mobility. Change was held up by financial constraints, especially after the First World War (see Chapter 4). It was held up by the churches, especially the Anglicans and Roman Catholics, who gained most from government funding for their schools and who tended to resist change. It was held up by the Conservative Party, who defended the privileged position of the grammar schools. And it was held up because there was little popular demand for change. For most working-class people, there was little perception that children would or could do anything other than manual work.

Whether middle or working class, most families expected girls to work for a few years and then marry. Even so there were parents, usually lower middle class, who would keep their daughters at school until 18 and then put them through two years of teacher training, a considerable financial sacrifice. Nurse training was rather more rough and ready, and many nurses dropped out after a year as they could then get jobs as assistant nurses. Nevertheless, it still entailed some financial sacrifice. Daughters in most upper middle and landed class families, before the First War, simply did not do paid work. Nevertheless, a few enlightened families in these social classes paid for their daughters to receive a university education. These must have provided most of the 1,000 women doctors there were in 1914. Much of the increase – to around 6,000 in the late 1930s – owed itself to growth in women's higher education between 1900 and 1920. By the 1920s there was strong resistance to further growth in the number of women university students, which hovered at around 25 per cent of the total throughout the interwar years. Most of these were destined for teaching.

Most working-class families made little more financial sacrifice for the career preparation of their sons than they did for their daughters. Throughout the whole period between 1900 and 1939, apprenticeships – the route into much skilled, and therefore higher paid, work – were entered by about 25 per cent of working-class boys. They entailed some financial sacrifice from parents because initial earnings were much lower than in other juvenile work, and therefore the youngster would bring in less income to the household. But earnings rose after the first couple of years. (Some girls were also apprenticed, for instance to hairdressing and dressmaking.) Skilled workers' children were more likely to be apprenticed, but this was not necessarily because skilled workers took more interest in their sons' specific careers, but rather because they could better afford the financial sacrifice. Most working-class parents seem to have been more concerned that their children had a job than with what it was or what its prospects were.

This is in sharp contrast to better-off middle-class parents. University was unusual outside upper middle and landed class families, although there was a long-standing tradition of greater university participation in Scotland. The eventual destination of many Scottish graduates was teaching, however, so university for many was simply an alternative to teacher-training colleges in England and Wales. In Great Britain as a whole, university and teacher-training participation, having doubled between 1900 and the early 1920s, remained at around 2.5 per cent of the population after that. But many other male careers besides teaching involved a financial sacrifice by parents. Large numbers of middle-class jobs, for instance as professional engineers or accountants, involved serving a 'premium apprenticeship'. In this a substantial premium was paid to the employer, the idea being that this ensured a wide training. Officer entry to the armed services also involved the initial laying out of money, particularly in the army, not to mention the taken-for-granted need for a public school education.

One division between working- and middle-class attitudes, therefore, was in their aspirations for male children. In this the relative lack of working-class concern for the future paralleled their lesser concern with saving.

Class

So far, class has been discussed as a label attached to certain occupational groups rather than as a social category which might give meaning to people's lives. As the latter, there are three ways of analysing it.

Marxist analysis sees class as all important. In this approach there is latent warfare in capitalist society between property owners, or capitalists, and the working class, whose interests are diametrically opposed. Capitalism will eventually collapse and the working class will triumph. Few British historians have ever been out and out Marxists, but Marxism's indirect influence has been considerable. Many historians have seen British society in the early twentieth century as grossly unfair, with the working class as the subject of that unfairness. Such historians have often seen the rise of the Labour Party as an inevitable result, as people became more aware of unfairness and concerned to remedy it. A focus on people's self-awareness of class as a spur to political change has therefore marked this approach. The third approach to analysing class has focused entirely on self-awareness – on people's understanding of class in general and their own class position in particular. It makes no assumptions as to the political results of this.

This section will continue with a discussion of class labels and will then turn to perceptions of class and their relationship to politics. Class position is usually taken as depending on the head of the household, in most cases up to the recent past male, so inevitably male occupations have tended to dominate the class labels assigned to families. The landed gentry and aristocracy are usually labelled 'upper class'. Aristocrats, or peers, had the right to sit in the House of Lords, but were not necessarily wealthier or socially distinct from other great landowners who were not ennobled and were therefore described as gentry. The latter might, however, be knighted, which entitled them to put 'Sir' before their names. The aristocracy was further complicated because wealthy businessmen and other prominent people might be ennobled, often because of political donations. But others of the same kind who had not been ennobled might also be labelled as upper class, especially if they participated in the London social round. Equally, plenty of such people were not interested in titles or socialising. 'Upper class' is, therefore, a fairly meaningless term if used to measure wealth or influence. It probably has most meaning as a status distinction – that is, as a mark of social esteem. Considerable importance was attached to having someone titled as patron or president of institutions and voluntary societies. In rural areas the landed gentry were strongly represented on local councils and in the magistracy which dealt with petty crime, but their influence was diminishing fast as agriculture declined and landed estates were sold off.

Middle-class occupations were discussed in an earlier section. As with the upper classes, 'upper middle' as a label had some correspondence with income but was also a status description. Male members of this class had usually gone to better-known public schools or expected to send their sons to one, and in Southern England, at least, spoke with what became known as 'received pronunciation' – that is, without a regional accent. At its lower end, the middle class shaded into the ranks of the working class. Grey areas here included self-employed workers, common in old-fashioned crafts like cobbling and in newer occupations such as electrical installation, and shopworkers, who along with salesmen comprised over 5 per cent of the occupied population. Employed manual workers unequivocally count as working class. Here the distinction between skilled, semi-skilled and unskilled is usually seen as important, although as already shown it did not always correspond to relative prosperity, since higher earners with large families could still be poor.

The Edwardian period had seen a burgeoning of middle-class fears of a militant working class. Kenneth Grahame's *Wind in the Willows* of 1908 is often read as an allegory of such fears, with the workers represented by the rampaging stoats and weasels who take over Mr Toad's comfortable riverside house. And the pre- and immediately post-war labour militancy seemed to provide evidence that such fears were justified. But then they subsided as Baldwin constructed an apparently apolitical Conservatism in which 'national character' and moderation were a force uniting all classes. So, in middle-class eyes, by the late 1920s and 1930s class conflict was not an important element in the class system.

On the face of it, middle-class attitudes reflected realities. Strikes increased to peaks just before and just after the war; from 1917 the threat of Bolshevism loomed and union membership and support for the Labour Party grew. But subsequently communism in Britain failed to take off, the Labour Party posed little threat to the established order when it came to office and labour militancy practically disappeared after the General Strike. Marxism itself had little influence on British intellectuals and even less on the Labour Party, which was particularly hostile to the Communist Party (see Chapter 4, 'National government 1931–1939').

Even in the strike-prone years between 1910 and 1921, however, middle-class fears were exaggerated. As Chapter 4 showed, labour militancy was primarily a response to short-term issues such as inflation and labour shortages, which gave workers a strong bargaining position. Even after the war, working-class support for the Labour Party was limited. The one group of workers who switched political allegiance more or less *en bloc* were the miners, but they were in a special position. Their industry had been extremely prosperous before the war and was unusually depressed after it. There was an undoubted shift among working-class intellectuals from nonconformism and Liberalism to ethical socialism, but for many workers the shift to Labour was not deep rooted, as was shown by the party's rout in 1931. The miners were exceptional also in that relations with employers, often good before the war, became transformed into bitter antagonism. But many workers, whether union members or not, retained reasonably positive relations with employers between the wars. The large combines which were emerging offered a limited degree of paternalism, for instance in the form of hospital subscription schemes and company sports grounds.

Some historians, however, have seen working-class identity as consisting not so much in political allegiances but in cultural practices. Patrick Joyce has pointed to a particular set of working-class attitudes displayed in, for instance, music hall and dialect literature. These incorporated a popular patriotism which was rooted in local identity, for instance as a Lancastrian, a Yorkshireman or a Londoner, all of which were also seen as embodying particularly British qualities of humour and steadfastness. As Joyce sees it, the working class were not deferential towards employers or the middle classes, but neither were they hostile. Ross McKibbin has pointed to another common element of working-class life, an inward-looking defensiveness. Contrary to the image of working-class sociability, many working-class people were extremely private and resentful of outside interference. This defensiveness arose partly from a perceived lack of opportunity to change their occupation or lifestyle. Working-class fecklessness, as the middle classes saw it – gambling and a lack of concern with education or saving – arose from the same source.

There are obvious overlaps between middle- and working-class identities. Local and regional loyalties, and sport which built upon those loyalties, both overrode class differences. Football was the main working-class sport, but most football clubs were owned and managed by middle-class businessmen in the locality. And in some cases, South Wales in particular, rugby was the main sport and a cross-class game. Support for cricket was also cross-class. Pubs, and a perception of them as embodying a Britain in which everyone – or all men – could enjoy a cheerful and open-handed environment, were another symbol of identity which transcended class. In fact pubs retained their own class divide in the different grades of bar (old-fashioned ones still have 'saloon' and 'public' bars, a division which used to be common). Nevertheless, an important component of the Conservative appeal to working men was the party's defence of the pub and its fancied embodiment of national character.

The pub was part of that 'imagined community' of Britain which emphasised patriotism. The monarchy, a particularly potent symbol which transcended class, was another. But, as shown earlier (see 'Identities: local and national'), the monarchy also represented another strand of Britishness which emphasised individual freedom and Britain's constitutional nature. This, too, was a strong element of working-class identity, as manifested in music hall songs and characters and dialect literature. As such it might be more critical of social relationships. But, Patrick Joyce argues, this did not embody class hostility so much as emphasise fairness. Clearly the growth of socialism from the 1900s strengthened the idea of class as an important division. But the deep-rooted nature of the ideas discussed above is suggested by the enormous popularity of Ramsay MacDonald in the 1920s. MacDonald played down class hostility and emphasised a gradual movement towards greater equality (see Chapter 4).

Many attitudes, therefore, were broadly shared by all classes and this overlap extended into life opportunities. Lower middle-class non-manual workers, for instance, often earned no more than skilled manual workers. Many lower middle-class children went to elementary school, and only a few to grammar or independent school. Indeed, only about half of children of professionals or managers went to such schools in the interwar period. This suggests that there was not always such a sharp divide between the classes in providing for the future. Many middle-class families had only a limited ability to save or to invest in their children's education. And many skilled workers did save in various ways, such as through trade union subscriptions which gave them a small pension, or by buying their own house.

The overlap of life opportunities promoted limited social mobility. Andrew Miles' figures suggest that in the 1900s about 10 per cent of manual workers' sons were in non-manual work when they married, while almost as many non-manual workers' sons went the other way. By the 1940s the rate of upward mobility had risen to about 25 per cent, while the downwards flow was static, so net upward mobility rose – which it had to as the proportion of non-manual jobs was gradually increasing. By the 1930s around 70 per cent of male workers were non-manual compared with almost 80 per cent in 1900. Female mobility was higher because women's non-manual work increased at a faster rate. Social mobility, therefore, softened class boundaries but was too slow to make a huge difference.

Notes

1. Feldman, D., *Englishmen and Jews: Social Relations and Political Culture 1840–1914* (London: Yale University Press, 1994), p. 381.
2. Quoted in Rose, *George V* (see Chapter 4), p. 343.
3. Shadwell, A., *Industrial Efficiency* (London: Longmans, Green, 1906), p. 80.
4. Rowntree, S. and Lavers, G., *English Life and Leisure* (London: Longmans, Green, 1951), p. 128.
5. Cronin, A. J., *The Citadel* (London: New English Library, 1983; 1st ed., 1937), pp. 169–170.

Further reading

Feldman, *Englishmen and Jews* is of exceptional value, especially on national identity. Halsey, *British Society* and Halsey and Webb, *Social Trends* (see Chapter 1) for much of the data in this chapter. Joyce, P., *Visions of the People: Industrial England and the Question of Class 1848–1914* (Cambridge: Cambridge University Press, 1991) is of great interest, although not easy to read. McKibbin, *Classes and Cultures* (see Chapter 1) is superb. Royle, E., *Modern Britain: A Social History 1750–1985* (London: Arnold, 2nd ed., 1997) contains much useful material, as does, on a larger scale, Thompson, F. (ed.), *The Cambridge Social History of Britain 1750–1950* (Cambridge: Cambridge University Press, Vols 1–3, 1990). Roberts, E., *A Woman's Place: An Oral History of Working-Class Women 1890–1940* (Oxford: Blackwell, 1984) is a classic of oral history. Zweiniger-Bargielowska, *Women* (see Chapter 1) has valuable chapters.

Other sources: Alderman, G., *Modern British Jewry* (Oxford: Clarendon Press, 1992); Bourne, G., *Change in the Village* (London: Duckworth, 1955; 1st ed., 1912); Brown, K., *The British Toy Business: a History since 1700* (London: Hambledon, 1996); Cannadine, D., 'Stanley Baldwin and Francis Brett Young' in Cannadine, D. (ed.), *In Churchill's Shadow* (London: Penguin, 2003); Cherry, S., *Medical Services and the Hospitals in Britain, 1860–1939* (Cambridge: Cambridge University Press, 1996); Floud and Johnson, *Cambridge Economic History* (see Chapter 1); Hatton, T. and Bailey, R., 'Women's Work in Census and Survey, 1911–31', *Economic History Review*, Vol. LIV, pp. 87–107 (2001); Hunt, *Labour History* (see Chapter 2); Lynch, M. (ed.), *The Oxford Companion to Scottish History* (Oxford: Oxford University Press, 2001); Miles, A., 'How Open Was British Society? Social Mobility and Equality of Opportunity 1839–1914' in Miles, A. and Vincent, D. (eds), *Building European Society* (Manchester: Manchester University Press, 1993); Millward, R. and Bell, S., 'Infant Mortality in Victorian Britain: the Mother As Medium', *Economic History Review*, Vol. LIV, pp. 699–733 (2001); Moore-Colyer, R., 'Towards "Mother Earth": Jorian Jenks, Organicism, the Right and the British Union of Fascists', *Journal of Contemporary History*, Vol. 39, pp. 353–371 (2004); More, *Industrial Age* (see Chapter 1); More, *Skill* (see Chapter 3); More, C. 'Workers' Careers and Length of Service *c*. 1860–1910', *Historical Studies in Industrial Relations*, No. 7, pp. 99–117 (1999); Morgan, K., *Rebirth of a Nation: Wales 1880–1980* (Oxford: Oxford University Press, 1982); Morris, J., 'The Strange Death of Christian Britain: Another Look at the Secularisation Debate', *Historical Journal*, Vol. 46, pp. 963–976 (2003); Pember Reeves, M., *Round About a Pound a Week* (London: Virago,

1979; 1st ed., 1913); Perry, C., 'In Search of H. V. Morton: Travel Writing and Cultural Values in the First Age of British Democracy', *Twentieth Century British History*, Vol. 10, pp. 431–456 (1999); Roberts, R., *The Classic Slum: Salford Life in the First Quarter of the Century* (Harmondsworth: Penguin, 1973); Treble, J., *Urban Poverty in Britain 1830–1914* (London: Batsford, 1979); Vincent, D., 'Mobility, Bureaucracy and Careers in Early Twentieth Century Britain' in Miles and Vincent, *European Society*; Williamson, *Baldwin* (see Chapter 4).

Chapter 7

THE SECOND WORLD WAR: BATTLES AND STRATEGY

The course of the war

Hitler's invasion of Poland was to launch a war which ultimately was to far exceed in scale the war of 1914–1918. But for over seven months little happened – the so-called Phoney War. The Germans quickly conquered Poland, while the British Expeditionary Force (BEF) went to France in accordance with pre-arranged plans to form part of the front with the much larger French army. The Phoney War ended when Germany invaded Denmark and Norway in April 1940. Allied attempts to resist in Norway were unsuccessful, although the German navy was seriously mauled, with ten destroyers sunk. The failure in Norway was the immediate cause of the fall of Chamberlain and his replacement by Churchill and a fully representative Coalition government, in itself one of the major events of the war (see Chapter 8; and box, 'Winston Churchill').

As the government changed, the German attack in the west began, on 10 May. The German *Panzer* (tank) divisions broke through the French lines and raced to the Channel coast which they reached on 20 May, thus cutting off a mass of French and British troops. The British commander, Lord Gort, took the correct decision to retreat. The BEF's ten divisions fought no major battle and contributed little to the defence of France but, with few tanks, there was not much they could do. The BEF succeeded in holding a narrow pocket leading to the French coast at Dunkirk, through which 200,000 British and 140,000 French soldiers were evacuated between 27 May and 4 June. The French still held a line along the Somme, and there were around 100,000 British troops still in France. As France's defence crumbled, they too were safely evacuated.

In the six weeks from the start of the German invasion of the west, Britain's strategic position had been utterly changed. Italy had come into the war on 10 June, and large Italian armies in her North and East African possessions threatened Britain's position in Egypt and her colonies in East Africa. Equally important, the Italian navy made the whole of the Mediterranean a no-go area for merchant shipping. British trade to and from India, Australia, New Zealand and the Far East had to be routed via the Cape of Good Hope, adding thousands of miles to the journey. The need to strengthen Britain's Mediterranean fleet added to the demands on the Royal Navy.

The most immediate danger was the threat of invasion. For a short time Hitler made serious preparations for this. The German air force's failure in the Battle of Britain in August and September (see box, 'The Battle of Britain') reduced its attractiveness, and with the onset of autumn he shelved the invasion plans. Instead Hitler's restless mind,

Military affairs: The Battle of Britain

It has been well said that the Battle of Britain, as Germany's attempt to gain air superiority over Britain in the summer of 1940 came to be called, involved two contrasting air forces. The first was technically up to date, aided by the latest and most sophisticated communications equipment and was well led. The other had a mixture of up-to-date and aging aircraft designs, an inefficient communications system and was poorly led with no coherent strategy. The first was the RAF, the second the German air force (*Luftwaffe*).

In other words, much of the popular image of the battle as a few gallant British pilots facing the modern *Luftwaffe* is a myth. The British pilots were both few and courageous, and the German fighters were modern. But the German bombers were showing their age, while Hermann Goering, the head of the *Luftwaffe*, had no coherent strategy once it was clear that the RAF would not be quickly defeated. British rearmament had probably been most effective in its production of modern fighters, the Spitfires and Hurricanes; radar gave the British an enormous advantage as they could locate approaching aircraft; and Hugh Dowding, the Fighter Command chief, controlled the battle with great skill, always keeping a reserve of fresh aircraft and pilots. The initial German attempts to knock out fighter airfields turned into attacks on London. These day attacks wreaked devastation but cost the Germans heavily in aircraft losses. In the autumn of 1940 through to the summer of 1941 the *Luftwaffe* went over to night attacks on cities, the Blitz. The Blitz caused major damage to houses, shops and offices and killed many people, mainly civilians. But it was never a serious strategic threat. City centres were the main target, but city centres contained little industry so industrial production was not significantly affected. East coast ports were closed for a time, because of the threat to shipping, causing congestion in west coast ports; but while serious, the situation was never critical.

The failure of the *Luftwaffe* to knock out Britain's fighters precipitated Hitler's decision not to invade Britain, and that in turn encouraged him to turn on Russia. But invasion would have been incredibly risky for Germany even if Britain had lost air superiority, and Hitler's thought processes, while inscrutable, are likely to have led him towards Russia sooner or later. It was always to him the greatest threat, and offered the greatest prizes in land and resources.

aggression and ceaseless urge to activism led him towards Russia. Expansion eastwards was a bedrock ambition of his; he also argued that he should eliminate what he saw as the ever-present threat from the east and then turn his attention to finishing off Britain. Admiral Raeder, his naval chief, suggested early in 1941 that Germany had a golden opportunity to defeat Britain in the Mediterranean and Middle East but Hitler was not persuaded.

Raeder's concern was partly because North Africa and the Mediterranean were areas of achievement for Britain, helping to sustain morale over the winter of 1940–1941. Italian forces in Libya and Ethiopia were badly officered and strung out in isolated outposts. Their army and air force had obsolete equipment, even by the standards of the not very well-equipped British army. As a result, and helped by the brilliant generalship of Richard O'Connor, the Italians suffered a series of major reverses, losing 130,000 prisoners by

February 1941 in North Africa and then being routed in East Africa. Success here was compounded by naval victories. In July 1940 Churchill had taken a ruthless decision, but in military terms a correct one. The British fleet attacked the French fleet, now under the control of the technically neutral Vichy regime but an obvious potential threat, at Mers-el-Kebir in North Africa. This sent a signal to America which was taken seriously: Britain was not giving up. Then severe defeats were inflicted on the Italian navy over the winter of 1940–1941. These actions ensured that, although Britain's naval position still remained fraught, there was no chance of Britain's surface fleet being overwhelmed.

In other respects, the winter of 1940–1941 was the most difficult of the war. German submarines were already taking a heavy toll in the Battle of the Atlantic (see box 'The Battle of the Atlantic'), while at home German air attacks, the so-called Blitz, brought civilians into the front line (see Chapter 8).

Following the Italian defeats in North Africa, in February 1941 Hitler sent Erwin Rommel, one of his best generals, with a small German force, the *Afrika Korps*, to stiffen Italian resistance. Simultaneously, there were a series of other demands on the British forces in North Africa. The British resolved to aid Greece, which was holding out successfully against an unprovoked Italian attack, in case the Germans joined in. The Germans did. British forces were not enough to defend Greece and Britain had to evacuate it, and then Crete, with heavy losses. In the summer of 1941 Britain invaded Iraq, which had a pro-German government, and Syria to liquidate the Vichy forces there. The overstretch told on the British army in North Africa and Rommel gained the upper hand (Fig 7.1).

In global terms North Africa and the Middle East were relegated to sideshows when on 22 June 1941 Germany attacked Russia. Churchill immediately declared Russia an ally, but for a long time there was not much that the British could do to help. Considerable sacrifices were made to send convoys to Russia, containing a mass of material ranging from clothing to fighter planes to trucks. Running them was another burden on the Royal Navy, which had to guard against threats from Norwegian-based submarines, surface ships and aircraft, and contend with atrocious weather. Apart from this aid the Russians had to stand against the German army alone.

There were further setbacks at the end of 1941. On 7 December the Japanese declared war, striking first at Pearl Harbour and destroying a large part of the American fleet. They also quickly overcame British strongholds in the area, culminating in the surrender of the great naval base at Singapore on 15 February 1942. British naval power had already been emasculated by the sinkings of the battleship *Prince of Wales* and battlecruiser *Repulse* in December. By May 1942 the British had also been chased out of Burma. In spite of Japanese aggression over a number of years in China and elsewhere, very little had been done to strengthen British positions in the Far East, for the simple reason that other demands were so pressing. Yet in the military thinking of the time Singapore had been accorded a higher importance than anywhere except the defence of Britain itself. The outcome was strangely ironic: the fall of Singapore and other British territories had little effect on the way Britain waged the war. The Americans brought Japanese expansion to a halt by their naval victory at Midway in June 1942. From then on the Pacific war was almost entirely an American concern, with some help from Australia and New Zealand. The British concentrated on retaking Burma, although they did not start an effective offensive there until 1944.

Military affairs: The Battle of the Atlantic

The threat to shipping was posed most strongly by German submarines, although aircraft, mines and from time to time surface ship commerce raiders were also important. The resulting conflict was the Battle of the Atlantic, a long-drawn-out war of attrition. It is usually seen as starting in 1940 after Germany occupied France, as submarines could then be stationed on the French west coast and could easily reach the Atlantic trade routes. The effect, apart from the direct losses caused by submarines, was that convoys had to take long diversions to minimise the submarine risk. They also had to be large in order to concentrate the relatively few escort vessels, and this meant that they formed up slowly. All this exacerbated the restrictions on merchant ship carrying capacity arising from port congestion and the need to take the Cape route to the Far East.

The Royal Navy had anticipated the possibility of submarine attack in a future war but thought that convoy and their underwater detection device, ASDIC (now called sonar), would counteract it. This indicates a failure to learn fully from the lessons of the First World War, since many submarine attacks were carried out on the surface, where the low profile of a submarine made it hard to detect, especially at night. However, the German navy had also failed to learn the lesson and gave submarines a low priority early in the war.

Fortunately, the terrible losses of the winter of 1940–1941 were not repeated until 1942, because in the summer of 1941 Britain began to read the German naval cipher, encoded on the famous Enigma machine which the Germans had thought impregnable. There were still long periods when the British could not read the naval Enigma and sinkings remained high until spring 1943. But other measures all made the submarines' task more difficult and increased their casualty rate. Long-distance aircraft – although they were in desperately short supply, partly because of Harris and Portal (see box, 'Strategic bombing'), until late 1942 – escort carriers and better quality escort vessels all helped, as did improved training of escort crews.

Churchill said that the submarine threat was the only thing during the war that kept him awake at night. Was it so serious? The German successes were achieved with a remarkably small number of boats and, on the face of it, a larger number could have had a disastrous impact. But this would have happened only if the Allies had not reacted at all. In practice, many improvements, such as better air cover, could have been made earlier than they were and in the case of utmost emergency probably would have been. Only a massive increase in the number of submarines would have threatened defeat to Britain, and once the invasion of Russia started Hitler simply did not have the resources to build them. Even so, 35,000 merchant seamen died as a result of enemy action.

Japan's attack finally prompted Hitler to declare war on the USA, which had been growing increasingly active in its aid to the Allies, escorting North Atlantic convoys and extending Lend Lease to Russia. It was his stupidest action ever, as it solved Roosevelt's problem with the isolationist lobby (see later section, 'Friends and allies'). The Americans had already agreed, in staff talks in 1941 which anticipated the scenario now unfolding, that the war against Germany should take priority. Japan, however

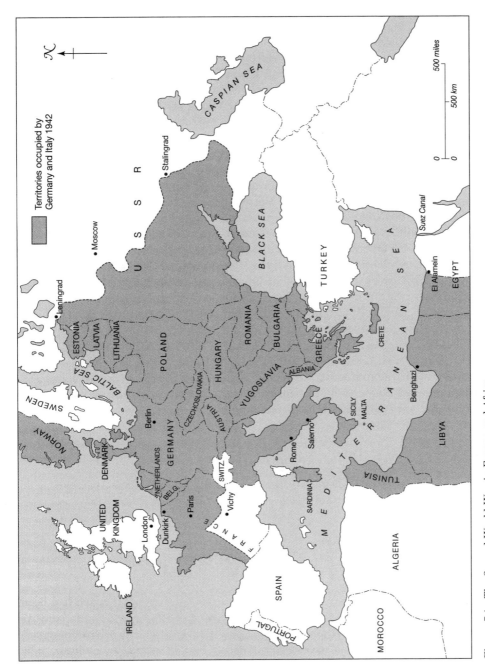

Figure 7.1 The Second World War in Europe and Africa
Source: Cootes, R. J., *Britain since 1700*, 2nd ed., Longman (1982), p. 292

widespread her conquests, had such a small economic base relative to the Allies that she was correctly seen as the lesser threat.

Joint strategy was agreed by the British and American chiefs of staff in a series of conferences over the remaining years of the war. They constituted the Combined Chiefs of Staff and, with much disagreement over means and some backsliding, they kept to the concept of Germany first. Disagreement arose largely because of British insistence on what became known as the Mediterranean Strategy (see box, 'Alan Brooke and the Mediterranean Strategy', later in chapter). The taking of the initiative by the Allies in North Africa began with two successes in autumn 1942. Bernard Montgomery, Britain's new general there, had received heavy reinforcements. At the Battle of El Alamein, named after a railway station on the line west from Alexandria, he used them effectively and, when the German and Italian forces broke in early November, Alamein became a major victory and a psychological boost to the British people. Immediately afterwards British and American troops landed in French North Africa, still ruled by Vichy. After some scrappy fighting the Vichy authorities capitulated, but North Africa was not cleared of enemy forces. Hitler poured troops into Tunisia, in the middle of the North African littoral. The British and Americans closed the ring slowly, with the German and Italian forces finally surrendering in early May 1943. There were over 250,000 prisoners. Then Anglo–American armies invaded Sicily in July and the Italian mainland in September. Mussolini was overthrown and the new Italian government surrendered, but the Germans had occupied all of Italy, up which they slowly retreated, fighting a series of defensive battles, until the end of the war.

While plans were being made to attack Sicily, the Allies at last won the Battle of the Atlantic – the submarine attack on Britain's supply routes which had continued since 1940. Also in 1943 the strategic bombing offensive against Germany, another long-term campaign, entered a new level of intensity. It was to continue to escalate until almost the end of the war (see box, 'Strategic bombing').

Military affairs: Strategic bombing

The most controversial British military campaign was the strategic bombing of Germany. The special position given to bombing goes back to the pre-war belief that it was a war-winning weapon. In spite of the evidence from the Blitz that it was not, the belief persisted among many, including Churchill, at least until late 1941 and in some cases until the end of the war. In the period after the fall of France, the belief was in part a psychological necessity, as Germany's hegemony seemed unassailable by any other means of warfare. Hopes that Germany might be successfully blockaded were much lower now that Hitler had control of much of Europe. Some people believed that mass insurrection in occupied countries might overthrow Germany, but Churchill was realistic enough to see that this was not an option. Belief in bombing remained.

Ironically, soon after Churchill had authorised a large increase in the bomber force, photographic evidence in late 1941 demonstrated that British bombing was hopelessly inaccurate. However, a new rationale emerged and was developed by Bomber Command: the destruction of German cities would make life intolerable for the Germans by 'dehousing' them. Bombing need not be particularly accurate. Churchill was never again persuaded that bombing was a war-winning weapon in itself, but it had other uses for him. It was a major propaganda weapon in persuading the British people that they had some hope of ultimately defeating Germany. It supported Churchill in withstanding Stalin's constant reproaches that the Allies were not fighting Germany seriously. Churchill gave Stalin photographs of bombed German cities, which the Soviet dictator seems to have enjoyed studying. Finally, bombing could be used in negotiations with the Americans. The United States Army Air Force (USAAF) put its faith in day bombing, while the RAF bombed almost entirely by night. By presenting their activities as complementary, the illusion of a combined offensive was created: the 'bomber barons', as the bomber chiefs have been nicknamed, were happy; and the USAAF would support the policy of giving Germany priority over Japan. In reality, each air force carried on largely independently.

One reason for this failure to cooperate was the chief of Bomber Command from early 1942, Air Chief Marshal Arthur (Bert) Harris. Harris's influence was almost wholly malign. He was suspicious of technological developments, and although bombing became far more accurate, this did not distract him from area bombing. For long periods of time, when asked to concentrate on particular classes of target, he failed to do so, pleading operational exigencies such as the weather. And he constantly intrigued to gain the maximum resources for his force without regard to other needs. Also culpable here was Portal, the RAF's Chief of Staff. Portal is often praised, but it is hard to see why. In 1942 he led resistance to the use of bombers for convoy protection work, a switch that would have prevented thousands of tons of sinkings and saved many lives. And although there was considerable scepticism within the air staff about Harris's claims for the results of bombing, Portal failed to prevent Harris from disobeying orders.

Bombing on the scale of the RAF and USAAF obviously had a major impact on the German war effort. Although night bombing was amazingly ineffective at destroying industrial capacity, Hitler devoted huge resources to anti-aircraft guns and fighters. There seems little doubt, however, that a smaller effort by the RAF would have tied up almost as many German resources at far less cost; that Harris's campaigns, especially the infamous 'Battle of Berlin' over the winter of 1943–1944, caused the RAF appalling losses; and that from late 1944, had Harris done what he was told and systematically attacked the German transport system, the war might have been measurably shortened.

Meanwhile, a massive build-up of British, Canadian and American troops was taking place in Britain as a prelude to the invasion of Normandy. The Germans were successfully deceived as to the invasion's whereabouts, and it was launched on 6 June 1944, immortalised as D-Day. The logistical effort was vast – 7,000 vessels from landing craft to battleships providing fire support, together with over 11,000 aircraft; 150,000 soldiers landed on the first day. German defensive skills meant that advance was slow for the first two months, but the German front then collapsed and by September the Allies were in Belgium and Northern France. Fighting then got bogged down and a major advance was only resumed in February 1945, with the Rhine crossed in March. During 1944 Allied bombers had also won air superiority over Germany. US bombers concentrated on bombing German synthetic petrol plants (they converted coal into petrol) and the transport system; British bombers largely continued their area bombing campaign, with intermittent attacks on transport.

By now the only question was when the war would end. On 7 May 1945, after Hitler's suicide, German forces surrendered. Victory in Europe (VE) day was celebrated on 8 May. The Japanese war continued, and British troops recaptured Burma. The main action, however, was nearer Japan on which atomic bombs were dropped by American planes in early August. Japan surrendered on 14 August.

Running the war

In military histories of the war, the focus is usually on the battles and the generals who fought them. The reality, of course, was more complicated. Battles were fought because strategy dictated that actions took place in certain theatres of war. Strategy was the outcome of debate and disagreement. And for most of the war the resources to fight the battles were limited. How was strategy decided, and how did the resources to implement it come into being?

The machinery of government settled down between Churchill's accession to the prime ministership and early 1941, at which point it reached a more or less stable form. The main agency for actually running the war was the Chief of Staffs Committee (COS). Its role was summarised by Alan Brooke, who chaired the COS from early 1942 to the end of the war: 'to think out what theatres of war were necessary, what the allocation of forces should be for them and to prepare the plans for the operations in that theatre. All this work had to be done in close consultation with the Government, and Government approval had to be obtained on all major issues. Finally it was up to the COS to issue the actual orders or directives to the Commanders in each theatre.'[1] The COS reported directly to a committee of the War Cabinet, the Defence Committee (Operations), although in practice this often merged with the War Cabinet itself. The latter was a group of, usually, five of the most senior ministers, including Churchill. The War Cabinet, however, was responsible not just for sanctioning military strategy, but also for integrating it with political, financial and economic needs. In other words, it had many other responsibilities and rarely challenged Churchill on military issues. So 'close consultation with the government' meant with Churchill, who was also Minister of Defence and had his own strong opinions. However, in spite of many disagreements, there are very few cases of Churchill overriding the COS's views, although in the early stages of the war this may partly have been because exhaustion on their part led to their agreeing with him. The COS became more independent when Brooke came on to it. His willingness to stand up to Churchill led to huge rows but ensured that the latter's wilder flights of strategic fancy never took off (Fig 7.2).

There was one very important gap in the COS's span of control. This was strategic bombing. In theory it was as subject to COS control as any other sphere of

Figure 7.2   Prelude to Alamein: Churchill visited Cairo, in Egypt, in August 1942 where he and Alan Brooke (behind Churchill) reorganised the Middle East command structure. Jan Smuts is beside him; behind Smuts is Arthur Tedder, air commander in the Middle East. © Bettmann/CORBIS

operations: it was discussed, sometimes heatedly, by the COS and agreement of a kind was reached. But the reality was different: General John Kennedy, Director of Military Operations for most of the war, thought that 'the bombing policy . . . was settled almost entirely by the Prime Minister himself in consultation with Portal [the Chief of the Air Staff] and . . . try as we would, we never succeeded in bringing this important . . . ingredient of victory under their [the COS's] control'.[2]

There were, therefore, both strengths and weaknesses in Britain's central control of the war. However, there was one other great strength. This was the ability to link strategic need with production possibilities, and vice versa. The counterpart to the Defence Committee (Operations) was the Defence Committee (Supply), again a committee of the War Cabinet. This committee was mainly concerned with establishing principles. Various subsidiary bodies put these into operation, until in 1942 a Minister of Production was appointed with general oversight. The system broadly worked, although until May 1941 it was complicated because Max Beaverbrook was Minister of Aircraft Production. His abrasive personality stymied cooperation with others; it was claimed that he produced more planes at a vital time, although modern scholars suggest that he did not even manage that. Otherwise, key figures cooperated. The most important after Churchill was Ernest Bevin, Minister of Labour and a member of the War Cabinet. As time went by, labour became the factor of production that was scarcest, even more so than shipping or finance. As a result, Bevin became crucial in pointing out what it was,

People and politics: Winston Churchill

Winston Churchill regularly tops the poll as the greatest Briton ever. He was an MP for 64 years and held offices of Cabinet rank for a total of 28 years. A survey of his career has to mention many things: his brilliant oratory; his dynamism; his constant flow of new ideas; his ability to discern the really big issues; and his humour. It also needs to mention the less positive aspects: his impetuosity; his occasional spectacular misjudgements; and his colossal egoism.

Elected as a Conservative MP in 1900, Churchill 'crossed the floor' of the House of Commons – an expression meaning to change parties without an intervening election – in 1904 to become a Liberal, as a result of his disapproval of tariff reform. He quickly rose to become Lloyd George's first lieutenant in pushing through the Liberal welfare reforms. In 1912 he became First Lord of the Admiralty. When war began he supported the unsuccessful Gallipoli campaign, and as a result of its failure became marginalised and left the government in 1916. Brought back by Lloyd George, he served in various offices in the Coalition between 1917 and 1922. By now the radicalism of his initial conversion to Liberalism had left him. Churchill was one of the chief exponents of intervention in Russia against the Bolsheviks and in 1926, when Chancellor of the Exchequer, he supported a hard line during the General Strike. Preceding this he had changed parties once more, moving back to the Conservatives, but his changes of allegiance and association with Lloyd George left many Conservatives mistrusting him. In the 1930s this was compounded by two major misjudgements. One was his taking the lead in the Conservative revolt over Baldwin's India policy. The other was his attempt to derail Baldwin's quick action in forcing Edward VIII to abdicate. In both cases few historians would now defend Churchill's views, but whether right or wrong, his views antagonised the solid centre of the Conservative Party. This made it more difficult for Churchill's arguments for further rearmament and a firmer line against the dictators to have any effect, and he was out of office from 1929 to 1939. By the late 1930s his glittering early career seemed to have come to a full stop. A biography of him up to 1939 is aptly subtitled *A Study in Failure*.

At the outbreak of war, however, Churchill's long experience and anti-appeasement record led to an invitation to join Chamberlain's Cabinet, once again as First Lord of the Admiralty, in a limited broadening of its political base. After the débâcle of Norway weakened Chamberlain's position, Churchill was invited to become Prime Minister. In spite of his right-wing reputation, Labour supported him because he was associated with the attempt to build a united political front against fascism.

As with all his roles, Churchill threw himself wholeheartedly into his latest one: Prime Minister of a beleaguered and isolated Britain at war. Here both his ability to adjust his attitudes according to his role and his ability to see the big issues came to the fore. He stepped back from any great involvement with the home front, allowing Clement Attlee, the Labour leader, to make the running in developing a raft of left-leaning social policies for post-war implementation. To Churchill, winning the war was more important than left or right in domestic affairs. He fought tirelessly to involve America in the war: his reliance on America has been questioned (see main text, 'Friends and allies'), but US involvement was arguably the most effective single way to victory. He also understood the importance of having a mechanism for matching production with military and civilian needs (see main text, 'Running the war').

His strategic insight is more questionable, although again he got some big things right. He realised that uprisings in continental Europe would never overthrow Hitler and gave resistance movements encouragement but only limited resources. From late 1941 he realised that strategic bombing was not a war-winner but continued to give it a high priority, probably largely to boost domestic morale and to strengthen his hand in negotiations with Russia. He realised the importance of Ultra (see p. 134) and gave it practically unlimited resources. But he was weaker in his assessment of purely military issues. He was obsessed with Norway (as was Hitler), although in reality it was a strategic dead-end. Furthermore, he was constantly overoptimistic in estimating the scope of operations which Britain could undertake, the disaster in Greece perhaps being the most serious example of this. After 1941 Alan Brooke was able to curb Churchill's scattergun approach and keep him focused on the Mediterranean Strategy and, later, on the Normandy landings. Churchill had many great qualities, but to suggest, as some do, that he was also a strategic genius is absurd.

Churchill's greatest achievement was to be the irrepressible symbol of British resistance, to the British themselves and to the outside world. His speeches, freighted with memorable phrases, helped to keep up morale. He was almost tireless, remarkable for a man who was in his late sixties when he became Prime Minister. His conversation was brilliant and his character often endearing, helping to bind people's loyalty to him even when other aspects of his behaviour infuriated them. In 1941 Brooke recorded an evening at Chequers, the Prime Minister's country residence: Churchill 'trotted round and round the hall giving occasional little skips to the sound of the gramophone. On each lap near the fireplace he stopped to release some priceless quotation or thought.'[3] To Brooke and others, these characteristics made up for the times when Churchill was rude, selfish and overbearing. And in spite of these less savoury characteristics, Churchill would listen to other opinions and to rational argument. His wartime decisions were not a matter of whim.

The final years of Churchill's political career were an anti-climax. His main achievement as Leader of the Opposition from 1945–1951 was to allow younger men to modernise the Conservative Party even though he often disapproved. In 1951–1955, as Prime Minister, he clung to power, depriving Anthony Eden, for long the heir apparent, of the prime ministership until the latter was a sick man (see Chapter 11 box, 'Anthony Eden and Suez'). Churchill was knighted in 1953, but unlike most other former prime ministers he refused a peerage and remained in the Commons until 1964, as MP for Woodford which he represented for 40 years.

and what it was not, possible to produce, while the Ministry of Labour produced labour supply forecasts which allowed a degree of forward thinking.

The organised control mechanisms of the Second World War contrast with the more ad hoc ways in which things developed in the First World War. Although at its peak the war effort in that war was massive, that in the Second World War had to be greater, for longer, and under more adverse circumstances. The ability to match production with strategic needs – even if in the case of strategic bombing these were exaggerated – was therefore a major bonus. It contrasts sharply with Germany, where only from 1941 were the beginnings made of any rational planning of war production. And, however much Churchill interfered in military strategy, the successful mechanism for running the war reflects great credit on his ability to see the big issues.

Effective methods for deciding on the allocation of resources would not be much use if the resources were lacking, and many of those resources had to come from overseas. In addition to food, there were many other essential imports: cotton and wool, steel (as Britain was short of iron ore), specialised machinery of all kinds and, increasingly, aircraft and munitions as American production of these increased. Most important was oil. Road transport used petrol, and was important, although railways carried far more freight traffic than today. But most of all, petrol and oil were needed for the RAF's planes and the Royal Navy's ships. It was Britain's allies, and the Empire, which provided many of those resources.

Friends and allies

When war broke out, Britain and France were not at war alone. Poland was soon defeated and dismembered by Germany and Russia, but numbers of Polish and Czech airmen, fought along with the RAF. Later, Polish prisoners captured by the Russians were freed when Russia was forced into war, and Polish ground forces reformed and fought with Allied armies. After the German occupation of much of Europe, the occupied countries contributed fighting men, merchant shipping and some naval vessels to the war effort. Foremost amongst these were de Gaulle's Free French forces. Churchill supported de Gaulle strongly against the Americans, who were much more lukewarm. De Gaulle repaid British support with rudeness and ingratitude.

To these allies were added the countries of the Empire. India and the colonies had no choice: they were included in the British declaration of war. The Dominions were now autonomous, however, unlike in the First World War: all declared war, although South Africa only after a change of government – Jan Smuts, the new Prime Minister, became an important source of advice to Churchill. By and large, 'Britain' and 'British' as used here include Empire forces. But in reality Empire troops played an important part in all the big campaigns except France in 1940: South African, Australian, New Zealand and Indian troops in North Africa; the last three also in the Far East; Canadian troops in the 1944–1945 campaign in Western Europe; and crews from all nationalities in the RAF. At sea, the Royal Canadian Navy provided escorts for a large proportion of Atlantic convoys, while the Australian and New Zealand navies were engaged against the Japanese.

In the long run, Britain's most important ally was the USA. America quickly bore the main burden of the war against Japan. However, it was not until the later stages of the campaign in Europe that America's contribution in the land war against Germany exceeded that of Britain. Russia's contribution to the war was, of course, incalculable, but she was wholly engaged in fighting the war on the Eastern front. Her direct contribution to Britain's war effort was nil, and Russian contributions to allied strategy were largely confined to demands for resources or for the rapid invasion of France. Later in the war there was some coordination of offensives, but there was nothing like the close and constant cooperation seen between Britain and America.

Although the military contribution of allies was significant, and in the case of America and Russia vital, they were also essential for the provision of resources. In the First War, Britain's continued large exports and the capital she held abroad could provide her with foreign currency for imports, although even then Britain needed to borrow from America. But the demands of the Second World War were much greater and Britain's overseas capital much diminished. Before the fall of France, the policy was to attempt to keep up exports, but after the summer of 1940 they fell away. Britain could also run up debts abroad. Most Empire and Commonwealth countries still used sterling as their trading currency and kept their reserves in sterling, called 'sterling balances'. Australia and New Zealand allowed Britain to accumulate debts in the form of additional balances and paid for their troops serving overseas. South Africa gave some financial help. Meanwhile, India, and the other Empire countries still ruled by Britain, had less choice in the matter and their sterling balances accumulated whether they liked it or not, as did Egypt's, where much British wartime spending was concentrated. India and Egypt became the main holders of sterling balances.

However, the sterling balances did not pay for the scarcest goods of which Britain had the most need – those that came from the Americas. American goods were desirable because only the USA had the technical resources to provide vast quantities of munitions; in addition, the USA and other American countries which used dollars provided the nearest sources of supply for oil and foodstuffs, a vital fact given the shortage of shipping. Canada, the main dollar country after the USA, was a major source of imports, including war stores such as trucks. Canada allowed Britain to pay for many of its Canadian imports with sterling, which from the Canadian point of view meant accepting a debt in a foreign currency. But Britain still had to pay for many goods in Canadian dollars and by early 1942 these were running out, at which point Canada made a gift to Britain of C$1 billion, or about £220 million.

The Canadian dollar shortage could be overcome by Canadian generosity; the American shortage was not so simple. Various American laws of the 1930s, intended to keep America out of a European war, prevented American firms extending loans to non-Americans at war who wished to buy American goods. Goods could only be bought on a 'cash and carry' basis. So Britain had to find dollars or gold, the universally acceptable medium of exchange. The slow pace of military preparation in 1939 and 1940 was, in part, because of the need to husband dollars and gold. When Churchill came to office, oil, munitions and steel were imported freely from America, at the cost of rapidly running down Britain's foreign currency reserves. By the end of 1940 they were virtually exhausted.

At that point, Britain became financially dependent upon America. The mechanism, which evaded America's restrictive laws, was Lend Lease. America would 'lend' Britain munitions, food and other goods, for an initially unspecified 'consideration'. The Lend Lease bill became law in March 1941 and, with a few hiccups, Britain's problems of finding overseas currency virtually ceased for the duration of the war. Equally important, Britain had access to the products of the world's largest and most technologically advanced nation, whose munitions production was increasing rapidly. Lend Lease was hymned by Churchill as the 'most unsordid act in history'.[4] Recent historiography has often been more critical, and the many ramifications of the American alliance have been most strongly criticised by John Charmley. His view is provocative but forces us to examine carefully the simple Churchillian narrative of American generosity – a narrative which legitimates Churchill's own role in soliciting American support. Charmley's arguments can be summarised as follows. Churchill's strategy from the moment he came into power was predicated on an American alliance. But there is no hard evidence that Roosevelt ever planned to enter the war. That America eventually did was due to Pearl Harbour and Hitler's stupidity. Rather, a key American concern was to ensure that the British Empire was weakened, as a trading entity and more generally. In order to achieve this, Britain's own dollar holdings were strictly monitored so that Britain could remain in economic thrall to America after the war. Furthermore, Charmley suggests that the American dislike of de Gaulle hampered British attempts to forge a post-war policy in Europe.

Certainly the American President, Franklin D. Roosevelt, and other American policy-makers were anti-imperialist and, in addition, had a rather exaggerated idea of the value of imperial preference (see Chapter 5, 'Empire and Commonwealth'). Behind those beliefs lay both principled ideas about self-determination and the value of free trade and unprincipled ones about gaining greater access to American manufactures in Empire markets. And some fairly sordid American actions took place in late 1940, culminating in the sending of an American cruiser to South Africa to collect all available gold. The original 'consideration' for Lend Lease was to be the winding-up of imperial preference, although when agreement was finally reached in 1942 this was watered down. (By now Lend Lease was called Mutual Aid, as it also involved Britain paying many of the costs of US forces stationed in British possessions.)

The watering down of American demands points to weaknesses in Charmley's argument. In part, they depend on a particular reading of Roosevelt's character and aims. Roosevelt was undoubtedly devious, but most commentators would agree that he also had a deep-rooted concern for liberal democratic principles and ideals, and a justified fear that precipitate action would jeopardise any help to Britain at all. In September 1939 an opinion poll found that just two and a half per cent of Americans supported American entry into the war on the Allied side, while 30 per cent thought that America should have nothing to do with either side and almost 40 per cent that goods should be sold equally to either side on a cash and carry basis. (Fortunately only 0.2 per cent thought that America should favour Germany.) Although opinions shifted towards the Allies as the war went on and Germany's aggression became more blatant, it was a mountain to climb, and opposition to American involvement was fostered by a large isolationist lobby. So Roosevelt had to show to the American people that pro-British actions such as Lend Lease had some pay-off for the United States.

One possible extension of Charmley's underlying argument is that, since Britain was so weak in 1940, the best course of action would have been to make peace with Hitler then – a course of action discussed within the government when Churchill came to office. The late Alan Clark is one writer who has suggested this. Behind it lies the idea that Britain and the West were landed with one appalling dictatorship, namely Soviet Russia, rather than another, Nazi Germany. The quick answers to it are that Russia remained appalling while Stalin was alive, subsequently becoming unpleasant but not genocidal; and that arguably Hitler, with his probably limitless ambitions, was a far more deadly neighbour than Russia ever became.

What is true is that importing lavishly from America from the summer of 1940 – that is, before Lend Lease was arranged – ran a major risk by assuming that ultimately America would help before Britain's dollar reserves ran out. However, it was also a period when invasion threatened and munitions were urgently needed. If Britain had tried to go it alone, it could have eked out its dollars for a while, but only with a greatly diminished war effort. And if in those circumstances Britain had still held out and Russia and America still come in, it would have meant that Britain was a junior partner from the start. As it was, Britain was remarkably successful in imposing on the Americans her own strategic conception of the war (see box, 'Alan Brooke and the Mediterranean Strategy').

Military affairs: Alan Brooke and the Mediterranean Strategy

Brooke was possibly the most important wartime personality on the British side after Churchill yet receives only a passing mention in many histories. A gunner in the First World War, he became Chief of the Imperial General Staff, that is chief of the army staff (see main text, 'Running the war') in December 1941, replacing Sir John Dill. Dill was a brilliant soldier but his caution grated on Churchill. Brooke was also cautious but better able to stand up to Churchill's tirades. He was intelligent, dynamic and irascible. The army held him in awe, even the bumptious Montgomery deferring to him.

Brooke was one of the chief exponents of the 'Mediterranean Strategy', whose value has been much debated. It started from the fact that the British were in Egypt and had built up large forces there. They were there initially for strategic reasons which are often forgotten. These were to defend the Suez Canal and the oil which flowed from Iran and Iraq. After Italy entered the war, the canal became valueless as the Mediterranean was closed anyway except to the heavily armed convoys which supplied Malta. But the successful 1940–1941 campaign against the Italians in North Africa ignited new hopes among military planners – to clear the enemy out of North Africa altogether and use it as a springboard to attack Southern Europe. The arrival of the *Afrika Korps*, however, made this aspiration much more difficult to fulfil.

▶

Brooke took over and developed this strategy, which chimed in with Churchill's own preconceptions. Both hesitated to meet the full strength of the German army in Northern France. For Churchill this aversion was atavistic, born of his memories of the carnage of the Western front in the First War. For Brooke it was more reasoned. Germany's interior lines of communication meant she could quickly switch Eastern front divisions westwards in the event of an invasion. The Allied problem in invading Northern France would be to build up forces quickly enough to meet this threat. To Brooke, therefore, it made sense to engage and tie up as much of the German army as possible elsewhere. An invasion of Italy would achieve this.

Brooke and Churchill faced bitter battles with the American chiefs of staff, who proposed a frontal attack across the English Channel. In 1942 Roosevelt resolved the situation, by insisting on the invasion of Vichy, North Africa. The American chiefs then reluctantly went along with the 1943 invasion of Italy.

Military historians have written books on the correctness or otherwise of this strategy. On the one hand, it was clearly not decisive in its impact on the German army, accounting for only a fraction of the casualties the latter suffered in Russia. On the other hand, its total military impact was still considerable. A measure of the German losses in North Africa was their nickname for the final surrender in May 1943 – 'Tunisgrad', echoing the Stalingrad disaster of a few months earlier. Italy was then knocked out of the war, greatly reducing the navy's commitment in the Mediterranean. And over the whole Italian campaign Germany suffered around 450,000 casualties. A recent analysis by two American military historians, Williamson Murray and Allan Millett, concluded that the British view was correct. The Allies could not have successfully invaded France earlier than 1944.

Brooke was made a Field Marshal in 1944 and became Viscount Alanbrooke in 1946. Typically, Churchill gave him barely a mention in his six volume memoirs of the war.

American attempts to weaken the British Empire were remarkably unsuccessful. Of course, the Empire was weakened because post-war Britain was economically weak, but who believes that Britain either could have held or would have wished to hold on to the Empire in the post-war years of European decolonisation? Charmley's suggestion that Britain lost opportunities to influence post-war Europe is interesting, although as he points out, this was as much because of Churchill himself as American dislike of de Gaulle. And the latter's incredible prickliness and the continued post-war unwillingness of British politicians to involve themselves in Europe (see Chapter 11) suggest that American wartime policies can have made little ultimate difference.

In the later stages of the war Churchill did become more and more preoccupied with the future of Europe. His preoccupation stemmed from uncertainties about Britain's other main ally, Russia. As Russia started to reconquer territory, it seemed to Churchill vital to define post-war responsibilities. However, his and American attempts to gain some influence over the future of the countries of Eastern Europe failed, as Russia was soon to dominate all its European neighbours. In retrospect it seems clear that this result was more or less inevitable, although Russia had not planned its precise post-war strategy in advance. When the Allies met at Yalta in February 1945, Stalin agreed to free elections – and may have done so genuinely, believing that they would lead to Communist governments. It was only after he was proved wrong that the Soviets turned to control by force and intimidation.

In relation to Germany itself, Russia seemed genuinely open to the notion of some form of joint control after the war, although agreement on what form this should take was never reached. However, Yalta did see military lines of demarcation agreed. Ultimately these were to solidify into a political division, but at the time this was not the intention.

The balance sheet of war

Britain's military prowess and her leaders' strategic judgement have been the subject of much debate. Some of the main campaigns and leaders are discussed in the boxes. What is the overall verdict?

The first seven months of war, the Phoney War, are often written off as the last gasp of Chamberlain's worn-out government: a period during which Britain failed to rearm vigorously or turn its economy over fully to war production. While there is some truth in this, it is also a judgement based on hindsight. The argument for limiting military action was that Britain could not turn over entirely to a war economy, because she still needed to export to keep up an inflow of foreign currency, necessary to buy food and raw materials. The French army, which was considered to be the premier European army, would with the help of the BEF prevent the German army from attacking west-wards. Italy would continue to be appeased. And Germany would be crippled through naval blockade, which in the First World War had had a good claim to be one of the main agencies of victory, and bombing which was considered the new war-winning weapon. This argument now seems foolish and overoptimistic, and to some extent it was. But it seems so now because Germany won a smashing victory over the French army which was neither predicted nor predictable.

The German breakthrough was achieved by a narrow margin. If it had not been achieved, and French and British forces had held on to a continuous line in Northern France, then judgements on the Phoney War period might be very different. However, once the breakthrough had happened French strategy was revealed as hopelessly flawed, while the British, culpably, had never discovered how flawed it was. The French had no strategic reserve with which to counter-attack the German forces. French divisions were tied up in the Maginot line in North-Eastern France or strung out along the rest of the lengthy front.

Defeat in France was followed by a major defensive victory, the Battle of Britain. It shows that pre-war rearmament was not always inadequate, since the technology was conceived and developed before the war. And the campaigns against Italian forces in North Africa were a brilliant and often forgotten victory. The subsequent decision in early 1941 to aid the Greeks was a serious mistake for which the responsibility must be shared: politicians urged it and senior military commanders agreed. It, and the subsequent campaigns in Iraq and Syria, hampered an effective attack against Rommel. The Iraq/Syria campaigns did, however, have a rationale which is often forgotten: oil. At that time Iraq and Persia, as Iran was then commonly called, were the only significant Middle Eastern oil producers, with the most important refinery complex at Abadan on the Persian Gulf. Middle Eastern oil was not, by mid-1941, being shipped to Britain because of the heavy cost in terms of tanker tonnage, but Abadan was the main source of supply for North Africa itself and for India. Iraqi oil on its own was not vital but Iraq's proximity to Persia made it too important to ignore, while Syria was a possible threat to both Egypt and Persia.

Aspects of British military performance have often been criticised, but the navy, justly, has been criticised least. It was integral to the war effort. In the early stages its value was largely confined to its skill in evacuating the army, from Norway, France, Greece and Crete. But even in this period there were positives – the sinking of a large proportion of Germany's destroyer fleet in Norway and the crippling of the Italian navy in 1940–1941. Whereas in the First World War the superiority of Britain's fleet led to extreme caution lest Britain's dominance be threatened, in the Second World War a much weaker fleet was more boldly handled, since risks had to be taken to achieve anything. The Royal Navy's biggest disaster, the sinking of the *Repulse* and *Prince of Wales* by the Japanese in December 1941, occurred because a political decision was taken by the government, before war broke out with Japan, to send them to the Far East. It was a final attempt to continue the policy of deterring the Japanese by a show of strength. It failed but, unlike Greece, it was probably a worthwhile gamble.

The most cogent criticism directed against the army was that, as in the First War, it was inflexible. British army training emphasised strict adherence to orders; by contrast, German troops down to the level of the private soldier were trained to act autonomously in a crisis. The contrast is strange given the self-image of the British as independent-minded. In Egypt and Libya in 1941–1942 tactical rigidity allied to poor equipment – British tank design was notoriously bad – helps to explain British failures. When Montgomery took over the Eighth Army in Egypt, however, Britain had built up a large quantitative advantage in equipment and numbers. Montgomery deserves credit for its effective use. Victory at Alamein was one result, and his techniques then became the lynchpin of British tactical doctrine. British forces ground their way through North Africa, Italy and North-West Europe supported by intensive air operations and concentrated artillery fire. The method was blunt but, with the increasingly lavish munitions supply made possible by Lend Lease, it compensated for deficiencies in infantry training and was relatively economical in terms of the lives of the attackers.

One major British achievement was 'Ultra', the codename for high-grade signals intelligence, much of it provided from interception of enemy signals encoded on the Enigma machine. In the North Atlantic, Ultra enabled the Allies to route convoys around U-boat packs and drastically cut losses. But victory in the Atlantic battle was achieved by a variety of means (see earlier box, 'The Battle of the Atlantic'): if Ultra had not

Figure 7.3   Prelude to victory: American built Sherman tanks of Britain's 2nd Army advance on Bremen a few days before the German surrender. © CORBIS

existed, the Allies could have stepped up their efforts to defeat the submarines – for instance, by introducing more long-distance aircraft – and possibly might have had to slow down the build-up of troops for Normandy; but they would not have lost the war (Fig 7.3). Ultra helped significantly in other campaigns, particularly in the Mediterranean, but cannot be seen as decisive.

Ultimately, what was decisive from 1942 was one thing: the massive Allied superiority in every weapon of war and in the lifeblood of modern war, oil. The Allies made mistakes and launched wasteful initiatives, of which strategic bombing was the most egregious, but they could afford these mistakes. Hitler made even more, and Germany could not afford them. Up to 1942, however, it is possible to argue that Hitler could have won. Therefore, the importance given in national mythology to Britain's fight for survival in 1940–1941 is justified. By her existence in those years, and by her agency in bringing America into the war, Britain ensured Hitler's ultimate defeat. And in 1940–1941 she and the British Empire did this virtually alone.

Notes

1. Quoted in Danchev, A. and Todman, D. (eds), *War Diaries of Field Marshal Lord Alanbrooke 1939–1945* (London: Weidenfeld and Nicolson, 2001), p. 648.
2. Kennedy, J., *The Business of War* (London: Hutchinson, 1957).
3. Quoted in Danchev and Todman, *War Diaries*, p. 194.
4. Quoted in Howlett, P., 'The war-time economy, 1939–45' in Floud and McCloskey, *Cambridge Economic History* (see Chapter 1), Vol. 3.

Further reading

Addison, P., 'Churchill and the Price of Victory' in Tiratsoo, N. (ed.), *From Blitz to Blair: A New History of Britain since 1939* (London: Weidenfeld and Nicolson, 1997) is shrewd on the Charmley thesis; for a summary of this, see Charmley, J., 'Churchill and the American Alliance' in 'Churchill in the Twenty-First Century' (Proceedings of a Conference held at the Institute of Historical Research), *Transactions of the Royal Historical Society*, 6th Series, Vol. XI (2001). Hastings, M., *Bomber Command* (London: Michael Joseph, 1979) is a readable and critical study. Howarth, S. and Law, D. (eds), *The Battle of the Atlantic: 1939–1945* (London: Greenhill, 1994) is authoritative. Murray, W. and Millett, A., *A War To Be Won* (London: Harvard University Press, 2000) is an excellent military history. See Overy, R., *The Battle* (London: Penguin, 2000) for a succinct study of the Battle of Britain and Overy, R., *Why the Allies Won* (London: Cape, 1995) for outstanding analysis.

Other sources: Bell, C., 'The "Singapore Strategy" and the Deterrence of Japan: Winston Churchill, the Admiralty and the Dispatch of Force Z', *English Historical Review*, Vol. CXVI, pp. 604–633 (2001); Bidford and Graham, *Firepower* (see Chapter 3); Casey, S., *Cautious Crusade: Franklin D. Roosevelt, American Public Opinion and the War Against Nazi Germany* (Oxford: Oxford University Press, 2001); Charmley, J., *Churchill: The End of Glory* (London: Hodder and Stoughton, 1993); French, D., *Raising Churchill's Army: the British Army and the War against Germany 1919–1945* (Oxford: Oxford University Press, 2000); Howlett, W., 'New Light Through Old Windows: a New Perspective on the British Economy in the Second World War', *LSE Working Papers in Economic History*, No. 2/92 (1992); Kennedy, *Rise and Fall* (see Chapter 5); Lane, A. and Temperley, H. (eds), *The Rise and Fall of the Grand Alliance 1941–1945* (London: Macmillan, 1995); Reynolds, D. *et al.* (eds), *Allies at War* (London: Macmillan, 1994); Sayers, R., *Financial Policy 1939–1945* (London: HMSO and Longman Green, 1956); Sherwood, R., *The White House Papers of Harry L. Hopkins* (London: Eyre and Spottiswoode, 1948); Terraine, *Business in Great Waters* (see Chapter 3); Webster, C. and Frankland, N., *The Strategic Air Offensive against Germany 1939–1945*, Vols 1–3 (London: HMSO, 1961).

Chapter 8

THE SECOND WORLD WAR: POLITICS AND SOCIETY

Politics and planning

Initially the Chamberlain government soldiered on, broadened by the addition of Churchill and Anthony Eden, who had left the government in 1938 and was seen as an anti-appeaser. Neither Labour nor the independent Liberals would serve under Chamberlain, however. The government's war strategy, discussed in Chapter 7, had a rationale but gave the impression of complacency, which was fatal when the Norway débâcle occurred. The dramatic scenes in the House of Commons on 7 and 8 May 1940 have often been recounted: Leo Amery, a long-standing Conservative critic of Chamberlain, quoting Cromwell's 'in the name of God, go'; the aged Lloyd George asking Chamberlain to give an example of sacrifice; the division on Labour's motion of censure in which, although Chamberlain still had a majority, 40 Conservatives voted against him and 80 abstained – a massive rebuff.

Chamberlain resigned. To succeed him, the choice was between Churchill and Lord Halifax, the Foreign Secretary. Churchill wanted the job, Halifax did not, and his position in the Lords was an added complication. The old government had technically been National but Churchill's new one really was, with a substantial Labour presence, including two out of the five in the War Cabinet, and Liberal representation. Ironically, the MPs who were initially least reconciled to Churchill were the Chamberlainite majority of the Conservatives. Chamberlain himself remained for the time being in the Cabinet and loyally supported Churchill, which helped ease the transition. Gravely ill, Chamberlain soon retired and Churchill took over the leadership of the Conservatives. He was to lead the party he had once deserted for a further 15 years (Fig. 8.1).

With all the parties in coalition, the war saw an electoral truce. There were challenges to it, particularly from the Common Wealth Party. Common Wealth was founded in 1942 by an ex-Liberal MP, Sir Richard Acland, with a socialist programme, including widespread nationalisation. Three MPs were elected at by-elections. Common Wealth's temporary success was partly due, no doubt, to the British electorate's hobby of punishing incumbent governments at by-elections for no particular reason besides the fact that they are there. But it was also a protest against the government's lukewarm reaction to the Beveridge Report, discussed below, and an indication of the shift in popular feeling.

Clearly the truce did not mean complete harmony between the disparate parties in government. There were, however, only a few real ructions. This was partly because

ALL BEHIND YOU, WINSTON

Figure 8.1   A 1940 David Low cartoon in the *Evening Standard* symbolised national unity: to Churchill's left are Attlee, Bevin and Morrison – all Labour men. Courtesy of Solo Syndication/Associated Newspapers

Churchill did little to oppose the development of left-leaning policies for the future. But it was also because the war had changed national perceptions, as the Common Wealth successes indicated. Conservatives realised that they could not resist these changing perceptions and sometimes shared them.

Discussion of permanent social and governmental change became formalised in 1941 with a Cabinet Committee on Reconstruction, followed by a Ministry of Reconstruction in 1942. But in practice discussion proceeded among many bodies – political parties, interest and pressure groups, the relevant ministries and individuals acting more or less on their own account. Chief among the latter was Sir William Beveridge. Beveridge was a senior civil servant turned academic administrator, of Liberal sympathies and egomaniacal tendencies. Ostensibly, he chaired a subcommittee of the Reconstruction Committee. He used this as a vehicle for his own ideas, expressed in his famous report on 'Social Insurance and Allied Services'. Although this recommended a free health service, discussed in Chapter 9, the detail in it concerned the cash benefits obtained through state insurance – unemployment, old-age pensions and others.

Beveridge was an adept publicist, which helped to make a report on such apparently unexciting topics into a best seller and ensured that its main recommendations became widely known. The report was published in December 1942, a timely moment, just after Alamein, when the British people could begin to sense victory and were looking for a reward after three years of shortages and sacrifice. Much in Beveridge was not actually new. Many people were already covered by state insurance for unemployment and old-age pensions, although only the old and now inadequate Lloyd George scheme was available for those over 70. Beveridge suggested that these schemes become more comprehensive, and added family allowances as well as a number of lesser benefits. Finally, he insisted that benefits be at least at subsistence level, to minimise the numbers of those who had to fall back on the Poor Law. Benefits were to be financed by the traditional method of flat-rate insurance, to which workers and employers contributed, the government adding a further contribution (family allowances would not be dependent on insurance, however). Beveridge's scheme was, therefore, potentially redistributive in that benefits were likely to be evenly shared over the population but income taxpayers, who were better off, would contribute to the government's share of the costs. On the other hand, the extent of redistribution was limited because all employees made some contribution, while the flat-rate principle meant that payments were by no means generous. This was explicitly designed to encourage the better off to make their own private provision, and in particular to encourage the continuation of private saving for old age.

The Beveridge Plan was one – very important – area where there were different party reactions. Although the plan was by no means wildly socialistic, the Conservative Party was lukewarm and Churchill would not endorse it. As a result, in 1943 backbench Labour MPs launched a massive parliamentary rebellion against the government over it. Bowing to the wind, Churchill made Lord Woolton, previously the Minister for Food and technically non-party (he was to become a liberal-minded Conservative), Minister of Reconstruction. On behalf of the government, Woolton endorsed the main thrust of Beveridge in a White Paper of 1944. It was a blueprint for post-war social insurance but came too late to save the Conservatives from being labelled as uncaring.

One vital predicate on which Beveridge relied needs separate discussion. This was the assumption of full employment, meaning in practice a low level of unemployment by historic standards. This enabled Beveridge to claim that his scheme would not be too expensive. Given the interwar experience of high and continuing employment, how was Beveridge able to legitimise this crucial assumption?

The answer lies with John Maynard Keynes. Keynes' theory that government spending, financed by borrowing, could soak up unemployment had a corollary. The corollary was to make Keynes' ideas central to government finance during the war, and to give Keynes himself enormous prestige. As a result, his ideas on the treatment of unemployment, scouted before the war, rapidly became not just respectable but accepted by many as tantamount to a law of nature.

The corollary was simple. Keynes' theory rested on the belief that economic depressions were caused by a deficiency of demand, due to a tendency to save too much. If the government borrowed and then spent the money, it would absorb these savings and translate them into demand. In wartime the problem was the opposite. Government spending was virtually unlimited and, added to private spending, was inflationary, since demand would exceed the economy's capacity to supply goods. This was at the root of the inflation of the First World War. The remedy – the corollary of Keynes' remedy for depression – was first for the government to maximise its revenue through taxation and second, since there were political limits to taxation even in wartime, to minimise private spending and maximise private saving. The 1941 Budget was the first to fully deploy Keynes' ideas. Taxation went up to unprecedented levels on higher incomes and on the few items of consumption still in reasonable supply, notably alcohol and tobacco. At the same time, there was massive publicity, and moral pressure, to encourage saving and to make 'voluntary' contributions to finance the war – competitions between towns to raise money for aircraft building being a striking example.

Keynes' wartime policies helped to peg inflation at far lower levels than in the First War. This success helped his remedy against depression to become intellectually respectable. Respectability was further aided because the failure of appeasement called into question other interwar assumptions, such as the belief in the inevitability of unemployment. Mindful also of the public demand for firm statements about post-war employment policy, in 1944 the government issued a White Paper on employment policy, accepting as 'one of their primary aims and responsibilities . . . the maintenance of a high and stable level of employment after the war'.[1]

Like employment policy, discussion of post-war education achieved considerable political agreement. It was carried out under the aegis of R. A. Butler, another progressive Conservative, and the resulting Education Act was passed in 1944. The leaving age was to be raised to 15, as had been planned before the war. There was a consensus that all children should go to a specialised secondary school rather than simply continue after 11 in a separate section of their elementary school. There was also a consensus that fees should be abolished for the 20 per cent or so of children who proceeded to grammar or, in some cases, technical schools and continued after 14. Behind these consensuses lay a variety of factors. One was an emphasis on abolishing obstacles to meritorious children getting a grammar or technical school education. This received strong support from education professionals among whom 'national efficiency', that old Edwardian concern, was still alive under different names, and who were concerned that 'national intelligence' was not being sufficiently developed. Civil servants, often a source of caution, realised that the country's mood called for substantial changes and therefore accepted a bill which appeared radical. The churches were also players. An acceptable compromise was reached over integrating the many church-supported schools into the state system in return for a degree of Christian instruction in all schools, although achieving this took up a huge amount of Butler's time.

The 1944 Act did not specify what type of post-11 education should be used by local authorities, but in practice most adapted their existing system. The result was 'tripartitism', in which children would be assessed and assigned to 'modern' (later usually called secondary modern) or grammar schools at 11. Since most professionals believed that there were limits to the intellectual development of the majority of children, they supported selection. In theory, between the ages of 11 and 13 children had the possibility of moving between the two or to the third type, technical schools, but in practice this did not happen much. The actual, rather than official, amount of change was quite limited. Access to grammar schools was widened, but not much because before the war the fees of poorer children had been completely or partially waived. Eventually, good quality modern schools did appear but this depended on resources not legislation. The content of schooling was not essentially changed.

Much of the optimism about the possibilities of post-war change was born of a belief in planning. Not for nothing did Beveridge call his own proposals a 'plan'. Planning had come into vogue in the 1930s as a catch-all word for desirable ways of organising the Britain of the future. It was accepted by most of the left, and many Liberals, as well as by reforming Conservatives such as Harold Macmillan. Political and Economic Planning (PEP), an influential pressure group, was set up in 1931 and produced a number of reports. Its membership ranged across the political spectrum and included academics and progressive businessmen. Further to the left, the apparent successes of Russian industrialisation in the 1930s had strengthened support for central economic planning. Apart from being a technique for realising social and economic change in general, planning was also thought of as the correct way forward for urban and rural development. This was not new – outside the military, the word 'planning' had first been used in connection with housing development. However, wartime thinking, encapsulated in the Town and Country Planning Act of 1944, envisaged far greater control over the physical face of Britain. The planning of cities would ensure both efficiency and a greatly improved urban environment. Planning the countryside would ensure areas for urban recreation and – although this was only legislated for in 1947 – the safeguarding of land for agricultural production.

Women and families

Over the last 30 years there has been a major shift in the perception of women's lives in the Second World War. In 1974 Arthur Marwick suggested that the war accelerated change in women's lives and consciousness. Since then, however, historians have poured cold water on his ideas. If the war did have effects, it was not those which Marwick had suggested.

As with the First World War, there was a big change in women's experience of paid work, and as with the previous war, most of those changes were temporary. Large numbers of jobs were created in munitions, but they were mainly semi-skilled and involved no progression. The majority of wartime women workers – over 70 per cent – had actually been employed before the war, since most unmarried working-class women did paid work as a matter of course. For many the war simply prolonged a temporary period of employment which they would normally have expected to leave on marriage. So there was continuity, but also disruption because hours were long and the work might involve moving and living in dreary lodgings. To many women, war work was often boring and certainly arduous, and they had no desire to continue it after the war.

Even more disruption was caused to many women and their families by evacuation. Evacuation was born of the intense, and in hindsight exaggerated, pre-war fear of bombing. Elaborate plans were prepared and activated on 1 September 1939, even before war broke out. Over 800,000 unaccompanied children, and over half a million mothers with pre-school children, left cities for small towns and country areas, to be billeted on the inhabitants. The plans were elaborate, but little thought had been given to the human side and stories abounded of long train journeys in carriages which, as many then did, lacked lavatories.

To the inevitable culture clash involved in the meeting of city and country and, quite often, working class and middle class was added the trauma of upheaval for children, many of whom had never been away from home before. As a result, a mythology developed in some receiving areas. Quite how widespread the mythology itself was remains unclear, but it certainly coloured both contemporary and later accounts of evacuation. In this mythology, lice-ridden and bed-wetting slum children, completely untrained in all normal habits of social interaction, invaded pleasant homes. Like most myths, there were small elements of truth. City children, and not only those from poor areas, were more prone to head lice than country children, and indeed still are, for a variety of reasons. Bed-wetting, hardly surprisingly, was quite common immediately after the initial trauma of evacuation, but later surveys suggested a stable level of only a few per cent of children. A crackdown on claims for extra laundry allowances – payable if the child wet the bed – in the Welsh town of Llantrisant cut the level sharply, suggesting over-reporting for financial reasons.

Not surprisingly, after the first exodus many evacuees soon returned, particularly as bombing did not materialise. When it did, in 1940, evacuation became better organised and more permanent. Children were medically inspected, which provided evidence to counter myths such as those above, but did not actually kill them off. The plentiful reminiscences of evacuation show how mixed experiences really were. Some mothers and children experienced unsympathetic hosts, but general lack of sympathy was itself another myth since many evacuees were treated with kindness. The essential problem for evacuees was that their normal life was utterly changed, while at the same time they were in the middle of totally unfamiliar surroundings. Soon after war began, the family of Barbara Pym in Oswestry, Shropshire, received a family of five with no obvious problems, but the mother was 'desperately unhappy' and returned with her children to Birkenhead after four days. While many evacuated children enjoyed the countryside, others missed the familiar amusements of cities such as cinemas and an active street life.

Rationing was another disruption for women, although any adverse effect on poorer families was reduced by the limitations of their pre-war diet. In general, it was accepted both because of its perceived fairness and because it was well administered. Surveys indicate overwhelming support – in 1942, 91 per cent of housewives approved. This was a tribute to the Ministry of Food and its head between 1940 and 1943, Lord Woolton, popularly known as Fred. Woolton, who had run a department store chain, was a master of publicity, coining the slogan, 'We not only cope, we care.'[2] Slogans like this can seriously backfire unless they are honoured, and it is an indication of the Ministry's efficiency that they were. However, many goods such as household utensils remained unrationed and became increasingly scarce. Scarcity manifested itself in

Military affairs: The Blitz

The Blitz – the large-scale German bombing of cities – began in early September 1940 but had been preceded by a number of smaller raids on urban areas. The idea that it was a reprisal for British raids is a myth, as is the idea that it was primarily designed to terrorise civilians. Attacks were initially directed at military and industrial targets, which was why much German bombing was directed at ports. With heavy loss rates the *Luftwaffe* quickly switched to night bombing, and it became easiest to aim at city centres. London was attacked heavily, as were major ports and a number of inland cities, notably Coventry. In relation to its population Hull, easily accessible from Germany, was the most heavily bombed city. Attacks trailed off in the spring of 1941 as Hitler prepared for the invasion of Russia but there were intermittent later periods of bombing. Then, in June 1944, V1 flying bombs – primitive cruise missiles – were launched at London, followed by V2 rockets from September. These killed around 9,000 people out of a total of deaths from bombing of 62,000.

In spite of the casualties, German bombing had no significant long-term impact on industrial output. As the far greater British bombing effort was to confirm, workers were more resilient than anticipated, while modern factories were mainly outside city centres. In Britain, port closures were compensated for by the drastic reduction in imports which had been dictated by submarine warfare and the shortage of foreign currency. Even so, bombing killed many, destroyed a quarter of a million homes and damaged nearly 4 million. How did people cope?

Newspapers propagated an image of carrying on and to a considerable extent this was justified, as the limited impact of raids on production shows. Nevertheless, there were cracks in morale. Large numbers of people trekked nightly out of cities such as Plymouth and Southampton which endured several consecutive raids. In the East End of London, which was also raided heavily, there were anti-semitic rumours about Jews occupying more than their fair share of places in shelters. Like Bomber Command later, however, the *Luftwaffe* did not understand that it was the frequent repetition of raids on the same town which had the most psychological impact and the most effect on production. Constantly switching targets decreased overall disruption. Only London was raided consistently, and it was so large that, like Berlin later, individual raids had little impact on the city as a whole. The other main influence on morale was the efficiency or otherwise of local authorities. For instance, in Southampton and in the East London borough of West Ham, those in senior positions were incompetent and inadequately prepared, and then failed to handle the aftermath of the raids properly. In Poplar, also in East London, the leadership was excellent and the borough had the lowest casualties per weight of bombs in the East End.

The Blitz stimulated heroism, not least by the firemen who were always in the front line, and also exposed cowardice and inefficiency. The stoicism of the majority had a favourable impact on American opinion and confirmed an existing British self-image, thus helping to sustain national morale. In reality, though, stoicism was also the dominant reaction of German citizens to Allied raids later in the war.

queues which formed when such goods were on sale, as well as in the limitations of choice imposed by the customer-retailer tie of food rationing (see box, 'Rationing and consumption').

An overwhelming theme of wartime life for women, and their families, was disruption. Many young married women who had expected to make a home were at work; evacuation disrupted the lives of both evacuees and those on whom they were billeted; scarcity involved shortages and time-consuming queues. Perhaps greatest of all was the disruption induced by the absence of over 5 million men who, during the course of the

---

Society and economy: Rationing and consumption

The story of civilian consumption mirrors the story of the war effort as a whole. The overriding priorities of the war were to supply the fighting services with men and munitions and to save shipping space. To do that, civilian consumption had to be drastically cut. In its peak years, 1943–1944, munitions output was around six times the level of 1939. Civilian consumption, however, had fallen to around 80 per cent of its pre-war level – to less, per person, than in the years immediately before the First World War.

The critical component in this was rationing. Here as elsewhere, the Chamberlain government had done more than it is often credited with. Food rationing, the mechanisms of which drew on First War experience, was ready at the beginning of war, although not introduced until 1940. It depended on ties between consumers and retailers, with people so far as possible registering at their local shops. (Before the age of the supermarket, most had to register at least at a separate grocer and butcher.) Rations were flat rate with hardly any exceptions, differential energy requirements being catered for by bread, potatoes and meals eaten out, which were all off the ration. Perishable commodities whose supplies fluctuated, notably fish and vegetables, were likewise not rationed. Food rationing was therefore relatively simple: coupons were used at first but were an unnecessary complexity and were soon discontinued. In 1941 clothes rationing was brought in, and this involved coupons since there was no consumer-retailer tie. Petrol rationing, instituted at the start of the war, affected far fewer people as private motoring was still a minority occupation.

Rationing was not just a means of economising on scarce supplies. It was a vital component in controlling inflation and, most important of all, persuading people of the essential fairness of the war. Inflation was tacked partly through Keynesian fiscal measures (see main text), but controlling prices to prevent wage pressures was also seen as necessary. However, price control when demand was high, which it was because of high employment, had one simple outcome. Supply fell short of demand and the temptation to sell goods on the black market at uncontrolled prices became too great. For many commodities, some leakage on the black market was accepted and the extent was controlled by police and legal action. For the basics, this was not enough. Both the anti-inflation strategy and the perception of fairness would have been shattered if basic food expectations had not been met at controlled prices: hence rationing was essential.

It is a truism that rationing made the British diet better. This was achieved in various ways. The average diet became healthier, because the consumption of meat and fats was reduced while the extraction rate of wheat increased so that the almost universal white bread of pre-war was transmuted into brown. Controlled prices, and increased wages, meant that the diet of poorer working-class consumers was improved simply because they could buy more. Finally, the decline in total food availability focused attention on vulnerable groups. Encouraged by interwar developments in nutritional science, policies to increase vitamin, calcium and protein intake were introduced. From 1940 expectant mothers and those with babies under one became entitled to free or subsidised milk, as did all children up to the age of 18. From 1942 free fruit juice and cod liver oil, or vitamin pills, were distributed to expectant mothers and children under five. Food policy, therefore, extended as the war went on from simple rationing to a degree of social engineering which was facilitated by the ever-growing powers of the state.

war, served in the military. Many other men spent nights away from home, serving as firewatchers or in other war-related capacities.

The perception of most women, then, was not of the war opening opportunities but of it closing them down. As a result, far from the 'modernisation' of attitudes suggested by Marwick, many women simply wanted a stable family life. This may be one of the reasons for the post-war boom in births which broke the pre-war trend of decline (see Chapters 6 and 12). And although the need for maximum labour effort had led the government to encourage women to work, governmental attitudes were essentially similar to those of many women. The government saw the family as central. Family allowances were the lynchpin of a policy often described as 'pro-natalist'. This had been stimulated by the pre-war fall in births, which had led many contemporaries to predict gloomily a future population decline. More generally, the Beveridge Plan assumed the centrality of the family as a unit. Married women's insurance rights were, to a large extent, dependent upon husbands' contributions, even if the wife worked. Feminists at the time criticised this but it was generally accepted.

Culture and society

Historians' perceptions of the impact of war on British society and social relations have changed over time. Early accounts stressed social and cultural solidarity, which manifested itself in the reforms, and plans for reform, discussed earlier. One of the most famous of these was Richard Titmuss's account in 1950, *Problems of Social Policy*. As time went by historians have chipped away at this interpretation. In fact, to believe some historians wartime Britain was little more than a seething hotbed of class dissension, strikes and petty crime. Where does the truth lie?

Certainly there was a fairly sharp reduction in income inequality, between social classes and between men and women, during the war and the immediate post-war period. Between 1937 and 1951 labour income as a proportion of national income rose from 65 per cent to 71 per cent, while profits and rental income decreased accordingly. 'All labour income' includes salaries so does not tell us specifically about manual workers; but we also know that skilled manual workers' pay, as an proportion of average male pay, rose from 68 per cent to 77 per cent, and unskilled from 45 per cent to 54 per cent. So both groups had a larger share of a bigger cake. This effect was accentuated by the increase in tax rates, which bore more heavily on higher incomes, and also by the fall in unemployment, which benefited manual workers more than the middle classes. Finally, female manual workers' earnings as a proportion of those of men rose from 52 per cent to 61 per cent over the period. However, this may partly reflect changes in the composition of women's work, in particular the shift towards higher paid white-collar work.

Significant though the shifts in income were, they did not change all sorts of basic relationships. Unskilled men still earned only around half the male average; working-class women earners were even worse off; profits and rental income still went to the owners of wealth who were concentrated among the better-off middle classes and the very wealthy. So, in purely material terms, there is truth in both a story of greater equality and a story of remaining inequality. Much of the debate about wartime social relations, however, focuses on changes in perceptions and attitudes.

There were certainly still tensions, of a familiar kind, centering around work. Although strikes decreased in the early part of the war, they increased later albeit never reaching the levels of the First World War. As in the First War, the strikes were largely economic in nature, and indeed attitudes towards civilian work remained strongly economistic except during the post-Dunkirk crisis when productivity increased. As an example, someone whom the author knew was conscripted from domestic service to assembly work. She recounted how the management, when establishing a standard output level for setting piece rates on a particular component, would initially select her: they sensed that she was more compliant and would work faster, thereby establishing a high output level which would result in a lower piece-work rate. The other women workers would urge her to slow down. Such implicit bargaining behaviour was deeply ingrained among management and manual workers. As with strikes, they suggest that attitudes were not totally consensual, but they do not tell us much, if anything, about class divisions.

Ross McKibbin has suggested that one group among which there was change was young working-class men, who developed a more challenging and sceptical attitude towards authority. Like all judgements based on fragmentary evidence, it may be true but is hard to measure. In the army, where there were large numbers of young working-class men, there are suggestions of a shift towards closer officer–men relations than in the First War – something which does not directly contradict McKibbin's view but gives a different perspective. The changes started at the top. Montgomery in particular, but also other prominent generals such as Brian Horrocks, made it their business to be seen by their troops and, as far as possible, explain their thinking in talks to the troops. Lower down, in spite of the persistence of hierarchical authority structures, more mechanised and less labour intensive forms of warfare threw officers and men continuously together. The fighting was done by small groups in tanks, bombers and infantry platoons, not by mass advances. The contacts thus engendered carried on after the war in a long-lasting network of regimental and other combat group associations.

The above suggests that in the military, at least, there was a strong common purpose combined with a limited lowering of class boundaries, but that this did not necessarily occur consistently in other walks of life. Analysis of political activity and media comments paints the same ambiguous picture. The Common Wealth Party's temporary surge in support suggests some hostility to class boundaries and support for a collectivist restructuring of society, but may in part just have been a bout of by-election horseplay on the part of the electorate. The media, by and large, subscribed to a generally optimistic and consensual view of the war, and the government rarely used its potentially draconian powers of censorship. This consensus was mostly con-cerned with the moral unity of Britain during the war, and only intermittently with plans for social reconstruction. When the latter was an issue, there was predictable support for Beveridge, but otherwise there was no strong leftwards tendency. The left-leaning talks of J. B. Priestley on the BBC have sometimes suggested otherwise, but closer analysis has suggested that its output was predominantly politically moderate. The government's main gadfly was the *Daily Mirror*, which was developing as the pop-ular left-leaning newspaper, with a serious edge, which it was long to remain. The *Mirror* espoused a more critical attitude towards both the government, and post–war recon-struction, than most newspapers, but was as pro the overall aims of the war as anyone.

In one respect, most of the media, the government and the population were at one in taking, after mid-1941, a respectful line towards Russia. Thus, in a 1943 Gallup poll, 50 per cent of respondents thought that Russia had done the most to win the war, as against 42 per cent naming Britain. Apart from being a reasonable assessment, it does suggest underlying feelings which converted into a vague but widespread belief in state intervention and social reform.

The more pessimistic interpretations of national consensus referred to in the first paragraph of this section, however, look at other statistics which might suggest a lack of concern among many people for anything besides personal gratification. Crime increased by over 50 per cent, with youth crime increasing faster. The Blitz saw considerable looting, including some by ARP (Air Raid Protection) wardens. On the other hand, food rationing received strong support and large-scale black marketeering was far lower than in the United States. But one reason for this support may have been the strength of British controls, which rendered evasion difficult. So food rationing worked and ful-filled one of its prime aims, which was fairness, but it was supported because it worked, as much as working because it was supported. Conversely, clothes rationing saw widespread use of minor evasions, such as the use of precut coupons (retailers were meant to cut coupons from ration books themselves, to avoid the sale of coupons). The increase in illegitimate births by 25 per cent, and in annual divorce rates from 1 to 5 per 100, suggests another type of rebellion against conventional morality.

Rather than see these things as indicating a state of rampant and selfish individual-ism, however, it may be more realistic to regard them as an almost inevitable reaction to wartime conditions. Bombing caused temporary chaos and offered almost irresistible temptations to the light-fingered. The inevitably petty rules of rationing rendered some offences against it equivalent, in most people's minds, to minor traffic offences today. And for women and men, the combination of the latter's abundance when in nearby camps, and long absence when abroad on duty, makes it fairly remarkable that illegitimacy and divorce did not increase faster. Robert Mackay's recent study concludes that many of the apparent social tensions of wartime were minor and that there was, as older interpretations suggested, a considerable degree of national solidarity.

Conclusion

Much of this chapter has ranged around one central historiographical debate – how far was there consensus in wartime Britain? It has revealed that a degree of consensus often existed, but its strength was widely different depending on the subject. We now need to clarify what those subjects were.

Jose Harris has pointed out that there was an almost universal belief in the rightness of the war. This was different to the First World War, when there were sceptics who, if not in the mainstream of politics, were at least respectable. In many people this belief might simply be the result of old-fashioned patriotism, but that was not the only motive because others felt disgust for fascism and Nazism, and that might be their main reason for supporting the war. So belief in the rightness of war engendered a consensus which transcended political divides.

Most people must have had some conception of post-war Britain, and for many this would have been better developed and more considered than equivalent conceptions in the First War, when post-war reconstruction was only seriously considered from 1917. In the Second World War, the fall of Chamberlain had ushered in a widespread condemnation of the past and, since then, there had been five years to think about the future. Yet in spite of that condemnation, many people seem to have had a 'traditional' conception of post-war Britain. There was a widespread longing for a simple, private, family life. The increase in divorce showed that such ideals did not always work in practice, but it was not a refutation of those ideals. This longing for privacy and family life was not, perhaps, totally consensual, because some people did want more radical change, but probably so many subscribed to it that it formed a sort of consensus. It dovetailed with another belief, which was complex and probably not often consciously articulated, and which Jose Harris has suggested was also widely held. This was the belief that Britain's atomistic and pluralistic society, not a modernised, carefully regulated one, was part of what was being fought for. It was a conception of Britain as a society in which differences were accepted and live and let live held sway, and which was free from minute and pervasive government intervention. Both these beliefs were deeply conservative, but with a small 'c'. They were more or less independent of formal political affiliation.

This modest consensus was strengthened by one other thing, the renewed status gained by Parliament. It could be seen as embodying the 'imagined community' of Britain

discussed in Chapters 1 and 6, in which individual liberty was underpinned by constitutional government. Churchill's emphasis on the importance of the Commons, the
defiance shown by its continued sitting even after the Commons chamber was bombed
and the reality that Britain continued to have opposition parties and by-elections all
contributed to this.

Yet if these conceptions were widely held, why were people willing to put up with
drastic limitations on freedom? Full-scale military conscription was instituted as soon
as war began, with little of the controversy of the First War (a more limited scheme
had been introduced in the spring, before war began, and this was more controversial).
The Emergency Powers (Defence) Act of 1940 gave the government sweeping powers,
including the power to conscript labour. Censorship of the press was already in place
by virtue of a pre-war act. Part of the reason for acceptance was the consensus over
the need to fight. Part was the fact that powers to direct labour were used carefully
and sparingly and, as strikes and the continuation of day to day wage bargaining show,
the civilian pattern of work was not changed as much as might seem. Part, though, was
probably because people were unaware of the degree of self-censorship of newspapers,
usually voluntary but reinforced in the case of awkward customers like the *Mirror* by
the threat of more draconian action.

One thing, however, seems clear. Limitations on freedom were not accepted because
of any great conversion to the idea of an organic community, which had attracted some
British intellectuals for 50 years (see Chapter 1). Although Beveridge himself was attracted
to the idea of a stronger state involving, for instance, permanent direction of labour,
the parts of his plan which caught the attention were the benefits given in return for
insurance payments. These were fully in tune with the predominantly contractarian
traditions of the British people. The Beveridge Plan was interpreted as an agreement
that they would enrol in a gigantic insurance company from which, because of the subsidy from general taxation, the less well-off would take out more than they put in, and
vice versa. Predictably, therefore, many Conservative MPs were lukewarm, and it is
not clear how many solid Conservative voters actively supported it. 'Consensus' over
social reforms meant that the Labour and Liberal parties and a majority, but not necessarily all, of the electorate supported them. Equally important, however, it meant that
senior civil servants and a fair number of senior Conservatives either actively supported
them or at least acquiesced because they thought reform inevitable. They thought this
for all sorts of reasons.

One reason was the post-Dunkirk criticism of pre-war governments which made modest and piecemeal reform seem not to be an option. Another was the public approval
of Russia, and the by-election successes of Common Wealth, suggesting a change
in the public mood which appeared greater than it actually was. Another was that, whether
or not they approved of reforms, those in senior political or governmental positions
realised that the wartime rhetoric of fairness could not just be forgotten afterwards.
And another was because many of the reforms were not, in spite of appearances,
so radical after all. As the discussion in the 'Politics and planning' section shows,
many reforming measures developed from pre-war ideas and plans. These might have
been generated by pressure groups, interested parties or civil servants themselves. So

when all the other reasons listed above made large-scale change seem inevitable, all these groups sensed victory and pressed that much harder for their ideas. The consensus for post-war reform, therefore, was perhaps most importantly a consensus among those with influence.

Notes

1. Quoted in More, *Industrial Age* (see Chapter 1), p. 250.
2. Woolton, F., *The Memoirs of the Rt Hon. The Earl of Woolton* (London: Cassell, 1959), p. 203.

Further reading

Donnelly, M., *Britain in the Second World War* (London: Routledge, 1999) is a good survey. Harris, J., 'Great Britain: the People's War?' in Reynolds, *Allies at War* (see Chapter 7) and Harris, J., 'Political Ideas and the Debate on State Welfare' in Smith, H. (ed.), *War and Social Change* (Manchester: Manchester University Press, 1986) are thought-provoking and important; see also other essays in Smith. Mackay, R., *Half the Battle: Civilian Morale in Britain during the Second World War* (Manchester: Manchester University Press, 2002) is a valuable recent study. Zweiniger-Bargielowska, I., *Austerity in Britain: Rationing, Controls and Consumption 1939–1955* (Oxford: Oxford University Press, 2000) has a host of important insights.

Other sources: Harris, *Welfare State* (see Chapter 2); Harvey, A., *Collision of Empires: Britain in Three World Wars 1793–1945* (London: Hambledon, 1992); Lowe, R., *The Welfare State in Britain since 1945* (Basingstoke: Palgrave Macmillan, 3rd ed., 2005); McKibbin, *Classes* and Ramsden, *Churchill and Eden* (see Chapter 1); Stewart, *Burying Caesar* (see Chapter 4); Thorpe, *Labour Party* (see Chapter 4); Weight, R., 'State, Intelligentsia and the Formation of National Culture in Britain 1939–45', *Historical Research*, Vol. 69, No. 168, pp. 62–82 (1996).

Chapter 9

THE YEARS OF CONSENSUS? POLITICS 1945–1974

Introduction

Churchill was anxious to keep the Coalition in being after the European war ended in May 1945, but Labour bowed to the widespread demand in the party for an election. Churchill headed a caretaker government until the result was declared on 26 July. Labour's huge victory astonished virtually everyone, although Gallup polls had shown a Labour lead since the early 1940s: but no one then took much notice of polls. Labour polled 2 million votes more than the Conservatives, gaining 393 seats to the latter's 210. The Liberals got just 12. Ever since, historians have tried to explain the result.

The roots of Labour's success lay in their inclusion in government in 1940. In the 1930s Labour's support, after its temporary collapse in 1931, had been growing steadily in local elections, but at national level they still ran a poor second in the 1935 election. When Labour was invited to play a major role in government, it could no longer be convincingly portrayed as the 'unpatriotic' or 'dangerous' party as it had been in the 1930s. Churchill tried to do this in 1945 and his attempt met with general criticism. The British experience of war was the other main contributor to Labour's success: 1940 had not only brought Labour in but, in many people's eyes, had discredited the governments of the 1930s, which were predominantly Conservative. Furthermore, the wartime rhetoric of fairness translated itself into a belief in the need for a major shift in social policy. Not surprisingly, Labour was seen as the best party to carry this out, and they strengthened their claim by stressing their ability to improve housing, one of the major election issues.

The economics of Labour

While social reform was probably the highest priority for most Labour voters, to significant groups within Labour the party's nationalisation plans were of most importance. Furthermore, Labour's broader economic policy was critical both to the extent to which it could realise its other policies and to its popular support. In the 1930s the government's economic powers were seen as limited and unemployment levels of 10 per cent or more were accepted. But since then, much of the rhetoric of reconstruction, including the acceptance of Keynesianism (see Chapter 8), had suggested that governments possessed a magic wand to cure economic ills. Labour's own emphasis on planning strengthened expectations still further.

Labour's economic policies can be divided into two: the longer-term policies for reconstruction; and the day to day policies concerned with raising revenue and guiding the economy.

The most prominent long-term policy was nationalisation. Public ownership was in Labour's constitution as 'Clause IV' (see Chapter 4). It had got there for a variety of reasons, and many in the party did not originally take it very seriously, but to Labour's left it was serious. The left's resurgence in the party in the 1930s had led to various industries being nominated for nationalisation; the contents of the list were dictated not so much by economic theory as by which elements of the party thought they would gain most from public ownership. Foremost were the miners. For them, nationalisation would remove the limitations which lack of profits imposed on the coal industry, namely an inability to pay decent wages or provide good conditions of work.

Nationalisation was cloaked in a rhetoric of modernisation which could appeal to the public and which many in the party genuinely believed. Major industries such as coal were said to have 'failed the nation' and, given its interwar record, this was a plausible claim. Interwar practice, whether Conservative or Labour, also favoured large economic entities which were believed to be more efficient, London Transport being an example. So nationalisation was not as revolutionary as all that.

It proceeded quickly, with acts passed nationalising the Bank of England and coal in 1946, railways, long-distance road transport and electricity in 1947, gas in 1948 and iron and steel in 1949. (In some cases the actual handover date was the subsequent year.) Gas and electricity were partly owned by municipalities, so here one form of public ownership was substituted for another. In other cases compensation in the form of government stock was relatively generous. The Conservatives were fairly quiescent, fighting over gas and road transport but only opposing iron and steel bitterly. They had some grounds for this as there was far less support for nationalisation from the iron and steel unions, since industrial relations in the industry were good.

Most nationalised industries were formed into 'public corporations' on the interwar model developed for London Transport by Herbert Morrison, then leader of London County Council. Management was vested in boards of directors who were nominated by the government. The government ultimately controlled pricing and investment but in theory delegated as much as possible. Management and unions, therefore, remained on opposite sides of the fence – a fact which suited the unions who cherished their continued right to bargain.

Nationalisation could be represented as part of a wider project of planning the economy, even if in practice it was also dictated by political and sectional interests. 'Planning' had become accepted by many as necessary and progressive before and during the war (see Chapter 8). There was, however, never an economic master plan but rather various different types of planning. The post-war British economy was being run at high pressure, as export demand, government spending and pent-up private demand all competed for resources. To keep down inflation, Labour continued to use the physical controls which had governed wartime output and consumption. Many foodstuffs were still rationed and commodities such as steel and basic chemicals allocated by licence. Exports could therefore be prioritised, necessary because of the constraints on the balance of payments, discussed below. The alternative was allocation by price – normal in a free market – but this would have involved price increases. While physical controls eased in the late 1940s, recent historiography suggests that Labour still saw them as a necessary part of its economic armoury. They also contributed to what were seen as desirable social ends. Building licences meant that public housing could be favoured over private, and new factories in the Midlands and South-East could be discouraged in favour of factory building in regions of former heavy unemployment.

There were other strands to Labour planning. Visits to American factories by managers and trade unionists were encouraged under the aegis of the Anglo-American Council on Productivity. Although their ultimate effect was probably limited, they were a recognition that low levels of British manufacturing productivity compared with American necessitated more than just reorganisation. A new planning body, the Ministry of Economic Affairs, formed in 1947 under Stafford Cripps might have developed such initiatives. But then in November he replaced Hugh Dalton as Chancellor and subsequently yet another facet of planning, Keynesian demand management, became dominant.

Both productivity drives and physical controls were in part addressing the same thing – the desperate need to earn foreign currency. Lend Lease had been abruptly ended on Japan's surrender, while exports had been minimised during the war and would take time to restore. Britain required dollars, in particular, to buy all the things which only the United States and other dollar-area countries could supply. A large American loan tided things over but it had a price. Britain had to promise that by mid-1947 it would restore the convertibility of sterling, which had been controlled during the war, into other currencies. The American terms were dictated by their belief in the desirability of restoring world-wide free trade.

While Dalton, as Labour's first Chancellor, is generally agreed to have made mistakes in his fiscal and monetary policies, it would probably have been impossible to close the gap between imports and exports. When convertibility came it was a débâcle. Traders and bankers did not want to hold sterling, and since they could now freely sell it, they did. Britain's foreign currency reserves were rapidly running out and, after five weeks, convertibility was suspended. By now, American attitudes were changing. Marshall Aid, a programme of economic assistance for Europe, was on the horizon and Britain was one of the beneficiaries.

Before that, Cripps as Chancellor had embraced Keynesianism with enthusiasm. The Keynesian answer to excess demand was a budget surplus to remove spending power from the economy. This meant no significant reduction in taxes, in spite of falling defence expenditure. Controls also continued as rationing was tightened once more, while a wage freeze was agreed with the unions. The policy was broadly successful, but there was still a gap between imports and exports and in 1949 Britain devalued sterling against the dollar, from a rate of £1 = $4.03, to £1 = $2.80. The effect of devaluation was to cheapen – and thus boost – exports but correspondingly increase the price of dollar imports.

The welfare state

With the dismantling from the 1980s of nationalisation, it is the welfare state which remains Labour's enduring legacy. The term itself was coined in Germany as one of abuse. Towards the end of the 1940s it started to become regularly used in the modern and positive sense. It is hard to define, but most definitions would include the concepts of state provision of, and citizens' rights to, education, social security, shelter and health services.

Education had already been essentially settled on a cross-party basis in 1944 (see Chapter 8), so Labour's first major contribution was the codification of the main Beveridge proposals in the 1945 Family Allowances Act and the 1946 National Insurance Act. The biggest beneficiaries of the Acts were pensioners and, through family allowances, mothers. However, the Coalition's agreed endorsement of Beveridge in 1944 had been less generous with some benefit levels than he suggested and these restrictions were carried forward under Labour. As a result of restricting some benefits, it was necessary to provide extra support for those with no additional resources and this involved the continuation of means testing. The mechanism was codified by the National Assistance Act of 1948.

Housing and land use are dealt with in the accompanying box, 'Houses and plans'. Apart from social security the really big change was health.

On the face of it, the creation of the National Health Service (NHS) was a huge and revolutionary undertaking. The jumble of interwar health care – independent general practitioners (GPs) and hospital consultants, local authority and voluntary hospitals, financed by a mixture of fees, insurance subscriptions and donations – was replaced by a unified, free service. Hospitals were organised under 14 regional hospital boards and doctors became paid by the state, although the option of patients paying privately remained. National insurance provided a proportion of the cost, but much less than general taxation.

The earthquake involved in establishing the NHS, however, masks long-term imperatives which pointed towards change. Daniel Fox has pointed out that these imperatives drove a model of health care which became ubiquitous across the developed world.

Politics and government: Houses and plans

As after the First World War, housing was one of the key post-war issues. From 1939–1945 virtually no houses had been built and large numbers had been destroyed or damaged. Labour's popularity in 1945 owed a lot to its realisation of how important housing was to many people and its promises to do something about it. Unfortunately, with such a resource-intensive activity as house building it was impossible to increase output rapidly. Furthermore, Nye Bevan, the responsible minister, emphasised quality rather than quantity – almost certainly a mistake as it enabled the Conservatives to counter-attack on the issue with their pledge at the 1950 Party Conference to build 300,000 houses a year.

While Conservative governments were triumphantly successful in meeting this, they shifted the emphasis from public to private housing. However, they accepted that public housing (popularly called council housing) had a significant role and initially increased subsidies for it. In 1957 they tried to liberalise the housing market with the Rent Act, a bold attempt to decontrol rents on privately owned rented property when there was a change of tenancy, and allow controlled rents to be raised within limits. Many controlled rents had been fixed in 1915, and after years of inflation this produced perverse incentives: for tenants, to stay in the same house even if their circumstances changed; for landlords, to spend the minimum on repairs. However, decontrol failed to encourage private landlords to build new property for rent. After scandals over slum landlords, the Conservatives lost their nerve and again encouraged council house building. Rent controls were then stiffened under Labour, although they had come to accept private house building for sale. So housing remained an area where there was some consensus but also continuing dispute.

The emphasis on numbers of dwellings continued into the 1970s. By then there was little real physical shortage of houses with acceptable facilities and most really low quality housing had been demolished. Indeed, the word 'slum', in common use until the 1960s, has become an historical term. Housing issues therefore changed and the Thatcherite break with the old consensus over housing raised protests at the time but became politically uncontroversial (see Chapter 11). As home ownership grew, the most salient issue became the violent fluctuations in house prices, which were first evident in the early 1970s. These have been partly caused by inflation and by interest rate changes, but one element has been constraints on land supply, preventing the rapid building of houses as prices rise.

The first land use planning Act was in 1909, but all through the interwar period planning controls were weak, particularly outside large towns. As a result, the interwar building boom often desecrated the countryside. 'Ribbon development' occurred along main roads while much of the south coast was built over. Pre-war demands for stronger land use planning dovetailed with wartime pressures to conserve agricultural land, while there were dreams of rebuilding bombed cities with houses and industry neatly separated.

One post-war result was new towns – and in the 1960s the new city of Milton Keynes – and the provision in many small and medium-sized towns of public housing for former city slum-dwellers. With some exceptions these new or uprooted communities seem to have been successful. But more important was the Town and Country Planning Act of 1947, the basis of much subsequent legislation. In essence, this brought all development under much tighter local authority control. In 1955 one extension was to ask local authorities to designate 'Green Belts' around cities in which new building was sharply restricted. With development in other rural areas also constrained, these environmental controls have helped to save Southern England, the area under most pressure, from resembling the sprawl of, say, rural northern Italy. But land prices have been forced up, so British housing, by continental standards, is not only expensive but also often lower quality. Land use controls have come, therefore, at a heavy price. (See also Chapter 12 box, 'Rural Britain 1945–2000'.)

At its root lay the belief that the medical services should be organised in regional hierarchies. This belief existed because, from the early twentieth century, medical science had made astonishing strides and for the first time it was reasonable to believe that hospitals could consistently cure many diseases. Therefore, it seemed sensible to organise services in regions sizeable enough that each could sustain the most specialised expertise and technology.

Fox suggests that many pre-war experts accepted that such a model should be established in Britain and that sooner or later this would have happened anyway. Of course, the particular structure taken by the NHS also reflects pre-existing patterns, wartime and post-war bargaining, and personal prejudices. Thus Aneurin (Nye) Bevan, the Health Minister, insisted on a 'free at the point of service' model, rather than one common on the continent in which patients reclaimed fees through their insurance provider. Arguably the British system is the cheapest to administer. On the other hand, doctors' lobbying led to the sidelining of plans in which local authorities would have taken a leading role in the organisation of the health service. Under these plans GPs would increasingly have worked together in clinics, as favoured on the continent. Instead, most GPs continued in the traditional one-person practice, which only gradually gave way to larger groupings. The British model was one which, along with other aspects of the NHS, focused on cure rather than prevention.

Bevan bargained with and bullied the myriad interests involved to establish the NHS in 1948. Almost immediately the government was confronted with a major problem: cost. In 1948–1949 the NHS bill exceeded estimates by 40 per cent. The spending should be put in perspective – the NHS cost no more than three and a half per cent of national income, one-third the cost of defence. But initially this spending appeared both uncontrolled and almost uncontrollable. Among the unexpectedly heavy costs were those for dental and optical treatment. In an age when dental hygiene was almost unimaginably deficient, many poorer people never went to dentists, waiting until their teeth fell out or had to be extracted, when they bought a set of dentures. Spectacles were often bought without prescription, to save money. The NHS's free service was therefore irresistible to the public; by 1953 it had provided 6 million sets of dentures and 26 million spectacles. These were a convenient target for the many Labour ministers who objected to Bevan's unwillingness to rein in the health budget – at the expense, of course, of other departments.

As a result, the price the government paid for teeth and spectacles was more than just financial. By early 1951 yet another national economic crisis loomed as the Korean war led to a massive rearmament programme, the expense of which was increased still further by a war-related rise in raw materials' prices. Hugh Gaitskell, the new Chancellor, proposed charges on dentures and spectacles. Bevan, by now Minister of Labour, resigned. The split was the forerunner of years of dissension in the Labour Party. Bevan actually had much justice on his side in his argument that the planned defence spending was both unrealistic and unnecessary, but his personal attacks on Gaitskell caused great bitterness. The creation almost simultaneously of the NHS and a damaging party split were fitting legacies for a man who combined genius with irresponsibility.

Labour 1945–1951: a summary

The Labour governments of 1945–19451 were heroic in their achievements. Whether one agrees with those achievements or not, they were astonishing in their scope. Moreover, they were brought about by politicians who, in many cases, had held senior office from 1940 onwards. It was not surprising that, when the Labour majority fell to five in the 1950 election and the Conservatives started harassing tactics in the Commons, the strain began to tell. Attlee was considering another election from the spring of 1951. Apart from collective governmental tiredness, his motive seems to have been the honourable one that the country needed the stability of a government with a larger majority, whatever that government might be. In October 1951 he took the plunge. Labour actually had a small majority of votes but, because of the vagaries of the electoral system, the Conservatives got more seats. Churchill would form the next government.

People and politics: Clement Attlee

Clem Attlee came from a prosperous middle-class family which supported charitable work in the East End. He argued himself out of the Christianity which had motivated his family's charity into a belief that only radical political change could tackle social problems. After a brief spell as a barrister, he inherited enough money to work more or less full time in politics, joining the Independent Labour Party (the ILP; it was affiliated to the Labour Party, and was politically on its left). He served with distinction in the First World War, ending it as a major. In 1922 he was elected for Limehouse in the East End, which he made a safe Labour seat – one of the few to survive the 1931 disaster.

In 1935 Attlee became Labour leader, replacing George Lansbury. His election owed itself partly to the shortcomings of the other contenders: many MPs distrusted Herbert Morrison and were concerned about Arthur Greenwood's drinking. Attlee was regarded as colourless and safe, yet he became the Labour Party's definitive leader – the one who led it in its years of greatest triumph (Fig 9.1).

Attlee had a successful war as Churchill's deputy, virtually running the home front. As Prime Minister, he enjoyed advantages. Labour was largely united after the war, with the few far left dissidents marginalised. The government had the strong support of the unions, who dominated the Party Conference. And Attlee was unconditionally supported by Ernest Bevin, Labour's strongman. But Attlee was undoubtedly an outstanding Prime Minister. He let ministers get on with their job, shifting them only if they failed. He did not give much lead on economic issues, though, and did not query the 1950–1951 rearmament programme, which was to cause so much trouble. After the 1951 defeat Attlee lost some of his grip on the party, which was riven by Bevanite faction-fighting.

Attlee's own political views were firmly on the left. But his famous taciturnity and general air of calm meant that he was widely seen as a moderate, and he was one of Labour's biggest electoral assets. Socially he was conservative, and his beloved wife

▶

Figure 9.1 Attlee (right of picture) confers with Ernest Bevin at the first meeting of the United Nations General Assembly, 1946. © Hulton-Deutsch Collection/CORBIS

Vi, who drove him about hair-raisingly on his election campaigns, was a Conservative in all but name. (There is an interesting comparison with Churchill, whose wife Clemmie was at heart always a Liberal.)

Attlee died in 1967, a monument to both the earliest years of Labour and its period of greatest achievement.

How far were Labour's achievements based on the social and cultural solidarity engendered by the war? As Chapter 8 suggests, there was probably less solidarity than was once thought, but there was widespread support for welfare reforms and for a greater degree of fairness. Of course, many of the components of the welfare state had been assembled before the war: by the Liberals before 1914; by the brief period of post-1918 reconstruction; and by the interwar Conservative and National reforms, some of the latter based on Labour plans from the 1929–1931 government. Beveridge revitalised these components and added others, and Labour's measures were based on his blueprint. The NHS was more obviously a creation of Labour, and particularly of Nye Bevan. But nonetheless, one central fact of the period was that all Western and Northern

European countries in the post-war era quickly moved towards some sort of comprehensive welfare state. Labour's achievements may have been heroic but they were not unique.

In judging Labour's overall performance, there are obvious things to criticise. Whether nationalisation was right or wrong, it was not part of a coherent plan for economic reconstruction. Indeed, one of its aims, to reinvigorate older industries such as coal and the railways which had suffered from a lack of investment, completely failed: little money was available and for years they soldiered on without much change. Housing (see earlier box, 'Houses and plans') is another candidate for criticism, but economic conditions were so limiting that not much more could have been achieved.

Because it is so easy to criticise some of Labour's own priorities, other possible errors may go unnoticed. So it is worth stressing that the economy was constantly held back by the continued high level of manpower retained in the military, and later by rearmament. The armed services still had 1 million men in 1949, and in 1951 defence spending took 8 per cent of national income. This may have been necessary, but its effect on the economy was significant. On the other hand, Labour's failure to achieve a major long-term improvement in British productivity levels cannot really be held against the government. There was some awareness of the problem, which is more than can be said for the early years of the Conservative government.

In other ways, Labour's economic achievements were quite considerable. Full employment, however, was not one of them. As shown in the accompanying box, 'The economy 1951–1973', full employment was a product of high post-war world demand and investment. There was a steady rise in output under Labour, but given domestic and world demand this too was not surprising. Labour achieved two things: the huge gap between imports and exports was virtually eliminated; and inflation was controlled at a reasonable rate, given the pressure of demand. Two planks of policy played a part in both achievements. Rationing restrained domestic demand, as did Cripps' move after 1947 to a full-blown Keynesian anti-inflationary policy involving a large budget surplus. Whether Conservative policies would have been better or worse overall is unknowable, but almost certainly they would have involved more rapid decontrol and thus higher prices. In addition, the unions would probably have been less cooperative in restraining wage demands. There are economic arguments for decontrol – that goods allocation is more efficient if determined by price rather than government fiat – but inflation would have been an almost certain result. A policy of decontrol could have been compatible with closing the payments gap, but success in this would have necessitated a fiscal policy as austere as that implemented by Cripps.

Control of inflation, however, involved other forms of control out of which the Conservatives could and did make political capital. Ina Zweiniger-Bargielowska has shown how women, who had generally welcomed rationing during the war, started to turn against it soon afterwards. Rationing started to be relaxed after the height of Crippsian austerity was passed in 1948, but meat, fats, sugar and sweets rationing continued until after 1951. Price controls also continued, keeping down inflation but exacerbating shortages. By the late 1940s there was widespread discontent with the continuing sparseness of goods in the shops. Politically, therefore, Labour paid a high price for controls

Society and economy: The economy 1951–1973

Given the Conservatives' criticism of controls before 1951, it is not surprising that they quickly dismantled them after coming to power. They could do this and still reduce inflation because raw material prices fell as the Korean war simmered down, while Labour's huge rearmament programme was scaled back. The Conservatives were still committed to managing the economy, however, which might mean keeping inflation down by suppressing demand, but might also mean pumping up demand if unemployment threatened. As a management tool, the Conservatives re-emphasised monetary policy, which had been downplayed under Labour. At this period, monetary policy usually meant adjusting interest rates, which the government influenced through the Bank of England, upwards to restrict demand or downwards to expand it. Monetary policy might also include attempts directly to control the money supply, for instance by pressure on banks to restrict advances.

The emphasis on monetary policy has led to much debate as to how far Conservative governments were 'Keynesian', but the debate is theoretical and has little bearing on the wider debate about consensus. Conservative governments still thought that unemployment mattered and that even small rises in unemployment necessitated some sort of stimulus, whether fiscal or monetary. The irony, as Robin Matthews showed in a famous article in 1968, is that low levels of unemployment were actually very little to do with fiscal or monetary stimulus, but were mainly a result of the high post-war investment and the expansion of world trade.

One important reason for this was trade liberalisation. In 1944, at Bretton Woods, Britain and America aimed to establish a world economic system which would prevent the revival of interwar protectionism. However, Britain's system of Commonwealth tariff preferences meant there was political pressure not to liberalise too quickly. Her dire post-war financial position also made her cautious. But America was now the world's banker and her wishes were paramount, so the Bretton Woods system continued until the early 1970s. Currencies were fixed in value against each other, although the role of gold in the system was downgraded. Devaluation was discouraged although allowable. Currencies were to be convertible, although following the 1947 débâcle sterling only became freely convertible in 1958, and even then some controls persisted. Trade liberalisation was the other plank of Bretton Woods. From 1947 it got underway under the aegis of the General Agreement on Tariffs and Trade (now the World Trade Organisation).

As has been seen, Britain devalued sterling early on, in 1949. The new rate, £1 = $2.80, seems to have been about right, although arguably it could have been a bit higher to reduce the inflationary impact of raw material price increases. Subsequently, over a long period, exports on average more or less matched imports. However, this did not eliminate crises over the possibility of another sterling devaluation. They arose because much trade was still denominated in sterling, a state of affairs which produced 'invisible' export earnings for Britain through commission on payments. (In trade, services are invisibles, as opposed to goods, which are visible.) If the traders and bankers holding sterling feared devaluation, they would sell it. Interest rates then had to be raised to make holding it more attractive. Therefore, interest rate rises to defend sterling were superimposed on other interest rate changes intended to accelerate or slow down economic activity in Britain. These alternations of economic stimulant and retardant were pejoratively referred to as 'stop-go'. In the 1960s stop-go came to be seen as a serious problem, acting to discourage investment plans. Most economic historians now disagree with this diagnosis. On balance, government fiscal and monetary intervention is thought to have had a mildly smoothing effect, in spite of defects in timing. More important, other European countries at this time experienced bigger economic fluctuations, but their levels of investment and overall growth rates were still higher than those of Britain. Therefore, historians' attention has turned to Britain's slow underlying growth rate.

Over the period 1951–1973 Britain's average growth rate was 2.8 per cent per annum. Income per person rose by over 50 per cent in the same period, an unprecedented increase in living standards. But because European growth was so much higher, countries such as Germany and France, historically poorer than Britain and the first devastated by bombing, were by the 1960s as wealthy or more so. However, several historians have pointed out that, as American technology spread, it was likely that European countries would catch up; Britain's post-war productivity gap with America was smaller and therefore its catch-up potential was less. Jim Tomlinson has extended this insight into a general critique of declinism, as it has been christened, pointing out that other perceived problems of the 1950s and 1960s such as 'stop-go' and inflation were no worse than in many European countries. Tomlinson's argument calls into question not just standard historiographical accounts of the period but also the private beliefs of many at the time, including Macmillan and Wilson, even if both portrayed a public optimism. Other historians, however, still share their belief that Britain's failure to raise productivity faster was a major problem. What, according to this more pessimistic interpretation, was the problem?

During the interwar period Britain, once the apostle of free trade, had become a protected economy. Externally there were tariffs, internally a proliferation of price fixing agreements between companies in the same business. This was in line with contemporary thinking which stressed excessive competition leading to price reductions as one factor in the depression. But the result in a post-war world of high demand was less incentive to modernise and more opportunity to take the easy way of increasing prices. As shown in the main text, British governments became increasingly concerned with strengthening competition. Cartelisation extended into the labour market via trade unions. Part of the post-war consensus was an acceptance by governments of their desirability. The unions had reciprocated with wage restraint between 1948 and 1950. By the 1950s, and with a Conservative government, the unions were less conciliatory, but inflation remained relatively low and wage demands were usually modest. In the 1960s, however, both political parties began to view unions as part of the wider problem of uncompetitiveness, both because of high wage demands and because of inefficient working practices. Stephen Broadberry and Nick Crafts are among historians who have broadly accepted this diagnosis, suggesting also that a fragmented bargaining system exacerbated problems.

▶

Some historians also see training and education, from shopfloor to management level, as systemic weaknesses of the British economy. It is possible to overstate this: although Britain historically had low levels of university participation, some areas which had been weak, such as chemistry, developed successfully. The apprenticeship system, responsible for training skilled workers in engineering and some other industries, was not as comprehensive as Germany's but many responsible companies ran it well. But in general British training of manual workers was deficient, and was not helped by the failure to develop technical schools, the hoped-for third leg of the tripartite system in education. At a higher level, university education in engineering was limited and much training was on the job. This meant, perhaps, less stimulus to disciplined management thinking about alternative methods of production. It may also have contributed to relatively low levels of research and development spending outside the defence industries.

– maybe even the price of losing office – when a slight softening of the policy might have tipped the balance.

The creation of the NHS remains Labour's greatest legacy. Faults can be found with its organisation, but any structure would have had imperfections. When voters shifted towards the Conservatives, it was not because of the welfare state or nationalisation, but more on the narrow, but human and understandable, grounds of lack of freedom of choice.

Post-war consensus

Debate about post-war consensus has both echoed and developed from the debate about wartime consensus. The focus of the debate about post-war is not so much on whether consensus embraced the British people as a whole, but on whether there was a consensus among the political elite. If there was, of course, it existed because it embodied views which both major parties attributed to the people.

Historians who support the idea of consensus identify a number of major components. On the economic side, there was an acceptance by the Conservatives of the nationalisation of major industries, while Labour tacitly accepted limits on the amount of future nationalisation. There was an acceptance by both parties, dating back to the 1944 White Paper, of full employment and the need for government economic action, if necessary, to realise it. There was an acceptance that the trade unions had an important role to play and should be consulted over economic policy. And there was an acceptance of the welfare state, with relatively little deviation from the pattern established in 1945–1948. Consensus, to those historians who believe in its existence, extended into wider areas of foreign and Commonwealth policy. There was a consensus that Russia was the main potential threat and that, by and large, the United States was the chief guarantor against that threat. There was also a developing consensus that, sooner or later, most of Britain's remaining colonies would become independent. A catchy word for consensus over economic policy was coined in the 1950s: Butskellism. It is a play on the names of two leading moderates, the Conservative R. A. (Rab) Butler and Hugh Gaitskell, Labour's leader after Attlee.

If a consensus existed, it was clearly one which, on domestic issues, followed the agenda laid down by Labour in 1945–1948. So to make such a consensus possible, the Conservatives had to adapt. They had adapted considerably during the war, for example accepting, if reluctantly, modified Beveridge-type welfare reforms. After the war Churchill gave little lead on domestic policy. The running was made by reformers such as Butler, Harold Macmillan and Oliver Lyttleton. In the 'Industrial Charter' of 1947 all the points above which related to the economy and economic management were accepted. The acceptance of these collectivist policies was combined with a rhetoric of choice and freedom: further nationalisation was opposed, rationing was to be lifted and public expenditure, and therefore taxation, was to be reduced. There was some opposition to the collectivist part of the charter from free-market Conservatives, but it was strongly supported at the Conservative Party Conference in that year.

Support at the conference highlights two things. First that, in spite of the limits to wartime solidarity, there was a clear sense among many Conservatives that the world had moved in a more collectivist direction. Second, that the party was now full of young members, shifting its centre of gravity from the retired regular army officers and Indian civil servants, and their wives, who had formerly played a big part, especially in Conservatism in Southern England. There had been a drive to modernise local branches and increase membership in the late 1930s, but it had been set back by the war. It was given new impetus by Fred Woolton, the successful wartime Minister of Food. This was a period when the membership of both major political parties peaked, the Conservatives with around 3 million members in 1952.

There seems, therefore, formidable evidence for the existence of consensus, strengthened by the fact that the Conservatives did very little when in office to undermine these pledges. Historians who argue against consensus point to various things. There was the continued preference of Labour in the early 1950s for controls; there was a – very brief – period when Labour's defence policy involved unilateral nuclear disarmament; and education, one of the policy areas over which there was most agreement during the war, became a political battleground. These were moderately big issues. There was also constant party strife over details, such as the amount of money spent on welfare, the precise mechanisms for maintaining stability in the economy, the balance between public and private housing, the speed of decolonisation and so forth. But party strife will exist even if there is agreement over broad areas. In a two–party system in which one party is out of office, that party does not have much rationale for existence if it fails to oppose the other one. When there is considerable agreement, opposition means taking the remaining differences and magnifying them.

The author therefore concludes, as do many other historians, that there was a wide area of post-war political consensus. And, given the experience of wartime, this is not very surprising. After the war as during it, even Conservatives who did not agree with widespread government social and economic intervention thought they had to accept it, while there were plenty of Conservative activists who did agree with it. Furthermore, as shown elsewhere in this chapter, later on there was also much consensus on an issue which increasingly came to the forefront: the modernisation of the British economy.

Conservatives in power 1951–1964

The Conservatives' tacit acceptance of many of Labour's policies constrained their ability to bring in radical change. Domestically, therefore, they aimed to differentiate themselves from Labour as much as possible where they could, while reassuring the voters that the welfare state was safe in Conservative hands. In addition, no major challenges would be mounted to the trade unions or nationalised industries.

The Conservatives carried out their promise to denationalise (the old term for privatise) steel and long-distance road haulage, but denationalisation went no further. The trade unions were treated with kid gloves. Walter Monckton, the Minister of Labour from 1951–1955, was on the left of the party. He preferred to settle industrial disputes by negotiation, and has been seen as encouraging overgenerous wage increases. But they actually remained quite low in the period, after a brief upsurge during the Korean war, and in practice Monckton's good relations with union leaders may have contributed to continued wage moderation.

Apart from limited denationalisation, the Conservatives differentiated themselves by getting rid of most of the physical controls that affected consumers. Food rationing ended in 1954 and in that year a list of Conservative achievements could claim that 'Austerity has gone the way of shortages, black markets, controls, power cuts, identity cards [another wartime innovation] and ration books.'[1] The existence of widespread consensus can divert attention from the appeal of the Conservative attack on the post-war world of drabness and austerity. Whatever the economic arguments for controls, it was politically foolish of Labour to continue as late as the 1955 election to advocate their restoration. The other major area of differentiation was the Conservative stress on home ownership, which dovetailed with rhetoric about individualism and freedom. This had begun in a limited way before the war when the phrase a 'property-owning democracy' was coined.[2] It was popularised after the war by Anthony Eden.

On the other side of the fence, the Conservatives kept faith with the welfare state, as they had to if they were to lay to rest the ghosts of the 1930s. Over the period from 1951 to 1964 welfare spending edged slowly upwards as a proportion of national income, from around 14 per cent to around 16 per cent, most of the increase being accounted for by education. Given the need for new hospitals, the stagnation of health spending shows that it had relatively low priority. Behind this lay both the high costs of the early years – leading to a Treasury focus on controlling NHS expenditure – and, perhaps, relatively low expectations by the public once the principle of free access was established. However, in 1962 the Hospital Plan aimed to spend heavily in order to rationalise and update hospital provision, although it was largely left to Labour to carry it through. Social security spending also rose slowly, basic benefits remaining low. The major innovation, in 1959, was that insurance contributions were linked to earnings to provide a modestly enhanced pension, although contributors could opt out of this and into an occupational pension scheme. That, home ownership and the rise in education spending was some underpinning for Conservative rhetoric in the mid- and late 1950s about an 'opportunity' state: an emphasis not just on the provision of basic welfare but on the state also providing opportunities for individual advancement.

In the early 1950s Labour had internal disputes, discussed later. These and the Conservatives' obvious, if modest, successes gave the latter another election victory in 1955. By then Anthony Eden had succeeded Churchill as Prime Minister. Eden failed tragically over Suez (see Chapter 11) and was replaced by Harold Macmillan. Macmillan restored confidence in foreign policy. At the same time, most people enjoyed increasing prosperity, unemployment remained low and Labour continued its internecine quarrels. In 1959 a Conservative government was elected again, with a further increase in its majority.

People and politics: Harold Macmillan

In spite of the languid aristocratic exterior he cultivated in later life, Harold Macmillan came from a mercantile background. The family firm was Macmillans, the publishers, and Macmillan was an excellent man of business, as he first demonstrated in politics during the Second World War, when he carried out a variety of important organisational and diplomatic tasks. His reputation for efficiency was sealed when as Minister for Housing from 1951–1954 he achieved the magic target of 300,000 houses built in a year (Fig. 9.2).

Macmillan's political odyssey was more complex than that suggests, however. After showing great bravery in the First World War, he became Conservative MP for Stockton, an industrial town in the North-East, in 1924. The sacrifices made by the working classes during the war, and the unemployment of the interwar years, had a major impact on Macmillan's thinking. By the 1930s he was firmly on the left of the Conservative Party, and attracted by planning. After the war he contributed to the Conservatives' 'Industrial Charter' (see main text, 'Post-war consensus'). One other characteristic was a well-developed ability to remember personal grievances. Both Rab Butler and Anthony Eden were targets in later years for resentments Macmillan had conceived many years earlier.

By 1955 Macmillan was Chancellor, and it seemed had reached the culmination of his career since Eden, a younger man, was Prime Minister. But Eden's fate was sealed by Suez and a serious operation. The senior members of the party (there was then no formal election) preferred Macmillan to Butler.

They were probably right. In his first years as Premier, Macmillan was brilliant. Having been regarded in the 1930s as an overserious bore, he had made himself into a witty parliamentary performer – a trajectory Harold Wilson also followed. Macmillan also greatly enjoyed diplomacy and soon achieved *rapprochement* with America after Suez. With that and economic prosperity, he earned the newspaper tag of 'Supermac'

▶

Figure 9.2 Macmillan in his alert businessman mode, as Chancellor of the Exchequer in 1955. © Bettmann/CORBIS

and led the Conservatives into a third election victory in 1959. Subsequently, he tried to move the party forward, and also tackle Britain's economic problems, by emphasising modernisation. But this was unsuccessful (see main text) and by the early 1960s his magic touch had deserted him. Like Eden, he broke down through illness but retained enough control to deny Rab Butler the premiership a final time in 1963. He ended an extremely long life as Lord Stockton, dying in 1986.

Macmillan symbolised the distance the Conservatives had travelled in their journey leftwards. Like Baldwin, he was good at blurring this reality and thereby keeping more old-fashioned members and voters happy. In Macmillan's case, the trick was achieved by making the party imagine it was led by a world-weary aristocrat when in fact it was led by a shrewd and sometimes devious businessman of progressive views.

In spite of his election victory, Macmillan was not complacent about the underlying state of the economy. With his early history as an opponent of *laissez-faire* capitalism, he saw weaknesses in Britain's post-war economic performance. To counter these, the Conservatives adopted two strategies, which although not necessarily contradictory were very different in emphasis.

One approach was a drive to enhance competition by an attack on the cartelised nature of British industry (see earlier box, 'The economy 1951–1973'). The Restrictive Practices Act of 1956 aimed to test before the Restrictive Practices Court the many price-setting agreements between British firms. Most such agreements were subsequently dropped. The retail version of these agreements was Resale Price Maintenance (RPM), the enforcement by manufacturers, on retailers, of prices at which goods had to be sold. This was made illegal in 1964.

More attention, however, was focused on a different approach – the attempt to cement the post-war consensus by strengthening economic planning. Macmillan was inspired by the apparent achievements of French indicative planning, which set targets rather than imposed physical controls. In 1962 the government set up the National Economic Development Council (NEDC, nicknamed Neddy), on which government, industry and trade unions were represented, and which was paralleled by 'Little Neddies' in individual industries. It was complemented by the National Income Commission (NIC – therefore Nicky), also of 1962, which reviewed wage settlements referred to it by the government. Neddy and Nicky had several aims. They aimed, of course, to improve the economic growth rate, but they also aimed to involve the unions in setting a national norm for wages. This second aim sprang from growing concern at the possibly malign effects of unions. By the early 1960s pay settlements had started to increase. The resulting inflation threatened to make British goods uncompetitive, destabilise the balance of payments and force the government into politically unpopular fiscal and monetary restraint (see box, 'The economy 1951–1973'). So Neddy and Nicky together were intended to control the unions' excesses, while keeping them happy by showing the government's commitment to consensus. Unfortunately, although predictably, the unions enthusiastically participated in Neddy and refused to have anything to do with Nicky.

Neddy and Nicky also fitted in with a wider political agenda. This was the Conservatives' attempt to project themselves as the party of modernisation. In 1955 there had been a huge scheme to update the railways, the Modernisation Plan, whose excesses had to be reined in after a few years. With marvellous zaniness, the plan contemplated the possibility of nuclear-powered locomotives, although accepting that they were not very likely. But while it is tempting to poke fun, the plan was a serious attempt to modernise part of Britain's infrastructure. Then the first nuclear power station, Calder Hall, started operation in 1956, while Britain's first motorway, a stretch of the M1, was opened in 1959. Both were given great publicity. Macmillan made modernisation a more coherent part of his strategy, the NHS's Hospital Plan of 1962 being one example. Central to the strategy was the attempt between 1961 and 1963 to join the European Economic Community (EEC; see Chapter 11). The EEC was seen both as modern in itself and also as another way of forcing British industry to modernise by subjecting it to more competition. Neddy and Nicky were its complements on the domestic front.

Macmillan is most famous for a speech he made near the beginning of his premiership, in 1957, in which he said, '. . . most of our people have never had it so good'.[3] The speech is often taken as implying a facile optimism about the economy. In fact, he went on to point out in it that the economic scene was troubled by the threat of inflation. Modernisation aimed to counter inflation by raising productivity, which would also have many other benefits: so modernisation was not just political rhetoric but a real, if unsuccessful, attempt to grapple with underlying problems.

By 1962–1963 the popularity of Macmillan, and the Conservatives, was waning. The application to the EEC was turned down early in 1963; only a few months later John Profumo, the Secretary of State for War, deceived the House of Commons over his relationship with Christine Keeler, a prostitute who was allegedly also involved with the Soviet Naval Attache. Accompanied by lurid rumours about sex and spies, the Profumo affair gave enormous enjoyment to the general public but further sapped confidence in the government. Later that year Macmillan underwent an emergency prostate operation and felt he must retire. Partly through Macmillan's intrigues, the new Conservative leader, and therefore Prime Minister, was Alec Douglas-Home, who resigned his peerage to be eligible for the job. Douglas-Home was popular but, as an ex-peer and archetypal country gentleman, quite the wrong person to project an image of modernity. Labour narrowly won the election of October 1964, ending 13 years of Conservative rule.

Labour 1951–1970: dissent, revisionism and government

In contrast to the harmony of the 1940s, Labour during the 1950s had experienced internal dissent which anticipated increasingly bitter disagreements in the future. In the 1940s Labour's policies appealed to most in the party, right and left. However, after 1950 this unity started to fragment and foreign policy, in particular, became a bone of contention. In the late 1940s all but a few on the extreme left in the party had accepted the need for continued partnership with America, as Soviet behaviour became increasingly aggressive. But in the 1950s doubts arose as to the extent of that partnership.

Aneurin Bevan's resignation in 1951, ostensibly over health charges, was ultimately about the level of spending on rearmament. Over the next few years Bevan and his followers, the 'Bevanites', opposed the party leadership on other foreign policy issues. Bevan's opposition later simmered down but foreign policy continued to arouse party controversy, with a group of Labour left-wingers supporting the Campaign for Nuclear Disarmament (CND), founded in 1958. With trade union leaders moving to the left, the 1960 Party Conference supported unilateral nuclear disarmament, although this was reversed in 1961.

More positively, the centre and right of the party had evolved ideas which took Labour beyond nationalisation and welfare – both issues on which the Conservatives had outflanked them. These ideas were encapsulated in Tony Crosland's *The Future of Socialism* of 1956, which endorsed Keynesianism, rather than nationalisation and controls, as the means of economic management, and pointed to Labour's future as lying in the extension of equality of opportunity, in particular through education. This chimed in with a shift within Labour towards support for comprehensive schooling.

One final, and perhaps vital, ingredient in Labour's election victory of 1964 was its leader from 1963, Harold Wilson (see box, 'Harold Wilson'). Broadly accepting Crosland's revisionism, as it was tagged, Wilson added a rhetoric of modernisation. This paralleled the Conservatives, but Wilson was a far more plausible standard-bearer of modernisation than Douglas-Home. In a famous speech at the 1963 Party Conference, he talked about the new Britain to be 'forged in the white heat' of a revolution in planned, scientific, industrial growth.[4] 'New Britain' became the title of a collection of his speeches. Planning was a consistent theme – a clever sop to traditional Labourites. In practice, Labour now leaned much more towards indicative planning.

People and politics: Harold Wilson

Few prime ministers came to office with the hopes entrusted in Harold Wilson. How was it that so many of these hopes were frustrated and that many historians see Wilson, and the Labour governments he led, as failures?

He was born in 1916 into a middle-class family. Wilson later liked to claim working-class origins, and some of his wide popular appeal lay in his apparent pipe-smoking ordinariness. In fact, as a factory manager, his father earned £350 a year, at least twice the earnings of a well-paid manual worker. Wilson briefly lectured in economics at Oxford before being drafted into the Civil Service for the war and becoming a Labour MP in 1945. As President of the Board of Trade from 1947, he gained political credit by getting rid of some of Labour's apparatus of controls. Early in 1951 Wilson joined Nye Bevan in resigning over Gaitskell's imposition of prescription charges. Wilson had argued against Labour's huge rearmament programme – the root of the resignation crisis – and had much good sense on his side. The resignation had portentous consequences. Until 1964 Wilson was seen as an ally of the left. In reality he was always a moderate (Fig. 9.3).

When Attlee retired after the 1955 election, Hugh Gaitskell became Labour leader and Wilson Shadow Chancellor. He became a formidable parliamentary performer – a master of economic argument and a witty and devastating speaker. In 1963 Gaitskell died. In the subsequent leadership election among MPs, Wilson won with the support of the left.

Many of Wilson's problems in the Labour governments of 1964–1970 stem from the effectiveness of his attacks on the Conservatives. By constructing a rhetoric of modernisation that far outdid theirs, he elevated the hopes of both the party and the country that Britain's economic problems could be overcome. He then spent three years grappling with balance of payments crises. In retrospect, it would probably have been best to devalue at once, and to have immediately reduced Britain's excessive world-wide defence commitments (see Chapter 11). Devaluation would not have solved the underlying economic problems (see box, 'The economy 1951–1973'), but it might have

▶

Figure 9.3 Harold Wilson with the Beatles (from left John, George and Paul) in 1964, a few months before he became Prime Minister. The juxtaposition emphasised Labour's modernity and (relative) youth. © Hulton-Deutsch Collection/CORBIS

provided a better base for confronting them. Wilson was also faced with the leftwards shift of parts of the Labour Party. America became increasingly unpopular with the left as the Vietnam war intensified. Unfairly, Wilson got no credit with them for resisting American pressure for Britain to contribute to the war. Instead they turned against him.

Britain faced so many problems during Wilson's 1974–1976 premiership that few commentators single him out for blame. He showed his political skills by defusing the issue of EEC membership but left much of the hard grind of government to his senior colleagues, Denis Healey and Jim Callaghan.

Ultimately, perhaps, Harold Wilson's main failing was his optimism: he thought he could always find a solution to problems, and thereby raised too many expectations. The problems themselves were hardly his fault. There are some similarities with Lloyd George: the optimism and the facility with expedient solutions, which ultimately gave both a reputation for deviousness. But unlike Lloyd George, Wilson set great store by party unity. All agree that, personally, he was one of the kindest of men. In this he has been compared with Baldwin – but Baldwin, with great political courage, supported causes unpopular in his party. Wilson preferred to give way.

Labour came into office with few firm commitments, but Wilson had whipped up many expectations. Since the Conservatives had maintained the welfare state, Labour could only satisfy its activists – and justify its own criticisms of the Conservatives – by spending more on welfare. Between the early 1960s and 1970 government spending rose from around 35 per cent to over 40 per cent of national income. Pensions were raised early on, and bringing the Hospital Plan to fruition increased spending on the NHS. In higher education, the number of students doubled. At that time all students were funded and provided with maintenance by government, with obvious effects on expenditure. As with the NHS, the growth in higher education was not just a result of Labour's initiatives. The Robbins Report of 1963 had already recommended a large increase in student numbers, which had been accepted by the Conservatives, who had also established seven new universities. Labour's specific contribution, which took up the idea of modernisation, was to develop polytechnics, originally intended to focus on scientific and vocational subjects. At school level, Crosland as Secretary of State for Education drove forward comprehensivisation, with pupil numbers in comprehensives rising from 10 per cent to over 30 per cent of the total. Comprehensives had become accepted by educational professionals and within the Civil Service – just as tripartism had only 20 years earlier – and the Conservatives tacitly accepted them too. During their period in office between 1970 and 1974 the proportion of comprehensive pupils rose again, to over 60 per cent.

Comprehensivisation and the extension of higher education were one part of the revisionist agenda. Another was a series of liberal reforms in criminal justice, race relations, divorce and other areas. Some of these were government sponsored, while others were introduced by private members but tacitly supported by the government. They are discussed in Chapter 12.

Whatever the achievements of social reform, the Labour governments of 1964–1970 have ultimately been judged by their handling of the economy. Although the Conservatives had left the balance of payments in a difficult position in 1964, Labour decided not to devalue sterling. The decision has been much criticised, but fixed rate currencies were then seen as a vital part of the world economic order (see earlier box, 'The economy 1951–1973') and hence currency stability was seen as a test of government economic competence – particularly telling for Labour since it had carried out the devaluation of 1949. Instead Labour pinned its hopes on strengthening the Conservatives' indicative planning machinery and encouraging industrial modernisation. Two new ministries – the Department of Economic Affairs (DEA) for planning and the Ministry of Technology – were formed, and in 1965 the DEA brought out a 'National Plan' which projected a sharp increase in growth. With increased welfare spending and the optimism generated by the plan, it was a good time for Labour to strengthen its wafer-thin parliamentary majority of three, and another election in March 1966 increased this to 97. From then on, things went downhill.

Continued sterling crises forced government spending cuts, reining back the growth of welfare. Nevertheless, devaluation – from £1 = \$2.80 to £1 = \$2.40 – became inevitable in November 1967. Parts of Labour's modernisation strategy survived these crises. Renationalisation of steel had been in the 1964 election manifesto as a sop to the left.

When renationalised, it was reorganised into one huge corporation, and this emphasis on size also lay behind government encouragement of various private sector mergers. The idea was to produce firms which were large enough to compete world-wide. Financial incentives encouraged factory building in, and business relocation to, regions where old industries, notably coal, were declining, a policy which could be partly justified on social grounds. The crises meant that the National Plan went out of the window, however. Instead, the government became increasingly concerned about the trade unions. Once bastions of the political right in the Labour Party, the unions had been jealous of their liberties but willing, between 1945 and 1951, to moderate pay demands. Since then they had moved to the left and, as the Conservatives had found, were unwilling to enter into voluntary agreements. Barbara Castle, the Secretary of State for Employment and a Wilson ally, produced a White Paper (a document outlining likely legislative changes), *In Place of Strife*, early in 1969. This set out some – fairly mild – proposed legislation on strike ballots and legal delays before a strike could be called. The unions predictably opposed it and, since they were entrenched in the Labour Party, with many powerful allies, it never reached Parliament.

Labour's post-war unity was becoming increasingly frayed. The dissent of the Bevanites had been primarily over foreign policy. This continued, with growing hostility to America's war in Vietnam and, by extension, to Britain's alliance with America; but it was joined by increasing conflict over domestic issues such as union reform.

The Heath government 1970–1974

Few governments came to power with such detailed plans for the reform of British institutions as did that of Edward (Ted) Heath. Few left office more ignominiously, with some of their most important plans in shreds – failures which were to have major repercussions in the future.

Heath, who was elected Conservative leader when Douglas-Home stepped down after the 1964 defeat, was essentially a liberal moderniser in the Macmillan mould, although his stiff personal style and lack of charm and bonhomie obscured his similarities to Macmillan. With the impetus to modernise even more urgent because of its failures under Macmillan and Wilson, detailed plans seemed essential. They included a strengthening of competition, entry to Europe and trade union reform. For most of the late 1960s Labour's unpopularity was such that a Conservative victory seemed inevitable. Eventually Labour regained much electoral support, reflecting apparent improvements in Britain's economic performance after devaluation, and prompting Wilson to call an election in 1970. Labour, however, lost.

One of Heath's first actions was to apply again for entry to Europe. After Macmillan's failure in 1963, Labour had dropped its earlier opposition and attempted to join, but de Gaulle had vetoed this in 1967. Heath was a strong pro-European and, like Macmillan, saw European Community (EC) membership as a galvanising influence on British industry. British membership was agreed in the summer of 1972, with formal accession in 1973. In the long run, entry was to be immensely important, and its many implications are discussed in Chapters 10 and 11.

The modernisation drive extended to the NHS and local government. The resultant reorganisation of the NHS was overcomplex and resulted in increased costs; much of it was unwound in the 1980s, while many of the local government reforms did not last much longer (see Chapter 10). In their wider social policy the Conservatives remained committed to the welfare state. Indeed, social spending in real terms rose rapidly, partly because of the expensive reorganisations but also because of a continued sharp rise in education spending. In other respects too, such as its attitude to race relations, the government remained firmly within the liberal consensus. Another area of consensus, albeit of a very different nature, was policy towards Northern Ireland, where Catholic protests over civil rights had become a full-scale guerrilla war. This is discussed further in the next chapter.

One major area of reform was policy towards the unions. The government wished, in particular, to target unofficial strike action, seen as a major problem, by making unions responsible for such action and liable to fines before an Industrial Relations Court if it did not cease. However, the Trades Union Congress (TUC) opposed the Industrial Relations Act, passed in 1971, by ordering unions not to register under it, thus severely damaging the Act's credibility. Other provisions such as 'cooling-off' periods before strikes also ran into trouble.

Union reform was in part an attempt to restrict unions' ability to gain large wage increases. It was, therefore, an attempt to attack inflation: Macmillan's old bugbear. What damaged this attempt more than union defiance of the Act, however, was their unfettered ability to keep winning such increases. One critical incident was a strike by the National Union of Mineworkers (NUM) early in 1972. Although the coal industry had been severely pruned in the 1960s, coal was the main fuel for power stations. By cutting supplies to these through aggressive picketing, the union brought overwhelming pressure on the government and achieved a large pay increase. But unemployment was also rising, reaching 4 per cent in January 1972 – a rate which then seemed unacceptable in the light of the long-standing commitment to full employment.

By early 1972, therefore, there were strong pressures on the government to rethink its policies. John Ramsden has argued that one other pressure was the likely prospect of entry to the EC. While it was hoped that this would galvanise British industry, industry needed to be in a fit state to respond to the stimulus. The result was what came to be seen as a 'U-turn': the government wholeheartedly embraced planned growth and attempted to cooperate with the unions. The U-turn's apparent sharpness was exacerbated because, before the 1970 election, Harold Wilson had seized upon a limited degree of right-wing Conservative rhetoric to invent 'Selsdon man', an archetypal right-wing figure, named after a meeting of Conservative shadow ministers at the Selsdon Park Hotel. The U-turn then lived on in political mythology because, as Conservatives looked back on the failures of the Heath years, the policy shift of 1972 was seen as a seminal and disastrous turning point. In reality, the Conservatives' policies from 1972–1974 were in many ways a rerun of Macmillan's policies between 1961 and 1963, while the 'right-wing' shift of 1970–1972 was largely imaginary. So there was a U-turn, but it was much less dramatic than often portrayed.

The government's new strategy had three main elements. One was an expansionary fiscal policy, beginning in 1971 and accelerated in 1972. By sharply increasing government spending it was hoped, Keynesian style, to boost the growth rate. The second, the Industry Act of 1972, gave increased powers to intervene directly in industry. The third was direct control over wages, prices and dividends.

The third element had precursors in a brief pay pause in 1961 and a longer one under Labour in 1966–1967, both intended to stabilise the balance of payments. The rationale for Heath's policy was more like that for Macmillan's abortive NIC: expansion was likely to cause inflation, which in 1972 was already high, and wage and price control was therefore necessary to curtail it. Heath spent much time consulting the TUC but could not reach agreement. So in November 1972 the government froze wages, prices and dividends for 90 days, subsequently restricting increases. Although the unions protested, there was wide public support and no initial challenges. But ultimately this policy, and the expansionary fiscal policy, were to have momentous consequences.

Domestic inflation in Britain had been rising since devaluation, which pushed up raw material costs and also, by reducing the prices of British goods to the outside world, made firms more susceptible to pressure for higher wages. Even the higher unemployment of 1971–1972 had not reduced wage pressure. Existing inflation was then exacerbated by sharp rises in the money supply, partly caused by the removal of direct controls on bank lending. The resulting rapid increase in borrowing was encouraged by interest rates remaining lower than the rate of inflation, making them effectively negative. Then in 1972 the Bretton Woods system of fixed exchange rates broke down due to American withdrawal and sterling floated. It depreciated against most currencies, thus further pushing up import prices, which were already rising sharply due to high world demand for raw materials. The government's expansionary fiscal policy exacerbated these inflationary forces. Finally, between late 1973 and 1974 oil prices, already rising, quadrupled due to restriction of output by OPEC, the oil producers' cartel.

In November 1973 Heath announced the continuation of the prices and incomes policy, allowing limited increases. The miners challenged it with an overtime ban which restricted coal supplies, in order to win a much larger rise. The government and the TUC negotiated, trying to preserve elements of the government's policy, which the TUC realised still had much popular appeal. However, Heath decided there was no option but an election. In an atmosphere of tension – the government had put industry on a three-day working week to conserve electricity, and the miners had now gone on strike – Labour became the party with the most MPs, although it did not have an overall majority. Early in March 1974 it took office.

Almost 30 years of post-war consensus had ended. Its ending was not immediately apparent, but the previous 12 years or so had sealed its fate. Over that period inflation had increased sharply, as had the incidence of strikes. For all the high hopes of successive modernisation drives, growth rates had not significantly increased. Two foundations of consensus now seemed to be built on sand. Keynesianism as an agent of economic regulation had broken down. In spite of a government fiscal surplus in 1969 and 1970, which should have restricted demand, wages had increased sharply. When unemployment had subsequently increased, wage rises accelerated further. The finger of suspicion for this state of affairs was now firmly pointed at the unions. They had been seen as part of the consensus, but there appeared to be little or no reciprocation by them in terms of wage restraint.

The Heath government did not itself wish to break the post-war consensus, but to revive it, although this underlying intention has been obscured by the mythology of the 'U-turn'. Heath, however, was Prime Minister at a time when the factors listed above were fatally weakening consensus, but before this fact was fully understood. Nevertheless, his government was responsible for some of its own misfortunes. World-wide inflation and the oil crisis were major factors over which it had no control. But it was responsible for poorly thought-out trade union legislation and the massive rise in government spending from 1972, which added to inflationary pressures. By 1973–1974 senior Conservatives were debating the apparent 'ungovernability' of Britain – a rather pathetic abnegation of responsibility.

Notes

1. Quoted in Zweiniger-Bargielowska, *Austerity* (see Chapter 8).
2. Quoted in Rhodes-James, *Eden* (see Chapter 5), p. 101.
3. Quoted in Turner, J., *Macmillan* (Harlow: Longman, 1994), p. 228.
4. Quoted in Ziegler, P., *Wilson* (London: Weidenfeld and Nicolson, 1993), pp. 143–144.

Further reading

Ball, S. and Seldon, A. (eds), *The Heath Government 1970–1974* (Harlow: Longman, 1996) is a very good. Burk, K. (ed.), *The British Isles since 1945* (Oxford: Oxford University Press, 2003) is a valuable set of essays. Dutton, D., *British Politics since 1945* (Oxford: Blackwell, 2nd ed., 1997) is a good survey. Hollowell, J. (ed.), *Britain since 1945* (Oxford: Blackwell, 2003) has a host of essays on many post-war topics. Lowe, R., *The Welfare State in Britain since 1945* (Basingstoke: Palgrave Macmillan, 3rd ed., 2005) is readable and authoritative. Ramsden, *Churchill and Eden* and Ramsden, *Winds of Change* (see Chapter 1) are outstanding. Thorpe, *Labour Party* (see Chapter 4) is a good survey. Tomlinson, J., 'Economic Policy' in Floud and Johnson, *Cambridge Economic History*, Vol. 3 (see Chapter 1) is particularly useful, and see other essays in this volume. Turner, *Macmillan* and Ziegler, *Wilson* are both excellent.

Other sources: Broadberry, S. and Crafts, N., 'UK Productivity Performance from 1950 to 1979: a Restatement of the Broadberry–Crafts View', *Economic History Review*, Vol. LVI, pp. 718–735 (2003); Cherry, G., *Cities and Plans: The Shaping of Urban Britain in the Nineteenth and Twentieth Centuries* (London: Arnold, 1988); Clarke, P., *The Cripps Version* (London: Penguin, 2002); Clegg, H., *The Changing System of Industrial Relations in Great Britain* (Oxford: Blackwell, 1979); Fox, D., 'The National Health Service and the Second World War' in Smith, *War* (see Chapter 8); Hall, P., *Urban and Regional Planning* (London: Routledge, 3rd ed., 1992); Harris, K., *Attlee* (London: Weidenfeld and Nicolson, 1982); Matthews, R., 'Why Has Britain

Had Full Employment Since the War?', *Economic Journal*, Vol. 78, pp. 195–204 (1968); More, *Industrial Age* (see Chapter 1); Morgan, K., *Labour in Power 1945–51* (Oxford: Oxford University Press, 1984); Sanderson, M., *Education and Economic Decline in Britain: 1870 to the 1990s* (Cambridge: Cambridge University Press, 1999); Tanner, *Labour's First Century* (see Chapter 4); Weiler, P., 'The Conservatives' search for a middle way in housing 1951–64', *Twentieth Century British History*, Vol. 14, No. 4, pp. 361–390 (2003); Wilson, H., *The New Britain: Labour's Plan* (London: Penguin, 1964).

Chapter 10

THATCHERISM AND AFTER: POLITICS 1974–2000

Inflation and monetarism

The breakdown of the post-war consensus was to usher in a period of rapid change in important areas of British life. Consensus had broken down in part because of the economic problems, real or perceived, of the 1960s and early 1970s. One of those problems, inflation, continued throughout the 1970s and had major effects on the national psyche. By 1980 prices were about four times those of ten years earlier, and drastic action to tackle inflation seemed justified. Rampant inflation coincided with intellectual shifts which promised new solutions. Many Conservative MPs adopted a more free-market economic philosophy, and this was usually linked to the acceptance of monetarism. In fact there is no necessary connection between the two, but nonetheless the term 'monetarist' is often applied to the whole set of ideas.

The free-market views of the 1970s had antecedents in the 1950s and 1960s, when one element of the Conservative modernisation strategy was to increase competition. But this had always omitted serious consideration of nationalised industries, while bodies such as the National Economic Development Council (NEDC), set up under Macmillan, were antithetical to strong free marketeers. Then the Heath government had constructed its maze of controls from 1972 onwards, creating even more of a gap between rhetoric and reality. In internal party debate in the late 1960s, more radical Conservatives such as Nicholas Ridley had suggested selling off large chunks of nationalised industry. But these ideas were suppressed and, after 1970, only some tiny denationalisations had taken place (such as a brewery in Carlisle, a legacy of government efforts to control drinking by munitions workers in the First World War!). After the Conservative defeat in 1974, the immediacy of inflation meant that the rise of monetarism overshadowed the growing acceptance of free-market views.

Monetarism is not the same as monetary policy, which is as old as central banking (in Britain, the first half of the nineteenth century). In the 1970s monetarism was a recent theoretical development within economics. It used the tools of monetary policy – that is, interest rates to control demand in the economy and various technical measures involving banking reserves and sales of government stock. But it had as its ultimate target money supply, with the aim of reducing its rate of growth. To extreme exponents of monetarism, inflation was altogether dependent on the rate of growth of the money supply and would therefore also be controlled.

Two politicians who were influential in spreading monetarist views were Sir Keith Joseph and Enoch Powell. Joseph was a well-intentioned Conservative politician and intellectual, with much support among Conservative MPs. Powell had been a Conservative minister, but by the 1970s he was a maverick demagogue with considerable popular support. Although in February 1974, having resigned his seat, Powell had urged Conservatives to vote Labour, his support for monetarism still commanded attention. While Joseph and Powell's championship of monetarism was important, it was the abject failure of the Heath government to control inflation which drove many Conservatives towards what promised to be a magic solution.

Monetarism was not just a preserve of Conservatives, but was an intellectual trend which was increasingly influential within the Treasury and the Bank of England, although with them it was yoked with the belief that any policy instrument that might work should be deployed against inflation. As such, the Labour governments of 1974–1979 could not ignore it, and continued the policy, initiated in 1973, of setting targets for the growth of money supply. Monetarism also fulfilled another function for the Labour government. Unemployment had risen, largely because of the shock that the oil price rise had delivered to the world economy, leading Labour activists to call for higher government spending to reduce it. But the government faced international selling of sterling in 1976, and although this could have been accommodated by letting sterling float downwards, such a course of action would exacerbate inflation. Instead the government borrowed from the International Monetary Fund (IMF) to support the pound, although this carried a price in terms of restrictions on government spending. The government, therefore, needed policy arguments to justify a move away from the simple Keynesian orthodoxy that higher unemployment could be met by more government spending, financed by borrowing. A partial acceptance of monetarism provided such arguments. It was encapsulated by James Callaghan, the Prime Minister, at the 1976 Party Conference when he stated that the government could no longer 'just spend [its] way out of recession . . .'.[1] He then attributed increasing rates of inflation in the past to such spending.

The importance of inflation in the 1970s cannot be overstated. Its impact on politicians, opinion-formers in the media and the public made the drastic policies of the early Thatcher years conceivable, if not popular. In spite of its importance, the focus of economic historians on economic growth has precluded, at the time of writing, much analysis by them of why inflation in Britain was so acute.

Labour 1974–1979

On taking office in March 1974, Labour was confronted with a set of problems which almost rivalled those of the 1945 government. Coal supplies to power stations were restricted and inflation was on an upward trend. Northern Ireland was still a major problem to any government that was in power (see box, 'Northern Ireland'). Harold Wilson was also obliged to do something about Britain's membership of the European Community. He had opposed the Conservative application to the Community, despite his own earlier application, on the grounds that the terms were wrong. This was an opportunistic stance, but was also an attempt to straddle the divide in the Labour Party over membership. To make life even more difficult, Labour was in a minority in the House of Commons, although it had more seats than the Conservatives. One reason for this was an upsurge in support for the Scottish and Welsh nationalist parties (see Chapter 12) and for the Liberals. Together they now had 23 seats, thus introducing new complications into the two-party political minuet which had characterised the previous 30 years.

Finally, Wilson now faced internal dissent from the left which harked back to the Gaitskell years. The left's power in the constituency parties and the unions had increased. The radicalisation and increasing anti-Americanism caused by the Vietnam war, the apparent failures of Wilson's moderate policies in 1964–1970 and the challenge posed to the unions by Heath were all factors. The shadow cabinet was elected by the Parliamentary Labour Party (PLP) which was far less left-inclined, and Wilson, as leader, appointed the cabinet himself. But the strength of the left within the party could not be ignored.

Some problems were dealt with quickly. The miners' pay claim was generously settled. Wage increases then proceeded more or less unchecked in 1974, partly because it was the easiest option and partly because they could, with some justice, be blamed on the Conservatives. With a degree of calm restored to the country after the near panic of the later Heath era, Wilson called another election in October 1974, emerging with a small overall majority. He then secured what many see as his outstanding success: finessing the left's opposition – in which they were joined by some Conservatives – to

Politics and government: Northern Ireland

Home Rule in 1920 reserved most powers except defence, foreign policy and taxation to the government of Northern Ireland, known as Stormont after its move to the monumental parliament building there in 1932. Of the province's million and a quarter inhabitants in the 1920s, around two-thirds were Protestant and the rest Catholic. (The Protestant proportion has now shrunk to 53 per cent of a total of around 1.7 million.) The Protestant party, the Unionists, had a permanent parliamentary majority and local government boundaries were redrawn to give Protestants control even in areas such as Londonderry where there were more Catholics. The result of political domination was discrimination against Catholics, particularly in public housing allocation. Catholics also bore the brunt of unemployment, which remained relatively high even during the boom years of 1945–1970 as the shipbuilding and linen industries declined.

In spite of discrimination and unemployment, there was little sustained protest before the late 1960s. A campaign of violence between 1956 and 1962 by the Irish Republican Army (IRA), the illegal relic of Southern Ireland's war against the British between 1919 and 1921, gained minimal support. During the later 1960s, Catholic political activists began civil rights campaigns, in part inspired by those for black civil rights in the USA. Tension was inflamed by Protestant counter-marching and police brutality and,

▶

following sectarian violence in 1969, British troops were sent in. The IRA split and a more militant group, the Provisionals, quickly became dominant, gaining significant Catholic working-class support. Between 1969 and 1972 violence escalated dramatically, with Protestant paramilitary groups joining in. In the peak year of 1972 there were 467 deaths, mainly from shootings and bombings. With the loss of control by Stormont, the British government introduced direct rule from Westminster in 1972. The Sunningdale agreement of 1973 to reintroduce devolved government, involving moderate elements from both religious groupings, was scuppered in 1974 by a Protestant workers' strike and direct rule was reinstated.

Violence slowly decreased for a variety of reasons: the security services improved their intelligence, while the Northern Irish economy was reconstructed on the basis of huge subsidies from the rest of the UK. By the late 1980s, 65 per cent of regional income came from public expenditure. As public sector employment grew, there was an erosion of the working class from which paramilitary groups gained most support. Simultaneously, the British government shifted towards collaboration with Eire, culminating in the Downing Street Declaration by the two governments in 1993. This recognised the right of the Northern Irish people to self-determination, while Eire accepted that its claim to Northern Ireland must go. It was removed from the constitution in 1998.

The IRA tacitly accepted that violence had no future. It declared a ceasefire in 1994 which, although broken in 1996, was reinstated in 1997 and has remained since. In 1998 the Good Friday Agreement reinstated a devolved Northern Irish government incorporating Sinn Fein, the IRA's political wing. Problems over the IRA's decommissioning of arms subsequently led to the suspension of devolution. With further IRA moves towards demilitarisation, however, violence except by rogue splinter groups seems off the agenda.

Why has Northern Ireland been so different to mainland Britain? Sectarian politics lived on in Liverpool and the West of Scotland until the Second World War, but never involved significant violence. Conversely, there were upsurges of violence in Northern Ireland between 1920 and 1969. In all three cases, Irish Catholics (or Catholics of Irish origin) lived alongside communities with very different traditions. But Northern Irish Protestants always perceived a threat from Southern Ireland, while Westminster, glad to be free of Irish problems, provided no check on discrimination against Catholics. So compared to the mainland, attitudes on both sides were hardened. However, until the late 1960s Northern Ireland avoided sustained violence. The main Catholic party, the Nationalists, remained rooted in an old-fashioned hostility to partition and this negative attitude may have encouraged Catholic apathy.

In the late 1960s, however, the political ferment of the civil rights movement, the Provisional IRA's claim to 'defend' Catholic areas and the presence of British troops gave the demand for Irish unification renewed saliency. Perhaps equally important, pressure from Westminster for reform and widespread criticism of police brutality weakened and divided the Unionists – who had themselves started on the road to liberalisation. As so often, the time of greatest vulnerability for repressive governments is when they start to reform.

the European Community. James Callaghan, the Foreign Secretary, renegotiated the terms of entry modestly in Britain's favour. He and Wilson portrayed themselves as neutral while edging towards support of continued membership. The final ingredients were acceptance of a referendum on membership, while allowing the Cabinet to divide over the issue. Wilson and Callaghan ultimately supported membership, and the referendum in June 1975 delivered a 2:1 majority in favour.

Wilson's other victory – fittingly, an essentially tactical one – was to temporarily neutralise the left. Tony Benn, who as Viscount Stansgate had renounced his peerage, was a technocrat who had moved steadily leftwards. He was appointed Industry Minister when Labour came to power, and had pushed the idea of a National Enterprise Board (NEB) which would, effectively, act as a vehicle for nationalising manufacturing industries. After the referendum Benn, a keen anti-European, lost political momentum and in 1975 Wilson moved him to the Energy Ministry, on the face of it an important ministry because of the development of North Sea oil, but a less politically controversial one. The NEB was launched without Benn and confined itself largely to bailing out financially crippled firms – something the Heath government had already been doing. The left, however, did not go away, although their influence during the rest of the government's term of office was limited.

Although Labour had agreed a 'Social Contract' (originally it was called a Social Compact) with the unions in 1973, by which the latter would moderate wage increases in return for increased social and other benefits, the unions had taken little notice of the moderation side of the equation. Eventually, however, the two most powerful union leaders, Hugh Scanlon and Jack Jones, grew concerned that high inflation – it peaked in August 1975 at an annual rate of 27 per cent – was potentially destabilising. In July 1975 a pay limitation policy was agreed, which until 1978 had some success. It may have played a part in reducing inflation, although this remained relatively high. Reduction was also helped by monetary controls and a recovery after 1976 in the value of sterling, which cut import prices.

Harold Wilson retired in March 1976 – not surprisingly, he had felt the strain of the last two years – and was replaced by James (Jim) Callaghan, another centrist. Apart from the continuing economic problems, Callaghan had to grapple with Labour's loss of its Commons majority due to by-election defeats. In 1977–1978 there was a 'pact' with the Liberals – support in return for some modest policy concessions – but this broke down. However, the Scottish and Welsh nationalists supported the government because bills for devolution, which had been government policy since 1975, were still in progress. But on 1 March 1979 devolution was rejected in referenda, removing the nationalists' grounds for support. The Conservatives put down a motion of no confidence, winning by one vote. A government defeated in the House of Commons on a confidence motion was a rare occasion in modern British politics, and an election became inevitable.

Among the electorate, the government's credibility and popularity had been damaged by a strike wave over the winter of 1978–1979, the so-called Winter of Discontent, which represented an effective rejection of the pay policy. Labour's defeat in the 1979 election was to usher in 18 years of Conservative rule.

The Labour governments of 1974–1979 were caught in multitudinous storms. In some ways their situation is comparable to that facing the post-war Coalition in 1918–1922: escalating inflation and intransigent unions, with the perennial issue of Ireland in the background. Even Labour's initial reaction, to let inflation rip because there were so many other problems to address, was similar. Subsequently, the government struggled to find a way to moderate inflation while keeping elements of the post-war consensus; its partial conversion to monetarism was more a matter of expediency than a firm intellectual switch. However, as Andrew Thorpe has commented, it marked the ideological bankruptcy of the right of the party. The apparently easy option offered by Keynesianism – economic growth plus low unemployment and moderate inflation – was now discredited. That being so, the sidelining of the old policy prescriptions of the left – planning, controls and nationalisation – was much more difficult to justify. Wilson won tactical victories over the left, and Callaghan with his close links to the unions kept the show on the road a little longer. Defeat in 1979, however, was to open the way to a resurgence of the left within the Labour Party.

Thatcher and after

Margaret Thatcher had replaced Heath as Conservative leader in 1975. Her eleven and a half years in office from 1979 was a longer continuous term than any Prime Minister since Lord Liverpool in the early nineteenth century, and longer in total than any Prime Minister had served since Lord Salisbury left office in 1902. The record of her governments still polarises opinion. Since they are so recent, the verdict on their ultimate importance is as much that of journalists and political scientists as of historians. Most agree that they were very significant. The Labour governments of 1974–1979 had merely seen elements of the post-war consensus called into question. The Thatcher years saw a radical and self-conscious break with much that had gone before. To the left, this break took the form primarily of an attack on the achievements of the Labour movement in general, and the Attlee government in particular: specifically, an attack on trade unions and nationalisation. Others perceived the government as conducting a wide-ranging attack on vested interests, and therefore to be genuinely radical and not just the wielder of a right-wing bludgeon.

Paradoxically, the doctrine which had become the new rallying cry for many Conservatives – monetarism – was to prove one of the least enduring legacies of the Thatcher years. Geoffrey Howe, her first Chancellor, yoked it in his 1979 budget to tax changes aimed at increasing incentives by shifting the burden from direct taxation (taxation on incomes) to indirect (VAT and excise duties on drink, tobacco and petrol; in tax language these are indirect, although they appear fairly direct to most people). VAT was virtually doubled, from 8 per cent to 15 per cent; income tax was reduced from 33 per cent to 30 per cent; and the top rate of tax was lowered from 83 per cent to 60 per cent. Monetarism was represented by an increase in interest rates and a tightening of money supply growth targets. In 1980 the Medium Term Financial Strategy (MTFS) set out a coherent monetarist policy. The rate of growth of the money

People and politics: Margaret Thatcher

Born in Grantham in 1925 of a modestly prosperous, but far from wealthy, shopkeeping family, Margaret Thatcher read chemistry at Oxford. Subsequently, she became a barrister. Formidably hard-working, she combined motherhood, the law and political activity, with an emphasis on the third.

Mrs Thatcher became Minister of Education in the Heath government in 1970. Her approach was not particularly controversial – comprehensivisation continued at a rapid rate – and her support for right-of-centre economic policies was muted. However, as a junior Cabinet minister she had limited opportunity to express opinions contrary to the government line. After the two 1974 election defeats, Conservative MPs were becoming disillusioned with Heath and attracted by monetarism (see main text, 'Inflation and monetarism'). Margaret Thatcher's alliance with the guru of monetarism, Keith Joseph, gained her the support of the right, while her silence on many issues meant that centrists did not view her as too extreme. In the subsequent leadership election, in 1975, Heath was defeated as party leader and Margaret Thatcher elected (Fig. 10.1).

Figure 10.1 Margaret Thatcher (left) with Queen Elizabeth at the Commonwealth Conference in 1979. Also visible is Daniel Arap Moi of Kenya. © Bettmann/CORBIS

The conversion of many Conservative MPs to monetarist and free-market views strengthened her ability to carry these through. Nevertheless, it took political courage to persist with policies which, in the early 1980s at least, were often unpopular, including with many of her own ministers. Some would say this also reflected obstinacy or simple lack of feeling. However, her actions were tempered by a shrewd appreciation of political realities. She drew back from danger areas such as education vouchers, and when in office kept her scepticism about Europe within limits. She does not, however, seem to be a person of great self-insight and fell into the trap of many with power of believing too strongly in her own wisdom. In her later years in office she increasingly bullied her ministers and eroded their willingness to support her in the 1990 leadership election, although by all accounts she treated her personal staff with great consideration. The increasingly strident rhetoric of those years came to bedevil Conservatism in the 1990s and beyond, leaving it associated with a negative attitude towards the welfare state and perceived as out-of-touch even after the internal quarrels over Europe had died down (see main text, 'Conservatives and Europe 1990–1997').

Her greatest strength was that her views usually mirrored those of many ordinary people, even if many others rejected them. They were fairly simple: militant patriotism, belief in people keeping what they earned and dislike of bureaucracy and trade unions.

The verdict of history is still provisional. Eric Evans sees her period in office as almost entirely reprehensible, although he is not much kinder about her immediate predecessors or successors in government. John Campbell's biography is more measured, awarding her both pluses and minuses. Peter Clarke's verdict is penetrating. Whatever one thinks of Thatcherism, her contribution to the changes it wrought were the conviction that she was right, and the ability to 'locate and mobilise a constituency'[2] behind ideas which others originated.

She was created Baroness Thatcher in 1992.

supply was to be reduced year on year. Government borrowing was also to be reduced and deviations in both it and money supply were to be met by automatic corrective action. Thus the Keynesian response to unemployment, increased government borrowing, was in theory ruled out. In practice, the subsequent recession meant the government still ran a deficit and had to borrow in the early 1980s, although taxes rose sharply in 1981.

The first three years of the Thatcher government saw an agonising squeeze on manufacturing industry. An international recession had followed a second large increase in oil prices. North Sea oil was now coming on stream and, as a result, sterling rose rather than fell as in the mid-1970s, thus making exports less profitable. The rise was exacerbated by the high interest rates called for by monetarism. As a result, unemployment increased rapidly to 3 million. Inflation was substantially reduced, although there is debate as to how far this was caused directly by high interest rates, and how far by the rise in unemployment in which other factors were involved. Subsequently, the MTFS became steadily less important. It was increasingly apparent that money is such an elastic commodity that attempting to control supply was extremely difficult, if not impossible. Furthermore, interest rates were subject to influence from Mrs Thatcher, who was always worried about the effect of high interest rates on the home owners' vote, many home owners having mortgages. By the late 1980s the stabilisation of sterling's level against other European currencies had become the main anti-inflationary policy instrument.

Monetarism went along with a belief in freer markets. The policy initiatives flowing from this in the 1980s included privatisation, the name given to the sale of nationalised industries; the strengthening of incentives through tax reductions; and attacks on vested interests including the unions.

In opposition, the Conservatives had been extremely cautious in their policy statements. This was tactically sensible, since by the late 1970s Labour was so unpopular that there was no point in the Conservatives making risky promises. But even in private there seems to have been little real planning for privatisation, and certainly little conceptualisation of what it might actually achieve. Initially, limited privatisation, mainly of stakes in manufacturing and oil companies which had been acquired over the years, seems to have been viewed simply as a convenient means of reducing government borrowing. As confidence grew, policy in the mid-1980s moved towards selling off large nationalised industries, notably gas and British Telecom – government owned since the Post Office had started providing telephone services in the late nineteenth century. At this stage, a belief in promoting popular capitalism through wider share ownership was added to the continuing desire to raise money. The belief that private enterprise would increase efficiency was always there, but at first the mechanisms for this were ill defined, since private monopolies may have little more incentive to efficiency than public ones. As time went by, the mechanisms became better defined: as an interim step, regulation would mandate price reductions; the ultimate aim was to promote new entry to industries, thus fostering competition.

Privatisation is an enduring legacy of the Thatcher years. The restructuring of taxation is another. Economic recovery after 1982, and the revenue flowing from taxation on North Sea oil, meant that direct taxation could be further reduced. By 1988 it was 25 pence in the pound, while the top rate of taxation on income had been reduced to 40 pence. Since the Second World War, levels of direct taxation in Britain had been among the highest in the West. The cumulative reductions reversed this position, although indirect taxation rose sharply to compensate. It remains unproven as to whether this shift had any real effect on incentives to work, the reason often advanced for it, although obviously it can be defended on other grounds.

The attack on vested interests, and particularly trade union privileges, was the final plank of economic reform. By the late 1970s there was widespread support, including among many trade unionists, for reform. But, as with privatisation, the Conservatives were sparing with policy prescriptions. One reason for this was the continued influence in the party of legatees of consensus such as Jim Prior. Another was Heath's failure to make reform stick even after detailed planning, a failure which occurred in part because the unions had the industrial muscle to take on the government, not just over reform but over pay as well. The Conservative response was to accept that reform would have to be gradual and confrontations prepared for.

The first Conservative Employment Act, in 1980, restricted lawful picketing to the pickets' own place of work – significant because of the miners' use of secondary picketing in the earlier coal strikes. The 1982 Act made sympathetic strikes illegal and removed unions' immunity from civil actions, thus making them liable for damages if they carried out illegal actions. In 1984 pre-strike ballots were made mandatory and later Acts in 1988 and 1990 banned the 'closed shop', which compelled union membership. It was the 1982 Act which was crucial, making it possible to levy large fines on the National Union of Mineworkers (NUM) in their 1984–1985 strike. The government had ducked out of an earlier confrontation with the miners, backing down after threatening to close a number of collieries in 1981. By 1984 they had built up coal stocks and took on the miners, led by the left-winger Arthur Scargill, over the issue of colliery closures. The government was aided by the refusal of most miners in Nottinghamshire and other Midlands pits to strike – in an echo of the earlier Spencer Union (see Chapter 4), they founded their own Union of Democratic Mineworkers. The coal strike's collapse was symbolic of how far the unions had been tamed. But, apart from the Conservative legislation, the decline in manufacturing employment had weakened the unions and the NUM's failure, dramatic as it was, was only one part of a larger picture. Other unions were adapting to the new situation, in some cases by moving towards closer relations with employers.

The government did not just take on the unions. At one time or another it confronted a host of interest groups, which were not always politically on the left (Fig. 10.2). Early on, the strong pound's effect on manufacturing led to bitter complaints from the Confederation of British Industry (CBI). Its president in 1980 promised a 'bare-knuckle fight' with the government[3] – which came to nothing. In 1986 the 'Big Bang' in the City of London abolished various restrictive practices in securities' trading. As part of the deregulation of financial services, its long-term impact was beneficial, but its immediate effect was to disrupt a cosy monopoly. Another special privilege was academic tenure, by which university lecturers virtually had a life freehold of their jobs. It was abolished for new members of staff in 1987.

The Thatcher revolution had limits, the main one being the welfare state. It was chipped around the edges, but when more radical changes were proposed, caution ultimately sidelined them.

The only real exception was housing, where the sale of council-owned property at lower-than-market prices was encouraged. Since existing council tenants were advantaged, the measures were popular with most of those affected. They fitted in with one strand of the government's ideology, the emphasis on popular capitalism. Removing large chunks of the housing stock from public ownership also dovetailed with the drive to freer markets, since difficulties of access to housing were held to have impeded labour mobility. To further encourage the latter, from 1988 the private housing market was made more viable by freeing rents and securing landlords' rights over new rented

Figure 10.2   The miners' strike: Arthur Scargill (open-necked) and Tony Benn (on Scargill's left) at a rally in Nottinghamshire – ironically the stronghold of working miners – in 1984.
© Bryn Colton/Assignments Photographers/CORBIS

property. The biggest chips around the edges were inflicted on social security. As an instance, short-term earnings related benefits, for sickness and unemployment, were abolished in 1982 and everyone went straight on to flat-rate benefit. In the same year increases in old-age pensions were linked to prices instead of earnings. Over time, as real earnings increased, the relative value of pensions shrank – the single person's pension was 23 per cent of average male earnings in 1981 and 15 per cent in 1993. In 1986 the government modified the State Earnings Related Pensions Scheme (SERPS), which had been introduced in 1975 with all-party support to replace the rather limited 1959 scheme for enhancing the basic pension. The original plan had been to abolish SERPS but this had been widely opposed, including by employers. Instead, subsidies to employees to opt out of SERPS into private schemes were introduced.

In spite of all the changes, social security spending as a percentage of total public spending jumped from 25 per cent in 1981 to 32 per cent in 1991. Behind this lay long-term factors such as the inbuilt increase in pension costs as pensioners lived longer and more people retired with earnings related pensions. The rising cost of social security indicates that financial pressures as well as ideology motivated the cuts in provision, without which the cost would have risen far more.

There were two prongs to the government's policies on education. One was the attempted raising of educational standards, which in Conservative rhetoric were slipping because of modern educational methods. A national curriculum, and testing for all children at the ages of 7 and 11, were pushed through in 1988, against the opposition of teacher unions. The over-elaboration of the early national curriculum was later relaxed. The other prong was choice. In 1980 parents were given the right to choose schools, but this right was constrained because local authorities could set limits on school size. In 1988 schools were allowed to expand numbers to their physical capacity and could opt to become grant maintained – that is, free of local authority control. Cumulatively these changes were substantial, but the Conservatives ducked introducing education vouchers, which would have given total parental choice. They were too politically risky, because if parents had been allowed to top up vouchers with fees, differences in the quality of schools would have been legitimated. Of course, parents could always buy private education, but only about 5 per cent could afford it, so to most people it appeared an irrelevance. Throughout all these changes, education increased its share of public expenditure, from 12 per cent to 14 per cent between 1981 and 1991, as children stayed longer at school and the number of those going on to higher education increased.

In 1992 the Major government aimed to make parental choice more effective by introducing league tables to measure school achievement. Subsequently, these also became an instrument of measurement and reform in the NHS. The Blair government carried forward many Conservative reforms, for instance by devolving responsibilities still further from local authorities and encouraging more diversified types of school. Comprehensivisation was comprehensively dead. In higher education too, there was continuity from the late 1980s onwards. The rise in the numbers attending higher education (see Chapter 12) had substantial public spending implications. The Conservative response was to reduce higher education funding for students and to freeze maintenance grants, topping them up with loans. Labour drastically intensified the policy in 1997 by abolishing grants and introducing fees. It is an interesting example of how a new government's political impetus allowed it to carry out radical policies.

As with education, but more dramatically, spending on health increased its share of public expenditure, from 11 per cent to 15 per cent. It is a truism that health spending in developed countries is likely to increase faster than other spending. Medical technology, in the form of machines and drugs, becomes more sophisticated and more expensive; people live longer; and there are only limited staff efficiency savings which can be made (in economists' language, labour productivity will only increase slowly). Conservatives broadly accepted the logic of this and reforms were devoted to attempting to obtain better value from the increasing amounts spent. This culminated in the 'market reforms' put forward in a 1989 White Paper and implemented in 1991. The 'internal market' meant that either District Health Authorities or GPs who had elected to manage their own budgets would 'purchase' health care from hospitals. While the Labour government of 1997 purported to change much of this, in reality the essential quasi-market structure remained even if responsibilities within it shifted.

Much in the NHS has remained since its beginnings. Its foundation is still the tax-financed system, free at the point of provision. Collectively, the changes of the 1980s and 1990s aimed to eliminate two of the big perceived problems of the old system. One was the relative weakness of primary health care, in particular the lack of incentives for GPs to practise preventive medicine. The other was the lack of any real knowledge of how well hospitals actually treated patients and with what resources. The cost of the changes was higher administrative spending.

Since many of the Thatcher reforms occurred later in her period in office, the fact that she held office for so long was vital. In her early years mounting unemployment made the government unpopular. But Labour was unpopular too, the gainers being the Liberal/Social Democratic alliance (the Alliance; see later section, 'Labour 1979–2000: decline, reconstruction and power'). The Falklands war swung support back to the government, which also gained increasing credit for economic recovery and the reduction of inflation. By splitting the anti-government vote, the Alliance's effect in the 1983 election was to boost the number of Conservative seats. Labour made some recovery between 1983 and the election of 1987 but the result was similar. Subsequently, however, support for the Conservatives eroded rapidly because of the unpopularity of the 'poll tax', the nickname for the flat-rate tax on adults which replaced the old rating system in local government. Conservative MPs feared electoral defeat and Mrs Thatcher's leadership was challenged. Although not defeated, it seemed likely that she would be at a second ballot. She resigned in November 1990 and was succeeded by John Major.

Politics and government: Local government in the twentieth century

For the first 70 years or so of the twentieth century local government consisted of independent councils in larger towns and cities, known as county boroughs, and separate county councils covering everywhere else. County boroughs often ran much of the urban infrastructure – tramways and later bus services, gasworks and later electricity supply, and so forth. The pattern of mixed public and private provision, which at national level was to develop in the interwar period, was already well established at the beginning of the century in this so-called municipal socialism.

For most of the century local government responsibilities increased, although in exercising them local authorities were usually the agent of central government which provided much of the finance. Housing provision was undertaken in a modest way before the First World War, and on a larger scale after it. Educational provision was transferred from School Boards to local authorities in 1902, and they played an increasing role in health care (see Chapters 2 and 6). Except in London, the police were also a local responsibility. After 1945 nationalisation removed gas and electricity provision and the NHS absorbed health care. But in other ways the post-war years of consensus greatly enlarged the activities of local authorities. Council housing became even more important, as did councils' responsibilities for planning (see Chapter 9). Traffic growth meant more spending on roads. Education budgets also grew and social service provision burgeoned as the number of elderly increased.

This growth in activity raised problems of structure and finance. The post-war concern with modernisation led to a belief that larger units and 'strategic' authorities would deliver better services and plan more effectively. One result was the reorganisation of London local government into fewer authorities and a strategic Greater London Council, implemented in 1965. This was followed by the 1969 Redcliffe–Maud proposals for drastically reducing the number of authorities. However, the Heath government designed its own reforms, in which smaller borough councils were subsumed in the counties and responsibilities then split between two levels. The Redcliffe–Maud proposal for strategic authorities for large conurbations was adopted, but they were abolished by the Thatcher government in 1986. In the 1990s unitary authorities on the Redcliffe–Maud lines were finally established in some areas in England and throughout Wales.

By 2000 the result of 35 years of change was a mess. The mess arose partly from conflicts. Modernisation and strategic planning – slogans as much as thought-out policies – conflicted with political imperatives. Thus fear of the strength of unitary local authorities lay in part behind Conservative hostility to them in the early 1970s. But later the Thatcher government came to dislike strategic authorities as fostering local government empire building. The biggest conflicts arose because of money. Local authorities' revenue base was the narrow one of rates – taxes levied on property, so central government subsidy had been necessary from the earliest years. But as their responsibilities grew either this subsidy had to increase or rates grew rapidly – unpopular with both business and householders. From 1958 central governments made regular attempts to curb local government expenditure, and the difficulty in doing this has led the attempts to become more and more drastic. These restrictions and increasing central government interference in, for instance, housing and education has led many to lament the decline of local government autonomy.

But in truth local government in Britain has always carried out policies which originated with central government, and the latter has always seen local government as subservient. Recent changes have merely exacerbated this tendency.

Thatcherism in perspective

Thatcherism was a radical attempt to break away from the consensus of the 1950s and 1960s. Chronologically, monetarism was its first component. Monetarism gained its political salience because of the inflation of the 1970s, but ultimately became unimportant. The enduring economic impact of Thatcherism was in its application of free-market ideas, always an undercurrent in post-war Conservatism but one whose scope had previously been limited. Under Mrs Thatcher they were applied to the nationalised industries and unions in particular, but extended to other areas too.

Nationalised industries had become part of the consensus and before 1979 had been a no-go area for significant political debate, even though both parties accepted that competition was desirable in other areas of the economy. Trade union privileges had originally been even more sacrosanct. But the implicit contract by which unions moderated wage demands, in return for the welfare state and nationalisation, was always fragile. In part, this was because most union members' attitudes were grounded in the long-standing British belief that rights did not entail obligations, and so they did not perceive a contract in the first place. But it was also because union leaders, who had originally accepted certain obligations, increasingly rejected them from the mid-1950s onwards. As a result, unions' conduct of their affairs had become a matter for political debate, as Chapter 9 showed. However, unions proved both too intransigent and too strong for governments. The Labour governments of 1974–1979 had reinstated the contract in a more overt fashion, but the unions' delivery of wage restraint came far too late to prevent much of the inflation of the period. Therefore, the contract appeared one-sided and, anyway, it broke down spectacularly in 1978–1979. This gave the Thatcher government popular support for trade union reform.

In the case of both privatisation and trade union reform, however, the government initially acted cautiously, and this caution was an important strength of Mrs Thatcher. In part, it happened simply because the government did not have detailed policies in many areas and developed its reforms as they became politically possible and as its own ideas developed. This was particularly the case with privatisation. In the case of trade unions, the caution was more pragmatic; Heath's attempt to reform too quickly enjoined a step by step approach. This caution extended into reform of the welfare state. Some members of the government, including Mrs Thatcher herself, believed that more competition between providers would have been beneficial. But in both education and health, an all-out free market would have meant accepting that the better-off could purchase better standards of care. So far as this was limited to the small existing areas of private health and education, few took much notice. But any large-scale extension would have meant that not just the poorest but many ordinary people would have been left with a basic service only. This was thought to be too politically risky and, since opinion polls have consistently shown overwhelming support for the NHS, this judgement was probably correct.

Housing was different. Originally an integral part of the welfare state, the growth of private housing illustrated that people were willing to pay more for housing if they could achieve higher standards. But, in addition, most people were willing to accept different standards for housing in a way they were not for health or education. The Thatcher government understood this and its housing reforms were broadly popular. Social services were different again. The cuts mainly affected the out-of-work – always a minority – and pensioners. The relative value of pensions shrank only slowly, however; and since this was the golden age of the company pension, which had spread widely since the war, the retirement prospects of many people were still improving. As a result, the reforms were politically acceptable.

Thatcherism may have been a radical break with consensus but what were its ultimate effects? Manufacturing declined relative to other sectors, but it has done so throughout the western world. Given the long-standing inefficiency of much British manufacturing, decline was likely anyway, but Conservative policies between 1979 and 1982 concentrated the decline in those years with a correspondingly sharper cost in unemployment. The dependence of trade unions on manufacturing means their influence would probably also have declined, but Thatcherism must have made a difference by breaking their power so dramatically and effectively. Their effect on inflation, and their potential for causing inconvenience and worse through strikes, was quite large. So lower inflation has been one probable result of Thatcherism, although some of the gains were thrown away in the late 1980s boom. And the generally positive impact of freer markets, including privatisation, on economic growth is agreed by most economists. On social security Thatcherism can claim prescience. Even Germany, the stronghold of welfarism, was by 2005 making radical cuts in unemployment benefits. But the combination of social security reform and tax changes in Britain sharply increased income inequality.

All this suggests a more neutral conclusion on Thatcherism, and the subsequent adoption by Labour of many of its policies, than is often made either by keen Thatcherites or by her critics. There were positive and negative effects which might not have occurred without her. But many changes were likely to have happened anyway over time.

Politics and government: The Civil Service in the twentieth century

As late as 1939, the British Civil Service was not that different from the Civil Service of the late nineteenth century. It was notionally a meritocracy, with entry by competitive examination. In practice, the upper ranks tended to be filled by graduates from Oxford or Cambridge, who had previously gone to public schools. There were few senior civil servants who were qualified in science or economics. It had grown substantially over the First World War and some functions, such as administering pensions and unemployment benefit, employed large numbers of routine clerical staff. But other vital departments such as the Treasury and the Foreign Office remained small. In theory, civil servants were non-political, there simply to carry out the will of their political masters. In practice, senior civil servants tended to have an agenda of desirable changes and those deemed impossible or undesirable. In departments such as the Home Office, or the Colonial Office between the wars, much routine legislation and the imparting of particular directions to policy was initiated by civil servants. The Treasury, which had overall control of spending, had one main policy aim – to keep it down.

However, the influence of civil servants on policy should not be exaggerated. Thus the Treasury's interwar hostility to increased public spending in order to tackle unemployment was shared by most Chancellors of the Exchequer. During the era of appeasement, senior civil servants' views on foreign policy themselves differed and, anyway, it was increasingly dominated by Chamberlain. When the political will was there, major reforms could be carried out. The Liberals' welfare reforms are an example. When needs must, as in both the world wars, Treasury views on economy were largely forgotten. The ultimate supremacy of political will was dramatically illustrated by the post-war Labour government. Whatever the views of senior civil servants, nationalisation took place, the welfare state was instituted and Britain was set on the path to nuclear weapons. One result of Labour's reforms was that the Civil Service, hugely swollen during the war, remained very large – around three-quarters of a million in 1950.

By comparison, change was relatively slow in the consensus years of the 1950s and 1960s. By the latter decade, Britain's perceived relative economic decline was also becoming an issue. The alleged resistance of the Civil Service to change was a target for critics, particularly in the Labour Party. The criticisms led to the Fulton Inquiry which reported in 1968, but recommendations such as more specialist senior staff were instituted only slowly and patchily. Britain's entry to the European Community, however, did make a difference. Departments such as Agriculture, Environment and Trade and Industry grew because European policies and directives were particularly important in their areas of competence. More fundamental changes finally arrived in the wake of Mrs Thatcher. With her visceral dislike of an over-large state, the Civil Service was likely to be a target for reform. As with other controversial Thatcherite policies, it took time and the 'Next Steps' initiative was only launched in 1988. It carried on under John Major and, in keeping with the new consensus, under Labour after 1997. The administration of many routine functions was hived off into semi-autonomous 'agencies'. The Civil Service proper is now largely a policy-making core. Agencies were followed by privatisation, for instance of much government computing.

This aroused little public concern but a lot of academic controversy. However, much of the routine work carried out by civil servants since the First War arose because of historical accidents rather than any logical apportionment between Civil Service, semi-autonomous government agencies or the private sector. The National Health Service has always been semi-autonomous. Education has always been directly controlled by local government, if financed partly by central. Warships and armaments have always been partly constructed by private firms. Popular lack of concern with 'Next Steps' may be quite rational, seeing it merely as a rejigging of functions among providers.

Conservatives and Europe 1990–1997

John Major won the leadership election following Margaret Thatcher's resignation, to become Prime Minister. Broadly speaking, he shared her economic views but was somewhat more liberal in social policy. His government quickly defused the poll tax issue, replacing it with a tax on houses graded according to their value. In spite of the onset of a serious recession, a rise in unemployment and the Labour revival (see next section), the Conservatives held on narrowly to win the 1992 election. Like Mrs Thatcher, John Major came from a lower middle-class background, but whereas she had remade herself as an imperious upper middle-class housewife, his image was classless and this was popular with many people. More important, Labour was still vulnerable to accusations that they were a 'tax and spend' party. With the Conservatives' re-election, however, John Major's troubles were just beginning.

In the late 1980s Nigel Lawson, the Chancellor, had come to believe that one antidote to persisting inflation was for Britain to join the Exchange Rate Mechanism (ERM), which kept European currencies within a narrow band of value against each other. Major succeeded him as Chancellor in 1989 and in 1990 persuaded Margaret Thatcher – somewhat against her own wishes – that Britain should join. The timing proved unfortunate. Britain was already in recession as interest rates had risen to stabilise sterling before entry. They then had to remain high to sustain sterling's value. So the recession intensified, with unemployment reaching almost 3 million. However, belief that sterling's level within the ERM was too high led to currency speculation against it and Britain's withdrawal from the ERM on 'Black Wednesday', 16 September 1992. Sterling then fell sharply. The government had staked its credibility on this policy, claiming that unemployment was a necessary price to pay for economic stability. Its reputation for economic competence was destroyed.

In retrospect, Black Wednesday's economic effect was almost wholly beneficial. The high interest rates of 1989–1992 had delivered what Thatcher's governments never achieved – the almost complete suppression of inflation. With high unemployment and commodity prices depressed, there was no danger of sterling's fall stoking it up again. The fall also gave a boost to manufacturing. In 1992 the government introduced inflation targeting which may have contributed to the continuing low levels of inflation.

Other Conservative initiatives which might have proved popular – the extension of quasi-market reforms in health and education and continued increases in spending in these areas – were not enough to counteract criticisms. Nor was the government able to initiate politically attractive privatisations because there were few candidates left. The sale of the remaining coal mines in 1994 was preceded by substantial closures, which did not play well politically. Railway privatisation in 1996 resulted in sales to business consortia, leading to accusations of excessive private profit making, a contrast to the popular capitalism of earlier privatisations.

These issues paled, however, besides the increasing problem that Europe posed the Conservatives. The European context is discussed in Chapter 11. Euro-sceptics particularly disliked the idea that sterling would join other European currencies in the single currency that would succeed the ERM. Major's policy was to keep options open, thus reassuring the Euro-enthusiasts in the party, but not tying Britain down. There was, of course, a real issue of sovereignty, but the bitterness of the debate within the party had other causes. Lady Thatcher's resentment at her exclusion from power led her to use Europe as a stick with which to beat John Major, and her more extreme supporters echoed her views. The issue was divisive enough to mean that the Conservatives could never present a united front. The press, where the influence of Lady Thatcher's followers was still strong, turned against the Major government. It prominently reported numerous sexual peccadilloes, and a few financial malfeasances, among Conservative MPs, leading to accusations of sleaze.

But even if Europe and sleaze had never come to the forefront, the Conservatives would probably have been defeated. In 1964 Labour had accommodated themselves to prosperity and won the election because enough people believed Labour could manage prosperity better – and because people were fed up with the party in office. In 1997 Labour had accommodated themselves to Thatcherism. The party convinced enough people that they could run the economy safely, and that they could manage the welfare state better. That done, then as in 1964 the desire for fresh faces and a change was probably all they needed to win. But to get to that position, Labour had had to make many changes.

Labour 1979–2000: decline, reconstruction and power

Defeat in 1979 ushered in a period of trauma for Labour. The left had gained ground in the party, for a variety of reasons (see earlier section, 'Labour 1974–1979'). Callaghan resigned in 1980 and Michael Foot was elected as leader. Foot was a veteran left-winger, but was seen by some as a potential healer of the party's divisions. Instead, these grew worse when early in 1981 a new system for electing the leader was set up. Now constituency parties, unions and MPs all participated, rather than just the latter. It was a victory for the left, who saw their strength as lying outside the parliamentary party, and was followed by the formation of a new party, the Social Democratic Party (SDP), by despairing Labour right-wingers.

In the early days of socialism, Social Democrat parties were Marxist – indeed, the first British SDP metamorphosed into the Communist Party. But after the Second World War European Social Democrats transformed themselves into moderate left-wing parties, and it was such parties that the new SDP hoped to emulate. Initially it gained substantial popular support but lost momentum with the revival of Conservative fortunes sparked by the Falklands war. It fought the 1983 and 1987 elections in alliance with the Liberals, and this grouping, known as the Alliance, almost overtook Labour in votes in 1983, although it slipped back in 1987. Subsequently, in 1988, the SDP merged with the Liberals to form the Liberal Democrats.

Politics and government: The Liberal Party 1945–2000

In the 1930s the Liberals had lost their last remaining strongholds in local government and in 1945 just 12 Liberal MPs were elected, falling to six in 1951. The party had a reservoir of support among nonconformists and among those who saw themselves as moderate and independent. But with both the major parties moving towards moderation, there was not much space left in the centre of politics.

Nevertheless, the party held aloof in 1951 when Churchill, who retained a tenderness for Liberalism, offered them a place in a new coalition. Between 1951 and 1964 they experienced occasional flurries of support in by-elections, with Conservative voters seeing them as a safe way of punishing the government during periods when it was unpopular, but achieved little else. In the late 1960s, however, the Liberals made progress in certain badly run local councils where dedication to local issues could gain them support. This 'community politics' hardly added up to a convincing programme for national government but in the long run helped to provide a basis of local strength and a cadre of activists.

Then space began to open up in the centre. The initial impetus to Liberal (and Nationalist) revival was probably the widespread public dismay at the strikes and

▶

inflation associated with both the other parties in government. The Liberals gained 19 per cent of the national vote in February 1974 but, because these votes were evenly spread, they did not translate into many parliamentary seats. Their brief period of support for Labour in 1977–1978 set the Liberals back, as the government's unpopularity rubbed off on them, and in 1979 they lost votes. They were galvanised in the 1980s, however, by Thatcherism and by Labour's left turn. The Liberals and the SDP together gained 25 per cent of the vote in 1983, although still winning only 23 seats. But with Labour's growing moderation, it became clear that two centre parties was one too many. Merger with the SDP in 1988 produced the Social and Liberal Democrats – known as Liberal Democrats from 1989.

In the 1990s the new party continued to prosper, at least in comparison to the previous 60 years, gaining 46 seats in the 1997 election. They were helped by a tacit agreement with Labour that the parties would not compete strongly in certain seats. This, in turn, reflected Tony Blair's apparent wish for a coalition of the centre and left. For the Liberal Democrats one necessary condition was proportional representation, which they saw as the safest way to end the perpetual squeeze of the first-past-the-post system on minority parties. Labour's keenness for cooperation lessened after their overwhelming victory in 1997. Nevertheless, with Conservatism, for many voters, tainted by Thatcherism and seemingly unable to modernise, the Liberal Democrat appeal seemed better established.

It is a cruel reality that the actual policies espoused by the Liberals at any one time have probably been quite unimportant to many Liberal voters. Broadly speaking, the party's stated social and economic policies have usually been somewhere between the two main parties, apparently endorsing its claim to moderation. Liberals have been distinctive for many years in their keen pro-Europeanism, in supporting political decentralisation and in espousing civil liberties – none of them on the evidence very interesting to most voters. In practice, most votes for Liberals have probably been votes against extremism and against violent alternations of policy. Although this has brought the party little political joy, their substantial support from the mid-1970s suggests that 'moderation', however vague that idea be, is widely popular.

The initial successes of the SDP, and the Alliance, highlighted the weakness of Labour in the early and mid-1980s. Their 1983 manifesto was a confused document, memorably described by the Labour MP Gerald Kaufman as 'the longest suicide note in history'. Hardy perennials of the left such as nuclear disarmament, withdrawal from the EC, nationalisation and a large increase in public expenditure were included. After Labour's catastrophic defeat, Neil Kinnock became leader. Kinnock had been firmly on the left, but in the early 1980s had become committed to healing the divisions in the party. Although he could be an inspiring orator, electoral gains for Labour were held back by the successes of Thatcherism in the mid-1980s, the continued attractions of the Alliance and his own weakness as a parliamentary performer. But with great political courage, and the suppression of many of his own long-held beliefs, Labour was reconstructed. Change was relatively slow before 1987 but accelerated after Labour's further heavy electoral defeat in that year.

Reconstruction under Kinnock involved two policy shifts. One was back to areas of the moderate middle ground which Labour had occupied for most of the 1950s and 1960s. Unilateral nuclear disarmament was ditched, as was hostility to the EC. An essentially Crosland-like policy towards public expenditure – that it should only rise as resources allowed – was put forward. Since the 1980s had seen substantial economic recovery, while inflation had been sharply reduced, a return to revisionism seemed appropriate (see Chapter 9, 'Labour 1951–1970: dissent, revisionism and government'). Labour's other shift was equally significant. The party tacitly accepted both privatisation and most of the Thatcherite trade union reforms. In the terminology of the 1960s and 1970s, the party had moved sharply to the right. Or to put it another way, the right was the new centre.

These shifts were accompanied by a drastic adjustment in Labour's public image and method of forming policy. Its new image became one of besuited respectability, while its 'democratic' structures were downgraded in favour of more control by the party leader. (In fact they never had been very democratic, being susceptible to the influence of union block-votes at the annual conference, horse-trading and general skulduggery.) These changes, often seen as the work of Tony Blair, were well underway before he became leader.

Labour had high hopes at the 1992 election but was narrowly defeated. Kinnock resigned and, after a short interlude under the moderate John Smith, who died of a heart attack in 1994, Tony Blair was elected leader.

Blair continued along the path already hewn out by Kinnock, and therefore portrayals of him as taking Labour even further to the right are simplistic. In part this image owed itself to a set of rhetorical devices. Blair invented 'New Labour', intended to further distance the party in the popular mind from its associations with trade unions and declining manufacturing industry. More lasting was the banishment of Clause IV, the 'socialist objective' in the party constitution which, although vague, could be read as committing the party to the nationalisation of everything (see Chapter 4, 'Labour in power'). It was replaced in 1995 by a new Clause IV, which was inclusive enough to satisfy most in the party. While most electors had probably never heard of the old Clause IV, it always had the potential to be used against Labour. Perhaps more importantly, ditching it was a signal to newspaper proprietors and editors, and opinion-formers in general, that Blair was serious about Labour's new direction.

Subsequently, Labour gave few hostages to fortune in terms of specific policy commitments. Initially, when they came to power in 1997, some of the Conservative quasi-market reforms, particularly in health, were undone, but after the 2001 election very similar reforms were pushed forward vigorously. Labour was also ultra-cautious over spending commitments, over which they had been successfully attacked in the 1992 election. They pledged to adhere to Conservative spending plans in the first two years in office. As economic growth continued, Labour was subsequently able to maintain quite high spending levels without sharply increasing taxes, while Keynesianism in a modified form reappeared in the so-called golden rule. By this, government revenue is planned to equal expenditure over an economic cycle – meaning that a government fiscal deficit during a recession could be tolerated. A few – important – areas of policy remained more distinctly Labour, however, notably those under the control of Gordon Brown, the Chancellor. While direct taxes remained historically low, there was some reduction in income inequality via the tax system. And within a continuing market economy framework, there was a renewed use of tax and other incentives in an attempt to increase productivity. One other economic measure took to its logical conclusion the inflation targeting introduced by the Major administration. Labour gave sole responsibility to the Bank of England to control inflation via the adjustment of interest rates – a prerogative shared with the Treasury since the 1930s. Since the government set the inflation target, it still had ultimate control, but the move cleverly distanced it from potentially unpopular decisions.

Conclusion: a new consensus

Most commentators agree that, by the 1990s, there was a new political consensus. As in the 1950s and 1960s, the major parties continued to quarrel fiercely; but their quarrels concealed much fundamental agreement.

There was a general acceptance that the workings of the market were largely beneficial. In contrast, from the 1940s to the early 1970s there had been broad agreement on a range of areas which were to be protected from competition: the labour market because of the privileged position of the trade unions; nationalised industries; and the major agencies of the welfare state. By the late 1990s only the latter was protected, and even here quasi-market reforms had made substantial headway. Labour's imposition of a minimum wage in 1999 was a relatively minor interference in the labour market. In other respects, such as employment rights, the British labour market remains relatively unregulated compared to Europe, and Labour supports this.

The other economic policy element of the post-war consensus which went was Keynesianism, broadly interpreted to mean an agreement that unemployment would be kept at low levels. Its initial replacement was monetarism, which was primarily focused on inflation, but this has been discredited. Later policies still focused on inflation, but (at the time of writing) it was controlled by the Bank of England through interest rates. However, Keynesianism has been partially reinstated, in the acceptance of fiscal deficits during recessions. The continuing emphasis on the control of inflation points to the importance of the 1970s in the genesis of the new consensus. The level and virulence of inflation gave political credibility to Thatcherism, but it also had a longer term influence on policy-makers, who have remembered the inflation of the period even if the public have largely forgotten it.

If unions did retard growth from the 1950s to the 1970s, and if macroeconomic policy has become more effective, Britain's growth rate relative to other western countries should have improved. This has happened, so the new consensus seems to have delivered some benefits. Whether or not microeconomic policy – and particularly that old bugbear, training and the level of skills – has improved to the same extent is more questionable.

It is less widely understood that the post-war consensus over relatively high levels of welfare spending was never really breached. In real terms, health expenditure almost doubled, and education spending rose by 50 per cent, over the 18 years of Conservative government. The Conservatives constantly attempted to rein back the growth of the other main spending area, social security, but this increased too. While Labour continued to increase spending on the first two, it also attempted to curb spending on the third, for instance by carrying forward Conservative efforts to encourage the unemployed to return to work. Behind this lie certain basic facts. By the 1970s government spending in Britain and other Western European countries was approaching 50 per cent of national income. Taxation in Britain was lower – the shortfall being made up by borrowing – but taxpayers still objected to the level they paid while high government borrowing increased interest rates and exacerbated inflation. So if social security spending had increased faster, either taxes or borrowing would have had to increase further. The constant chipping away at social security provision, therefore, can be seen as an almost inevitable concomitant of increased spending on health and education and not, ultimately, a 'right-wing' policy. Similar policies have been carried out in other European countries, not necessarily by right-wing governments.

Notes

1. Quoted in More, *Industrial Age* (see Chapter 1), p. 266.
2. Clarke, P., 'The Rise and Fall of Thatcherism', *Historical Research*, Vol. LXXII, pp. 301–322 (1999), p. 315.
3. Quoted in Grant, W., 'Pressure Groups', in Hollowell, *Britain since 1945* (see Chapter 9), p. 373.

Further reading

Campbell, J., *Margaret Thatcher: The Iron Lady* (London: Pimlico, 2003) is excellent. Clarke, 'Rise and Fall' is exceptionally perceptive. Dunleavy, P. *et al.*, *Developments in British Politics* (Basingstoke: Macmillan, 6th ed., 2000) – this and earlier editions are all valuable. Major, J., *The Autobiography* (London: HarperCollins, 1999) is a useful guide to day to day developments during his premiership. Thatcher, M., *The Downing Street Years* (London: HarperCollins, 1993) is largely concerned with scoring points off her ministers.

Other sources: Dutton, *British Politics* (see Chapter 9); Dutton, *Liberal Party* (see Chapter 2); Evans, E., *Thatcher and Thatcherism* (London: Routledge, 1997); Floud and Johnson, *Cambridge Economic History* (see Chapter 1); Gamble, A., *The Free Economy and the Strong State: the Politics of Thatcherism* (London: Macmillan, 1988); Keogh, D., 'Ireland 1945–2001: between "Hope and History"' in Burk, *British Isles* (and other chapters in *ibid.*) (see Chapter 9); Lowe, *Welfare State* (see Chapter 9); Patterson, H., 'Northern Ireland since 1945' in Hollowell, *Britain* (and other chapters in *ibid.*); Tanner, *Labour's First Century* (see Chapter 4); Thorpe, *Labour Party* (see Chapter 4); Ziegler, *Wilson* (see Chapter 9).

Chapter 11

BRITAIN AND OVERSEAS
1945-2000

Post-war problems

Britain ended the Second World War with huge debts and equally huge responsibilities. The immediate cessation of Lend Lease after Japan surrendered on 14 August 1945 made the financial constraints even more serious. Yet unless she abandoned much of war-torn Europe, and much of Asia where post-war responsibilities were shared with the USA, Britain had to maintain large numbers of military personnel in far-flung parts of the world. In Indonesia, for example, obligations to the ruling Dutch, whose exiled government was a wartime ally, necessitated up to 90,000 British troops being used against a colonial revolt.

These temporary responsibilities exacerbated the difficulty of conceptualising Britain's longer term role in the world. It was one of the three main victors of the war. (France and China considered themselves victors, but were not taken so seriously in this role by Britain and the other two, the United States and the Soviet Union.) As such, and in keeping with its historic imperial role, it seemed clear that Britain would continue to play a large part in world affairs. European reconstruction and a final end to German aggression were vital aims. Security in the eastern Mediterranean and the Middle East were seen as essential to safeguard the trade route to the Far East through Suez. It was accepted that parts of the Empire would soon become independent but other parts were seen as ripe for development.

Overlaying the first two of these issues were Britain's relations with the United States and the Soviet Union. America had long ties of friendship with Britain. There were no such ties with Russia, but its popularity had been enormously boosted during the war. While many diplomats and politicians were wary of Russia, in the immediate aftermath of war it still had to be accepted as an ally. Irrespective of that, it could not be ignored as it occupied most of Eastern Europe, Eastern Germany and part of Austria. Peace treaties or settlements for all these countries had to be worked out. Conversely, the ending of Lend Lease was symbolic of American ambivalence towards Britain and Europe immediately after the war. Truman, who had been pitchforked into the presidency when Roosevelt died early in 1945, was at first politically weak and faced a resurgence of American isolationism.

Over the next three years many of these issues were clarified. They were clarified in a way which set the pattern for both international relations, and to a considerable extent Britain's own world role, for a further 40 years. Whether the direction Britain took was the only option is a moot point, but most historians see it as more or less inevitable, given the circumstances as they were then perceived.

Clarification occurred because the Soviet Union became regarded as fundamentally antagonistic to western democracy. As a result, the United States, fearing the global implications of a hostile Russia, became willing to take both the financial and military lead in contesting it. From what we know now, it seems likely that Russia's initial intentions were not so much aggressively hostile as defensive, although its leaders were also concerned to seize opportunities when they could. However, the fairly brutal Soviet way of going about things made it understandable that Britain and America put the most pessimistic interpretation on Soviet behaviour. For example, free elections in Eastern Europe, agreed at the Yalta Conference in early 1945, were soon vitiated by Communist bullying and intimidation. As the West had virtually given up on Eastern Europe, Britain's main causes for concern were Greece, Turkey and Iran, all sensitive areas because of their proximity to the Middle East. In 1945 and 1946 Russia's attitude towards Turkey and Iran was threatening and aggressive. In Greece, there was civil war between the communists and the government, Britain supporting the latter with a substantial military commitment.

By early 1947, with the financial situation still dire, Britain felt constrained to pull out of Greece. By now American attitudes had changed and Truman enunciated the 'Truman doctrine': the United States must support 'free peoples who are resisting attempted subjugation by armed minorities or outside pressure'. His target was the Soviet Union and its clients. Encroachment beyond the countries of Eastern Europe would be resisted.

America took over Britain's Greek commitment and then, in the summer of 1947, accepted that drastic measures would be needed to combat communist influence in Western Europe. At the root of this was Europe's failure to recover economically. The US initiative, the Marshall Plan, took the form of large grants to European countries to help overcome the shortage of dollars and facilitate economic recovery. It went along with the reintegration of the American and British zones of occupation in Germany, with the French zone joining later. Fearing a western bloc which would include most of a revitalised Germany, in June 1948 Russia put pressure on the West by cutting off western land access to Berlin, which was jointly occupied but within the Russian zone. America and Britain's riposte was the Berlin Airlift – a huge and successful 11-month effort to supply Berlin by air, with the RAF carrying a quarter of all supplies.

In all these dramas Ernest Bevin, the Foreign Secretary, played a major part. The same was true of the formation of a western defensive military alliance, the North Atlantic Treaty Organisation. For internal political reasons, it was important for the United States' government that initiatives involving it in Europe should be seen to come from Europe. Bevin had taken the lead in establishing the Treaty of Brussels, a defensive alliance between Britain, France, Belgium, the Netherlands and Luxemburg signed in March 1948. Truman could then sell the North Atlantic Treaty to the American people and their representatives. Signed a year after Brussels, and allying the USA, Canada, the Brussels signatories and other European countries, it was historic. For the first time the USA was bound by treaty to Europe – a treaty which has lasted to the present day.

Military alliance was stimulated, of course, by the perceived Russian threat, with the Berlin blockade adding urgency. But it also reflected the failure of the grandiose wartime plans to ensure lasting world peace. These had originated with the Atlantic Charter of early 1941 agreed by Churchill and Roosevelt, which put forward democratic freedoms and non-aggression as international principles to be established after the war. In part, the charter was a political gesture which gave hope to the British while reassuring the Americans that, if they should fight, it would not be for the narrow principle of defending the British Empire. But it also formed the basis of the United Nations (UN), set up with high hopes in 1945 to replace the League of Nations. The UN's effectiveness was quickly stymied, however, because any of the five permanent members of the Security Council (Britain, the USA, the Soviet Union, France and China) could veto its resolutions and, predictably, the Russians and the western nations usually lined up on different sides. So unfortunately it degenerated into a forum for international name-calling.

The exception to its impotence was the conflict in Korea between 1950 and 1953 which set the final seal on the Cold War, as the continued tension and mistrust between the West and Russia became called. The Korean war started with a Soviet-sponsored attempt by Communist North Korea to occupy South Korea. When this occurred, Russia was boycotting the UN, so the western dominated Security Council (China then being represented by non-communist Taiwan) condemned the action and, under the auspices of the UN, the non-communist world intervened. Although America was the main participant, Britain made a significant military contribution. It was also an expensive one. Rearmament had started in 1948–1949 and Korea accelerated it. All this strengthened the distrust among the Labour left of the government's foreign policy and provoked damaging resignations from the government (see Chapter 9).

But before this happened Ernest Bevin had died. His vast, if controversial, contribution is assessed in the accompanying box.

People and politics: Ernest Bevin

Ernest (Ernie) Bevin was born into extremely poor circumstances in Winsford, in deepest rural Somerset, in 1881. Like Ramsay MacDonald he was illegitimate, but unlike MacDonald, who prospered in the excellent Scottish educational system and became a pupil-teacher, Bevin left school at the age of 11. Like many young countrymen and women, he moved to the nearest large town, in his case Bristol, becoming a (horse) van driver. And, in another trajectory followed by many young working-class men and women at the time, he progressed through nonconformity into socialism. He successfully organised local van drivers into the Dockers' Union and, in 1911, became a full-time union official.

After the First World War, Bevin masterminded the Dockers' amalgamation into the Transport and General Workers' Union, which became Britain's largest trade union and which he led. After the Labour Party split from MacDonald in 1931, Bevin became a major influence on its policies. He epitomised the idea of the 'labour movement', in which the trade unions were as important a component as the Labour Party itself. While the party moved left in the 1930s, Bevin was essentially a pragmatist. As the dictators threatened peace, he helped to move Labour from its semi-pacifist stance of the early 1930s. He also conceived a loathing of communism. He saw communists as anti-democratic and motivated purely by their own agenda and not by the everyday needs of working people.

In 1940 Churchill asked Bevin to become Minister of Labour, in which role his contribution to the war was incalculable. Bevin pushed the British people to the limit of mobilisation for war, but not beyond. His insistence that employer-worker consultation and such practical benefits as factory canteens should go along with conscription of labour meant that industrial peace was maintained.

His appointment by Attlee as Foreign Secretary was a last-minute decision. Most people would see it as inspired. Bevin immediately took the line that British interests, and the British Empire, must be robustly defended. In his view this would benefit the inhabitants of the Empire, as well as Britain. Both this concern and his early suspicion of Soviet expansionism motivated his interest in Middle East security. But as Russia seemed to become more and more intransigent, it was Europe which held centre stage. As the USA emerged from its period of temporary post-war isolation and became concerned to hasten European recovery, it was Bevin who took the lead in forging European cooperation and opening the way for America assistance.

Bevin's robust policy was expensive because it led to greater military commitments. Arguably, however, Britain eventually received substantial recompense for its costs through the Marshall Plan. Immediately after the war, however, there was significant dissent from many Labour MPs at policies which, they believed, were merely propping up capitalism when a socialist alternative was available. As the brutal reality of Soviet control in Eastern Europe became apparent, most of this dissent was silenced, although by the time of the Korean war it had surfaced again. A more interesting alternative was argued by Attlee himself in 1946. This was to abandon Britain's commitments in the eastern Mediterranean and Middle East, on the grounds that when India became independent, the Suez route would become less strategically vital. Bevin countered this with the argument that the Middle East itself could become a vital area for Britain, both as an oil producer and as a market. And, most of all, Britain could not afford to let the Soviet Union dominate the area. Attlee dropped the issue but, in the long run, his argument was to prove prescient.

Ernie Bevin was built on a heroic scale. This was the case physically – of average height, he weighed 18 stone in later years – but, more important, mentally and morally. In retrospect, his overall foreign policy stance can be criticised for perpetuating British illusions about its strength which resulted in it following expensive policies such as the independent nuclear deterrent (see box, 'The nuclear option'). On the other hand, given Russian actions at the time, the policy of firmness towards the Soviet Union – which necessitated Britain taking the lead in European defence in order to strengthen the US government's hand in its internal debates – would to most people seem the correct one.

The Cold War 1950–1990

The Cold War was to dominate British defence policy for 40 years and was a major ingredient in foreign policy. Its context was set by the Soviet Union and the United States. It is now clear that, as in the 1940s, Soviet policy was more defensive, and more influenced by Russia's perception of its own weakness and isolation, than was thought at the time. However, Soviet behaviour continued to send mixed messages, so it was understandable that the West frequently saw it as aggressive and expansionist. Furthermore, the successful western resistance to aggression in the Korean war encouraged the belief that firmness was the correct way to deal with Soviet adventurism. Soon after the war broke out in 1950, the USA set up the North Atlantic Treaty Organisation (NATO) to solidify the Atlantic alliance (see previous section, 'Post-war problems').

After Stalin's death in 1953, the new Soviet leadership was dominated by Nikita Kruschev who aimed, with some success, at reducing tensions. But he could not resist the temptation, for propaganda reasons, to inflate Russia's real nuclear strength. As a result, and with continuing tensions over Berlin and Cuba, the West continued to be suspicious. After Kruschev's fall, Leonid Brezhnev dominated the leadership until 1982. In the 1960s the Soviet Union aimed to translate Kruschev's paper nuclear forces into real ones, with the aim of negotiating *détente* – that is, improving relations with the West – from a position of strength. But the impact of *détente* in the 1970s was severely weakened by the Soviet penchant, reminiscent of 1945–6, for meddling in areas such as Africa which the West saw as beyond Russia's legitimate sphere of influence. This tendency culminated in 1979 with the Soviet invasion of Afghanistan. In 1980 Ronald Reagan, the new, right-wing American President, took the recent Soviet record as signalling the restarting of the Cold War (the term having gone into recess since the 1960s). There followed a period of US rearmament before, in 1985, Gorbachev began a process of radical reform in the USSR accompanied by the intention to systematically improve East–West relations. This culminated in the collapse of the entire Soviet system between 1989 and 1991.

Britain's relations with the USA started with the fact that continuing American membership of NATO was seen as critical. Since the Americans wanted Europe to make as large a military contribution to NATO as possible, this mandated a substantial British commitment. NATO, of course, was not just a defensive military alliance but also a signal to the USSR that political meddling in Western Europe was not welcome. Nevertheless, fears of Soviet attack were at times quite considerable, so the military commitment was a very real one and involved the bulk of British armed forces being dedicated to NATO.

British–American relations were, however, more complicated than that. The USA prized Britain as NATO's foremost European champion. This meant that it wanted Britain to join in European integration. Britain was much more lukewarm, and tended to believe that it had a 'special relationship' with the USA. But from the point of view of the Americans, their support for sterling in times of crisis meant that Britain did not so much have a special relationship as a special dependence. From 1979 the special relationship re-emerged on slightly more equal terms.

Finally, Britain's defence policies were set within a domestic and a colonial and Commonwealth context. Domestic political constraints included the challenge from the left (see box, 'The nuclear option', later in this chapter) but this was rarely very significant. It was much more important that both Conservative and Labour governments consistently followed an almost identical policy of nuclear deterrence and commitment to NATO. But both parties also had to work within other constraints. One was the continuing Commonwealth commitment, which wound down in the 1960s before flaring up in the Falklands war. From 1969 the army commitment in Northern Ireland impacted on defence spending. But more important were the claims from other spending priorities, especially welfare. So finance was a perennial problem which had significant implications for defence spending and hence foreign – and colonial – policy.

The 1950s and 1960s saw Britain, in the context of these constraints, coming to terms with the end of its 'Great Power' status. One positive aspect of this was the strengthening of NATO. Germany's entry, which went along with the acceptance of German rearmament, took place in 1955. This owed a great deal to Anthony Eden as Foreign Secretary, who devised the formula by which Germany and Italy would also join the Brussels Pact, which then became the Western European Union (WEU). (The WEU never, in practice, played an important role independent of NATO and from 1999 was subsumed into the European Union.) One apparently negative aspect of Britain's reduced position was Suez, but this ultimately reinforced realities even if at the time it was a humiliating climbdown (see box, 'Anthony Eden and Suez').

One area where Great Power illusions lingered after Suez was an inexpensive and relatively harmless one – summitry. Even before he returned to office, Churchill hankered after face to face meetings of world leaders – summits – as a means of thawing the Cold War. He was foiled in his attempts, but Macmillan, who loved diplomacy, carried on the idea. He successfully rebuilt relations with the USA after Suez, and then engineered a summit conference in Paris in 1960. It was, however, a dismal failure. But Macmillan's stress on negotiation had some positive impact in the partial nuclear test-ban treaty, which he had long supported and which was signed in 1963. As with his attempts at summitry, which began before the 1959 election, electoral calculations were a factor. He believed there were Liberals who supported nuclear curbs and could be lured to the Conservatives by stressing Britain's eagerness to limit nuclear proliferation.

The special relationship with America was downplayed in the 1960s and 1970s. In part this was because Wilson wished to avoid – and skilfully succeeded in so doing – any involvement in Vietnam; while Heath, of all post-war British prime ministers, was least enthusiastic about the USA. Under Margaret Thatcher the special relationship took on a renewed significance, although probably more in her mind than in that of Reagan. From 1978 NATO had instituted a programme of installing medium-range missiles, including the Tomahawk cruise missiles, as a reaction to new Soviet missiles. Britain's role in this new period of Cold War tension was to support Reagan's rearmament programme – without itself spending much more on arms – and to face down a resurgence of anti-nuclear protest as the missiles were deployed. All this was to end, however, with the Soviet collapse.

People and politics: Anthony Eden and Suez

Like Ramsay MacDonald, his rival as the best-looking Prime Minister of the twentieth century, Anthony Eden was also one of the unhappiest and unluckiest.

Eden came from a Durham family of landed gentry. Like many young officers who survived the First World War, he ended it with a keen sympathy for the working class and a commitment to peace. Entering Parliament in 1923, he became a youthful Foreign Secretary in 1935. He advocated a firm line against the dictators within the framework of appeasement. He resigned in 1938 – in effect over Chamberlain's interference in foreign policy – and once war broke out this stand enhanced his reputation. Churchill made Eden Foreign Secretary again late in 1940. After his glittering early career, Eden then had to endure 15 years of unhappiness and growing frustration. He lost his eldest son in 1945, flying the dangerous supply route to the troops fighting in Burma, and his first marriage broke up. (Unlike MacDonald, however, he had a long and happy second marriage.) In office, again as Foreign Secretary, he was frustrated as Churchill clung on as Prime Minister, although he had foreign policy triumphs such as the deal over German entry to NATO (see main text, 'The Cold War 1950–1990').

Why was Eden so long seen as the Conservative heir apparent? From the mid-1930s to the mid-1950s he was immensely popular with the public because of 'the Eden charm . . . integrity plus friendliness'.[1] His natural and direct speeches and genuine cross-class sympathies echoed those of Baldwin, who influenced him in the 1930s. He was firmly on the progressive wing of the party, and in the post-war years this seemed an essential criterion for Churchill's successor. In 1955 Churchill finally stood down and Eden took over (Fig. 11.1). All agree that he was a poor Prime Minister. He interfered too much with other ministers, and his public charm was offset by too frequent private ill temper, exacerbated by ill health. And then came Suez.

The paradox of the Suez crisis was that in 1954 Eden as Foreign Secretary had accepted a diminished role for the Suez base (see main text, 'The end of Empire'). However, the new nationalist regime in Egypt under Nasser was mistrusted. Nasser's requests for Soviet financial aid and arms were inspired by the West's lukewarm attitude, but the result was to strengthen British mistrust. By early 1956 Eden wanted to get rid of him. Nationalisation of the Suez Canal by Egypt in July provided an opportunity. By itself, however, it was not a reason for war. The French, with a financial interest in the canal, the Israelis and the British cooked up a secret plan, the Sevres Protocol, by which Israel would attack Egypt, advancing towards the canal. France and Britain would intervene to 'safeguard' it. Although the intervention in November was militarily successful, it ran into other problems. Suez divided Britain, with 50 per cent approving but a large minority of 30 per cent disapproving. More importantly, Eisenhower, the American President, was firmly against it. Leaving aside the secret collusion, the operation was still of doubtful international legality, since it was not sanctioned by the UN. And Eisenhower accurately assessed Nasser as an Egyptian nationalist not a Soviet stooge, so there was no overriding western defence aim at stake. The USA punished Britain by refusing to support sterling. It came under selling pressure on the foreign exchange market and Britain had to end the operation.

Figure 11.1 Anthony Eden on the campaign trail in the 1955 election.
© Bettmann/CORBIS

Suez had many side effects. Pro-western Arab governments were put in a difficult position and France conceived an even stronger mistrust of Britain than usual. But its effects were not all negative. It emphasised that Britain could not afford to pursue an active military policy independent of America. And it further undermined, although it did not immediately end, Britain's lingering imperial pretensions. But it finally broke Eden's health. He resigned early in 1957 and was created Lord Avon. Suez's violence and illegality was an unhappy end to a career which had been devoted to peace and moderation.

The end of Empire

By the end of the war it was widely accepted that India would become independent in the fairly near future. What had been the lynchpin of Empire would soon be gone. But in spite of this, many politicians, Labour and Conservative, believed that much of the rest of the Empire – the colonies still under British rule – had a long-term future.

Initially it was hoped that India would follow a peaceful and measured transition to independence, but Britain's bad relations with the dominant Congress Party had allowed Jinnah's Muslim League to grow, with British support. Jinnah then pressed for partition of India, with the predominantly Muslim north-west and north-east becoming a separate state – Pakistan. A hard line by both parties meant growing inter-communal violence and decreasing hopes that Britain's original aspirations could be met. Lord Mountbatten, the Viceroy, speeded up the timetable for withdrawal. Partition and independence followed in August 1947 accompanied by a heavy death toll as millions of Muslims and Hindus moved from one part to another, sparking religious violence. Burmese independence followed in 1948. Much later, Bangladesh was to secede from Pakistan.

The lynchpin of Empire fell – and few in Britain really cared; the Empire's popular appeal had long been diminishing (see Chapter 5). Of those who did care, Churchill, once the guardian of British India, had resigned himself during the war to its loss. Other Conservatives, realising that India no longer had much resonance with the electorate, kept their opposition muted. And Labour's appointment of Mountbatten, a member of the Royal Family, helped to suppress right-wing discontent. Churchill denounced 'Scuttle' but it is doubtful that the Conservatives either could have, or really wanted to, behave differently.

Another pull-out took place in Palestine. Once part of the Ottoman Empire, Britain had taken it over as a League of Nations mandate after the First World War. Unfortunately, during that war Britain had made several rash promises to gain support for the war effort: to the Arabs, promising independence and to the Jews promising them a homeland in Palestine – the Balfour Declaration. Only by convoluted reasoning could these promises be made compatible, and the Arabs saw them as contradictory. Britain's chicanery was paid for in blood, since the two promissees were bitterly opposed. The interwar period saw intermittent inter-communal strife between Arabs and Jews. After the war British troops faced attacks from Jewish guerrillas while trying to keep the peace. With no settlement in sight and in the face of Britain's own economic difficulties, the government relinquished the mandate in 1947. A Jewish takeover of power and the long agony of Arab–Israeli strife followed.

The rest of Empire posed fewer immediate problems. Labour genuinely wished to develop the colonies which had stagnated economically between the wars. This was altruistic, but there was also self-interest. The 'sterling area' included the colonies and some other countries. Surpluses on their foreign trade could not be spent freely outside the area as sterling was not convertible to other currencies without the Bank of England's permission. So these surpluses helped to finance Britain's own desperate need for dollars, both during the war and after it. As a result, the colonies, although receiving some development aid from Britain, could not immediately reap the benefit of high war and post-war commodity prices. Instead of buying American goods, they piled up sterling deposits with the Bank of England. The policy helped to bail Britain out but stirred up resentment. The survival of the sterling area was an interesting reflection on America's inability to enforce its wartime demands for sterling convertibility, once the brief experiment of 1947 had failed.

The economic rationale behind post-war colonial development was a belief that commodity prices would remain high. But after Korea they fell. Given that moderates in the Conservative Party shared Labour's view that colonies would move towards independence, the changing economic circumstances provided a further impetus towards this. Furthermore, both Suez and a series of colonial military interventions showed that hanging on was expensive. Obviously there were other pressures towards decolonisation: nationalism within the colonies; and sniping from both Russia and America over Britain's continued imperial status.

Britain maintained certain principles in its policy towards decolonisation. Parliamentary government and British-style judicial systems would, it was hoped, enable ex-colonies to develop as democracies. Another principle was the establishment of federations, which should lead to stronger regional entities. On the whole, both principles were to be frustrated. Federations quickly broke up as nationalism asserted itself. Clearly Britain cannot be entirely blamed for the breakdown of democracy in many ex-colonies, or for their failure to develop economically. But the frequent reliance in colonial days on traditional leaders, and the lack of previous economic development, did not help.

Early to independence were the West African colonies of Ghana (independent in 1957) and Nigeria (in 1960) (Fig. 11.2). In both there had historically been more black participation in public life than elsewhere in Africa (see Chapter 5). In the Far East, Malaysia (independent in 1957) had necessitated a major military commitment during the Emergency of 1948–1960 to counter communist subversion, but even at this stage only slow decolonisation elsewhere was envisaged. Rapid French decolonisation after 1958, however, exacerbated attacks on Britain as a remaining imperialist power, and there were increasing fears in 1960 that anarchy in the ex-Belgian Congo would spill over elsewhere in Africa. These facts lay behind Macmillan's famous 'wind of change' speech in 1960 – the wind of change being decolonisation and the speech intended partly as a marker to the Conservative Party. Between 1960 and 1964, 17 colonies gained independence, including several West Indian islands and, in Central Africa, Malawi and Zambia (both in 1964). In both cases there were attempted federations which failed. In Central Africa, the remaining member of the federation, Southern Rhodesia (now Zimbabwe), resisted black majority rule and the white dominated government unilaterally declared independence (UDI) in 1965. Rhodesia remained a thorn in the side of British governments until settlement was reached in 1980.

The continuing imperial commitments of the 1950s also reflected Britain's belief that it still needed to project its power world-wide, and that it required extra-European military bases to do this. The Middle East was the fulcrum. In military thinking, the whole Suez area was conceived of a gigantic base blocking possible Soviet moves into the Middle East and Africa, and guarding both sea and air routes to the East. Britain retained substantial military commitments 'east of Suez', as the whole area from the Persian Gulf to the Far East was known. The commitments were partly a legacy of Empire, but also a result of Britain's membership of the South-East Asia Treaty Organisation (SEATO), set up in 1954 and essentially an anti-communist front. Another vital factor behind the Middle East presence was oil. With dollars short, sterling denominated oil from the Middle East, much of it produced by British firms, was more critical after the war than during it. Oil lay behind Britain's participation in an unsavoury secret operation in 1953, in collaboration with America, to ovethrow the nationalist Iranian Prime Minister Mossadeq and restore the pro-western Shah. And oil, in part, lay behind

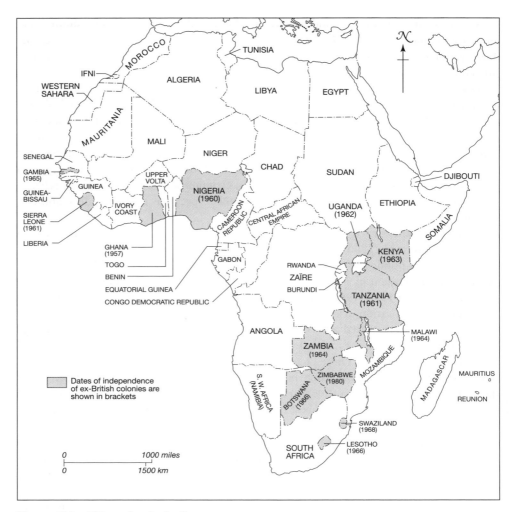

Figure 11.2   African decolonisation

the Suez operation (see earlier box, 'Anthony Eden and Suez'). Even after the failure of Suez, the Middle East remained important, with Aden becoming the main base and Britain remaining committed to the defence of the smaller Gulf states.

The decline of Empire did not, to many, mean the decline of the Commonwealth. When the 'White Dominions' became formally independent in 1931 (see Chapter 5), the Commonwealth became a union, with both a sentimental and a practical side, in which the British monarchy as head of state was the common denominator. In 1947 India wished to become a republic yet remain a member of the Commonwealth. The conundrum was solved by the monarch becoming head of the Commonwealth as an entity, and thus remaining as the uniting link. Most ex-colonies adopted the Indian solution.

Into the early 1960s the Commonwealth embodied important trade, investment and defence links, including those east of Suez. Thus, for example, Britain helped to defend Malaysia when from 1963 there was a 'Confrontation' with Indonesia over disputed territory. And the new multinational Commonwealth emerging from decolonisation appeared to symbolise a new post-imperial Britain. So in the early 1960s the Commonwealth could still be seen as both 'modern' and practical, and was strongly supported by Labour. But disenchantment grew rapidly. Many new Commonwealth nations joined the 'non-aligned' movement, whose non-alignment often seemed to consist of criticism of America and, by extension, its ally Britain. Economically, trade with Commonwealth nations was rapidly declining as a proportion of total trade, and Labour was turning towards Europe, The cost of 'east of Suez' commitments now seemed too high and in 1967 Britain planned a gradual pull-out from the Far East. After devaluation late in 1967 Roy Jenkins became Chancellor. Jenkins, a keen Europeanist, enforced further economies. The timetable for withdrawal was accelerated and all military commitments east of Suez were ended by the early 1970s.

After 1967 it is hard to see the Commonwealth as having any real role. As sentimental ties diminish, with Australia, for instance, only narrowly voting against becoming a republic in 1999, it seems destined to fade into insignificance.

Some important legacies of Empire remained in the form of scattered territories which sometimes had a sting in their tail. The Falklands are isolated islands in the South Atlantic with a tiny population, too small to sustain independence. Britain had made some cheese-paring defence economies in the area which encouraged the Argentine government in 1982 to assert the country's long-standing claim to the islands and invade them. Margaret Thatcher immediately decided on a full-scale military response. After some heavy fighting and the loss of a number of ships to air attack, the islands were recaptured. Domestically the Falklands war was an enormous success. Although the Conservatives had been recovering from their intense unpopularity of 1981, it helped to seal their electoral victory in 1983. Patriotism was still a powerful emotion.

Hong Kong also remained, having become an important economy in its own right. However, under a long-standing treaty most of it would be reclaimed by China in 1997. Within this framework, the British government had some success in the 1980s and 1990s in introducing democracy and reaching agreement with China that the territory would retain some autonomy after that date. Agreement was eased by China's own turn towards capitalism. The British Empire was once a global economic force, so there was a fitting coincidence between the handover of its last major outpost and China's increasing impact on the globalisation of world trade.

Britain and Europe

After the war, some European politicians looked to a complete reconstruction of relationships between European countries, seeing political integration as the only way to finally tame German militarism. Bevin, however, thought that political integration was impracticable. Like most British politicians, he believed that Britain still had a world role and a viable Empire, so he also thought that British involvement in Europe should be limited. Nevertheless, as has been seen, between 1945 and 1950 Britain was centrally involved in constructing a European defence community and in developing the European Recovery Programme, the formal name for the Marshall Plan.

For the time being, the more grandiose plans of European thinkers foundered on practicalities and their aim became more limited: to develop cooperation in functional areas. This gave rise in 1950 to the European Coal and Steel Community (ECSC), a supranational authority to pool the coal and steel output of France, Italy, Belgium, the Netherlands, Luxembourg and Germany. Britain held aloof for two reasons. The first was that Labour, having just nationalised coal and steel, was hardly likely to want to hand over control to an external authority. The other, more fundamental, reason was that Bevin had a rooted dislike of supranational bodies – authorities which were independent of national governments. He believed that European cooperation should be intergovernmental, through institutions which directly represented member governments. This belief was to become a leitmotif of British attitudes to European integration. In part it stemmed from deeply held views about the sovereignty of Parliament, to which was added the belief in Britain's world and Commonwealth roles. But additionally, most in Britain did not see the solution to German militarism in the same way as other Europeans did. To the British, the solution in the Second World War had come from a partnership of Britain and America. This was naturally still at the forefront of British politicians' minds when looking to future peace in Europe, particularly as potential Russian aggression was now added to the equation.

Bevin's attitude to Europe was shared by the Conservatives. In the late 1940s Churchill had flirted with the idea of Britain's participation in an integrated Europe. He infuriated Bevin who believed, correctly, that Churchill was playing party politics. Once the Conservatives were in power, from 1951, their attitude towards Europe became practically identical to that of Bevin. Eden's triumph in establishing the Western European Union in 1954 (see 'The Cold War 1950–1990') seemed to point up the superiority of the British method, since it followed the collapse of plans for a supranational European army.

Britain's hostility to supranational European integration was encapsulated in her reaction to the aftermath of the Messina talks of 1955, at which the ECSC countries agreed to discuss a more comprehensive union. Britain sent a civil servant, not a politician, to the negotiations in Brussels, later withdrawing him. By 1957 the European Economic Community (EEC) had been agreed, coming into existence in 1958. But by this time Britain's attitude to Europe was changing. Why?

In part, the success of the Brussels talks in establishing a major trading bloc itself mandated some British action, since Britain looked like being excluded. But there were deeper reasons. Macmillan, now Prime Minister, had always been more favourable than Eden to Europe, although he was no keener on supranationalism. Suez, the balance of payments crisis which accompanied it and the rapid decline of the Empire all pushed him and others towards a belief that, if Britain was to remain economically strong and have some voice in the world, Europe provided a framework in which it could do so. Macmillan's initial plan was to graft British ideas on to the EEC. His notion was to make it into a wider European Free Trade Area (EFTA), in line with the British 'Plan G'. Crucially, this would leave out food so as not to affect preferential agricultural trade arrangements with the Commonwealth. In 1958, however, de Gaulle, the French President, declared against any cooperation between the EEC and EFTA. Britain went ahead with the latter in 1959, but the other countries joining it were economic minnows compared to France, Germany and Italy.

In spite of British reservations, Macmillan was still drawn towards EEC membership. Plan G had in part been impelled by the notion that freer trade was vital to push British industry, still protected by a web of tariffs, into modernisation. Europe's rapid economic growth and Britain's continued economic sluggishness strengthened this line of reasoning. European competition would dovetail with Macmillan's other attempts to modernise Britain's economy (see Chapter 9). Furthermore, in spite of his efforts via summitry and the retention of the nuclear option to keep Britain on the world stage of diplomacy, the USA saw Britain's place as lying within the EEC, both to ensure Europe's continuing economic recovery and as a guarantor of a pro-American Europe. Finally, Europe to Macmillan was simply a big idea that could energise the Conservatives. In supporting Europe they would be a party which was in favour not just of economic modernisation but of modernisation in general. So in 1961 Britain applied formally to join the Community.

The obstacle to entry was summed up in two words: de Gaulle. The General was fiercely protective of France's position and particularly suspicious of Britain as a Trojan Horse for American influence. Britain's attempts to maintain the Commonwealth's agricultural trade preferences were another sticking point. Macmillan's likely acceptance of Polaris missiles (see box 'The nuclear option'), which would stymie any prospect of Franco–British collaboration over an independent nuclear deterrent, strengthened de Gaulle's suspicions and was probably the ultimate cause of his veto of Britain's application in January 1963.

Labour's commitment to the Commonwealth, the apparent reason for its opposition to Macmillan's application, was undoubtedly genuine, even if overemphasised for effect. By 1966, though, Labour was coming to view the Commonwealth as a nuisance rather than an asset. And the forces which had impelled Macmillan to apply were still there: the somewhat contradictory beliefs that the EEC held opportunities for British

Military affairs: The nuclear option

Britain was a leader in the prehistory of nuclear developments before the Second World War, but during the war it was the USA which had the resources to develop an atomic programme, as it was then called. After the war America reneged on an agreement to share its developments. In the context of this refusal and of fears that America was retreating into isolationism, Britain went ahead with her own nuclear programme. There was only limited debate about this, in spite of the certain expense. It seemed integral to Britain's ability to follow an independent foreign policy in the future or, as Ernest

▶

Bevin put it more earthily, 'We've got to have the bloody Union Jack flying on top of it'[2] – 'it' meaning the atom bomb.

Britain's first bomb was tested in 1952 and its delivery system, the so-called V-bombers, started to enter service from 1955. Britain's nuclear deterrent has always been technically independent, in that the ultimate approval for its use would come from the Prime Minister. In practice, it was regarded as part of the NATO equation of power and this was reinforced in 1957 by the Conservative defence review, the Sandys review, which opted for a defence strategy in which nuclear deterrence was central. Conscription, which had been dignified by the label National Service, was wound up. Cynics argued that the new strategy was a convenient excuse for cutting conventional forces to economise.

Nuclear deterrence was not a cheap option, however, as air-launched bombs from the V-bombers would soon be obsolete. Britain's attempt to develop its own long-range missile, Blue Streak, was abandoned as too expensive in 1960. Britain then obtained the promise of a new US missile, Skybolt, but that too was cancelled. At Macmillan's urging, America then agreed to sell Britain the technology for the Polaris submarine-launched missile. In all this the 'special relationship' was a factor, overcoming the fact that America was never particularly keen that Britain had a deterrent at all. And once Polaris was agreed, it was never truly an independent one again. As Harold Wilson joked, Polaris was a 'Moss Bros deterrent'[3] – although he went on to deploy it.

The defence review, and the deployment of the V-bombers, coalesced with other factors to produce strong anti-nuclear protests. These other factors included Britain's development of the fusion or hydrogen bomb by 1957, and the deployment, which went back to the late 1940s, of US nuclear bomber squadrons on British airfields. From 1958 the Easter marches held by the Campaign for Nuclear Disarmament (CND) to the nuclear research centre at Aldermaston in Berkshire became an annual pilgrimage for left-wing Labour MPs and many others. The Labour Party briefly adopted unilateral nuclear disarmament – disarmament by Britain alone – as its policy in 1960–1961, although it was fiercely opposed by the then leader, Hugh Gaitskell. The West's move from a policy of all-out nuclear retaliation to Soviet attack, to one of graduated response, defused anti-nuclear protest in the 1960s.

Civil nuclear power enjoyed widespread, and at first fairly uncritical, support from the 1950s when its use began. Britain designed its own systems – first the 'Magnox' stations, then the Advanced Gas-Cooled Reactors. Although possibly safer than American designs, they were undoubtedly more expensive. This expense slowed the civil nuclear programme from the 1970s. However, its cessation in the 1990s owed itself to the realisation that decommissioning involved enormous legacy costs and unquantifiable future safety hazards.

Although the left was more active in the Labour Party by the early 1970s, Labour's centre and right were firmly in charge of defence policy in 1974–1979 and accepted the need to modernise Polaris with the Chevaline programme. Since Chevaline was kept firmly secret, much more controversy accompanied the decision to station Tomahawk nuclear armed cruise missiles in Britain as part of the NATO response to Russia's new missiles. At much the same time, in 1980, the Conservative government took the decision to continue a submarine-based independent deterrent with the new Trident system, again acquired from America. As with all such programmes, it had a long lead time, only becoming activated in the 1990s.

In response to all this, there was a resurgence of CND and related peace movements, the best known being the woman's peace camp outside the Greenham Common airbase in Berkshire, where cruise missiles were based (Fig 11.3). Just four years after their deployment, a 1987 treaty with the Soviet Union, now a very different entity under Gorbachev, eliminated all such missiles in Europe and the last one left in 1991. Although Trident lives on for the time being, the very concept of deterrence in a post-Soviet age is problematical.

Figure 11.3   A 1960s CND poster. Image courtesy of The Advertising Archives

industry but would also push it to modernise; and strong American pressure which also highlighted Britain's own declining position in world affairs, to which European membership seemed to offer a substitute. Labour contained many anti-marketeers (the EEC was popularly known as the Common Market), but internal party conflict was avoided because de Gaulle again declared against Britain's entry in 1967.

By 1970 the situation had completely changed. De Gaulle had resigned in 1969 and the French were no longer hostile to British entry. Indeed, Britain now seemed valuable to them as a counter to Germany, whose seemingly unstoppable economic growth was making it ever more powerful. On the British side, the Conservative election victory had replaced Wilson, a moderate pro-marketeer leading a party with many anti-marketeers, with Heath, an enthusiastic supporter of the now renamed European Community (EC) leading a less divided party. Given future Conservative scepticism, the lack of Conservative opposition from Macmillan's first application to the early 1970s is interesting. There were, in fact, a number of Conservative opponents on the right of the party. But, like Heath himself, many of the post-war generation of Conservative MPs saw European unity as both a worthy aim in itself and one which could help attain the nirvana of economic modernisation. Moreover, the solid centre of the party, in those days, saw the prime Conservative virtue as loyalty – which meant following the leader.

Negotiation on British entry was still not easy. The Conservatives could not ignore the Commonwealth as otherwise they would infuriate their right wing who remained Commonwealth minded. Thus special arrangements for West Indian sugar and New Zealand butter were negotiated. In turn, the need to gain concessions on these led to British concessions on the issue of her own contributions to the EC budget, which mainly went to pay for the Common Agricultural Policy (CAP). The old British agricultural support system, developed in the 1940s, had accepted low world food prices and compensated British farmers for their higher costs. The CAP used import duties on food to support intervention – buying up European agricultural surpluses to raise prices. The policy increased food prices and was also expensive. Agriculture in Britain had been a small segment of the economy since the late nineteenth century, so subsidies to British farmers did not cost that much. In CAP, however, Britain had to help subsidise the large agricultural sectors of France and Italy. Thus entry to the EC would involve a large British contribution to the EC budget.

On 1 January 1973 Britain formally joined the EC. Labour's renegotiation of Britain's membership terms in 1974–1975 and the subsequent referendum on entry are discussed in Chapter 10. In spite of this renegotiation, Britain still made a substantial financial contribution to the EC and this became an issue with Margaret Thatcher. While not against the Community in the 1970s, she had never been an enthusiast. Asserting Britain's interests by reducing the country's contribution, while remaining in the EC, played better with the electorate than Labour's new policy of withdrawal, adopted when it swung left. And once Mrs Thatcher had started on this course, she would have lost face by abandoning it. After a series of temporary budget rebates Britain achieved a permanent formula for a reduced contribution in 1984.

Many commentators have criticised Margaret Thatcher for her stubbornness over the budget issue, which certainly reduced good feeling in the Community. Their criticism, however, depends in part on unproven assertions that Britain would have achieved significant budget rebates by following other tactics. However, it is true that Britain failed to radically reform the CAP, which everyone agrees was wasteful. (See also Chapter 12 box, 'Rural Britain 1945–2000'.)

The EC now renewed attempts to achieve greater integration in the form of the Single European Market (SEM) established in 1987, which aimed for a free internal market in jobs and services, as well as goods. This fitted well with Margaret Thatcher's general views and she supported it. But in potential, it strengthened the power of the Community vis-à-vis its member states. And since the European Parliament had been operating since 1979, although initially with very little power, the SEM encouraged the longer term development of supranationalism. This became manifest when European Monetary Union (EMU) was put on to the agenda in 1988. Margaret Thatcher opposed it as another step towards integration but, since the convergence of currencies was supported by Nigel Lawson, the Chancellor, and Geoffrey Howe, once her closest lieutenant, Margaret Thatcher became politically isolated. Her stance contributed to the weakening of her position, which resulted in her fall after the poll tax débâcle (see Chapter 10).

Britain and overseas in the 1990s

In 1991 the Soviet Union ceased to exist – a long-term result of its economic sclerosis, a short-term result of the reforming forces unleashed by Mikhail Gorbachev. Gorbachev had already signed arms limitation agreements with the West. The new Russian leader, Boris Yeltsin, carried the process of disarmament further forward. One result was another rapid rundown in Britain's armed forces as much of the Cold War defence apparatus, including the British army of the Rhine and the civil defence mechanism, was virtually dismantled. The cruise missiles were removed from Greenham Common in 1991.

Britain was still able to make a substantial military contribution to the American-led coalition in the 1991 Gulf war, the almost unanimous UN response to the invasion of Kuwait by Saddam Hussein, the dictatorial ruler of Iraq. Its resonances were to be long term, but in the 1990s it seemed to be merely a large-scale forerunner of a new role for Britain's armed forces, as interveners and then peacekeepers in civil wars or regional conflicts in which the international community had become involved. Britain was involved in these in Bosnia in 1992–1995 and Kosovo in 1999 – both conflicts which arose from the aftermath of the break-up of Yugoslavia. As a result of these new responsibilities, NATO retained a role – albeit a very different one to its function in the Cold War – as a command and control organisation.

It was only after the turn of the century that world-wide terrorism came to be perceived as a major threat and Iraq was to return to prominence as the target of another, much more controversial, American-led invasion which Britain also joined. The special relationship with America had been a factor in the Gulf war, in that Britain's military contribution was substantial. However, with the end of the Cold War, there seemed no reason why the special relationship should be of longer term significance, and it was much less prominent for most of the 1990s. After 2001, however, the Labour government's enthusiastic support for the 'War on Terror', which led to the invasion of Iraq, once more returned the special relationship to an important place in Britain's foreign policy.

The end of the Cold War, therefore, had resolved some problems and seen others emerge. Europe remained – an opportunity to many in mainland Europe, a problem to many in Britain.

As discussed in Chapter 10, Margaret Thatcher's departure destabilised the Conservative Party, with Europe becoming the fulcrum of discontent. New Conservative MPs in the 1980s tended to be more right wing than their predecessors, and the right wing was often associated with Euro-scepticism, as lukewarmness or downright hostility to the European Community was known. While she was Prime Minister, Mrs Thatcher had controlled and channelled this discontent through her own criticisms of Europe, although of course those criticisms had also exacerbated Euro-scepticism. Once she was out of office there was less constraint on the Euro-sceptics. As a result, internal Conservative criticism of Europe mounted, while by the late 1990s anti-European parties, notably the UK Independence Party, gained a significant number of votes.

But Europe itself was also changing. Historians have noted a renewed impetus towards political integration – the ultimate goal of Europe's founding fathers – from the mid-1980s. When the Single European Market was agreed, European leaders also insisted on an increase in powers for the European Parliament – although it remained relatively weak – and, more important, the European Commission, the central bureaucracy in Brussels. In 1991 significant further moves were made towards a more integrated European Union (EU) – the new overarching name – in the Maastricht Treaty. This established the 'Social Charter' – common labour laws also confusingly known as the Social Chapter. Maastricht also called for moves towards European Monetary Union (EMU) – that is, a single currency. Britain secured an opt-out from both of these, even though sterling at the time was aligned with other European currencies through the Exchange Rate Mechanism (ERM). In spite of the opt-out, which John Major could represent as carrying forward Thatcherite principles, ratification of the Maastricht Treaty by Parliament in 1992–1993 became a focus for bitter internal Conservative dissent. With Britain's departure from the ERM in 1992, her participation in monetary union became even more remote. EMU was established in 1999, with the new currency, the euro, following in 2002. But Labour's Chancellor, Gordon Brown, was lukewarm and kept it off the immediate political agenda.

In other respects, though, the Conservative defeat in 1997 reduced the impact of Euro-scepticism within the country. It did this partly because the Conservatives became a weak and impotent opposition, their own continuing disputes over Europe not helping. It did so also because Labour's domestic policy seemed, at first, exciting and fresh enough to keep people's minds off Europe. As the power and authority of the EU continued to grow, however, it has become clear in the new century that Britain's relationship to it is not an issue which will go away.

Britain and overseas in the post-war world: conclusion

In 1948 Churchill put forward the notion of Britain's 'three circles' of overseas influence. They were the Commonwealth and Empire, the English speaking world, notably the United States, and Europe: all those circles intersected, and within the area of that intersection lay Britain. His idea has been widely used by political commentators and historians. It neatly sums up Britain's position within the world, as it was seen by most British politicians and diplomats in the late 1940s and the early 1950s.

Since then much has changed. The Empire has gone and the Commonwealth has withered. There is little left now besides sentiment. Conversely, Britain's relationship with Europe has steadily grown in importance. But Britain's opting out of parts of European integration, and the consistent public scepticism towards the EU, means that its membership of this circle is still problematical. In the 1940s, and in spite of Churchill's occasional rhetoric to the contrary, most Britons saw Europe as a unstable chemical mixture, which had to be stabilised for Britain's own good, rather than an entity with which it had close emotional ties. And given the events of 1939–1945, this view is understandable. But since then there has been the advent of mass foreign tourism, which from the 1960s sent millions of Britons to Europe; a reorientation of British foreign trade so that Europe is now the dominant partner; the development of numerous joint European ventures such as the Erasmus programme for student exchanges; and the periodic re-election in Britain of European MPs – the MEPs. Yet in spite of all this, the British attitude to Europe still seems lukewarm.

Britain's reticence towards European integration is not unique in Europe. The French people, for instance, have not always favoured closer European links, while the Danes have always been lukewarm. However, other Western European governments – Germany, Italy, Spain and the Benelux countries – and their peoples have, at least until recently, been more relaxed.

Although Britain's lack of sympathy with Europe poses fascinating sociological and cultural questions, from the point of view of foreign policy the most interesting questions are raised by Churchill's second circle, the English speaking world. Subsumed within this circle was Britain's continuing world-wide defence role. While this arose partly from continuing Commonwealth commitments, it was also part of the West's barricade against Communist expansion. And within this circle, too, was the notion of a special relationship with the USA. This relationship, however, has always been perceived as more important by Britain than by the USA itself. From the American point of view, Britain's main function was to be a NATO partner – militarily the strongest, after the USA itself, but no more than that. Until the 1970s this American perception meant that, in their view, one of the most valuable things Britain could do was to join any political entity which Western European governments constructed – meaning, from 1958, the EEC.

By the late 1960s Britain seemed to have accepted that role, and terminating her 'east of Suez' commitments was part of that acceptance. Heath's enthusiasm for Europe, and Britain's economic problems from 1974 onwards, seemed to cement a reduced

British defence and Cold War role, as a loyal member of NATO but no more. But then Margaret Thatcher's enthusiastic embrace of the Reagan opposition to Soviet expansion, and Britain's own adventure in the Falklands, put its world role back on the agenda. In a rather less grandiose way, this was continued in the 1990s with the belief of Douglas Hurd, Foreign Secretary from 1989–1995, that Britain should 'punch above her weight' in world affairs.

What has lain behind this desire to stride on the world stage? In the late 1940s, and to some extent up to the mid-1950s, it was a comprehensible attitude. The realities of the Commonwealth, of Britain's trading links and of the need to knit together Western Europe against potential Soviet aggression all pointed towards a continuing world role. But after Suez, Macmillan's continued desire to cut a figure in diplomacy and Britain's attempt to cling to a nuclear deterrent now seem luxuries – and were not particularly desired by the USA.

The more modest world role assumed by the late 1960s appears a welcome but belated acceptance of the new realities. But then in the 1980s, realities again appeared to take a back seat. One obvious reason why Macmillan, and later Mrs Thatcher and (rather more modestly) Douglas Hurd, wanted to project Britain's world role was that this has usually played well domestically. For instance, during the Macmillan era it softened the potential opposition of the Conservative right to continuing military cutbacks and the ending of Empire. The only two big exceptions are Suez and, beyond the scope of this book, the Iraq invasion of 2003. But another, less cynical, reason is that politicians have genuinely believed that Britain ought to project itself on the world stage. Unfortunately, and leaving aside their own domestic political advantage, there seems no reason to suppose that they were correct. While Britain has undoubtedly played an important role as America's leading NATO ally, that role could almost certainly have been successfully performed in a more low-key way. After the mid-1950s the tangible benefits of Britain's periodic efforts to punch above her weight seem more or less nil, since countries such as Germany and Japan have hugely increased their share of world trade and their wealth with no such posturing.

Notes

1. Dennis Bardens, *Anthony Eden*, cited in Rhodes-James, *Eden* (see Chapter 5), p. 73.
2. Quoted in Bullock, A., *Ernest Bevin: Foreign Secretary 1945–51* (London: Heinemann, 1983), p. 352.
3. Quoted in Wilson, *New Britain* (see Chapter 9), p. 132.

Further reading

Bullock, *Bevin* is very good although not very critical. Campbell, *Thatcher* (see Chapter 10) is excellent. Reynolds, *Britannia* and Reynolds, D., 'Britain and the World since 1945: Narratives of Decline or Transformation?' in Burk, *British Isles* (see Chapter 9) are valuable and thought-provoking surveys. Tomlinson, J., 'The Decline of Empire and the Economic "Decline" of Britain',

Twentieth Century British History, Vol. 14, pp. 210–221 (2003) is very good on the turn to Europe. Turner, *Macmillan* and Ziegler, *Wilson* (see Chapter 9) are both excellent.

Other sources: Beaumont, R., 'The British Armed Forces since 1945' in Gunn, L. (ed.), *The Defense of Western Europe* (London: Croom Helm, 1987); Brown and Louis, *British Empire* (see Chapter 1); Clarke, P., *The Cripps Version* (London: Penguin, 2002); Cockcroft, W. and Thomas, R., *Cold War: Building for Nuclear Confrontation* (Swindon: English Heritage, 2003); Davis, R., ' "Why did the General do it?" De Gaulle, Polaris, and the French Veto of Britain's Application to Join the Common Market', *European History Quarterly*, Vol. 28, pp. 373–398 (1998); Evans, *Thatcher* (see Chapter 10); Hollowell, *Britain* (see Chapter 9); Kennedy-Pipe, *Russia* (see Chapter 5); Major, *Autobiography* (see Chapter 10); Owen, N., 'The Conservative Party and Indian Independence 1945–1947', *Historical Journal*, Vol. 46, pp 403–436 (2003); Pickering, J., 'Politics and "Black Tuesday": Shifting Power in the Cabinet and the Decision to Withdraw from East of Suez', *Twentieth Century British History*, Vol. 13, pp. 144–170 (2002); Thatcher, *Downing Street* (see Chapter 10); Young, J., *Britain and European Unity, 1945–1992* (London: Macmillan, 1993).

Chapter 12

SOCIETY 1945–2000

Class, occupation and voting

Class as an organising principle of British society seemed to reach its peak after the Second World War. Manual workers still comprised around 70 per cent of the male workforce, and 50 per cent of the electorate voted for Labour in 1945. This has often been seen as the culmination of a process in which the working class finally saw themselves as an entity with common interests.

As Chapters 8 and 9 show, however, although there was a desire in 1945 for more government intervention, it was not strongly based on the idea of class. The Labour Party itself stressed its cross-class appeal and there was widespread acceptance of the post-war ideal of a fairer society, with Labour gaining a significant middle-class vote. Furthermore, the Conservatives with over 40 per cent of the vote continued to attract many working-class voters. The unions, an influential element of the wider 'labour movement', seemed more definitely class based since they mainly catered for manual workers. But whatever their rhetoric, the unions' main concern had always been the promotion of the interests of their own members, not of the wider working class.

Nonetheless, it is true that in the 1940s and early 1950s the working class, meaning manual workers, remained fairly homogeneous and 'traditional' in outlook and lifestyle. It was still recognisably the working class of the 1930s, or even the 1900s. Manual jobs in older industries were still important. Union membership increased, partly because it became almost universal in nationalised industries. And in one area, housing, class identity was if anything strengthened as public housing provision grew. It was mainly taken up by working-class families, while the middle classes increasingly brought their own homes. By the late 1950s patterns were changing. Mining and railways shed labour rapidly, although an increase in manufacturing jobs slowed the overall decline in manual work. From the mid-1960s manufacturing employment also fell. The result has been a continuing shift in occupational structure. Male and female manual workers together, 64 per cent of the total workforce in 1951, fell to 38 per cent in 1991. As this was happening, real incomes steadily rose.

Growing prosperity had led American sociologists in the 1950s to put forward the 'embourgeoisement' thesis – that affluence would lead practically everyone to become middle class in their lifestyles and attitudes. An empirical survey in the 1960s led by John Goldthorpe suggested this did not hold for Britain. Compared to the middle class, manual workers had a different and more instrumental attitude to work, which they saw primarily as a means of earning money, and most still perceived themselves as working class.

Nevertheless, the steady reduction in the proportion of manual workers seemed to foreshadow the eventual redundancy of the very concepts of 'working class' and 'middle class'. However, class is dichotomous because self-identification with a particular class may be different from the label conferred by occupation. Just as a minority of manual workers in the 1960s identified themselves as middle class, so non-manual workers might identify themselves as working class. In the 1960s and 1970s the continued increase in union membership, especially among public sector non-manual workers such as civil servants, contributed to this since union membership has some correlation with perceived class position. Since the 1970s, however, Britain has unquestionably become a middle-class society as measured by occupation. And if occupation had remained the chief determinant of voting patterns, Labour would no longer be a significant political force. Instead, in 1997, it revived to gain 43 per cent of the popular vote. Why has the link between occupation and voting patterns changed since the 1940s?

At first patterns were slow to change, although Labour increased its share of the middle-class vote in order to win electoral victories in the 1960s. In the 1970s the increasing Liberal vote signalled a further shift since this came fairly equally from all parties. The Alliance of the 1980s and the Liberal Democrats of the 1990s continued to have cross-class appeal. The Conservative successes from 1979 onwards were dependent in part on working-class votes, but as has been seen the Conservatives always captured a proportion of such votes. The biggest change has been in the 1990s – the far greater propensity by the middle classes to vote Labour. Two explanations for this – Labour's move rightwards and the Conservatives' internal warfare over Europe – have nothing to do with class. But nonetheless the shift suggests that class now has far less connection with voting. This conclusion is strengthened because union membership, which had previously solidified the link, has declined from a peak of 54 per cent of the workforce in 1979 to 33 per cent in 1995.

Does class matter any more? Maybe in some ways it does. In spite of the decline of manual work, income distribution has changed very little over the last 50 years, as shown in the next section. But inequalities of income distribution have never seemed to play much part in class feeling. In the 1960s Gary Runciman demonstrated that most people in Britain compare themselves with others in a roughly similar position, rather than with those much wealthier than themselves. Indeed, there is not much awareness of how great disparities are. Even if people were aware, the fact of continued inequality might matter much less, because most people can now command a comfortable standard of living. However, there remain a fair number of people, in less well-paid manual jobs, in long-term unemployment or on sickness benefit, who are significantly disadvantaged. Ethnic minorities are a disproportionately large element of this group: in 2000 black unemployment was 15 per cent and Pakistani/Bangladesh 17 per cent, against an average of 5 per cent. The disadvantage is particularly marked in health, where there is a strong correlation between better health and higher income. The problem for such people is not just poverty, but the difficulty of moving out of it. Over time, there has been net upward social mobility; in other words, more working-class children have shifted their social class upwards over their working lives than middle-class children downwards. But nonetheless, upward social mobility in Britain has been relatively difficult to achieve compared with other developed countries.

Finally, many non-manual workers in Britain consider themselves working class. Perhaps this continued self-identification is merely a realistic appreciation of the continued inequalities in income. Or perhaps it owes itself to lingering myths of a solidaristic working class.

Work, incomes and consumption

In the 55 years since 1945 patterns of employment underwent radical changes, as shown in the previous section. The shift away from manual work was at first most evident among women, but has subsequently extended to men. In 1951 there were 7.5 million people in manufacturing, 750,000 in mining and about 1.75 million in finance and professional services. By 2000 the manufacturing workforce had fallen to around 4 million and miners to a few thousand, while there were over 5 million in finance and business services.

Almost as striking has been the increase in women's participation in paid work. The upsurge in the Second World War was followed, as it had been after the First World War, by a decline and then a period of relative stability. But since the 1950s there has been rapid change: 33 per cent of women over school age worked in 1951 compared with 54 per cent in 1998. From the 1950s, too, young people's participation in full-time paid work declined as more stayed on at school until 18 and the proportion going to university increased.

Finally, from the mid-1970s, there have been a set of related shifts. After 30 years of post-war full employment, unemployment increased to about 13 per cent in 1982. After falling sharply in the late 1980s, it reached 10 per cent again in 1993. High unemployment was associated with other forms of economic inactivity. Firms which reduced their workforces often did so by encouraging employees to retire early. The trend was facilitated by the buoyant stock market, which increased the value of pension funds, thus enabling companies to offer early pensions. So the 'activity rate' – the proportion in employment – of men above 60 fell. (Recently this trend has reversed, partly because of more employment opportunities, but also because longer lifespans and stock market declines have made it much more expensive to offer early pensions.) There was also a big rise in the numbers of those on incapacity benefits, from around 1 million – the long-term average – in 1980 to 2.4 million in the mid-1990s. Clearly this is not primarily because more people are ill or disabled. There certainly are large numbers of people, for instance ex-miners, who suffer from long-term illnesses, often related to their previous occupation, but these illnesses have always existed. Indeed, in the past there were far more people who did hazardous manual work and were more likely to have such an illness. Up to the 1980s, however, large employers would often continue to employ such workers in less onerous jobs. As competition and privatisation have squeezed employers, such opportunities have declined. Doctors' attitudes to such illnesses may also have changed. As a result, incapacity benefit has become, in part, a form of disguised unemployment. An increase also took place in the interwar years, another period of high unemployment.

Up to the 1970s the regional imbalances in unemployment which had characterised the interwar period were much less evident, as unemployment was low everywhere. In the 1960s the decline in mining jobs and other older industries had led to some increase in unemployment in South Wales, the North-East and Central Scotland, but newer manufacturing industries took up some of the slack. From the mid-1970s the picture was very different. Unemployment was particularly bad in the old industrial areas and the formerly prosperous West Midlands, where the car industry declined. Regional differences in average income levels per person mirrored unemployment. From the mid-1990s things changed again. Unemployment fell everywhere, although as noted above its true levels were masked because of incapacity benefit. Nevertheless, regional imbalances in income levels remained, with much higher average levels in London. Next most prosperous were the South-East and East Anglia.

Government policy had some bearing on these trends. As explained in Chapter 10, from the mid-1970s governments moved away from an emphasis on full employment. Then throughout the 1980s and early 1990s they chipped away at trade union bargaining power and unemployment benefit relative to average pay. Together this erosion led to the so-called flexible labour market of turn-of-the-century Britain. This fostered the proliferation of low-wage jobs which helped to mop up unemployment.

Governments were only partially responsible for the rise and subsequent fall of unemployment, however. It and other changes also depended on fundamental shifts in the world economy. In the long run, economic activity has shifted, from an initial focus on primary production – mainly food – first towards manufactures and finally towards the tertiary sector, or services. It has done so because production of food, and to some extent manufactures, has become 'commoditised'. They no longer need scarce or specialised factors of production, and therefore production has shifted to those areas which had an abundance of land (for food) or labour (for manufactures). In the case of food, this happened for Britain in the nineteenth century. But manufactures behaved differently. In some cases, notably textiles, where production techniques were relatively simple, manufacture was moving away from Britain after the First World War. But for most manufactures, the process was drastically slowed down by the depression and its aftermath. Tariff barriers proliferated, thus hindering the global division of labour. The world economy recovered after the Second World War but worldwide tariffs were slow to come down. On the face of it, unemployment increased in the mid-1970s because of the oil crisis, the consequent slowdown in growth and the unwillingness of governments to adopt Keynesian policies. In fact, the process of trade liberalisation had now reached a stage where much manufacture was destined anyway to shift from Britain. Whether the shift from manufacturing in Britain has gone further than it should have done is not the task of this book to answer. It has certainly gone further than in most European countries.

The shift towards services underpinned many of the employment changes in modern Britain. It was one cause of the unemployment of male manual workers. However, it

Society and economy: Rural Britain 1945–2000

A host of factors dictated a very different approach to agriculture after 1945 than after 1918, when wartime price support for foodstuffs had soon been dropped. By 1945 planning and government intervention were the norm, while many thought that basic commodities would remain scarce and expensive indefinitely. So price support for food-stuffs continued and was supplemented by grants and a scientific infrastructure to assist farmers in increasing productivity. The inception of the Common Agricultural Policy (CAP) in 1973 (see Chapter 11) changed the method of price support but not the under-lying policy, which was to increase food production at almost all costs. In its basic aim the policy was highly successful. Wheat yields, for instance, tripled between the 1930s and the 1990s. The cost, however, was high. It was not just a cost to the taxpayer, although that was substantial and increased with CAP. The focus on food production had a detrimental effect on the environment as price incentives dictated heavier fer-tiliser and pesticide use and larger fields to maximise machinery use. The centrality of food production meant there was only limited encouragement to diversify the rural economy.

The policy was supported by a powerful agricultural lobby. The Ministry of Agriculture and Fisheries (in 1955 it added Food to become MAFF) was notorious for its almost complete immunity to normal political control. It and the National Farmers' Union together ran agricultural policy. In the 1980s, however, the Thatcher govern-ment extended its attacks on consensus to agriculture, an approach which fitted in with its attempt to curtail the cost of CAP and eventually gained support within the EU itself. There were the beginnings of a more environmentally friendly farming policy with the designation of Environmentally Sensitive Areas in 1986, an approach which was subsequently expanded to include modest cost-restraining reforms in 1992. More radical reforms had to wait until the new century (2003). As a result, agricultural policy began to shift from its productionist orientation. But rural land use was also constrained by the strengthening movement for rural preservation, a reaction to uncontrolled interwar development. Its first post-war manifestations were the National Parks designated in 1948, and subsequently influential lobbying bodies such as the Council for the Protection of Rural England (CPRE) remained hostile to wider economic, and housing, development in the countryside. This stance was supported by many of the better-off who lived in rural areas, an attitude nicknamed 'Nimbyism' (not in my backyard). The Thatcher government was less willing to take on this wider constituency than it was to confront the now relatively small farming lobby.

In spite of these forces – first agricultural productionism then rural protectionism – the rural economy has diversified over the last 50 years. Light manufacturing, tourism and other service industries have sharply reduced the importance of agriculture. The car has enabled many to live in the countryside and work elsewhere, while many small towns have expanded their population substantially. But almost certainly less restric-tive planning policies would have encouraged these trends further and perhaps reduced house prices generally, to everyone's benefit. (See also Chapter 9 box, 'Houses and plans'.)

also facilitated the growth of women's employment because many of the occupations in which employment was increasing were those in which women's positions were already entrenched. These included finance, the media, the NHS, catering and retail. The actual jobs women did changed in diverse ways. On the one hand, part-time work – usually low paid – grew, from 11 per cent of working women in 1951 to around 45 per cent by 1990, since when it has stabilised. On the other hand, far more women became professionals. In 1961, 15 per cent of all doctors were women and just 3.5 per cent of lawyers. By 1990 half of all entrants to law and medicine were women, and the proportion has gone on increasing. But other higher status occupations, such as engineering and industrial management, were less permeable to women.

Economic shifts helped to provide the demand for more women to work. But social and educational changes have also led to radical adjustments in the once accepted norms that women mainly occupied lower status jobs and that married women stayed at home.

Most people seem to have enjoyed or at least not minded the jobs they have done. After youth, when typically jobs are changed rapidly, people tend to find a job which suits them. Manual workers seem to have experienced less job satisfaction than non-manual workers, but to some extent people did less satisfactory manual jobs such as fast-paced production line work because they paid better. In other words, there was a trade-off between money and satisfaction. As manual work has declined, it seems likely that overall levels of job satisfaction have increased. Women in the past typically found less satisfaction than men in paid work, although interaction with workmates was a compensation. Most women saw their jobs as primarily to earn money, and many female jobs were repetitive assembly work. As such jobs have declined, and more women have seen their work as a career, it can be inferred that their job satisfaction has increased.

Contrary to popular supposition, there has been no long-term trend towards a segmentation of work between well-paid, more permanent jobs and poorly paid temporary 'Macjobs' (so-called after the burger chain). There have always been plenty of low-skilled and impermanent jobs. In the 1950s and 1960s many were in manufacturing, and as this sector has shrunk jobs in services have become more visible. The recent trend towards more flexible labour markets has created more low-paid jobs but has not changed employment stability for most people. Conversely, the steady growth from the 1950s to the 1990s in company pension schemes and stronger employment protection laws also seem to have made little difference to employment stability. A different employment pattern may develop in the future but there is not much hard evidence for it yet.

Between 1945 and 2000 real income for everyone, rich and poor, increased by about three times on average. The fundamental reason for this was the growth of productivity, but there have been other reasons. Government's share of national income has fluctuated, and these fluctuations have correlated inversely with personal incomes. From 1945 until the early 1960s the trend was downwards, as defence spending fell, but in the 1960s and 1970s the increase in social security spending pushed it up again. Subsequently, the government's share fell again slightly. The other main influence has been the relative price of imports and exports. During the Korean war, and again during the 1970s, the price of raw materials – which constituted a large proportion of imports – spiked upwards, thus depressing incomes. And intermittently during the 1970s and 1980s sterling was abnormally weak, which had the same effect. Conversely, since the late 1990s it has been abnormally strong, which has boosted incomes.

While all incomes have grown, inequalities between the better and less well-off have not changed much. Over the wartime period such inequality was reduced (see Chapter 8), and during the 1960s and 1970s there was a further small reduction as pensioners were treated more generously while tax rates on high incomes increased. But much of this was reversed in the 1980s. Labour, after 1997, has promoted some limited equalisation again. One long-term reduction in inequality, however, was women's pay relative to that of men. From 52 per cent before the war, there was a wartime jump and then stabilisation until 1970 at around 60 per cent. By 1995, taking full-time pay only, it was 80 per cent. The Equal Pay Act of 1970 had some impact, but it was limited because many occupations were staffed mainly by women, thus making comparability with male jobs difficult. The shift of women into higher paid jobs was another positive factor. Even so, most commentators accept that discrimination of a hard-to-pin-down nature, such as differential opportunities for promotion, remained. The risk to employers of younger women taking maternity leave is, of course, an economic factor which has continued to constrain women's progression into higher paid jobs.

The distribution of wealth also changed. In the 1920s it is estimated that 1 per cent of the population owned 58 per cent of total wealth, and 10 per cent owned 88 per cent. By 1991 the comparable figures were 17 per cent and 47 per cent, and if the accumulated value of pension rights is taken into account, 10 per cent and 33 per cent. Death duties (now inheritance tax) reduced the share of the better-off, while the increase in home ownership spread wealth more widely.

If people earn more, they consume more. 'Affluence' has become one of the most widely used words in describing the culture associated with increasing post-war consumption. But what it actually means, and whether it has any explanatory value, is hard to say. Consumption has been increasing since the Industrial Revolution: many of the staple consumption items of the 1930s – gas cookers, radios and trips to the cinema, for example – were luxuries or undreamed of 50 years earlier. Nor can affluence be related to an increasing propensity to spend rather than save. Personal savings as a proportion of income were low in the first half of the twentieth century and then rose to the 1960s, often portrayed as the high point of affluence. All this suggests that terms such as affluence and consumerism may obscure more than they illuminate (Fig. 12.1).

Immediately after the war, consumption of goods was constrained by rationing. In any case, most people's priority was to replace the deficiency caused by wartime shortages of furniture, clothing and household utensils. From the early 1950s a more distinctive consumption pattern emerged. Controls ended, real incomes grew and the relative prices of many goods declined due to productivity increases and tax reductions. The most obvious change was the rise of the car: motoring expenditure, around 3 per cent of consumer spending before the war, was 8 per cent in 1965 and 13 per cent in 1994. There were around 2 million cars in 1950, increasing to 10 million by 1970 and 22 million by 1997. But spending on other categories shifted more slowly. Thus spending on 'household goods' rose from 6 per cent of the total in 1937 to 8 per cent in 1994, although with incomes increasing and relative prices falling, the actual volume of goods bought rose far more.

Figure 12.1 Carnaby St. in Soho in 1967 when it symbolised the burgeoning of youth culture, youth spending power and a 'modern' Britain. © Bettmann/CORBIS

Television ownership rose from virtually nil in the late 1940s to 52 per cent of households in 1958 and 99 per cent by 1977. Even in the mid-1960s, however, only 40 per cent had a refrigerator, but that too had risen to 99 per cent by the late 1990s.

As incomes rose, homes improved, thus absorbing the same, or a greater, proportion of spending. In addition, house prices and mortgage rates tended to increase faster than other prices, while rent subsidies fell. Spending on housing was around 10 per cent of income up to the 1960s, rising to around 15 per cent by the 1990s. Housing quality improvements are reflected in mundane statistics. Thus in 1951 only 60 per cent of households had a bath or shower, but by 1981 the proportion was over 95 per cent. In 1964, 8 per cent had central heating, and by 1990 over 80 per cent – the critical influence here being North Sea gas.

Sue Bowden and Avner Offer have helped us to understand the trajectory of durable goods penetration, and their insights are more valuable than vague generalisations about affluence. Goods can be thought of as time saving – washing machines, vacuum cleaners and so on – or time using – television, for example. Cars are both, depending on how they are used. Time-using goods have certain generic characteristics, including mild addictive powers and perceived status achieved by ownership. As a result, market penetration has been more rapid and less dependent on price than that of time-saving goods. Thus in 1958, when televisions were still relatively expensive, middle- and working-class household penetration were virtually identical, at 53 per cent and 51 per cent of households. Similarly car ownership, in spite of its cost, has risen far faster than practical necessity would dictate. The pattern reflects not so much increased leisure time, as average weekly hours of work have not changed much since the 1920s (although holiday time has increased), but the variety of satisfactions conferred by time-using goods.

In spite of the growth in consumer durables, the dominant trend in recent years has been the shift to the consumption of leisure services – holidays, eating out and so on. This has partly reflected a recent rapid fall in the price of durables, freeing income for other spending, and partly market satiation for time-saving durables. The theme of leisure activities is taken up in subsequent sections.

Women, men and families

Post-war Britain was full of young married couples. Compared to the interwar years, more people married, they married younger and they had more children. The fears of a declining population voiced in the 1930s were put to rest. Some of the reasons for these trends are obvious, but the extent of the contrast is still puzzling.

There had always been more women than men, thus making it likely that many women would remain unmarried, and this was exacerbated by the First World War. But far fewer men were killed in the Second World War, and over time this and better health care redressed the sex imbalance. After the war, too, jobs for men were plentiful. In the past women's work – especially domestic service – had often been more secure than men's, and it was the woman who put together some savings and a 'bottom drawer' which gave the wherewithal to embark on marriage. But this process took time. Now men's earnings seemed secure – and they were also higher than they had ever been. Early marriage became much less of a financial risk. Furthermore, from 1946 having children conferred an actual financial reward – the five shillings a week of the family allowance. The free family health care provided by the NHS was another bonus. Even so, after a shortlived post-war 'baby boom', the birth rate fell again. Almost certainly the acute post-war housing shortage was a factor here. For many young couples housing conditions were worse than before the war. But then from the early 1950s to the mid-1960s the birth rate rose, to around 18 per 1,000 people per year. Furthermore, the increase was more marked in the higher social classes, so although those in lower social groups still had more children, the differential reduced.

With falling adult mortality, more children grew up without losing a parent. The two-parent nuclear family, the theoretical western norm for centuries, seemed ubiquitous. However, by the mid-1960s another set of social changes was underway. Easier birth control – the pill was widely available from the early 1960s – was one agent. The birth rate fell rapidly again, to around 13 per 1,000 on average in the 1980s and 1990s. But other changes could not be put down to the availability of birth control. Conceptions outside marriage increased from the war onwards, although initially this usually led to marriage before the child was born. By the 1970s pre-marital sex was increasingly transmuted into cohabitation before marriage. In the late 1960s just 6 per cent of those marrying had lived together beforehand; by the 1990s it was 70 per cent. And, of course, many of those cohabiting split up without marrying. The increased incidence of such splits was accompanied by a steep rise in divorce. More people than ever got married in the 1960s, but whereas only 7 per cent of those married in 1951 were divorced after 20 years, 24 per cent of those marrying in 1966 were – and the proportion has continued to increase. The easing of divorce laws, for instance in 1969 and 1985, facilitated the change, but the subsequent increase in cohabitation shows that rising divorce rates were part of a trend to more temporary relationships.

The increasing prevalence of divorce does not mean that women and men have suddenly come to dislike one another. As suggested in Chapter 6, husbands and wives often had relatively low expectations of each other in the apparent golden age of interwar marriage. These attitudes did not disappear because of a world war. The 1953 study of the mining town of 'Ashton' describes what seem rather dismal marriages of convenience 'to which the development of affection and companionship is incidental'.[1] Such purely functional relationships represented an extreme example of the way in which the 'male breadwinner' model of marriage was transmuted into relationships in which there was only perfunctory contact between husband and wife.

Thirty more years were to see important changes as the proportion of married women doing paid work increased. Notoriously, however, men were slow to do more housework, and by the 1980s sociologists were recording the dissatisfaction of women with the 'double shift' – paid work and housework. Such dissatisfaction was obviously one reason for increased marriage breakdown. Paid work also increased women's experience of the world, thus making them more alive to the faults in a relationship. However, there are clear signs that male attitudes, seemingly the rocks on which many modern marriages are shipwrecked, are changing too. Thus, as recently as the mid-1980s, 52 per cent of fathers believed that their main role was to be the breadwinner; by the mid–2000s just 20 per cent did. And this attitudinal change has been reflected in practice: for instance, fathers now contribute one-third of parental child care.

While factors such as the increase in paid work for women and the easing of the divorce laws help to explain changes in marriage and childbearing patterns, common sense suggests that they were part of a wider change in which individuals felt less bound by once-accepted norms. These might be religious, or the norms of the local community or of wider society. So the decline of marriage and the rise of cohabitation have been seen as reflecting the rise of individualism: individual choice determines whether relationships are created or broken. 'Individualism' is so wide an explanation as to be virtually meaningless, however. The fact is that historians have not yet really got to grips with what combination of social, economic and cultural change lies behind this breakdown of norms. What is notable, however, is how little positive influence the state has had on the process. Child allowances may have helped raise the post-war birth rate but did not stop it declining later. Otherwise, the conception of the male breadwinner family, which lay behind much of the detail of the Beveridge Plan, was simply overtaken by events. Aspects such as the limitation on married women's pension rights were adjusted only when they became outdated because of the growth of women's work.

Meanwhile, the decline of marriage itself seems to have taken everyone, including the state, by surprise.

While marriage has declined, many couples do still get married and others remain unmarried but are in stable relationships. Has the decline of the male breadwinner conception of marriage led to more companionship in marriage or partnership, such as seemed so lacking between Ashton men and women 50 years ago?

As Chapter 6 shows, the companionate marriage was gaining ground in the interwar period, in the sense that husbands and wives increasingly shared home-based activities such as gardening. From the 1950s onwards the continued increase in home ownership also offered almost endless opportunities for DIY, a frequently shared activity which has barely registered on historians' radar screens. An even more central activity from the mid-1950s onwards, however, was TV viewing. In the 1960s housewives and employed men watched television for about two hours per day on average, the figures rising slightly over the next 20 years. Viewing seems the opposite of DIY in its passivity, but the viewing of many programmes – some game shows, *Z-Cars* and *Morecambe and Wise*, for example – was far more widely shared than most radio listening and therefore provided talking points. With the rise from the 1980s of VCRs and subsequently DVDs, and of multiple television ownership, opportunities for individualising viewing increased.

While this recent trend may have reduced family interaction, from the 1950s home-based leisure activities were supplemented by a growing number outside the home. The car was a major facilitator of these. To some extent it replaced excursions by public transport, bicycle or on foot. It also facilitated the growth of shopping as a leisure activity for the whole family, not just women, and promoted eating out – until the 1960s mainly a middle-class pursuit embarked upon with trepidation due to the dreadful standard of British catering outside central London. The huge increase in informal and family-based activities has probably not been paralleled in more organised forms of non-work activities, even though many activities which involve membership of an organisation or an active decision to participate have increased since the 1950s. Around 2 million people now give blood compared with half a million; membership of children's organisations such as Scouts and Guides has increased, although not by so much. On the other hand, membership of churches and political parties has declined. But given the far greater opportunities for informal leisure activities, it is quite striking that so many still participate formally. Volunteering seems to have increased between the 1970s and the 1990s and, on one count, almost half the population volunteered for some activity during the calendar year.

All this puts in perspective laments about the decline of neighbourliness and 'community' – laments which are not new. Relatively homogeneous working-class communities in which older women played an important part in transmitting cultural values, still important in the 1950s, have steadily declined. But in such communities relations with next-door neighbours were usually friendly but relatively formal, precisely because the close proximity of small terraced houses enjoined caution. Modern 'community' places more emphasis on interaction with immediate neighbours, and then a wider interaction with a range of more geographically scattered friends and

Society and economy: Religion in Britain 1945–2000

The second half of the century was characterised by a continuation of the slow fall in the number of participating church members which first became evident in the 1930s. At the same time, membership of other faiths grew as a result of immigration.

Religious membership (see Chapter 6), around 25 per cent of the population in 1950, was 17 per cent in 2000. But whereas Christians comprised the great majority of these in 1900 and 1950, by 2000 they comprised only three-quarters, or about 13 per cent of the population. Anglicans comprised about one-quarter of church members at the end of the century, compared with around 40 per cent at the beginning. Catholic Church membership had outstripped Anglican by 1980, although subsequently it has fallen as rapidly. More permanent gainers were Pentecostal and 'House' churches, the former associated particularly with communities of West Indian origin. Even so, in 2000 these together comprised only 0.6 per cent of the population. By comparison, Muslims were around 2.5 per cent.

The decline in the membership of most Christian churches is indisputable. But its slow and uneven nature has led to many disputes about why and when Britain became secularised. The usual suspect is 'modernisation' – a very vague term, broadly speaking referring to the growth of science and rationalism on the one hand, and more mundanely the growth of alternative attractions to church attendance. It does not, of course, explain the puzzling fact that the most 'modern' country in some ways – the United States – is far more religious than most of Western Europe. 'When' is almost equally difficult. The disengagement of the state from formal involvement with religion started well back in the nineteenth century and, in spite of Anglicanism's continued status as England's Established Church, after 1920 and Welsh disestablishment, there were few occasions when religion impinged much on politics in mainland Britain. Some see the 1960s as a crucial decade, as it is only then that absolute decline set in and relative decline became much more marked. Certainly it is tempting to see that decade as finally marking an end of a definably 'Protestant' Britain. The reader should go to the excellent review article by Jeremy Morris for pointers to recent thinking on both 'why' and 'when'.

In spite of membership decline, there is still a wide penumbra of belief. In the 1940s and 1950s about 80 per cent of adults believed in God. A sharp drop to 70 per cent took place in the 1960s since when it has remained much the same. But the proportion of those who positively asserted their non-belief has risen from 10 per cent to 27 per cent. The contrariness of the tides of faith is illustrated by belief in ghosts, which actually rose from 15 per cent to 30 per cent. The proportion of baptisms, around 90 per cent in the 1920s and 1930s, fell steadily from the 1950s, but even now around 45 per cent of infants are baptised, about 60 per cent of these in the Church of England. All these statistics suggest that many still have some vague Christian belief and there is a substantial legacy of formal adherence to the rites of Christianity.

acquaintances. Families, even if living further apart, are often still just as important. The losers are those without cars in areas, often of public housing, where the old matriarchy has broken down and other norms which might control interaction are lacking.

This section started with marriage and childbirth and finishes with old age and death. The twentieth century has postponed death for most of us. In 1901 the average expectation of life at birth was about 51; by the 1990s it had rises to about 77. Seventy per cent of the increase took place before 1950, largely because of public health improvements (see Chapter 6). From 1950 to 1980 the rate of increase slowed sharply, almost certainly because of one overwhelming factor – smoking. When Richard Doll first published his pathbreaking work on smoking and cancer in the 1950s, tobacco consumption had risen steadily over the century and the average consumption for men, including non-smokers, was over ten cigarettes per day. Serious public concern over health took time to develop. Male consumption stabilised, and women's consumption continued to rise, until 1970. For many years, therefore, smoking undid many of the benefits to health brought about by continued public health improvements – for instance, the reduction in air pollution brought about by the Clean Air Act of 1955 – and better health care. Since 1970 smoking has declined and by the mid-1990s around 25 per cent of men and 20 per cent of women smoked – around half the figures for the mid-1970s. Since 1980 the rate at which life expectancy has increased has once more accelerated.

As life expectancy increased, the number of those over 65 grew rapidly. In 1900 they comprised 4.7 per cent of the population, by 2000 over 16 per cent. Increasingly the elderly live alone – about 13 per cent in 1951, compared with about 35 per cent by the 1980s. This results partly from choice enabled by higher living standards. The state old-age pension is meagre but for many it is supplemented by private pensions, and so old age, while still one of the determinants of poverty, is also a time of modest prosperity for many. Contrary to myth, there is no evidence that families are less caring than in the past and plenty of evidence that grandparents, even if they live alone, frequently play a vital part in caring for grandchildren. Nor is there any trend to institutionalisation. At any time over the century the proportion of elderly in institutions has not exceeded 5 per cent.

Growing up

The influences which have shaped childhood and adolescence since 1945 have themselves changed radically – probably more than in the first 45 years of the twentieth century. Between 1900 and 1945 there was only slow change in living standards and educational opportunities. From 1945 living standards rose steadily, changing children's environment. And after slow change for the first 15 years or so, educational opportunities changed rapidly, in particular for girls and young women.

Family economics were changed from 1946 by family allowances. These were not paid for the first child but in 1977 were replaced with Child Benefit, which was. In 1946 family allowances raised incomes for a three child family on average earnings by almost 10 per cent. But over the whole period from 1945, average living standards rose by around three times and in the long term had a far greater effect on children's economic environment.

Over time the distribution of resources between age groups has changed. In the 1940s and 1950s resources for all children in larger and poorer working-class families were limited. Their childhood was still characterised by early responsibility, especially for daughters, and independent play in the street, unassisted by many toys, for all children. This diminished as homogeneous working-class neighbourhoods of terraced housing shrank and traffic increased. The dominant trend until the 1970s was the widespread adoption of a culture, middle class in origin and already spreading in the interwar years, in which childhood was a special period in which parents invested increasing resources in the form of toys, children's clothes and so on. As more mothers went out to work, paying for nursery care or childminding became another expense. However, parents also became increasingly willing to invest in keeping children at school, thus shifting resources up the age range. From the 1980s onwards, supporting children in higher education also became more and more significant, especially as government financial support for students was eroded from the early 1990s.

The state's role in all this, as with much else, was attempts to guide behaviour which ultimately had limited effect. Family allowances probably did have a positive effect on the birth rate, as was intended, but over time the impact was outweighed by other factors and in the 1970s the birth rate fell steeply. Governments have remained confused and ambivalent about the growth in the number of working mothers. They welcomed the addition to the workforce but were concerned about the effect of work on the cohesion of families and the bringing up of children. However, increases from the late 1960s in the number of playgroups, and from the 1980s in the number of nurseries, were almost entirely private initiatives. Only in the 1990s did governments start to introduce some financial support to parents for pre-school activity. One reason for this was the increase in the number of single parents, many of them unmarried: by the 1990s about one-third of births were outside marriage. Here again the state's role has been to react to trends which it neither expected nor could control. They are trends, of course, which must have a significant impact on the experience of childhood. From the child's point of view, there has been a reversion to the pattern common in the nineteenth century in which many children had one parent missing.

One area where the state inevitably had an impact was education, because it supplied all of it except that for the small proportion of children, fluctuating between 5 per cent and 8 per cent of the total, who have been educated privately. As described in Chapter 7, the tripartite organisation of education enshrined in the 1944 Education Act owed much to interwar ideas about different types of intelligence. It was elitist in that it endorsed selection at 11, with 'academic' children going to grammar schools, although it embodied genuine beliefs about improving standards for all children. The reality, however, was that the number of children taking higher level qualifications initially rose slowly. In 1961 only 6 per cent of state school leavers in England had one or more A level. From the 1960s growth was more broadly based, stimulated by an increase in the minimum school leaving age to 16 in 1972. By 1991 the equivalent figure was 19 per cent, with a further significant number gaining A levels at further education colleges.

Not surprisingly in the light of these figures, the numbers in full-time higher education – universities, teacher training and other vocational courses – also rose slowly. Just 2.7 per cent of the school-leaving cohort entered it in 1938, 5.8 per cent in 1954 and 8.5 per cent in 1962. With university expansion from the early 1960s and the subsequent development of polytechnics (see Chapter 9), the proportion had doubled to 15 per cent by 1972 but then there was a lengthy period of stagnation – partly because of teacher training cutbacks due to the falling birth rate cutting school rolls, partly because of funding restrictions in the difficult years of the late 1970s and early 1980s. Then, from the late 1980s, the proportion rose again to over 30 per cent by the mid-1990s, in spite of the ending of maintenance grants. The increase was fuelled by the rise in the number taking A levels 30 years earlier – now parents who had higher expectations for their children.

Factors behind the disenchantment of Labour with the tripartite system included changing views about the maturation of intelligence which suggested that selection at 11 – the 'Eleven Plus' – was too early and that many children were condemned to an inferior education in secondary moderns. The minimum school leaving age had been raised to 15 in 1947, but this was still too young for O levels, the equivalent in England and Wales to today's GCSEs. With working-class parental expectations still low and with plenty of jobs for young people, it was natural to leave school as soon as possible with no formal qualifications. And since middle-class children still took a big share of grammar school places, tripartism appeared to do little to enhance social mobility. So Labour's emphasis on this from the mid-1950s was another reason to support comprehensives (see Chapter 9).

However, comprehensives have not levelled social class differences in educational outcome. The grammar/modern school distinction has been replaced by differences between schools with different catchment areas. And one segment of schooling remains particularly unequal – private education. Thus 73 per cent of independent school leavers achieved at least one A level in 1991, compared to 20 per cent of comprehensive school leavers. Depending on one's point of view, this can be seen as a good thing as it enhances the stock of education in the country at no cost to the state, or a bad thing as it perpetuates inequality.

In spite of these caveats, the results of state intervention in education over the century are striking. Of those leaving school between 1900 and 1909, 71 per cent of boys and 85 per cent of girls gained no formal qualifications in their lifetime – including post-school qualifications. By 1997 less than 10 per cent of adolescents had no graded school examination results, while around 40 per cent of boys and 50 per cent of girls had at least five GCSE results graded A–C. This reversal of the sex differential is another striking feature, and points to a less positive aspect of modern education – the disenchantment with it of a significant number of adolescents, particularly male.

In spite of the continued sharp differences between social classes in educational outcomes, social mobility has actually taken place on a large scale. How has this occurred, if not through school? The answer, in a large part, is through work and work-related education. This is paradoxical because the entry to work, for most adolescents, continued to be a hit and miss affair. In the 1950s many working-class parents were still not much concerned with what job their child got, only that they got one. And as late as the 1980s, nearly half of a sample of female school leavers had one of three traditional female occupations as their desired job – nursing, hairdressing and clerical work. Once at work, however, relatively rapid post-war economic growth meant more frequent upgrading of skills and thus more social mobility. Up to the 1960s around 25 per cent of male school leavers still entered apprenticeships to skilled jobs, and these were often a stepping stone to the development of other skills. Whether they had been apprenticed or not, many people gained such skills through day release, evening classes or correspondence courses. The proportion of the population with a professional qualification as their highest qualification peaked among the generation leaving school in the 1950s, at 19 per cent of men and 13 per cent of women. This huge segment of the educational system has therefore been vital, but is unmentioned by most historians. From the 1980s apprentice intakes collapsed along with the decline of manufacturing. Other professional qualifications remain vital, however, as part of the process of up-grading skills.

In the inner life of adolescents, education and work may not always have featured highly, save that the latter increased their economic independence and thus their ability to escape parental restrictions. Such independence grew in the 1950s. The real earnings of the 15–24 age group were estimated to have increased by 50 per cent between 1938 and the late 1950s. These higher earnings fuelled high spending on items which still feature heavily today on that age group's spending list – records (later CDs), the cinema, cosmetics and footwear. A distinctive youth culture in which spending was an important part started to emerge in the 1950s and seemed fully blown by the 1960s. Both at the time and subsequently many commentators saw this youth culture as being heavily influenced by America. As Ross McKibbin has shown for the years before 1950, most of the easy assumptions made about American influence on music and many other things are simply wrong. Influence flowed both ways across the Atlantic. This was as true after 1950. Many areas of popular culture such as sport and popular newspapers were not influenced by American examples. Common observation suggests that young people's leisure and spending habits have many similarities across the developed world, but it also suggests that many habits are resolutely national and cut across age boundaries. Many British adolescents are not only enthusiastic about football, they are enthusiastic about their local, and often heroically unsuccessful, teams. Many Welsh adolescents, but only a few English ones, are enthusiastic about Rugby Union. Less happily, young people in Britain have also taken recently to an age-old British (and certainly not American) custom which had seemed to be declining – drinking too much.

Immigration and ethnicity

Immigration has intermittently been a significant social and political issue since 1945. It is an issue which has been inseparable from views about 'race', a biologically meaningless word which has nonetheless been part of common discourse for many years.

In the 1940s the pre-war assumption that white people were superior, or at least different, was held at all levels of society. The Royal Commission on Population of

1947 stated that larger-scale immigration 'could only be welcomed without reserve if the immigrants were of good human stock and were not prevented by their religion or race from intermarrying with the host population or becoming merged in it'. Yet this widely held belief in racial difference coexisted with another belief, explored in Chapter 6, that there should be equality of all before the law. The Aliens Acts of 1905 and 1919 had restricted the entry of non-British subjects but this did not apply to Commonwealth citizens, and the 1948 Nationality Act affirmed that 'colonial subjects' were 'full British citizens'. This dichotomy in official attitudes was mirrored at popular level. Many people deplored the strict segregation which the US military enforced among its troops in Britain during the war, but many were also concerned at interracial sexual liaisons. Kenneth Little, speaking to audiences of soldiers in the 1940s, observed that 'there was obviously a strong desire that coloured people (in the abstract) should be treated on terms of equality, and yet at the same time an equally strong reluctance to face the logical implications of equal opportunity'.[2] He found widespread uncertainty towards and some dislike of black people because of ignorance and cultural conservatism, but no systematic prejudice as in the USA.

The post-war years saw considerable migration into Britain, both from the Commonwealth and elsewhere, primarily because of the high demand for labour. Britain absorbed large numbers of European refugees between 1946 and 1951, notably Poles of whom there were 120,000 in 1954. Irish immigration was even more substantial. Britain and Ireland had retained the free movement of citizens in spite of Ireland's complete secession from the Commonwealth in 1949, and by the 1960s there were almost 900,000 Irish-born people in Britain, an increase of half a million since the 1930s. By comparison, in 1961 there were around 100,000 Asians born in India and Pakistan and about 170,000 black people born in the Caribbean (Fig. 12.2). Even if Britain lacked systematic prejudice, there was more than enough for most blacks and Asians. For example, a Jamaican immigrant arriving in Gloucester in 1950 was banned from some pubs, while finding lodging was very difficult. His landlord 'went through hell' for taking Jamaican lodgers.[3]

In spite of the relatively small numbers, Asian and black immigration was becoming controversial. Government ministers expressed occasional disquiet over immigration, but the benefits of a continuing supply of labour for low-paid jobs in, for instance, the NHS and London Transport initially quelled doubts. Then, in 1958, black immigration to two areas which had severe housing shortages – Notting Hill in West London and Nottingham – helped to spark off anti-immigrant riots. Although these were not an immediate stimulus to political action, they bolstered the arguments of right-wing Conservative MPs who called for restrictions on immigration. The government passed the Commonwealth Immigration Act in 1962, in which only those with employment vouchers guaranteeing a job were allowed in. Labour opposed the Act but in 1965, when in power, strengthened it by limiting the number of vouchers. By a final Conservative Act of 1971, all special privileges to primary immigrants – that is, those coming to take up employment – from Commonwealth countries were ended. However, immigration continued at high levels for some time, since dependents were allowed in. As many migrants were young adults, the ethnic minority population increased further due to a high birth rate.

Figure 12.2   A West Indian immigrant arrives at Victoria Station in 1956. © Hulton-Deutsch Collection/CORBIS

Post-war policy towards immigration and race was driven by several factors. There was a lingering belief that British citizenship was inclusive, but this was probably less significant to policy-makers than the economic advantages of immigration. Once the perceived problems posed by black and Asian immigrants made immigration a subject of public concern in the late 1950s, policy-makers shifted ground rapidly and restrictive legislation was brought in. As immigration declined, its saliency – and public concern about 'race' – also declined. In the early 1970s about 10 per cent of the electorate saw it as a key issue. This declined steadily to around 2 per cent in the early 1990s.

From the early 1990s immigration increased again. These new immigrants came from all parts of the world and included both legal and illegal economic migrants. The number of legal non-Commonwealth migrants grew from 1973 when Britain joined the European Community, and the free movement of EC citizens was stimulated by the Single European Act of 1985. They also included increasing numbers claiming asylum against persecution, which Britain was bound to honour having signed the Geneva Convention on the Protection of Refugees in 1951. Many asylum seekers were believed by sections of the press and public to be, in reality, economic migrants. Levels of concern about immigration rose again, around 25 per cent of the electorate seeing it as a key issue in 2005. As a result, politicians' interest in the subject also grew. There were a series of Asylum and Immigration Acts, starting in 1993, aimed at tightening up conditions for those claiming asylum. Similar political responses have continued in the new century.

While accepting immigration restrictions, Labour in the 1960s attempted to eliminate discrimination with the Race Relations Acts. The first, in 1965, was primarily voluntary and omitted the vital areas of employment and housing. These were included in the 1968 Act, and in 1976 another Act further limited the scope of discrimination and set up the Commission for Racial Equality to make investigations into discrimination more effective and to promote equality.

Discrimination was undoubtedly a heavy cross to bear for non-whites. While many owners of rented housing and employers discriminated, trade unionists also attempted to keep blacks and Asians out of certain manual occupations. So immigrants tended to get unskilled or semi-skilled manual jobs. This was partly due to their relative lack of skills, since many were from a rural background, but much was due to discrimination. Although the picture has changed significantly since the 1960s, earlier discrimination has been a long-term liability to blacks and Asians, because of the difficulty in Britain of achieving upward mobility (see earlier section, 'Class, occupation and voting').

Whatever the current concerns about immigration, attitudes to ethnic and religious differences have undoubtedly changed. Anti-semitism was fading throughout the period and is now confined to small groups. The major political parties played a part in this as both had many Jewish party members, although a residue of anti-semitism may explain the small number of Jewish Conservative MPs up to the late 1970s. But, symbolically, in 2003 Michael Howard, a practising Jew, became Conservative Party leader.

Official attitudes to other minorities, as manifested in the Race Relations Acts, had shifted by the 1960s while popular opinion often had not. Some Conservative candidates campaigned on a racist platform in 1964, although the party subsequently distanced itself from such attitudes by supporting the Race Relations Acts. The National Front, a far-right party, gained some support in the early 1970s. And in the 1979 election the three major parties had less than ten ethnic minority candidates between them, while by 2005 they had around 100, more or less evenly distributed. Clearly such candidates are not now seen as significantly diminishing electoral chances. In a different arena, the huge increase in the number of black footballers since the early 1980s has been accompanied, in the view of many sports commentators, by a sharp diminution of racism amongst spectators. Nonetheless, there has recently been another revival of the far right. It is mainly limited to areas of continuing unemployment, suggesting – as did the Notting Hill riots – that social and economic factors have played a part in racial problems.

How far the apparent decline of racism owes itself to legislation is a moot point. But the Race Relations Acts, by enhancing employment opportunities for ethnic minorities, have meant that most people have perforce mixed with those from other ethnic groups. Perhaps this has stimulated the belief that we are, after all, very similar whatever the colour of our skin.

The 'Liberal Hour'

The 'Liberal Hour' is a phrase often used for that brief period in the 1960s when a widespread sense of optimism over the future coincided with a number of socially liberal legislative reforms. Initially associated with John Kennedy's presidency in the USA, optimism was carried forward in Britain on the froth of Harold Wilson's rhetoric about a 'New Britain' and Labour's National Plan. By the late 1960s optimism about Britain's economic prospects had died and liberal optimism about reform had changed to pessimism over the Vietnam war.

The initial impetus to reform was associated with Roy Jenkins, the Home Secretary from 1965 to 1967. Among the reforms with which he was directly or indirectly associated were the second, and stronger, Race Relations Act of 1968 (see previous section, 'Immigration and ethnicity'). Abortion was legalised in 1967 through a private member's bill introduced by David Steele, a Liberal MP (and later Liberal leader) but given parliamentary time by the government. In the same year, local authorities were authorised to provide a Family Planning Service, and homosexuality between consenting males over 21 was decriminalised (lesbianism had never been illegal). An easing of the divorce laws – it could now be based on a period of separation as well as 'faults' such as adultery and cruelty – took place in 1969. Sexual and marital liberalisation was supplemented by the abolition in 1968 of the Lord Chamberlain's rights to read, and approve, stage plays before performance. Abolition was quickly followed by nudity on stage in *Hair*.

Jenkins and Jim Callaghan, the Chancellor from 1964, swapped places after devaluation in 1967. Callaghan was socially more conservative, and in this probably reflected popular views. By 1968 pressure for tougher restrictions on immigration had built up and the Race Relations Act was paralleled by such restrictions. Callaghan rejected the easing of criminal penalties on soft drugs in 1968 in the context of helping to halt 'the advancing tide of so-called permissiveness'.[4]

The Liberal Hour and the notion of a permissive society have encouraged the popular view of the 1960s as a decade of rapid social change. But there is nothing magical about a ten-year period, just because it happens to coincide with the beginning and end of a decade. Teenage preoccupations probably changed as rapidly in the 1950s as the 1960s. Sexual permissiveness seems to have changed at no faster a rate than before or afterwards. And pressure for legislative reform had been building up before the 1960s. Abortion and divorce reform were not new issues; decriminalisation of homosexuality had been advocated by the Wolfenden Report of 1957; literary censorship – applied to books deemed obscene – had been relaxed in 1958. Much of the legislative change relevant to women was to come, and this picked up on long-standing campaigns by women's organisations as well as the changes in working patterns discussed earlier in this chapter (see 'Work, incomes and consumption'). Thus in the early 1970s the Conservatives introduced a series of measures giving women greater rights to control of their children, and to marital property, in the event of marriage breakdown. They were preparing a Sex Discrimination Act when defeated in 1974. Labour passed a more comprehensive measure in 1975, setting up the Equal Opportunities Commission.

The Thatcher governments were less inclined to pass socially liberal legislation – reflecting the views of many Conservative activists, including Margaret Thatcher herself, and of much of the public. There were still many opponents, at least in theory, of permissiveness. But, at the same time, there were in practice radical changes in attitudes towards, for instance, children born outside marriage and marriage itself (see earlier section, 'Women, men and families'). Attitudes towards issues such as race relations and homosexuality were slowly changing too. Attitudes may have changed anyway whatever legislation had been passed, but it is hard to believe that the Liberal Hour did not have a long-term impact.

Identities: national and local

Most people saw the end of the war as an opportunity to rebuild a family life disrupted for six years by Hitler, Mussolini and Tojo. The war had not revived the militant patriotism of the Edwardian years, but it had reinforced an idea of Britain as standing for timeless values of peace and domesticity (see Chapter 8). It also reinforced the idea of Britain as a bastion of freedom and democracy, but to this was added a new ingredient – social and economic fairness. The aspiration for this became embodied in the welfare state. And it became widely accepted, even by the middle classes who quickly found that they benefited from welfare as well as paying for it through taxation. Richard Weight believes that by the early 1950s the political consensus was strengthened by a consensus about British identity and a widely held optimism about the future.

This contrasted with a short period of post-war pessimism generated by the seemingly never-ending austerity and rationing, exacerbated by the foreign policy tensions of the incipient Cold War. From 1946–1948 bread, freely available in the war, was rationed to enable Britain to feed its occupation zone in Germany. In 1947–1948 an appalling winter led to serious coal shortages. A Gallup poll suggested that 42 per cent of Britain's population would emigrate if they were free to do so.

The greater optimism of the early 1950s owed itself largely to Britain's much improved economic position. However, one aspect of the sense of national identity which underpinned it was new – an emphasis on a Britain which combined tradition with modernity. The 1951 Festival of Britain was intended not only to lift national morale but also to provide a showcase for Britain's modernity (Fig. 12.3). One of its chief features was the Skylon, a futuristic structure resembling 'a ballpoint pen suspended in midair'.[5] Scientific exhibits rubbed shoulders with tradition exemplified by Rowland Emmet's fantastically quaint 'Far Tottering and Oyster Creek' narrow-gauge railway. After the festival, modernity was emphasised in constant media reports on British projects such as the Comet, the world's first jet airliner, and nuclear power. By 1956, 65 per cent of people saw Britain as a world leader in science and technology.

The relative failure of these projects – several Comets crashed and the nuclear programme suffered a serious accident in 1957 which was hushed up – symbolised a wider failure to modernise economically. Macmillan's modernisation drive in the early 1960s was essentially an attempt to make up for earlier failure. Failure continued, however,

Figure 12.3   Almost the end of post-war austerity: the Festival of Britain, 1951. Image courtesy of The Advertising Archives

with de Gaulle's veto on EC entry and was compounded by Conservative presentational errors. But Harold Wilson re-energised modernisation in the mid-1960s with his 'New Britain'. This dovetailed with liberal social reforms and a less stuffy society – the 'Swinging Sixties' – to engender another period of optimism. But in 1967 devaluation marked an end to economic optimism, while the 'Liberal Hour' had run its course. When Britain joined the EC in 1973, it was a few months before the start of the oil crisis which ushered in ten years of economic stagnation and recession. The late 1950s onwards, therefore, can in hindsight be seen as a period when the widely shared post-war national identity, in which new elements were successfully grafted on to old, was increasingly dislocated. What emerged instead?

One thing which did emerge was Celtic nationalism. Both the Scottish National Party (SNP) and Plaid Cymru (PC), the Welsh nationalist party, had miniscule support in the 1950s. By 1974 PC had 20 per cent of the Welsh vote, the SNP 30 per cent of the

Society and economy: The media

The biggest development in the post-war media was the rise of television. Started by the BBC on a small scale before the war, it took off in the early 1950s as receivers became cheaper. In 1955 the Conservatives allowed the introduction of ITV, whose revenue came from advertisements not the licence fee. It was an easy way for them to demonstrate their commitment to choice and free enterprise while not interfering with the existing delicate balance – as they perceived it – of other nationalised industries. It was only in the 1980s that satellite broadcasting and cheap VCRs, and in the late 1990s that the internet, challenged television as the main form of electronic media. Cinema, once so dominant in British leisure habits, declined rapidly – admissions at their nadir in the late 1960s, falling to 5 per cent of the 1940s level.

The 1950s saw national newspaper sales peak, since when there has been a gradual decline. The tabloid format, once dominated by the *Mirror*, was adopted by the *Sun* – a transformation of the old *Daily Herald – Mail* and *Express* in the 1970s, and the *Sun* went on to overtake the *Mirror* as the biggest seller. (The adoption by most 'quality' newspapers of this format only came after 2000.) All these changes, and the increase in the 1970s in sex and scandal as selling points, were seen by many as marking the downgrading of press standards. But accusations that much of the British press was essentially frivolous date back to the early twentieth century. Newspapers have always been as much branches of the entertainment industry as organs of information.

Nevertheless, since newspapers also take political standpoints, the potential influence of such light-minded media has been a post-war issue, as it was in the 1930s when Baldwin confronted the press barons. Imbalance is an irredeemable function of news stories, however seriously presented, since no one at short notice can possibly have access to all the information needed to present an objective account. That is not a defence of light-mindedness but it suggests that a distribution of political standpoints is more important than that all media should be serious. In the early post-war years only the *Mirror* and the *Herald* were consistently Labour, and the latter was fading fast. But the *Mirror's* popularity was some antidote. In the 1980s the *Mirror* faded and the *Sun* moved right, so press Conservatism seemed more dominant. But in the 1990s 'New Labour' and Conservative disunity threw the field open and several newspapers became less dogmatic. This suggests that the press, however light minded, is open to persuasion. A variety of influences – editors, political journalists and the skill of politicians at putting their message across – ultimately form press opinion. And for most of the post-war period there seems to have been less influence from wilful owners than in the 1920s and 1930s.

The vagaries of the press threw even more onus on broadcasters to report news as objectively as possible. Broadcast news has certainly become more lively since the days of John Reith, and since the 1960s both major political parties have, fairly consistently, accused the BBC of bias. This suggests they may have got the balance about right. Certainly no one who has read autobiographies of news presenters can doubt that they seriously believe that they try to be objective. They could be accused of hubris – a belief in their own powers of objectivity when the circumstances do not in fact allow it – but in an imperfect world Britain has a media which preserves some balance amid much frivolity and, in broadcasting, a belief in the merits of objectivity.

Scottish vote, and both a number of parliamentary seats. Some of this support was ephemeral, a Scottish and Welsh version of the Liberal upsurge of that year which reflected disillusionment with both major political parties. But support had been growing earlier as the Welsh and Scottish economies faltered, the long-term decline of their coal-mining and heavy industry having reasserted itself in the 1960s. In solidly working-class areas which wished to register a protest against the Labour government of 1966–1970, the nationalists were preferable to the Conservatives. Economic grievances were not the whole story. In Welsh rural areas, English second-home owners forced up house prices. Scotland, with its own educational and legal systems, had always been more distinct from England both geographically and intellectually, but up to 1939 an imperial identity had linked the two. By the 1960s there was widespread intellectual support for a new relationship with England, exacerbated in 1965 by an insensitive government attempt to portray the Magna Carta as the foundation of British, rather than English, liberties.

The political upsets of the 1970s then put Labour into a position in which it needed support in Parliament from the pro-devolution Liberals and the nationalists. Therefore, it had to support devolution, the modern word for Home Rule, in which some powers over domestic affairs were given to local assemblies. However, national-ism was temporarily stilled in 1979 when modest devolution proposals did not gain enough support in referenda.

Mrs Thatcher revived it again. Most Scottish and Welsh coal mines closed, unem-ployment rose sharply and Thatcherism's individualistic tone ran counter to the com-munitarian image that the Welsh and the Scots had of themselves. In the latter case, as Richard Weight has shown, this was a myth invented in the 1960s. By the 1990s many, especially in Scotland, favoured outright independence not just devolution. Devolution, however, was what they got. Labour had promised it on the pragmatic grounds that it would help to maintain the United Kingdom. In new referenda in 1997, the Scottish Parliament gained 75 per cent of the vote on a 60 per cent turnout. The Welsh Assembly, with limited powers, gained just over 50 per cent on a 51 per cent turnout – that is, about one-quarter of the total electorate. The latter was hardly a ringing endorsement, suggesting that for many Welsh people the cultural ties with England were still strong.

Nationalism provided a new identity for many Scots and a smaller number of Welsh. What has been available to the English? The xenophobic nationalism of the far-right parties, the National Front in the 1960s and 1970s, and the British National Party in recent years, has only appealed to a small minority. Much more popular is a spec-trum of identities which descends in part from the rural nostalgia of the interwar period and also owes a lot to Britain's role in both the world wars, and particularly the Second. It encompasses the intense and continuing interest in the world wars, the manifold tentacles of the heritage industry and the modest nostalgia of John Major with his 1993 speech which talked of 'long shadows on county [cricket] grounds, warm beer, invincible green suburbs . . .'.[6]

What is striking about this diffuse national identity is that some of its ingredients have become far more widely available over the last 50 years. Access to rural or semi-rural locations, once limited for most people by transport constraints, has been transformed and has manifested itself in, for instance, the growing membership of the National Trust, from 23,000 members in 1950 to 2.4 million by 1998. In a related trajectory, popular access to, and knowledge of, the past has been transformed by similar forces and by television. Critics who focus on the partial picture of the past painted by the heritage industry almost entirely miss the point. All pasts are partial. The heritage industry may depict a British past in which military glory and the life of the wealthy in country houses played a large part. But by so doing it calls attention to a current state of affairs in which Britain is more or less free of war and in which all manner of people can visit castles and country houses on payment of a modest subscription. The messages purveyed by the heritage industry are actually incredibly varied. The burgeoning of popular history has therefore created the opportunity of a variety of national identities which are available to millions of people.

These national identities include militant patriotism, and an apparent resurgence of this took place under Mrs Thatcher. It manifested itself tangibly in the post-Falklands parades and ceremonial entry of homecoming ships to harbour, and rhetorically in the assertion of Britain's importance as a partner to America in the Cold War. But whatever Mrs Thatcher's own militancy, for many people the impact of her foreign policy was probably limited to a more diffuse patriotism generated by the undoubted fact that Britain's standing in the world was enhanced in the 1980s.

This sort of patriotism encompasses Britain and not just its constituent nations. So to some extent does the heritage industry, which gives individuals the opportunity to construct their own national identity, since that can be taken from elements of the past which encompass the history of Britain as a whole, not just England. So there are still factors, including the lingering if faded allure of the monarchy, which make for a British identity rather than a purely Scottish, Welsh or English one. Perhaps because of this, there has been little shift in the nationalist vote for a number of years. Equally, there is little evidence of a strong desire for a separate English identity. Attempts to popularise the flag of St George and St George's Day have made limited progress.

A continuing British identity coexists with local loyalties. As in the earlier twentieth century, these have been most evident in support for local sports teams. In 1953 the coal-mining town of Ashton (a fictional name but a real place) in Yorkshire, with a population of around 14,000, had an average attendance at local Rugby League matches of over 4,500. After the 1950s there was a general trend for attendance, especially in football, the most popular sport, to cluster around the strongest teams. But even teams in the second ranking football league regularly sustained crowds of 20,000 or more in the late twentieth century. The importance of locality has always gone beyond sport. Thus when Ashton men were discussing national subjects, 'they were dealt with . . . from the point of view of their relationship and importance to Ashton'.[7] Even in 1953, such intense parochialism was probably exceptional: mining towns had little in-migration, while miners had a preoccupation with work which limited their horizons. But the move away from gendered and work-oriented cultures often meant that horizons remained local but the subjects were different – schools and crime, for instance.

People and politics: Queen Elizabeth II

Elizabeth was born on 21 April 1926, a few days before the General Strike. It was only at the abdication of her uncle, Edward, in 1936 and her father's accession as George VI that she became heir to the throne. George's early death in 1952 made her a monarch at the age of 25.

By all accounts the Queen is intelligent without being intellectual, with a sardonic sense of humour. Her private interests are predominantly rural – dogs, country walks, horses and horseracing (but not betting). She is devoutly if unostentatiously religious. She has been happily married for almost 60 years. And she has a strong sense of public duty. In most of these characteristics she is the opposite of the majority of her subjects.

In spite or perhaps because of this, opinion polls show the Queen to be popular and widely respected. Attitudes to the monarchy as an institution, however, have changed over the 50 years of her reign. Elizabeth's accession, her Coronation in 1953 and her young family strengthened support for an already popular institution. Following a tradition started by Queen Victoria, the monarchy was seen as embodying the virtues of family life. The 1960s, however, saw a decline in outward marks of public respect. The playing of the National Anthem in cinemas and theatres decayed because audiences were no longer willing to stand through it, while fewer listened to the Queen's Christmas broadcast on television. From the late 1960s new advisers at the Palace encouraged more openness to press and television and there was a resurgence of support for the monarchy, reaching its peak at the Silver Jubilee in 1977 and the marriage of her eldest son, Prince Charles, and Diana Spencer in 1981. From then on things went downhill. Changing codes of behaviour by the media resulted in constant revelations about the private lives of the royal offspring and their spouses – which indeed strayed far from the rectitude displayed by the Queen, her father and grandfather. Elizabeth herself was criticised more frequently than in the past.

Were there alternative directions which the monarchy could have taken? Discussions of royal spending in the late 1940s briefly raised issues about whether the monarchy should remain ceremonial, or be more simple and 'democratic', on the Scandinavian model. The Labour government decided to support a level of spending that meant it could continue to be ceremonial. Then, in 1957, an article by Lord Altrincham, a forward-thinking young peer, attacked the monarchy for its social conservatism. But again, the debate was quietly buried. Both the family monarchy and the ceremonial monarchy were to become something of a hostage to fortune: the former for obvious reasons and the latter because as the monarchy became fair game for criticism, royal spending again became a target. Paradoxically, the British monarchy is, in a formal sense, highly democratic in that Elizabeth has been obsessive in her desire to make significant changes only in accordance with her governments' wishes. Nevertheless, the continuing importance of ceremony has perhaps obscured this.

What is the real importance of monarchy in the modern world? Constitutionally, it has a theoretical role in that a hung Parliament could force the monarch to choose the Prime Minister from rival party leaders. But most commentators would agree that the real significance of the monarchy throughout the twentieth century has been its

▶

role in constructing national identity. George V's importance was to be perceived as above both class and party: to be, with Parliament, the 'symbolic centre of the nation ... which guaranteed individual freedoms'.[8] George VI represented the moral unity, through a shared belief in both democracy and tradition, of a nation at war with fascism. Elizabeth's early years as Queen saw an optimism which mirrored the national mood at the time, in which tradition and modernity were combined in a 'New Elizabethan Age'. But since then her reign has lacked any such focus, and few would now see the Crown as central in guaranteeing freedom. As the world changed around her, the Queen's notorious reluctance to initiate change, however constitutionally correct, may have been a drawback. Altrincham's criticisms proved prescient as the monarchy became seen as less and less relevant.

Having said that, it is impossible to write off a monarch who had entered, according to rough and ready estimates by Brian Masters in 1972, up to one-third of her subjects' dreams. Historians, with Ben Pimlott's biography and a recent article by David Cannadine, are beginning to take the modern monarchy seriously, but even they find it hard to say quite why.

Nonetheless, most people's horizons have widened and this has led to one critical shift in British identities. As discussed elsewhere in the chapter, there has been an increased tolerance of minority views by the majority, whatever the behaviour or beliefs of certain prejudiced groups. This has encompassed greater racial tolerance, where football has become an exemplar of changed attitudes; the acceptance of women as entitled to an education and a career in the same way as men; and the acceptance of those with different sexual orientations in public life.

Another aspect of Britain's liberal inheritance which seems to have fared less well, however, has been the perception of Britain as a country embodying the rule of law and democratic freedoms. As suggested in Chapter 6, this was an important part of national identity earlier in the century. An apparent indifference to the limitations of freedoms introduced to combat the IRA and, after 2001, international terrorism seems evidence of its decline. But the acceptance of a fairly strong role for the state in Britain is not new. This has most obviously been the case in time of war, but continued beyond 1945 in the 'secret state' of the security services and the numerous heavily guarded defence installations of the nuclear age. Least obvious because most pervasive is Britain's long-standing punitive attitude to criminality. This suggests that democratic freedoms have always been interpreted by many in Britain to encompass a tolerance of dissenting opinions and the opportunity to constrain governmental lifespans through parliamentary elections, but not to mean a weak state.

Another liberal inheritance is hostility to armaments and, by extension, to war. The extent of this has varied. Suez split the country, and it split it because of real doubts about both its practicality and its legality, given the opposition of both the United States and the United Nations. In the extent of and reasons for opposition it was comparable to the second Gulf war of 2003. Most of the time, peace movements have encompassed a narrower constituency although in the late 1950s, and the late 1970s/early 1980s, CND

Society and economy: Crime in twentieth century Britain

In recent years crime has been one of the chief concerns of the public as expressed in opinion polls. On the face of it, that concern is justified. Between 1900 and 1997 the number of crimes recorded by the police rose about sixtyfold, and as a proportion of the population aged over ten, by about thirtyfold.

Criminal statistics, however, have long been regarded with almost as much suspicion as criminals. And recently, Howard Taylor has shown how crime statistics until at least the 1930s – the point when a serious increase began – were an almost completely meaningless artefact resulting from a desire to control government spending. With a fixed central government allowance for prosecution costs, local authorities faced paying for additional prosecutions and therefore leant on the police – locally controlled except for London – not to prosecute. Chief constables therefore discouraged their officers from recording all but the most obvious crimes. Thus the Metropolitan Police until 1931 used a 'Suspected Stolen Book' for so-called doubtful cases. When it was discontinued in 1932, the number of recorded larcenies tripled. This distortion of the figures extended even to murder. For long it was complacently assumed that Britain's low murder rate owed itself to our pacific national character. Taylor suggests that murder may have been grossly under-recorded. Coroners simply assumed accident or suicide with little investigation.

The gradual reduction of deliberate under-recording must account for much of the apparent fourfold increase in the crime rate between the late 1920s and the late 1940s. How far the further sevenfold increase until 1992 – since when it has dropped somewhat – is real is difficult to say. Police recording of some crimes, for instance rape, has continued to change, as has the willingness to report crime by the public. Crime surveys from the early 1980s suggest more stability than the reported figures, although some increases, such as in violent crime involving gun use, must be real. Furthermore, the rapid increase in the use of drugs since the 1960s and – after years of stagnation or decline – of drink consumption are both trends which are likely to have fuelled larceny and/or violence. However, large-scale incidents of collective violence have occurred sporadically during the century, not clustered at the end. They include riots associated with strikes, for instance in Tonypandy, South Wales in 1910, with race in 1919 and again in 1958, and with unemployment and police behaviour towards young blacks in 1981. Furthermore, everyday behaviour in the past was not always pacific. Violence by husbands against wives was frequent in rougher working-class areas. In Salford in the 1900s Robert Roberts recorded thugs casually burning the stock of a Jewish second-hand clothes dealer who had set up business there; the incident ignored by the police. In the early 1950s in the South Yorkshire coalfield there would usually be fights between young men from different towns on a Saturday night. Probably violent behaviour today has become less selective in its choice of victims or opponents and this makes more people feel threatened, but it does not necessarily mean there is more violence overall.

had substantial support. While, therefore, Britain's military past has shaped some people's identity, others have drawn explicitly from the liberal past. And this has not just been in their opposition to war – which might or might not be a liberal standpoint – but in their appeal to law and their reliance on democratic freedoms to make a protest.

CND was an early example of a loss of faith in one of the fruits of modernity, the power of the atom. And since the Heath governments, there has been a diminished emphasis on technological modernisation as manufacturing has shrunk. Yet in many ways Britain changed more between 1975 and 2000 than in the previous 25 years, for instance in occupational and class structure and gender roles (see previous sections). Occupational and class levelling has been reflected in an elision of cultural markers of class divides such as accent and clothing. This elision and its many concomitants, such as the growing ubiquity of Christian names in everyday social interaction, is one of the major cultural phenomena of the recent past with which historians have still to grapple.

Notes

1. Dennis, N. *et al.*, *Coal is Our Life* (London: Tavistock, 2nd ed., 1969), p. 183.
2. Little, K., *Negroes in Britain* (London: Routledge and Kegan Paul, 2nd ed., 1972; 1st ed., 1948), p. 255.
3. Online at http://www.bbc.co.uk/gloucestershire/untold_stories/african/living.shtml
4. Quoted in Lewis, J., *Women in Britain since 1945* (Oxford: Blackwell, 1992), p. 41.
5. Weight, R., *Patriots: National Identity in Britain 1940–2000* (Basingstoke: Macmillan, 2002), p. 200.
6. Major, *The Autobiography* (see Chapter 10), p. 376.
7. Dennis, *Coal*, p. 145.
8. Feldman, *Englishmen and Jews* (see Chapter 6), p. 381.

Further reading

Halsey and Webb, *Social Trends* for much of the data in this chapter. Lewis, *Women* and Zweiniger-Bargielowska, *Women* (Chapter 1) are both very good. Pimlott, B., *The Queen: Elizabeth II and the Monarchy* (Harper Collins, 2nd ed., 2002) is fascinating. Weight, *Patriots* is outstanding and highly readable.

Other sources: Alderman, *Jewry* (see Chapter 6); Bowden, S. and Offer, A., 'Household Appliances and the Use of Time: the United States and Britain since the 1920s', *Economic History Review*, Vol. XLVII, pp. 725–748 (1994); Cannadine, D., 'From Biography to History: Writing the Modern British Monarchy', *Historical Research*, Vol. LXXVII, pp. 289–312 (2004); Cherry, G. and Rogers, A., *Rural Change and Planning: England and Wales in the Twentieth Century* (London: Spon, 1996); Curry, N. and Owen, S. (eds), *Changing Rural Policy in Britain* (Cheltenham: The Countryside and Community Press, 1996); Frean, A., articles in *The Times*, 13.6.2005 and 16.6.2005; Goldthorpe, J. *et al.*, *The Affluent Worker in the Class Structure* (Cambridge: Cambridge University Press, 1969); Hollowell, *Britain* (see Chapter 9); Lynch, *Scottish History* (see Chapter 6); McKibbin, *Classes* (see Chapter 1); Marr, A., *My Trade* (London:

Macmillan, 2004); Masters, B., *Dreams about H.M. The Queen* (London: Blond and Briggs, 1972); More, *Industrial Age* (see Chapter 1); Morris, 'Strange Death' (see Chapter 6); Roberts, *Classic Slum* (see Chapter 6); Rosen, A., *The Transformation of British Life 1950–2000* (Manchester: Manchester University Press, 2003); Runciman, W. G., *Relative Deprivation and Social Justice* (London: Routledge and Kegan Paul, 1966); Taylor, H., 'Rationing Crime: the Political Economy of Criminal Statistics since the 1850s', *Economic History Review*, Vol. LI, pp. 569–590 (1998); Wynn, N. ' "Race War": Black American GIs in Bristol and Gloucestershire during World War II', *Regional Historian*, No. 14, pp. 23–30.

AFTERWORD

Historiography is the study of the writing of history, and this chapter starts with a brief study of some of the ways in which twentieth century British history has been written.

At the beginning of the century the dominant tradition in British historical writing was Whig. Whig history saw Britain's past as a story of progress: progress towards a country which was constitutional, prosperous, Protestant and imperial. Different aspects of these were emphasised according to the taste of the historian. As a way of writing national history, Whig history fell out of fashion in the interwar period. One fundamental characteristic of Whig history, however, is hard for historians to shake off. This is the habit of seeing the past as the unrolling of a story with an inevitable conclusion. The growth of the Labour Party has often been written in this way. In this version, as class consciousness replaced other factors as a predominant influence on voting, the working class inevitably migrated from the Liberals to Labour.

The rise of Labour became associated with another subject from which historians find it hard to escape Whiggism, the growth of the welfare state. In histories of welfare another characteristic of Whig history has often come into play – the belief that historical change tends towards the good. Since it is hard to see old-age pensions, better health services and so on as other than good, it is hard to write about their increasing provision as other than representing the triumph of right, and attempts to restrict them as the opposite.

Anyone who reads modern British history, however, can quickly see that, although there is often within it some underlying sense of progress, this is shot through with caveats and often downright pessimism. Indeed, much of twentieth century British historiography is not about progress but decline. One obvious decline has been in the absolute extent of the British Empire. Along with its decline, Britain's potential influence in the world has receded. Most historians of the subject, however, have not been pessimistic about decline itself. Of generally liberal inclination, historians are hardly likely to see decolonisation as bad. Similarly, realism suggests that a relatively small island is not likely to play a major part in world affairs for ever. Historians have, however, often been pessimistic about Britain's ability to manage decline. David Reynolds' *Britannia Overruled* is an example.

Decline is also a favourite theme of economic historians. As with the decline of Britain's world influence, economic declinism accepts that some relative decline was likely to occur, but is nonetheless concerned at Britain's failure at various periods to achieve growth rates equivalent to those of various comparator nations.

Economic historians are often concerned with the long term, but most historians deal with much shorter spells of time, or the history of particular events, movements or institutions. Many such historians of modern Britain also take a rather pessimistic stance. Many episodes, and longer periods, in the twentieth century are frequently portrayed as lost opportunities, or examples of persistent error. The First World War and much of the history of the interwar period have often been seen in this way. A brief interlude of historiographical cheerfulness then occurs, since one has to be quite perverse to see the outcome of the Second World War as a failure. And the post-war Labour governments still get positive marks from many historians. But from then until 1979 pessimism is again a persistent theme. This extends from the performance of governments and the economy to institutional history. In spite of the Whiggish early interpretations of the welfare state, for example, modern historians have drawn attention to the extent to which its coverage has been partial and its administration inefficient. Historians' opinions on the period after 1979 tend to be polarised. Some see Mrs Thatcher's governments as embarking on necessary reforms with a measure of success, while others see them as destructive and divisive.

Pessimistic approaches have different foundations for their pessimism. Some point to underlying structural problems which make change or adaptation difficult. Others point to the influence of individuals, perhaps adding to that the ideology which motivates them. Some see structures as constraining change but individuals as still responsible for making, or not making, it happen.

One distinctive approach, in which structure is of overwhelming importance, sees British society throughout the twentieth century as marked by profound and persistent inequity – in other words, not merely economic inequality, but pervasive unfairness. Historians who adopt this approach have usually been influenced to a greater or less extent by Marx. They are the greatest pessimists of all, and in recent years Thatcherism and Blairism have made them even more pessimistic.

There are other ways of writing modern British history, of course. One is to emphasise military triumph. In the most epic versions of this, of which Churchill's *The Second World War* is the exemplar, Britain is depicted as the saviour of western civilisation. For obvious reasons this approach is only relevant for a very short period, although other narratives can coexist with it. One such takes us back to the Whigs – but of the political kind, rather than historians. Famously, Whigs in the nineteenth century believed in adapting to the new so as to preserve the old. And one quite common historiographical approach is to emphasise the capacity to adapt in twentieth century Britain. It is a narrative of conservative adaptation – conservative because it aimed to conserve, but also because, some historians would say, it was practised very effectively by the Conservative Party. One historian whose works, on the history of the Conservative Party itself, embody this approach is John Ramsden. Historians of this persuasion coexist happily with those who emphasise the willingness of challengers to established structures to accept compromise, rather than insist of confrontation. Such historians tend to share one other Whig characteristic, a belief that Britain really was a constitutional state and that this was not just a figment of an imaginary 'Whig history'. So historians of this kind see structures as important, but in enabling change as well as hindering it. They also tend to see individuals as important in making structures work.

There are, of course, many other approaches which relate to individual periods or groups in the past. Women's history is an important one. Early versions of this were almost Whig-like in their portrayal of the subject as a history of liberation – although liberation in the future rather than a liberation already achieved. Subsequently, women's history has become much more nuanced, encompassing almost as many approaches as does the wider history of Britain itself.

Finally, there are those historians who question any interpretation which can be fitted within one of the broad approaches sketched above. A. J. P. Taylor, a professional maverick, is still the most famous of these. More recent examples include economic historians who have questioned the thesis of economic declinism, while John Charmley and a few others have questioned the heroic interpretation of the Second World War. Perverse though some of these opinions might seem, their existence ensures that historians of modern Britain will have plenty of work for many years to come as they ceaselessly rebut other historians and emerge with new interpretations of their own.

Britain and the world

Historians would agree that some decline in British power in the twentieth century has been inevitable. Furthermore, so far as the decline involved the countries of the Empire gaining independence, most would say it has been beneficial. But decline has occurred intermittently, not at a constant rate, and it has involved choices as to its pace and direction. Were the choices made wise or foolish?

Foreign policy always involved the search for security but in a changing context. One part of this context was the perceived need to defend the Empire. There were economic and strategic reasons for this, but sentiment and prestige also entered into it. After 1945 the extent of the Empire declined, although it briefly had a new role, which was to financially prop up a virtually bankrupt Britain. So defence of the Empire, or what was left of it, was still a concern until the economic disadvantages clearly outweighed the advantages.

Another part of the changing context was Britain's own economic position, which provided the wherewithal for military spending. Relatively strong although Britain's economy was in 1900, even then most politicians and diplomats perceived that isolation was not a long-term option. Isolation made defence of the Empire potentially too expensive. Defensive treaties with Japan, France and Russia quickly followed. In the 1920s Britain's economic position was weakened. Security seemed most cheaply assured by disarmament and the League of Nations. Many had doubts as to their real value, though, and Locarno was an attempt to put some teeth into mutual security in Europe. The vulnerability of these good intentions was exposed in the 1930s, when Britain's worldwide weakness, and perceived economic constraints on rearmament, led to appeasement in Europe and a frank acknowledgment that British interests east of India would depend on hope and Singapore. After the war, another perceived military threat loomed – Russia – and Britain could not possibly afford to defend herself alone. As Stephen Howe has pointed out, this led to a reversal of Palmerston's famous dictum that Britain had no permanent friends, only permanent interests. America and the other members of NATO became her permanent friends.

Economics, in part, also drove Britain's wish to join the European Community. The Community, it was thought, would provide both the economic security of a large free-trade area and a bracing cold shower of competition which would drive modernisation. But Britain had never mentally adapted to the other part of the Community's agenda, the vision of a supranational Europe which would end the rivalries of centuries. Both that mental limitation and the practicalities of the Common Agricultural Policy constrained a willing British acceptance of the Community.

If economic factors influenced the need for friends, ultimately these were also needed because of the real or perceived existence of enemies. While the treaties with France and Russia early in the century contributed inadvertently to Britain's involvement in the First World War, all these powers were involved because of German and Austrian aggression. On Germany's part, aggressive intentions persisted between the wars and Hitler added to them a lethal virulence. So Germany's bid for European hegemony shaped Britain's foreign policy for the whole period until 1945, and much else in British history via the economic and social changes caused by war. After 1945 the perceived Soviet threat replaced that of Germany. We now know that Russia was never, in intention, in the same malign league as Germany. However, its own actions frequently made it seem a threat and, given the failure of good intentions in the 1930s, the Western desire for a strong military response was understandable.

Economic and diplomatic considerations were themselves shaped by public opinion, encompassing not just the public's views so far as they could be ascertained but also newspaper opinion. For a long period between the wars, public support for peace and disarmament was something which politicians felt they could not ignore and with which they often agreed. After the Second World War, opinion polls and election results suggested that a majority of the public consistently supported a moderate level of armaments, including nuclear weapons, and security through the membership of NATO. CND, although sometimes gaining considerable support, was never significant in shaping policy. But military action by Britain which was not a direct response to aggression was much more controversial. Thus Suez and, in the present century, the war on Iraq polarised opinion. In this can be seen a long-term legacy of the pacific liberal tradition.

In spite of these constraints, politicians have still made real choices between different courses of action. One choice, the series of *ententes* in the 1900s, is much less criticised now than it was between the wars. There is general acceptance today that German aggression caused the First War, not alliance systems. A Gladstonian foreign policy might have kept Britain out of war, but the policy actually followed was reasonable in the circumstances. Conversely, foreign policy in the 1920s can be criticised for its trust in a non-aggressive Germany. Nevertheless, Locarno is quite favourably regarded by modern historians. As against the French policy of suppressing Germany, Britain's course of action offered a chance to bring Germany back into the comity of nations. Arguably it was a reasonable chance which was only doomed by world depression and its effects on German politics. Subsequently, the choice of appeasement was shaped by several factors as outlined above, and criticism of it should take these into account. Chamberlain's diplomacy, however, is hard to defend. Finally, only a few historians would criticise the decision to enter the Second World War.

After Chamberlain's eviction from office, there was one important choice: that between Churchill and Halifax as Prime Minister. Not only were the immense powers of the eventual choice, Churchill, used to maximum effect, but the possibility of an early peace was squashed. Halifax, as Foreign Secretary and a member of the War Cabinet, was tempted to explore peace terms as the Blitzkrieg unfolded. Churchill was not. Like all alternative scenarios, what might have happened is unknowable but if he had become Prime Minister Halifax would have been in a better position to carry his view.

Post-war foreign policy has often been criticised for involving too many commitments – not just to NATO, which most historians would accept as necessary, but also to nuclear weapons and, for some time, to a continuing imperial role. Britain has also been criticised for committing to Europe too late and too half-heartedly. But David Reynolds, one of those who has made such criticisms, accepts that the instability of the immediate post-war period, and uncertainty over the extent of US commitment, made abandoning Britain's world-wide role seem a risky option. There is a stronger case for saying that Macmillan's continuing dreams of superpower status were less justified by external circumstances. But Macmillan also had to perform a political balancing act: potential Conservative hostility to decolonisation could be neutralised by continuing to emphasise Britain's superpower status.

Decolonisation can be seen as one of the successes of British foreign policy – for Britain, if not for various dismally misgoverned post-colonial nations. The success lay in the ability to discard the Empire with so little opposition at home. Since it is a negative – by doing so Britain avoided the agonies of French and Portugese decolonisation – it is rarely noticed, but when assessing Britain's management of decline, it ought to be. Arguably Ireland has been Britain's only post-colonial trauma, and the totality of bloodshed has been far less than in, say, Algeria.

Most historians see European integration as positive, and therefore criticise Britain's lukewarmness. But it is possible to tell a different story, in which lukewarmness has not actually made much difference to anything, and in which political integration may have limits set by hostility to it within other European countries. The rejection in French and Dutch referenda of the proposed European constitution in 2005 makes this a more plausible story than it appeared in 2002 when the Euro was adopted.

There is one other way of looking at British foreign policy in the twentieth century. No one would deny that it has always been shaped by a conception of British interests, on the one hand, and by constraints set by economics, real or perceived external threats, and public opinion on the other. But, even if inadvertently, it has also been altruistic. Britain has never set out to wage large-scale wars of aggression. Twice in the first 45 years of the century the nation was disrupted, and many lives lost, to curb such aggression. Its curbing was seen as necessary for Britain; but it also benefited other nations. After the war Britain perceived the need to rebuild European defences, taking a lead in doing so and then in maintaining them. If Churchill's heroic interpretation of Britain's Second World War role as global saviour is too strong for modern tastes, they might at least accord Britain a role as a reluctant altruist.

Politics and possibilities

The twentieth century has seen a vast increase in the role of the state, in Britain and throughout the world. The usual, and probably correct, explanation for this is that a universal franchise brought with it electoral pressure for the reduction of inequality through welfare, as voters who benefited exceeded in numbers those who paid through taxation. But this took time to develop, because older political issues such as religion were also salient. Efficiency concerns were also involved. 'National efficiency', an idea which was gaining ground at the turn of the century, saw improved education, health and child protection as desirable to develop what would now be called 'human capital'. Furthermore, public provision by its scale reduced transaction costs – that is, the costs of doing business – for services such as health insurance adding to its attractiveness. In the interwar period this dovetailed with the retreat from untrammelled competition. Price-fixing agreements, already common among British firms, were extended into a belief that large-scale enterprises were better able to rationalise production and cope with economic difficulties.

The post-war Labour government inherited all these beliefs and added to them a concern with nationalisation driven by a key component of the labour movement, the trade unions. For political reasons, and in some cases because they genuinely agreed, the Conservatives fell into line and accepted Labour's further extension of the state's role. However, from the late 1970s the proportion of national income absorbed by the state stopped rising, although the inbuilt momentum of health, education and social security spending means that it has not fallen much. Furthermore, privatisation led to a fall in the proportion of the workforce employed by the state. Three factors coincided to halt the onward march of state intervention.

First, as state spending grew, so did the number of taxpayers. Thus the numbers who suffered from redistribution increased relative to those who gained. A proposition to the electorate based on rolling back the state came to have increasing attractions. Second, the efficiency advantages of size seemed to be increasingly outweighed by the disadvantages of monopoly and the potential for the state's safety net to lead to inefficiency in nationalised industries. Third, there was a perception that the twin crises in the 1970s of public spending and inflation, common throughout the developed world, were particularly acute in Britain because of union power. The special position of the unions went back to 1906, when the Trade Disputes Act confirmed what had begun to be established in the 1870s – that the state in Britain was neutral in industrial disputes. This was, of course, in sharp contrast to some countries at that time such as Germany. Baldwin deflected Conservative attempts in the 1920s to substantially reduce unions' legal rights, and such changes as were made were repealed by Labour in 1946. But increasingly in the 1960s and 1970s, untrammelled union power seemed to pose threats to efficiency and price stability, and with the 1974 miners' strike to parliamentary government itself.

These three factors together paved the way for change. However, some or all of them were salient issues in many other countries, so Britain's halt to the onward march of state intervention, while it happened earlier than most, was not unique.

Much of Britain's political history in the twentieth century can be seen as the working out of the trends outlined above. However, the political process itself was still important. It determined which party administered change, and therefore the timing and detail of the changes and how great were reductions in inequality. On a few occasions, more major issues still were at stake.

In the 1900s the Conservatives adopted tariffs, rather than redistributive taxation, as their solution to the problem of financing social welfare spending. Instead it helped to keep them out of power. Nevertheless, while the Liberals were the immediate gainers, the classic Liberalism of the mid-Victorian period was finished by the rise of welfare. Some historians go further and see the Liberal Party as doomed because welfare – and redistribution which was an inevitable concomitant – was becoming the main political issue, in which case working-class voters would see a class-based party as the most effective means of delivery.

However, others believe that Liberals and Labour could have continued to coexist. But in the real world the First War occurred and that, and their own divisions, instead gave the Liberals the kiss of half-life. Labour, however, was not a straightforward class party but one committed to gradualism. Although Ramsay MacDonald had something to do with this, there were also structural reasons behind it. Labour politicians had been brought up in a deeply rooted constitutional tradition and going outside it was not a road they wished to take. George V's actions and words helped to persuade them that the constitutional road was the correct one. Trade unions operated within a different sort of tradition, the tradition of bargaining, which had the same result. Bargaining was legitimated by the state and accepted by increasing numbers of employers, so unions did not seriously challenge the status quo.

Nevertheless, it was still important that the Conservatives dropped their Edwardian militancy and chose moderation. What would have happened if they had not, and if moderation had not been maintained by Baldwin? There might have been a resurgence of Liberalism leading to Labour/Liberal cooperation in government; but given the structural weaknesses of both parties, a more right-wing Conservative government could have taken office at some point. Alternatively, a weaker Conservatism could have opened up space for a much stronger fascist party.

Is the gloomy view of interwar governments taken by many historians justified? Britain's moderate Conservatism did, after all, have merits. In the guise of the National government, it made mistakes over rearmament and appeasement, but these were no more egregious than the mistakes made by the other political parties which were not in a position to implement their foreign policies. It made mistakes over the economy, but the 1930s depression was milder in Britain than in most industrialised countries. It constrained social spending, but in criticising this historians ignore the restrictions placed by party activists and many voters on taxation levels. In short, interwar governments showed the limitations, but also the merits, of conservative adaptation (see earlier section, 'Historiographical traditions').

Because of Labour's participation in wartime government, a large proportion of the electorate ceased to see it as a bogeyman, making its election in 1945 possible. Labour also gained from the more egalitarian climate engendered by the war. But it would be wrong to see the war as the sole springboard for a great leap in social welfare provision. It speeded change, but change had already occurred, and was likely to continue, within the context of the long-term forces outlined above.

Labour's challenge also forced the Conservatives to modernise themselves still further. Should they embrace Labour's reforms while cloaking the embrace in the language of choice, or take a more free-market stance, once a Liberal position but now appropriated by some Conservatives? The first course was chosen. It was not automatic but owed itself to a dedicated modernising lobby. The response was important, because it probably helped them gain their narrow election victory in 1951. By adopting the mixed economy and the welfare state they had, effectively, opted for consensus. Therefore, like other historians, the author sees the debate over this issue as otiose.

Running Labour's system effectively and removing controls was enough for the Conservatives initially but there was a felt need to do more. In the early 1950s technical and scientific modernisation, exemplified by nuclear power, was on the agenda. But by the late 1950s this seemed to be insufficient. Britain's economic growth remained slow and inflation, although low, was persistent. The pending demise of the Empire also suggested the need for a big idea which could galvanise the Conservative Party. In the early 1960s Macmillan extended modernisation to institutions, involving indicative planning, greater competition and entry to Europe as the next big idea. All these were taken up by Harold Wilson, who heightened expectations that he could deliver where the Conservatives had failed. Consensus, therefore, had extended to include modernisation. The Heath government finally achieved European entry but otherwise its failures marked the final derailment of the modernisation project. It also marked the derailment of conservative adaptation.

Why did conservative adaptation ultimately fail? Its interwar aspirations were modest: stability even if that included unemployment; and consensus over a pacific foreign policy, which eventually proved a mistake. Post-war adaptation, whether practised by Conservatives or Labour, was committed to a higher level of welfare spending which continued to grow because of welfare's success: as lifespans increased there were more elderly who were the biggest users of welfare services. A more active foreign policy also pushed up spending, although as time went by this became less important. However, conservative adaptation also ran into problems because of the perception of low growth and the fear that persistent inflation threatened sterling's stability. Jim Tomlinson has questioned whether this economic declinism was really justified. But the fact remains that many at the time held the view strongly, while no one can deny the traumas of the 1970s, which made the electorate willing to contemplate more radical change.

The road was therefore cleared for Thatcherism. But how radical was it? One element of the old consensus, the commitment to full employment, was already being downplayed by Labour from the mid-1970s. Other elements, notably the commitment to the NHS and to a wide panoply of other welfare services, have survived. Moreover, it seems likely that many of the changes which have occurred would have come in Britain sooner or later, given that other countries have pursued similar paths. But because of Margaret Thatcher they came fairly quickly, and sometimes brutally. Importantly, Thatcherism also involved a rewriting of the terms of organised labour's contract with the state. Again, the decline of some of the main sectors of union strength would probably have meant a decline in union power anyway, but Thatcherite reforms must have exacerbated this. Thatcherism was therefore important in accelerating change and in facilitating it by including the unions. And, even if Mrs Thatcher's own intellectual contribution to it was limited, both the facts of change as well as the name depended to a large part on her.

Thatcherism was also important because major areas of change, such as privatisation and union reform, were perceived by many voters as being successful. This did not compel Labour to change, but it increased the pressure for the party to do so. Neil Kinnock and Tony Blair carried change through but, as with the Conservatives in the late 1940s, Labour's own modernisation needed not just the leaders but a dedicated group of other modernisers. Labour's spell in office so far has shown no sign of reversing the general trend towards a more market-oriented economy, although there has been some reversal of the trend towards greater income inequality. Education policy, however, seems to put a pragmatic emphasis on improved outcomes above equality.

The cumulative change brought about by political action in the twentieth century has therefore been vast – although in some cases the changes have reversed earlier ones. Some historians, however, believe that more rapid change could have occurred if it had not been for the constraints introduced by the Civil Service. In David Reynolds' words, 'Whitehall stands out among bureaucracies in its ability to prevent sharp changes of policy.'[1] However, the extent to which the Civil Service has really inhibited change is questionable, given all the other influences in a democratic society, many of which have also tended to slow down the rate of change. It could be argued instead that the relative efficiency of a partially meritocratic and largely non-corrupt government bureaucracy has enabled large changes in the scope of government or in government policy – the growth of the welfare state, decolonisation, the changes needed in time of war – to be carried out surprisingly smoothly.

The extent of change over the whole twentieth century leads to the question of how far there has been any continuity between politics and government, and how people perceived them, in the early twentieth century, and these things today.

Britain is still a constitutional monarchy. But although the monarchy's real powers were limited even in 1900, its symbolism as an arbiter of fair play was important in a way it is not today. The power of the Lords was decisively reduced in 1911. Subsequently, its delaying power over legislation was reduced to one year in 1949, and in 1999 the voting rights of most hereditary peers were abolished. While this was a long overdue reform, it left the party in power more able to influence the composition of the Lords via the creation of life peers. So the Commons, and hence the party in power, are even more dominant in a system which was always notable for its relative lack of checks and balances.

This trend has been more marked than the apparent increase in prime ministerial power, which seems much more dependent on individual personalities than long-term trends. Lloyd George, Chamberlain, Churchill as a wartime but not a peacetime Prime Minister and Mrs Thatcher were all dominant prime ministers. But they have been interspersed with others who were not. Tony Blair, while more dominant than most, has also been heavily reliant on his Chancellor, Gordon Brown.

However, the supremacy of the Commons is today hedged with new restrictions, namely the increased powers of courts both in Britain and Europe. This exists because of Britain's adherence to international conventions. The European Human Rights Convention became enshrined in British law in the Human Rights Act of 1998, but as Britain had signed the Convention in 1953, cases before the Act had gone to the European Court of Human Rights. The European Court of Justice oversees the application of EU law, which has been long established as having precedence over national law. This is, of course, one reason why some have opposed Britain's membership of the EU so strongly.

What has not changed is the strength and depth of freely entered and independent associations – what it has become fashionable to call 'civil society'. The relative popularity of these associations has changed. Pressure groups have gained at the expense of political parties, for example. While many worry about the decline of the latter's membership, it is only since the new century that it has been accompanied by a significant decline in turnout at general elections. Nevertheless, to the extent that politics appears to excite less interest, Parliament is less the symbolic centre of the nation than it once was.

What has also not changed much is the dominant, if usually unexpressed, view that government exists in order to fulfil a contract with the people who put it in power. Of course, this has always been tempered by patriotism, and the duties people have accepted from patriotism. And in criminal justice the British have always tended to accept a fairly strong role for the state, which has spilt over into an acceptance of considerable limits on individual freedom during time of war and terrorist threat – in the 1970s the IRA, and after 2001 Al-Qaeda. But in other respects the state is still regarded as there to provide us with services. Since the inception of large-scale welfare, governments have tried to influence behaviour in order to reduce welfare costs. However, this has usually been pretty unsuccessful. Welfare, especially the NHS, exists for most people as a given to which they are entitled, and the development since the late 1980s of a government rhetoric of choice has stoked up such expectations.

Culture and society

The twentieth century has seen vast social changes. The life expectation of the average person and the quality of their housing has been transformed, as has much of what has been taken for granted in the surrounding world. Cars are now the most common form of transport. The layout of many towns and the pattern of shopping have completely changed. Holidays abroad, the preserve in 1900 of the upper and upper middle classes, have become increasingly common.

Politicians would like to take credit for many of these changes, but often they have been an almost inevitable concomitant of economic growth and the consequent growth of real incomes. Growth in incomes has been accompanied by some redistribution. But this has been limited and Britain is still a relatively unequal society economically, compared with some European countries.

Inequality lay behind the increasing salience of class as a factor in politics, at least up to 1945. But the impact of class has been mitigated because it is only one of the things that people have considered important. Furthermore, the meaning most people have attached to it has been constrained. Solidarity has usually been limited to members of the same union, or workers in the same factory or mine, not to the wider working class. Understanding of the broad picture of inequality has also been limited. And as some concept of a wider working-class interest grew, it was simultaneously undermined – slowly at first – by social mobility. Eventually this led to the working class, on most definitions, becoming an ever smaller minority of the population.

As class became less significant to most people, gender inequality became more so. A combination of economic change, personal choice and legislation – the latter often following rather than leading the other two – has produced rapid change concentrated in the last 40 years of the twentieth century. Married women now work as a matter of course and women's expectations of lifetime careers have radically changed.

Class and gender have been only two of the constructs out of which people have fashioned their identities. In 1900 family, locality, nation and Empire were all significant. For men more than women, work and leisure pursuits could be added. Religion for some, and political affiliation for many, were also important.

All these except Empire are still important today, although religion and a fixed political affiliation are less so. Women's, and more tentatively men's, identities are less constrained by expectations about gender roles, while the growth of middle-class occupations and higher education has meant wider expectations of potential careers for both sexes. Different ethnic groups maintain elements of their historic identity but are, surveys show, generally positive about subscribing to a British identity too. The growth of popular history has expanded conceptions of the locality, and the nation, to which people can relate. The growth of education and the diversification of the media has widened the interests from which many people construct part of their identity. So identities today are more differentiated, and the 'imagined community' of British people is more diverse.

In theory, however, Britain is a less tolerant society, since from the 1905 Aliens Act onwards free entry from other countries was restricted. But since the cumulative effect of immigration has still been large, Britain is today far more ethnically diverse than it was. And in spite of patches of intolerance, there is now more racial toleration. So in actuality if not in theory, more differentiated identities do seem to be accompanied by more tolerance of those identities. Terrorism, however, and the tensions and reactions it brings, is a major threat to this tolerance.

Note

1. Reynolds, *Britannia* (see Chapter 1), p. 305.

Further reading

Stephen Howe, 'Labour and International Affairs' in Tanner *et al.*, *Labour's First Century* (see Chapter 4). And see chapter bibliographies as appropriate.

APPENDIX
UK POPULATION AND EARNINGS

Year	Population
1901	38.2
1911	42.1
1921	44
1931	46
1941	
1951	50.2
1961	52.7
1971	55.9
1981	56.4
1991	57.4
2001	58.8

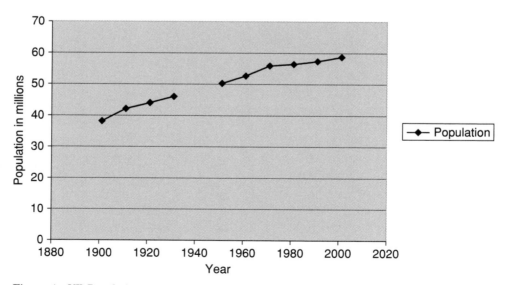

Figure 1   UK Population

Year	Average Earnings	Consumer Prices	Real Earnings*
1900	86	91	95
1910	93	96	97
1913	100	100	100
1920	278	245	113
1930	196	156	126
1940	271	180	150
1950	497	286	174
1960	949	425	223
1970	1801	633	285
1980	7586	2282	332
1990	17869	4304	411
2000	27702	5813	477

* Average earnings divided by prices

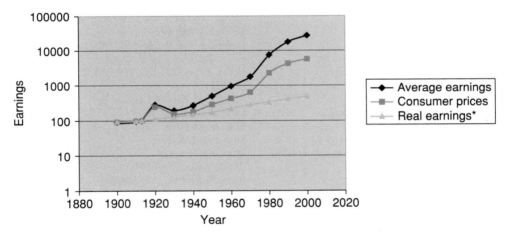

Figure 2   UK average earnings, consumer prices and real earnings
Source: Lawrence H. Officer, 'What were the UK Earnings Rate and Consumer Price Index then?' Economic History Services, September 2005, URL: http://eh.net/hmit/ukearncpi/.
Copyright © 2006 Lawrence H. Officer. All rights reserved

INDEX

abortion reform 241
Abyssinia (Ethiopia) 84
Acland, Sir Richard 137
administrative reforms 59–60
Afghanistan, Soviet invasion of 204
African colonies
   decolonisation 209, 210
   'Indirect Rule' 79
ageing population 234
agriculture
   agricultural workers 95
   cooperative marketing schemes 66
   protectionism 14, 226
alcohol consumption 106, 108
Aliens Act (1905) 94, 238
Alliance, SDP-Liberal 195, 196, 223
altruism 256–7
Amalgamated Society of Engineers 22
America *see* United States-British relationship
Amery, Leo 137
Anglicanism 92, 233
Anglo–French disagreement 73–4
anti-semitism 64, 94, 240
appeasement policy 82, 83–4, 85, 87–8, 206,
   255–6
apprenticeship system 111, 162
Armistice 43
Asquith, H.H. 19, 20, 26, 27, 30, 31, 41, 49
asylum seekers 239–40
Atlantic, battle of 119, 120, 122
Atlantic Charter (1941) 202
Attlee, Clement 62, 157, 158–9, 203
Austro-Hungarian Empire 30, 84
authority, attitudes to 146–7

Bagehot, Walter 1
balance of payments crisis 171, 172
Baldwin, Stanley 53, 54, 57, 58, 59, 63, 66, 70,
   71, 79, 93–4, 95, 257
Balfour, Arthur 16

Balfour Declaration 208
Battle of Britain 117, 118, 133–4
BBC *see* British Broadcasting Corporation
   (BBC)
Beaverbrook, Max 70, 80, 125–6
Benn, Tony 181
Berlin airlift 201
betting 106, 108
Bevan, Aneurin (Nye) 154, 156, 169
Bevanites 169, 172
Beveridge, Sir William 138–9
Beveridge Plan 138–9, 149, 154, 231
Bevin, Ernest 85, 126, 159, 201, 202–3, 212,
   214
'Big Bang', City of London 186
Birkenhead, Lord 49
birth control 104, 230
birth rate 230, 235
Black and Tans 51
'Black Wednesday' 194
Blair, Tony 196, 197, 260, 261
Blair government 188
   see also New Labour
Blitz, the 143, 147
Boer war 2, 3, 8, 10, 11, 13, 15, 16, 17
Bolshevism 74
Bonar Law, Andrew 26, 31, 49, 53
Bosnia conflict 217
Bosnia-Herzegovina, annexing of 30
Bourne, John 37
Bowden, Sue 229
Bowley, A.L. 98
Brett Young, Francis 93
Bretton Woods system 161, 175
Brezhnev, Leonid 204
Briand-Kellog Pact (1928) 75
British Broadcasting Corporation (BBC) 107–8
British Expeditionary Force (BEF) 32, 117, 133
British National Party 245
British Union of Fascists (BUF) 68, 94

Broadberry, Stephen 162
Brooke, Alan 124, 127, 131–2
Brown, Gordon 198, 218, 261
Brussels Treaty (1948) 201
Butler, R.A. 140, 163, 167
Butskellism 163

Callaghan, James 171, 178, 181, 195, 241
Campaign for Nuclear Disarmament (CND) 169, 214, 248, 250, 255
Campbell, John 184
Campbell, J.R. 57
Campbell-Bannerman, Henry 19, 29
Carson, Edward 26, 27
cartelisation 162, 167
Castle, Barbara 172
Ceylon 3
Chamberlain, Austen 49, 54
Chamberlain, Joseph 9, 15
Chamberlain, Neville 59–60, 66, 81, 82–3, 84–5, 117, 137, 256
Charmley, John 87, 130, 131, 132, 254
Cherry, Steven 105
children
    activities 109
    resources for 109, 235
    see also education
Children Act (1908) 18
Church of England 10, 11
church schools 140
Churchill, Winston
    Atlantic Charter 202
    Beveridge Plan 139
    at Board of Trade 18
    Britain's overseas influence 219
    Coalition government 49, 126
    Commons, importance of 149
    defection to Liberals 16, 126
    Edward VIII, support for 67, 126
    European integration 212
    First Lord of the Admiralty 126
    India policy 79, 126, 208
    and Labour Party 151
    Leader of the Conservatives 137
    Leader of the Opposition 127
    memoirs 85, 253
    Prime Minister 126–7
    Second World War 117, 119, 120, 122–3, 124–5, 126–7, 130, 131–2
    stands down for Eden 206
    summits 205
    welfare reforms 21

Citrine, Walter 83
City of London 61, 186
Civil Service, influence on policy 13, 29, 79, 192–3, 260
civil society 261
Clark, Alan 131
Clarke, Peter 184
class
    approaches to 112
    boundaries 147
    cross-class loyalties 114, 222
    disadvantaged groups 223–4
    identities 262
    income inequalities 223–4
    lower middle class 96–7, 112
    middle class 95
    occupations 112, 222–3
    social mobility 114–15
    upper class 112
    upper middle class 95–6, 112
    voting patterns 223
    see also working classes
Clause IV 19, 152
clubs and societies 107
CND see Campaign for Nuclear Disarmament (CND)
coal production 4, 5
    see also miners
Coalition government (1918) 42
    economies, pressure for 50
    inflation 50
    Ireland 51–3
    miners' claims 50–1
    reconstruction costs 50
    taxation 50
    unemployment benefit 50
Coalition (wartime) 31, 41, 47
cohabitation 230–1
Cold War 202, 204–5, 217–18
Common Agricultural Policy (CAP) 216, 217, 226, 255
Common Wealth Party 137, 147, 149
Commonwealth
    commitment to 205
    decolonisation 210–11
    EC 213, 216
    immigration 238–9
    White Dominions 78
Communist Party of Great Britain (CP) 68, 113
community relations 107, 232, 234
comprehensive schooling 169, 171–2
Confederation of British Industry (CBI) 186

conscription 31, 85, 149
Conservative-Liberal polarity 1, 45–7
Conservative Party
    change, slowness of 10
    communitarian tradition 9–10
    conservative adaptation 253–4
    election defeat 1997 195, 218
    election victory 1900 3
    election victory 1924 57
    election victory 1951 157
    election victory 1955 165
    election victory 1959 167
    election victory 1992 193
    franchise, extension of 10
    moderate Conservativism 258–9
    party history 253–4
    party membership 164
    religious toleration 10–11
constitutional monarchy 1, 247–8, 260
consumption
    cars 228
    diet 101
    durable goods penetration 229–30
    leisure services 230
    new housing 101
    post-war rationing 228
    shopping 101–3
    televisions 229
contraception 104, 230
convoy tactic 40–1
counties, in Britain 4, 8–9
Coupon Election (1918) 31, 49, 51
Cowling, Maurice 54
Crafts, Stephen 162
crime
    social tensions 147–8
    twentieth century Britain 249
Cripps, Stafford 153, 160
Cronin, A.J. 109
Crosland, Tony 169
Currie, Robert 55
cycling 107
Czechoslovakia, German invasion of 84–5

Daily Express 70, 71, 80, 244
Daily Herald 71, 93
Daily Mail 70, 71, 87, 244
Daily Mirror 147
Daily Telegraph 71
Dangerfield, George 22, 25, 27
Dawes Plan 74
De Gaulle, Charles 128, 130, 213, 243

decolonisation 256
    Africa 209, 210
    Commonwealth 210–11
    'east of Suez' commitments 209–10, 211, 219
    independence, advance to 75, 78
    India 207–8
    pressures for 208–9
    principles 209
    sterling area, survival of 208
denationalisation 164–8, 177
depression *see* economic depression
détente 204
devaluation, of sterling 161, 171, 172, 243
diet 101, 145
    see also rationing
Dill, Sir John 131
disarmament 75, 80, 81, 254
Disraeli, Benjamin 2
divorce 108, 231, 241
Doll, Richard 234
Douglas-Home, Alex 168, 173
Dowie, Jack 60
Downing Street Declaration 180
Dunkirk evacuation 117

earnings *see* income
'east of Suez' commitments 80, 209–10, 211, 219
EC *see* European Community
economic controls 152–3, 160, 165
economic declinism 259
economic depression
    employment stability 99, 100–1
    financial crisis 61–5
    and society 60–2
economic growth 161–2, 261–2
economic planning 141, 151–3, 167–8, 169, 172
Eden, Sir Anthony 17, 82, 127, 137, 165, 167, 205, 206–7, 210
education
    class system 110, 111
    comprehensive schooling 169, 171–2
    Conservative legislation 17
    elementary education 109, 110
    girls' education 110–11
    grammar schools 109–10, 140–1
    higher education, expansion of 111, 169, 171, 236
    league tables 188
    national curriculum, and choice 187–8
    private education 110, 236
    qualifications, increase in 235, 236

education (*continued*)
  reforms 1902 110
  religious 15
  school leaving age 109, 110, 140, 236
  selection at 11 235, 236
  social mobility 236–7
  technical schools 110, 140–1
  tripartite system 140–1, 235, 236
Education Act (1902) 15
Education Act (1944) 140–1, 235
Edward VII, King 4, 20
Edward VIII, King 67
EEC *see* European Economic Community
Egypt 80
Eisenhower, Dwight 206
El Alamein, battle of 122, 134
Elizabeth II, Queen 247
Emergency Powers (Defence) Act 1940 149
Empire, British
  in 1900 1–3
  in 1919 (map) 76–7
  American attempts to weaken 130–2
  defence of 254
  First World War, involvement in 32, 34
  glorification of 14
  interwar years 73–88
  popular support for 2, 3, 93
  see also decolonisation; White Dominions
Empire Day 93
employment
  reforms 18–19
  stability 99, 100–1, 227
  women's 46, 97, 101, 141, 224, 226–7, 231
Employment Acts 186
Entente Cordiale 3–4, 29
Equal Opportunities Commission 241
Equal Pay Act (1970) 228
ERM *see* Exchange Rate Mechanism
ethnic identity 262
ethnic minorities 223
  see also immigration
EU *see* European Union
Euro-scepticism 218
European Coal and Steel Community (ECSC)
  212
European Community (EC)
  Britain's entry to 178–9, 181
  budget issue 216–17
  and Civil Service 193
European Court of Justice 261
European Economic Community (EEC)
  attempt to join 168
  de Gaulle's suspicions 213, 216
  drawing towards 212–13
  Labour attitudes 213, 216
European Free Trade Area (EFTA) 213
European Human Rights Convention 261
European integration 256
  attitudes to 212
  resistance to 218, 219
European Monetary Union (EMU) 217, 218
European Union (EU) 218
Evans, Eric 184
Exchange Rate Mechanism (ERM) 193–4, 218

Falklands war 195, 205, 211, 246
family allowances 230, 234–7
Family Allowances Act (1945) 154
Family Planning Service 241
fascism 68, 94
Feldman, David 93, 94
Festival of Britain (1951) 242
'first past the post' electoral system 13
First World War
  aircraft, small impact of 39
  Allied superiority 39–40, 44
  American involvement 34, 40
  attrition strategy 39
  'balance of power', maintenance of 29
  Balkans, threat from 30
  casualties 32, 34, 44
  costs of 46
  economic factors 45
  Empire involvement 32, 34
  Gallipoli campaign 32–3, 37
  German aggression 30–2, 255
  Gladstonian peace policy 29, 32
  Hundred Days Allied attacks 36, 39
  media self-censorship 44–5
  naval rivalry 29, 30
  naval warfare 34, 36, 40–1, 43
  reconstruction 46
  tank deployments 39
  trench warfare 37–8
  volunteers 44
  Western Front 32, 33–4, 36, 37
  women's work 46
Foot, Michael 195
Fox, Daniel 154, 156
franchise
  expansion of 49
  right to vote 10, 12
  woman's suffrage 31
  see also suffragettes

Franco, General 84
free trade 4, 14, 15–16, 27–8, 80

Gaitskell, Hugh 156, 163, 171, 179, 214
Gallipoli campaign 32–3, 37
Gandhi, Mahatma 79
Geddes, Sir Eric 50
gender roles 262
General Agreement on Tariffs and Trade
  (GATT) 161
General Strike (1926) 57–60, 70
George V, King 21, 63–4, 71, 81, 93, 95, 248,
  258
George VI, King 67, 247, 248
German High Seas Fleet 40
Gibraltar 80
Gladstone, William 1, 11, 23, 28, 29
Gladstonian foreign policy 29, 32, 47, 255
Gold Standard 60, 61, 65
Goldthorpe, John 222
Good Friday Agreement 180
Gorbachev, Mikhail 204, 215
Gort, Lord 117
Government of India Acts 78–9
gradualism 55, 71
grammar schools 109–10, 140–1
Greece 119, 201
Green, Ewen 27
Greenwood, Arthur 158
Grey, Edward 29, 30

Haig, Douglas 34, 35–6
Haldane, Richard 32
Halevy, Elie 70
Halifax, Lord 137, 256
Hankey, Maurice 80
Hannington, Wal 68
Harris, Air Chief Marshal Arthur 125
Harris, Bernard 100
Harris, Jose 148
Healey, Denis 170
health care
  general practice deficiencies 105
  health insurance 20, 22
  hospitals 4, 105
  life expectancy 105
  mortality rates 105–6
  public health improvements 105
  see also National Health Service
Health Insurance Act (1911) 105
Heath, Edward (Ted) 172–5, 191, 205, 216, 259
Heath Government

EC membership 172
economic policy 174
expansionary fiscal policy 174, 175
inflation 174–5
miners' strikes 174
modernisation 173
NHS reorganisation 173
post-war consensus, ending of 175
prices and incomes policy 174, 175
trade union reform 173–4, 191
U-turn 174, 175
welfare state 173
'high politics', and change 54
historiographical traditions
  economic declinism 252–3
  pessimism 252–3
  structures 253, 254
  Whig history 252, 253–4
  women's history 254
Hitler, Adolf 83, 84–5, 87–8, 131, 135
  see also Second World War
Hoare, Sam 79
hobbies/interests 106–7
Holidays with Pay Act (1938) 68
Home Rule for Ireland debates 10, 11, 26–7,
  51, 179, 180
homes see housing
homosexuality 241, 242
Hong Kong 211
Horrocks, Brian 146
hospitals 4, 105
House of Commons 1, 261
House of Lords 17, 19–21, 23, 260
housing
  dwellings, numbers of 154, 155
  Green Belts 155
  home ownership 165
  new 101
  new towns 155
  Rent Act 155
  ribbon development 155
  standards 98–9
  subsidy schemes 69
  Thatcherism 186, 191
Howard, Michael 240
Howe, Geoffrey 182, 217
Howe, Stephen 255
Human Rights Act (1998) 261
Hurd, Douglas 220

identity see local identities; national identity
illegitimacy rates 106

immigration
  anti-semitism 240
  asylum seekers 239–40
  Commonwealth 238–9
  controversial nature of 238–9
  discrimination 240
  European 239
  increased 239–40
  Irish 238
  racism 237–8, 240
import/export gap 153, 160
In Place of Strife (White Paper, 1969) 172
incapacity benefit 224–5
income
  earnings, average 264
  inequalities 98, 99, 146, 223–4, 228
  real incomes, growth in 227–8
  rural and urban wage levels 95
Independent Labour Party (ILP) 11–12, 68,
    158
India
  Empire, in 1900 2
  Morley-Minto reforms 17
  partition and independence 78–9, 207–8
India Councils Act (1909) 17
individualism, rise of 231
Industrial Charter (1947) 163, 167
Industrial Relations Act (1971) 173
Industry Act (1972) 174
infant mortality 104
inflation
  Coalition government (1918) 50
  Heath Government 174–5
  and taxation 139–40
  Thatcherism 177–8, 182, 183, 184–5, 190,
    198
Inskip, Sir Thomas 87
International Monetary Fund (IMF) 178
Iran 201, 209
Iraq
  Gulf War, 1991 217
  Second World War 133–4
  US invasion of 217–18, 220, 255
Ireland
  Easter Rising (1916) 51
  Home Rule 10, 11, 26–7, 51, 179, 180
  partitioning, 1920 51–2
  see also Northern Ireland
Irish Free State 51–2, 78
Irish Nationalists 23, 27
Irish Republican Army (IRA) 51, 179–80
Irish Volunteers 27

isolationism 3
Italy 84, 117, 132

Japan 3, 80, 81, 86, 119, 134
Jarrow March (1936) 100
Jenkins, Roy 211, 241
jingoism 14
job satisfaction 227
Jones, Jack 181
Joseph, Sir Keith 178, 183
Joyce, Patrick 114
Jutland, battle of 34, 40

Kaufman, Gerald 196
Keeler, Christine 168
Kennedy, A.L. 81, 83
Kennedy, John 241
Keynes, John Maynard 61
Keynesianism 61–2, 66, 139–40, 151, 153–4,
    160, 169, 172, 175, 182, 184, 197–8
Kinnock, Neil 196–7, 260
Kipling, Rudyard 93
Kitchener, Lord 41
Korean war 201, 204
Kosovo conflict 217
Kruschev, Nikita 204

labour migration 99
labour mobility 97
Labour Party
  adjustment to 70
  Conservative reforms, continuation of 197–8
  EC membership 178–9, 181
  election defeat 1970 173
  election defeat 1979 181
  election defeat 1983 196
  election defeat 1992 197
  election victory 1945 151, 259
  election victory 1964 168, 169
  election victory 1974 179
  foundation of 11–12
  internal dissent 169, 172, 179
  left, neutralising of 181
  reconstruction 196–7
  Whig history 252
Labour Representation Committee (LRC)
    11–12, 17
language, and rhetoric 71
Lansbury, George 158
Lawrence, T.E. 33
Lawson, Nigel 193, 217
League of Nations 70, 75, 202, 254

leisure activities 232
Lend Lease 129–31, 134, 153, 200
Liberal Democrats 195, 196, 223
'Liberal Hour' 241–2
Liberal Imperialists 29
Liberal Party 195–6
  decline of 27–8, 53–4
  defections to 16
  election victories 1910 20–1
  election victory 1906 16
  failure of 68–9
  'high politics', and change 54
  Lockean tradition 9–10
  religious toleration 10–11
Liberal Unionists 9, 10, 14, 16
licensing laws 17, 108
life expectancy 105, 234
Little, Kenneth 238
Lloyd George, David 13, 19, 21, 30, 31, 40–1,
  41–3, 45, 49, 50, 53, 66, 73, 137, 171
local government 189–90
Local Government Act (1929) 105
local identities
  Irish and Catholic 90
  Jewish 90
  local loyalties 90, 246
  local media 89
  regional accents 89–90
  urban migrations 89
Locarno Treaty (1925) 74, 84, 255–6
Loch Mowat, Charles 53
Locke, John 9–10
London Transport 152
loyalty 2, 3
Luftwaffe 118, 143
Lyttleton, Oliver 163

Maastricht Treaty 218
MacDonald, Ramsay 54, 55–6, 63, 64–5, 70,
  71, 95, 114, 202, 258
Macmillan, Harold 141, 163, 165, 166–7, 168,
  173, 174, 205, 209, 212–13, 214, 216, 220,
  242, 256
Maginot Line 133
Major, John 189, 193–4, 245
Major government 188
Malaysia 209, 211
Malta 80
Manchester Guardian 13
manufacturing 2, 4, 224, 225
marriage
  companionate 106–7, 108, 232

decline of 231–2
divorce 108, 231, 241
increase in 230
married life 103, 106
married women, and paid work 103–4
Marshall Plan 153, 201, 203, 212
Marwick, Arthur 141, 145
Marxism 113
Masters, Brian 248
Matthews, Robin 161
May, Sir George 62
McKibbin, Ross 71, 106, 113, 146, 237
Means Test marches 68
media
  broadcast news 244
  consensual views 147
  newspapers, commercialisation of 70–1
  press censorship 149
  self-censorship 44–5, 149
  tabloid press 244
  television, rise of 229, 232, 244
Mediterranean Strategy 122, 131–2
Medium Term Financial Strategy (MTFS)
  182, 185
Mesopotamia (Iraq) 80
Middle East 201, 203, 209–10, 211, 219
Miles, Andrew 114
Millett, Allan 132
miners
  claims 50–1, 54
  strikes 22, 57–9, 113, 174
Ministry of Agriculture Fisheries and Food
  (MAFF) 226
Minto, Lord 17
Mirror 144
mobility 103
moderation, political advantages of 70–1,
  258
modernisation drives 152, 168, 169, 171, 172,
  173, 242–3, 259
monarchy
  constitutional 1, 247–8, 260
  decline in support for 247
  and empire 1–4
  modernisation of 64
  and national identity 93, 247–8
monetarism, and inflation 177–8, 182, 183,
  184–5, 190, 198
monetary policy 160–1
Monkton, Walter 164
Montgomery, General Bernard 122, 131, 134
Morley, John 17

Morris, Jeremy 233
Morrison, Herbert 152, 158
Morton, H.V. 93
Mosley, Oswald 68
Mountbatten, Lord 208
Munitions of War Acts (1915, 1916) 45
Murray, Williamson 132
Mussolini, Benito 84

Nasser, Gamal Abdel 206
National Assistance Act (1948) 154
National Economic Development Council
    (NEDC) 167–8, 177
'national efficiency' 8, 9, 15, 16, 18, 140, 257
National Enterprise Board (NEB) 181
National Front 245
National Government (1931–1939)
    agriculture 66
    communism 68
    economic recovery 65
    fascism 68
    formation of 62–3, 64–5
    Labour Party 66
    Liberal Nationals 66
    Liberal Party 68–9
    price raising policies 65, 66
    public corporations, creation of 65–6
    social reform 66, 68
National Health Service (NHS)
    creation of 154, 156, 159
    Hospital Plan (1962) 165, 168, 169
    reorganisation 173
    Thatcher government 188–9, 191
national identity
    British identity 245–6
    Celtic nationalism 94, 244–5
    diffuse 245–6
    heritage industry 246
    'imagined community', of Britain 93, 95,
        148–9
    and monarchy 93, 247–8
    'national character' 93–4
    political consensus 92–3, 94
    political moderation 94–5
    religion 91–2
    rule of law, and democratic freedoms 248
    rural nostalgia 93, 245
    tolerance 248
    war, hostility to 248, 250
    welfare state, and British values 242
National Income Commission (NIC) 167–9
National Insurance Act (1946) 154

National Unemployed Workers Movement
    (NUWM) 68
National Union of Mineworkers (NUM) 174,
    186
National Union of Women's Suffrage Societies
    (NUWSS) 23–4
nationalisation
    Labour economics 151–2, 159
    post-war consensus 163
    public corporations, creation of 65–6
    renationalisation of steel 172
    see also denationalisation
nationalism
    British 245–6
    Celtic 179, 181, 244–5
    see also national identity
Nationality Act (1948) 238
NATO see North Atlantic Treaty Organisation
naval warfare 29, 30, 34, 36, 40–1, 43, 119
Nazi regime 81, 83
Nazi-Soviet Pact (1939) 85
Near East post-war settlement 74
New Labour 197–8
New Liberals 9, 16, 21
Newfoundland 78
News of the World 13
'Next Steps' 193
Nigeria 3
Nivelle, General 34
nonconformism 16, 17, 22, 91–2
Normandy invasion (D-Day) 124
North Atlantic Treaty Organisation (NATO)
    201, 204, 205, 214, 217, 219, 220
Northern Ireland
    partitioning 26–7, 51–2
    sectarian violence 179–80
    see also Ireland; Ulster
Norway 127, 137
nuclear deterrence 203, 205, 213–15
nuclear power 214

O'Connor, General Richard 118–19
Offer, Avner 229
oil
    'east of Suez' commitments 209–10, 211, 219
    Iraq/Syria campaigns 133–4
    price rises 1970s 175
'opportunity' state 165
Ottoman Empire 30, 208
    former territories 75, 80
    Gallipoli campaign 32–3, 37
Ottawa agreements (1932) 78

Palestine 75, 80, 208
Pankhurst, Emmeline 23, 24
Parliamentary Labour Party (PLP) 179
patriotism 9, 113, 211, 246
  First World War 44–5, 47
'peace for our time' (Chamberlain) 84
Pearl Harbour 119
permissiveness 241–2
pessimism 252–3
Phoney War 113, 117
Pimlott, Ben 248
Plaid Cymru (PC) 244–5
planning see economic planning
Poland, German invasion of 85, 117
Polaris missiles 214
Political and Economic Planning (PEP) 141
polytechnics 171
Poor Law 4, 8, 18, 98, 100, 105
post-war consensus
  atomistic and pluralistic society, belief in 148
  breakdown of 177
  Butskellism 163
  collectivist policies 163–4
  Conservative adaptations 163
  local authorities 189
  nationalisation 163
  Parliament, status of 148–9
  party strife 164
  rightness of war, universal belief in 147
  Russia, threat from 163
  social reforms 149–50
  welfare state 163
Powell, Enoch 178
Presbyterian Church 10
Price, Christopher 87
Priestley, J.B. 147
prime ministerial power 261
Prior, Jim 185
privatisation see denationalisation
productivity 153, 159, 161–2
Profumo, John 168
'property-owning democracy' 165
Provisionals 180
public corporations 65–6, 172
  see also nationalisation
public opinion 255
pubs 91, 106, 108

Race Relations Acts 240, 241
racism 8–9, 94, 237–8, 240
radio 107–8
railway dispute 22, 23

Ramsden, John 58, 174, 253
rationing 46, 160
  and consumption 142, 144–5, 228
  and crime 147–8
  ending of 165
  post-war pessimism 242
Reagan, Ronald 204, 205
rearmament policy
  air rearmament, focus on 85, 86–7
  German threat 81, 82, 83, 85, 87–8
  slowness of 85–6, 87
Redcliffe-Maud proposal 190
Reeves, Pember 107
Reith, John 107–8, 244
religion
  Anglicanism 92
  belief 233
  Catholicism 91
  churchgoing, decline in 91, 233
  nonconformity 91–2
  Presbyterianism 92
  Protestantism 91
  religious ceremonies 92
  social function of 92
Representation of the People Act (1918) 49
'respectability' 106
Reynolds, David 252, 256, 260
Rhodesia 209
Ridley, Nicholas 177
Roberts, Elizabeth 92, 104
Roberts, Robert 249
Roosevelt, Franklin D. 58, 130–1, 202
Rose, Kenneth 64
Rothermere, Lord 70
Rowntree, Seebohm 98, 108
Royal Air Force
  Battle of Britain 117, 118, 133–4
  strategic bombing 86–7, 120, 122–3, 123,
    124–5
Royal Navy
  Atlantic, battle of 120
  limitations of 3
  naval warfare 29, 30, 34, 36, 40–1, 43, 119
Royal Ulster Constabulary (RUC) 51
Runciman, Gary 223
rural protectionism 226
  see also agriculture
Russia 74–5, 85, 129, 132–3, 147, 163, 200
  see also Soviet Union

Saddam Hussein 217
Salisbury, Lord 16

Salonika expedition 37
Samuel, Sir Herbert 57–8, 63
Scanlon, Hugh 181
Schlieffen Plan 32
Scottish National Party 94, 179, 181, 244–5
Second World War
    Allied superiority 155
    American involvement 119, 120–1, 122, 127,
        129–32, 134
    Chief of Staffs Committee (COS) 124
    disruption 144, 145
    evacuations 141–2
    Greeks, assistance for 133–4
    Hitler's eastwards expansion 117–18
    intelligence 134–5
    Iraq/Syria campaigns 133–4
    Keynesian employment policy 139–40,
        144
    Mediterranean Strategy 122, 131–2
    North African campaigns 118–19, 122,
        133
    overseas currency, need for 129–30
    politics and planning 137–41
    production, and strategic need 125–6,
        128
    rationing 142, 144–5, 147–8
    resources 128
    Royal Navy, role of 119, 134
    society 145–8
    strategic bombing 120, 122–3, 124–5
    territorial occupation 121
    War Cabinet 124, 125, 126
security, and economics 254–5
'Selsdon man' 174
Sevres Protocol 206
Sèvres Treaty (1920) 74
Sex Discrimination Acts 46, 241
Sheffield, Gary 37
Sherriff, R.C. 37
Simon, Sir John 66
Singapore 80, 86
Single European Market (SEM) 217
single parents 104, 235
Sinn Fein 51, 180
Smith, John 197
smoking 234
Smuts, Jan 128
Snowden, Philip 56, 62
Social Charter (EU) 218
Social Democratic Federation (SDF)
    11–12
Social Democratic Party (SDP) 195–6

'Social Insurance and Allied Services'
    (Beveridge) 138–9
socialism 55–6
socialist parties 11–12
South Africa 3
South-East Asia Treaty Organisation (SEATO)
    209
Soviet Union
    collapse of 204, 217
    expansionism 204
    threat from 201–2, 203, 255
    see also Russia
Spanish civil war (1936–1939) 84
Stalin 85, 123, 131, 133
state, role of 9, 70, 257–8, 261
State Earnings Related Pensions Scheme
    (SERPS) 187
Statute of Westminster (1931) 78
Steele, David 241
sterling, devaluation of 161, 171, 172, 243
'stop-go' 161
Stormont 179
Sturt, George 109
Suez 80, 131, 203, 205, 220, 248, 255
    and Eden 17, 165, 206–7, 210
suffragettes 23–6, 27
summitry 205
Sun 244
syndicalism 22

Tariff Reform 15–16, 27–8, 80
taxation
    inflation 139–40
    middle classes 50, 69, 99
    social reforms 69
    of wealthy 28
Taylor, A.J.P. 35, 37, 45, 254
Taylor, Howard 249
technical schools 110, 140–1
television 229, 232, 244
temperance lobby 14
Terraine, John 35
Thatcher, Margaret 182, 183–4, 185–9, 194,
        205, 211, 216–17, 218, 220, 226, 242, 245,
        253, 260, 261
Thatcherism 260
    education policy 187–8
    Europe 193–5
    free-market ideas 177, 190, 198
    health spending 188–9, 191
    housing 186, 191
    interest groups, confrontations with 186

Thatcherism (*continued*)
  miners, confrontation with 186
  monetarism, and inflation 177–8, 182, 183,
    184–5, 190, 198
  political consensus 198–9
  privatisation 185, 190, 191
  radical nature of 182
  social security 186–7, 192
  taxation 185
  trade union reform 185–6, 190–2
  unemployment 184–5
  welfare state 186–7, 191
Thorpe, Andrew 182
Times, The 71, 81
Titmuss, Richard 145
tolerance 248, 262
Tomlinson, Jim 162, 259
Town and Country Planning Acts 141, 155
towns, in Britain 4, 8–9
trade liberalisation 161, 175
trade supremacy 3, 4
trade unions 162
  bargaining 258
  Conservative-Liberal support for 11–12
  Heath government reforms 173–4, 191
  industrial disputes, low levels of 164–5
  and Labour Party 70
  legislation, 1927 59
  Social Contract 181
  strikes 1913–1914 22–3
  Thatcher government reforms 185–6,
    190–2
  and working class 222, 223
Trades Disputes Act (1906) 23
Trades Union Congress (TUC) 173
Transport and General Workers' Union
  (TGWU) 202
Trenchard, Hugh 'Boom' 86
Trident system 215
Truman, Harry S 200, 201
Turkey 74, 201

UK Independence Party 218
Ulster 23, 26–7
  see also Ireland; Northern Ireland
Ulster Presbyterians 26
Ulster Volunteers 27
unemployment 60–1, 184–5, 224–5
unemployment benefit 50, 69, 70, 71, 98,
  100
unemployment insurance 19, 98, 100
Union of Democratic Control (UDC) 47

Unionists, and Home Rule 10, 179, 180
United Nations, setting up of 202
United States-British relationship
  Empire, American attempts to weaken
    130–2
  First World War 34, 40
  invasion of Iraq, support for 217–18, 220
  NATO 204
  post-war 200–1, 203
  Second World War 119, 120–1, 122, 127,
    129–32, 134
  'special relationship' 204, 205, 214, 217–18,
    219, 220
US Army Air Force (USAAF) 123

Vansittart, Sir Robert 81, 87
Versailles Peace Conference 1919 73, 81,
  83, 84
Victoria, Queen 1, 2, 14
Victory in Europe (VE) day 124
Vietnam war 179
Vincent, David 99–100
voting patterns 13, 223
  see also franchise; suffragettes

'War on Terror' 217–18
Washington Naval Treaty (1922) 86
wealth, distribution of 4, 228, 257–8
Weight, Richard 242, 245
welfare reforms
  employment reforms 18–19
  health insurance 20, 22
  paying for 17
  pensions 18
  welfare of children 18
welfare state 165
  British values 242
  Heath Government 173
  post-war consensus 163
  Thatcherism 186–7, 191
  Whig history 252
Welsh Anglican Church 22
Welsh National Party 94, 179, 181, 244–5
Western European Union (WEU) 205, 212
Whig history 252, 253–4
White Dominions 2, 15–16, 32, 34, 78, 80
Wilhelm II, Kaiser 31
Williamson, Philip 58
Wilson, Harold 167, 169–70, 174, 178–9, 181,
  205, 216, 259
Wilson, Woodrow 75
'wind of change' speech (Macmillan) 209

Winter of Discontent (1978–1979) 181
women
    employment 46, 97, 101, 141, 224, 226–7, 231
    girls' education 110–11
    history 254
    shopping 101–3
    voting rights 23–6, 27, 46
Woolton, Lord 139, 142
working classes
    attitudes 113–14

conservativism 14–15
militancy, fears of 113
occupations 222–3
religion 14–15
urban populations 95
world affairs, Britain's role in 200, 219–20

Yalta Conference, 1945 133, 201

Zinoviev letter 57